William Wordsworth, Alexander Balloch Grosart

Prose Works

For the First Time Collected, with Additions from Unpublished Manuscripts. Vol. I

William Wordsworth, Alexander Balloch Grosart

Prose Works
For the First Time Collected, with Additions from Unpublished Manuscripts. Vol. I

ISBN/EAN: 9783744687966

Printed in Europe, USA, Canada, Australia, Japan

Cover: Foto ©Thomas Meinert / pixelio.de

More available books at **www.hansebooks.com**

THE PROSE WORKS

OF

WILLIAM WORDSWORTH.

FOR THE FIRST TIME COLLECTED,

WITH ADDITIONS FROM UNPUBLISHED MANUSCRIPTS.

Edited, with Preface, Notes and Illustrations,

BY THE

REV. ALEXANDER B. GROSART,
ST. GEORGE'S, BLACKBURN, LANCASHIRE.

IN THREE VOLUMES.

VOL. I.

POLITICAL AND ETHICAL

LONDON: EDWARD MOXON, SON, AND CO.
1 AMEN CORNER, PATERNOSTER ROW.
1876.

TO THE QUEEN.

MADAM,

I have the honour to place in your Majesty's hands the hitherto uncollected and unpublished Prose Works of

WILLIAM WORDSWORTH

—name sufficient in its simpleness to give lustre to any page.

Having been requested thus to collect and edit his Prose Writings by those who hold his MSS. and are his nearest representatives, one little discovery or recovery among these MSS. suggested your Majesty as the one among all others to whom the illustrious Author would have chosen to dedicate these Works, viz. a rough transcript of a Poem which he had inscribed on the fly-leaf of a gift-copy of the collective edition of his Poems sent to the Royal Library at Windsor Castle. This very tender, beautiful, and pathetic Poem will be found on the other side of this Dedication. It must 'for all time' take its place beside the living Laureate's imperishable verse-tribute to your Majesty.

I venture to thank your Majesty for the double permission so appreciatively given—of this Dedication itself and to print (for the first time) the Poem. The gracious permission so pleasantly and discriminatingly signified is only one of abundant proofs that your Majesty is aware that of the enduring names of the reign of Victoria, Wordsworth's is supreme as Poet and Thinker.

Gratefully and loyally,

ALEXANDER B. GROSART.

DEIGN, Sovereign Mistress! to accept a lay,
No Laureate offering of elaborate art;
But salutation taking its glad way
From deep recesses of a loyal heart.

Queen, Wife, and Mother! may All-judging Heaven
Shower with a bounteous hand on Thee and Thine
Felicity that only can be given
On earth to goodness blest by grace divine.

Lady! devoutly honoured and beloved
Through every realm confided to thy sway;
Mayst Thou pursue thy course by God approved,
And He will teach thy people to obey.

As Thou art wont, thy sovereignty adorn
With woman's gentleness, yet firm and staid;
So shall that earthly crown thy brows have worn
Be changed for one whose glory cannot fade.

And now, by duty urged, I lay this Book
Before thy Majesty, in humble trust
That on its simplest pages Thou wilt look
With a benign indulgence more than just.

Nor wilt Thou blame an aged Poet's prayer,
That issuing hence may steal into thy mind
Some solace under weight of royal care,
Or grief—the inheritance of humankind.

For know we not that from celestial spheres,
When Time was young, an inspiration came
(Oh, were it mine!) to hallow saddest tears,
And help life onward in its noblest aim?

W. W.

9th January 1846.

PREFACE.

IN response to a request put in the most gratifying way possible of the nearest representatives of WORDSWORTH, the Editor has prepared this collection of his *Prose Works*. That this should be done *for the first time* herein seems somewhat remarkable, especially in the knowledge of the permanent value which the illustrious Author attached to his Prose, and that he repeatedly expressed his wish and expectation that it would be thus brought together and published, *e.g.* in the 'Memoirs,' speaking of his own prose writings, he said that but for COLERIDGE'S irregularity of purpose he should probably have left much more in that kind behind him. When COLERIDGE was proposing to publish his 'Friend,' he (WORDSWORTH) had offered contributions. COLERIDGE had expressed himself pleased with the offer, but said, "I must arrange my principles for the work, and when that is done I shall be glad of your aid." But this "arrangement of principles" never took place. WORDSWORTH added: "*I think my nephew, Dr. Wordsworth, will, after my death, collect and publish all I have written in prose.*" . . . "On another occasion, I believe, he intimated a desire that his *works in Prose should be edited by his son-in-law, Mr. Quilli-*

nan."* Similarly he wrote to Professor REED in 1840: 'I am much pleased by what you say in your letter of the 18th May last, upon the Tract of the "Convention of Cintra," and *I think myself with some interest upon its being reprinted hereafter along with my other writings* [in prose]. But the respect which, in common with all the rest of the rational part of the world, I bear for the DUKE OF WELLINGTON will prevent my reprinting the pamphlet during his lifetime. It has not been in my power to read the volumes of his Despatches, which I hear so highly spoken of; but I am convinced that nothing they contain could alter my opinion of the injurious tendency of that or any other Convention, conducted upon such principles. *It was, I repeat, gratifying to me that you should have spoken of that work as you do, and particularly that you should have considered it in relation to my Poems, somewhat in the same manner as you had done in respect to my little volume on the Lakes.*'†

It is probable that the *amount* of the Prose of WORDSWORTH will come as a surprise—surely a pleasant one—on even his admirers and students. His own use of 'Tract' to describe a goodly octavo volume, and his calling his 'Guide' a 'little volume' while it is a somewhat considerable one, together with the hiding away of some of his most matterful and weightiest productions in local and fugitive publications, and in Prefaces and Appendices to Poems, go far to explain the prevailing unacquaintance with even the *extent*, not to speak of the importance, of his Prose, and the light contentment with

* 'Memoirs,' vol. ii. p. 466.
† Ibid. vol. i. p. 420.

which it has been permitted so long to remain (comparatively) out of sight. That the inter-relation of the Poems to the Prose, and of the Prose to the Poems—of which above he himself wrote—makes the collection and publication of the Prose a duty to all who regard WILLIAM WORDSWORTH as one of the supreme intellects of the century—as certainly the glory of the Georgian and Victorian age as ever SHAKESPEARE and RALEIGH were of the Elizabethan and Jacobean—will not be questioned to-day.

The present Editor can only express his satisfaction at being called to execute a task which, from a variety of circumstances, has been too long delayed; but only delayed, inasmuch as the members of the Poet's family have always held it as a sacred obligation laid upon them, with the additional sanction that WORDSWORTH'S old and valued friend, HENRY CRABB ROBINSON, Esq., had expressed a wish in his last Will (1868) that the Prose Works of his friend should one day be collected; and which wish alone, from one so discriminating and generous—were there no other grounds for doing so—the family of WORDSWORTH could not but regard as imperative. He rejoices that the delay—otherwise to be regretted—has enabled the Editor to furnish a much fuller and more complete collection than earlier had perhaps been possible. He would now briefly notice the successive portions of these Volumes:

VOL. I.

I. Political.

(*a*) *Apology for the French Revolution*, 1793.

This is from the Author's own MS., and is published *for the first time.* Every reader of 'The Recluse' and 'The Excursion' and the 'Lines on the French Revolution, as it appeared to Enthusiasts at its Commencement'—to specify only these—is aware that, in common with Southey and the greater Coleridge, Wordsworth was in sympathy with the uprising of France against its tyrants. But it is only now that we are admitted to a full discovery of his youthful convictions and emotion by the publication of this Manuscript, carefully preserved by him, but never given to the world. The title on the fly-leaf—'Apology,' &c., being ours—in the Author's own handwriting, is as follows:

A

LETTER

TO THE

BISHOP OF LANDAFF

ON THE EXTRAORDINARY AVOWAL OF HIS

POLITICAL PRINCIPLES,

CONTAINED IN THE

APPENDIX TO HIS LATE SERMON:

BY A

REPUBLICAN.

It is nowhere dated, but inasmuch as Bishop Watson's Sermon, with the Appendix, appeared early in 1793, to that year certainly belongs the composition of the 'Letter.' The title-page of the Sermon and Appendix may be here given:

A
SERMON
PREACHED BEFORE THE
STEWARDS
OF THE
WESTMINSTER DISPENSARY,
AT THEIR
ANNIVERSARY MEETING,
CHARLOTTE STREET CHAPEL, APRIL 1785.
WITH AN APPENDIX,
BY R. WATSON, D.D.
LORD BISHOP OF LANDAFF.
LONDON:
PRINTED FOR T. CADELL IN THE STRAND; AND T. EVANS
IN PATERNOSTER ROW.
1793 [8vo].

In the same year a 'second edition' was published, and also separately the Appendix, thus:

STRICTURES
ON THE
FRENCH REVOLUTION
AND THE
BRITISH CONSTITUTION,
AS WRITTEN IN 1793
IN AN
APPENDIX TO A SERMON
PREACHED BEFORE THE
STEWARDS OF THE WESTMINSTER DISPENSARY,
AT THEIR
ANNIVERSARY MEETING,
CHARLOTTE STREET CHAPEL, APRIL 1785,
BY R. WATSON, D.D.
LORD BISHOP OF LANDAFF.
Reprinted at Loughborough
(With his Lordship's permission) by Adams, Jun.
and
Recommended by the Loughborough Association
For the Support of the Constitution to
The Serious Attention of the Public.
Price Twopence, being one third of the original price.
1793 [small 8vo].

The Sermon is a somewhat commonplace dissertation on 'The Wisdom and Goodness of God in having made both Rich and Poor,' from Proverbs xxii. 2: 'The rich and poor meet together, the Lord is the Maker of them all.' It could not but be most irritating to one such as young WORDSWORTH—then in his twenty-third year—who passionately felt as well with as for the poor of his native country, and that from an intimacy of knowledge and intercourse and sympathy in striking contrast with the serene optimism of the preacher,—all the more flagrant in that Bishop Watson himself sprang from the very humblest ranks. But it is on the Appendix this Letter expends its force, and, except from BURKE on the opposite side, nothing more forceful, or more effectively argumentative, or informed with a nobler patriotism, is to be found in the English language. If it have not the kindling eloquence which is Demosthenic, and that axiomatic statement of principles which is Baconian, of the 'Convention,' every sentence and epithet pulsates—as its very life-blood—with a manly scorn of the false, the base, the sordid, the merely titularly eminent. It may not be assumed that even to old age WILLIAM WORDSWORTH would have disavowed a syllable of this 'Apology.' Technically he might not have held to the name 'Republican,' but to the last his heart was with the oppressed, the suffering, the poor, the silent. Mr. H. CRABB ROBINSON tells us in his Diary (vol. ii. p. 290, 3d edition): 'I recollect once hearing Mr. WORDSWORTH say, half in joke, half in earnest, "I have no respect whatever for Whigs, but I have a great deal of the Chartist in me;"' and his friend adds: 'To be sure he has. His earlier poems are full of that intense love of the people, as such, which becomes Chartism when the attempt is formally made to make their interests the especial object of legislation, as of deeper importance than the positive rights hitherto accorded to the privileged orders.' Elsewhere the same Diarist speaks of 'the brains of the noblest youths in England' being 'turned' (i. 31, 32), including WORDSWORTH. There was no such 'turning' of brain with him. He was deliberate, judicial, while at a red heat of indignation. To measure the quality of difference, intellectually and morally, between WORDSWORTH and another noticeable man who entered into controversy with Bishop WATSON, it is only necessary to compare the present Letter with GILBERT WAKEFIELD'S 'Reply to some Parts of the Bishop of Landaff's Address to the People of Great Britain' (1798).

The manuscript is wholly in the handwriting of its author, and is done with uncharacteristic painstaking; for later, writing was painful and irksome to him, and even his letters are in great part illegible. One folio is lacking, but probably it contained only an additional sentence or two, as the examination of the Appendix is complete. Following on our ending are these words: 'Besides the names which I.'

That the Reader may see how thorough is the Answer of WORDSWORTH to Bishop WATSON, the 'Appendix' is reprinted *in extenso*. Being comparatively brief, it was thought expedient not to put the student on a vain search for the long-forgotten Sermon. On the biographic value of this Letter, and the inevitableness of its inclusion among his prose Works, it cannot be needful to say a word. It is noticed—and little more—in the 'Memoirs' (c. ix. vol. i. pp. 78-80). In his Letters (vol. iii.) will be found incidental allusions and vindications of the principles maintained in the 'Apology.'

(*b*) *Concerning the Relations of Great Britain, Spain, and Portugal, to each other and the common Enemy, at this Crisis; and specifically as affected by the Convention of Cintra: the whole brought to the test of those Principles, by which alone the Independence and Freedom of Nations can be Preserved or Recovered.* 1809.

As stated in its 'Advertisement,' two portions of this treatise (rather than 'Tract'), 'extending to p. 25' of the completed volume, were originally printed in the months of December and January (1808-9), in the 'Courier' newspaper. In this shape it attracted the notice of no less a reader than Sir WALTER SCOTT, who thus writes of it: 'I have read WORDSWORTH's lucubrations* in the 'Courier,' *and much agree with him.* Alas! we want everything but courage and virtue in this desperate contest. Skill, knowledge of mankind, ineffable unhesitating villany, combination of movement and combination of means, are with our adversary. We can only fight like mastiffs—boldly, blindly, and faithfully. I am almost driven to the pass of the Covenanters, when they told the Almighty in their prayers He should no longer be their God; and I really believe a few Gazettes more will make me turn Turk or infidel.'†

What WORDSWORTH's own feelings and impulses were in the composition of the 'Convention of Cintra' are revealed with unwonted as fine passion in his 'Letters and Conversations' (vol. iii. pp. 256-261, &c.), whither

* Lucubrations=meditative studies. It has since deteriorated in meaning.

† Lockhart's 'Life of Scott,' vol. iii. pp. 260-1 (edition, 1856).

the Reader will do well to turn, inasmuch as he returns and re-returns therein to his standing-ground in this very remarkable and imperishable book. The long Letters to (afterwards) Sir CHARLES W. PASLEY and another—*never before printed*—which follow the 'Convention of Cintra' itself, are of special interest. The Appendix of Notes, 'a portion of the work which WORDSWORTH regarded as executed in a masterly manner, was drawn up by De Quincey, who revised the proofs of the whole' ('Memoirs,' i. 384). Of the 'Convention of Cintra' the (now) Bishop of Lincoln (WORDSWORTH) writes eloquently as follows: 'Much of WORDSWORTH's life was spent in comparative retirement, and a great part of his poetry concerns natural and quiet objects. But it would be a great error to imagine that he was not an attentive observer of public events. He was an ardent lover of his country and of mankind. He watched the progress of civil affairs in England with a vigilant eye, and he brought the actions of public men to the test of the great and lasting principles of equity and truth. He extended his range of view to events in foreign parts, especially on the continent of Europe. Few persons, though actually engaged in the great struggle of that period, felt more deeply than WORDSWORTH did in his peaceful retreat for the calamities of European nations, suffering at that time from the imbecility of their governments, and from the withering oppression of a prosperous despotism. His heart burned within him when he looked forth upon the contest, and impassioned words proceeded from him, both in poetry and prose. The contemplative calmness of his position, and the depth and intensity of his feelings, combined together to give a dignity and clearness, a vigour and splendour, and, consequently, a lasting value, to his writings on measures of domestic and foreign policy, qualities that rarely belong to contemporaneous political effusions produced by those engaged in the heat and din of the battle. This remark is specially applicable to his tract on the Convention of Cintra. . . . . Whatever difference of opinion may prevail concerning the relevance of the great principles enunciated in it to the questions at issue, but one judgment can exist with respect to the importance of those principles, and the vigorous and fervid eloquence with which they are enforced. If WORDSWORTH had never written a single verse, this Essay alone would be sufficient to place him in the highest rank of English poets. . . . . Enough has been quoted to show that the Essay on the Convention of Cintra was not an ephemeral production, destined to vanish with the occasion which gave it birth. If this were the case, the labour bestowed upon it was almost abortive. The author composed the work in the discharge of what he regarded a sacred duty, and for the permanent benefit of society, rather than with a view to any immediate results.'* The Bishop adds further these details: 'He foresaw and predicted that his words would be to the public ear what midnight storms are to men who sleep:

> "I dropp'd my pen, and listen'd to the wind,
> That sang of trees uptorn and vessels tost—
> A midnight harmony, and wholly lost
> To the general sense of men, by chains confined
> Of business, care, or pleasure, or resign'd
> To timely sleep. Thought I, the impassion'd strain,

* 'Memoirs,' as before, vol. i. pp. 383, 399.

> Which without aid of numbers I sustain,
> Like acceptation from the world will find.
> Yet some with apprehensive ear shall drink
> A dirge devoutly breath'd o'er sorrows past;
> And to the attendant promise will give heed—
> The prophecy—like that of this wild blast,
> Which, while it makes the heart with sadness shrink,
> Tells also of bright calms that shall succeed."*

It is true that some few readers it had on its first appearance; and it is recorded by an ear-witness that Canning said of this pamphlet that he considered it the most eloquent production since the days of Burke;† but, by some untoward delays in printing, it was not published till the interest in the question under discussion had almost subsided. Certain it is, that an edition, consisting only of five hundred copies, was not sold off; that many copies were disposed of by the publishers as waste paper, and went to the trunkmakers; and now there is scarcely any volume published in this country which is so difficult to be met with as the tract on the Convention of Cintra; and if it were now reprinted, it would come before the public with almost the unimpaired freshness of a new work.'‡ In agreement with the closing statement, at the sale of the library of Sir James Macintosh a copy fetched (it has been reported) ten guineas. Curiously enough not a single copy was preserved by the Author himself. The companion sonnet to the above, 'composed while the author was engaged in writing a tract occasioned by the Convention of Cintra, 1808,' must also find a place here:

* 'Poems dedicated to National Independence and Liberty,' viii.

† Southey's 'Life and Correspondence,' vol. iii. p. 180; 'Gentleman's Magazine' for June 1850, p. 617.

‡ 'Memoirs,' as before, vol. i. pp. 404-5.

'Not 'mid the world's vain objects that enslave
The free-born soul—that world whose vaunted skill
In selfish interest perverts the will,
Whose factions lead astray the wise and brave—
Not there; but in dark wood and rocky cave,
And hollow vale which foaming torrents fill
With omnipresent murmur as they rave
Down their steep beds, that never shall be still,
Here, mighty Nature, in this school sublime
I weigh the hopes and fears of suffering Spain;
For her consult the auguries of time,
And through the human heart explore my way,
And look and listen—gathering where I may
Triumph, and thoughts no bondage can restrain.'*

(*c*) *Letter to Major-General Sir Charles W. Pasley, K.C.B., on his 'Military Policy and Institutions of the British Empire,' with another —now first printed—transmitting it.*

The former is derived from the 'Memoirs' (vol. i. pp. 405-20). In forwarding it to the (now) Bishop of Lincoln, Sir CHARLES thus wrote of it: 'The letter on my "Military Policy" is particularly interesting. . . . Though WORDSWORTH agreed that we ought to step forward with all our military force as principals in the war, he objected to any increase of our own power and resources by continental conquest, in which I now think he was quite right. I am not, however, by any means shaken in the opinion then advanced, that peace with Napoleon would lead to the loss of our naval superiority and of our national independence, . . . and I fully believe that the Duke of Wellington's campaigns in the Spanish Peninsula saved the nation, though no less credit is due to the Ministry of that day for not despairing of eventual success, but supporting him under all difficulties in spite of temporary reverses, and in opposition to a powerful

* 'Poems dedicated to National Independence and Liberty,' vii.

party and to influential writers.' The letter transmitting the other has only recently been discovered on a reëxamination of the Wordsworth MSS. Both letters have a Shakespearian-patriotic ring concerning 'This England.' It is inspiring to read in retrospect of the facts such high-couraged writing as in these letters.

(*d*) *Two Addresses to the Freeholders of Westmoreland*, 1818.

The 'Mr. BROUGHAM' of these 'Two Addresses' was, as all the world knows, the (afterwards) renowned and many-gifted HENRY, Lord BROUGHAM and VAUX. In his Autobiography he refers very good-humouredly to his three defeats in contesting the representation of Westmoreland; but there is no allusion whatever to WORDSWORTH. With reference to his final effort he thus informs us: 'Parliament was dissolved in 1826, when for the third time I stood for Westmoreland; and, after a hard-fought contest, was again defeated. I have no wish to enter into the local politics of that county, but I cannot resist quoting an extract from a letter of my esteemed friend Bishop BATHURST to Mr. HOWARD of Corby, by whose kindness I am enabled to give it: "Mr. BROUGHAM has struggled nobly for civil and religious liberty; and is fully entitled to the celebrated eulogy bestowed by Lucan upon Cato—

'Victrix causa Diis placuit, sed victa Catoni.'

How others may feel I know not, but for my own part I would much rather be in his situation than in that of the two victorious opponents; notwithstanding the cold discouraging maxim of Epictetus, which is calculated to check every virtuous effort—'Ανίκητος εἶναι δύνασαι, ἐὰν οὐκ εἰς μηδένα ἀγῶνα καταβαίνῃς, οὗ οὐκ ἔστιν ἐπινικῆσαι

[=You may be invincible if you never go down into the arena when you are not secure of victory: Enchiridion, cxxv.]. He will not, I hope, suffer from his exertions, extraordinary in every way. I respect exceedingly his fine abilities, and the purpose to which he applies them" (Norwich, July 10, 1826). As Cato owed Lucan's panegyric to the firmness he had shown in adhering to the losing cause, and to his steadfastness to the principles he had adopted, so I considered the Bishop's application of the lines to me as highly complimentary' ('Life and Times,' vol. ii. pp. 437-8). It seemed only due to the subject of WORDSWORTH's invective and opposition to give *his* view of the struggle and another's worthy of all respect. Unless the writer has been misinformed, WORDSWORTH and BROUGHAM came to know and worthily estimate each other when the exacerbations and clamours of provincial politics had long passed away, and when, except the 'old gray head' of WELLINGTON, none received more reverence from the nation than that of HENRY BROUGHAM. In the just-issued 'Memoirs of the Reigns of George IV. and William IV.' by GREVILLE, BROUGHAM and WORDSWORTH are brought together very pleasingly. (See these works, vol. iii. p. 504.)

The Author's personal relations to the Lowthers semi-unconsciously coloured his opinions, and intensified his partisanship and glorified the commonplace. But with all abatements these 'Two Addresses' supply much material for a right and high estimate of WORDSWORTH as man and thinker. As invariably, he descends to the roots of things, and almost ennobles even his prejudices and alarms and ultra-caution. There is the same terse, compacted, pungent style in these 'Two Addresses' with his general prose. Bibliographically the 'Two Addresses' are even rarer and higher-priced than the 'Convention of Cintra.'

(*e*) *Of the Catholic Relief Bill*, 1829.

To the great names of EDMUND SPENSER and Sir JOHN DAVIES, as Englishmen who dealt with the problem of the government of Ireland, and found it, as more recent statesmen have done, to be in infinite ways 'England's difficulty,' has now to be added one not less great —WILLIAM WORDSWORTH. If at this later day—for even 1829 seems remote now—much of the present letter to the Bishop of London (BLOMFIELD) is mainly of historical noticeableness, as revealing how 'Catholic Emancipation' looked to one of the foremost minds of his age, there are, nevertheless, expressions of personal opinion—*e.g.* against the Athanasian Creed in its 'cursing' clauses, and expositions of the Papacy regarded politically and ecclesiastically in its domination of Ireland, that have a message for to-day strangely congruous with that of the magnificent philippic 'Of the Vatican Decrees,' which is thundering across Europe as these words are written. As a piece of vigorous, masculine, and o' times eloquent English, this letter may take its place—not an inch lower—beside a 'View of the State of Ireland,' and the 'Discoverie of the True Cavses why Ireland was never entirely subdued, nor brought under obedience of the Crowne of England, vntill the beginning of his Maiestie's happie raigne;' while the conflict with Ultramontanism in Germany and elsewhere and Mr. Gladstone's tractate give new significance to its forecastings and portents.

The manuscript, unlike most of his, is largely in

WORDSWORTH's own handwriting—the earlier portion in (it is believed) partly Miss WORDSWORTH's and partly Mrs. WORDSWORTH's. In the 'Memoirs' this letter is quoted largely (vol. ii. pp. 136-140). It is now given completely from the manuscript itself, not without significant advantage. It does not appear whether this letter were actually sent to the Bishop of London. There is no mention of it in Bishop Blomfield's 'Life;' and hence probably it never was sent to him. In his letters there are many references to the present topics (cf. vol. iii. pp. 258-9, 263-4, &c.).

II. ETHICAL.

I. *Of Legislation for the Poor, the Working Classes, and the Clergy: Appendix to Poems*, 1835.

This formed one of WORDSWORTH's most deliberate and powerful Appendices to his Poems (1835), and has ever since been regarded as of enduring worth. It has all the Author's characteristics of deep thinking, imaginative illustration, intense conviction and realness. Again, accept or dissent, this State Paper (so to say) is specially Wordsworthian.

It seems only due to WORDSWORTH to bear in recollection that, herein and elsewhere, he led the way in indicating CO-OPERATION as *the* remedy for the defects and conflicts in the relations between our capitalists and their operatives, or capital and labour (see the second section of the Postscript, and remember its date—1835).

II. *Advice to the Young.*

(*a*) Letter to the Editor of 'The Friend,' signed Mathetes.
(*b*) Answer to the Letter of Mathetes, 1809.

'Mathetes' proved to be Professor JOHN WILSON,

'eminent in the various departments of poetry, philosophy, and criticism' ('Memoirs,' i. 423), and here probably was the commencement of the long friendship between him and WORDSWORTH. As a student of WILSON's, the Editor remembers vividly how the 'old man eloquent' used to kindle into enthusiasm the entire class as he worked into his extraordinary lectures quotations from the 'Excursion' and 'Sonnets' and 'Poems of the Imagination.' Among the letters (vol. iii. p. 263) is an interesting one refering to 'Advice to the Young;' and another to Professor WILSON (vol. ii. pp. 208-14).

III. OF EDUCATION.

(*a*) On the Education of the Young: Letter to a Friend, 1806.

(*b*) Of the People, their Ways and Needs: Letter to Archdeacon Wrangham, 1808.

(*c*) Education: Two Letters to the Rev. H. J. Rose, 1828.

(*d*) Education of Duty: Letter to Rev. Dr. Wordsworth, 1830.

(*e*) Speech on laying the Foundation-stone of the New School in the Village of Bowness, Windermere, 1836.

In these Letters and the Speech are contained WORDSWORTH's earliest and latest and most ultimate opinions and sentiments on education. Agree or differ, the student of WORDSWORTH has in these discussions—for in part they have the elaborateness and thoroughness of such—what were of the substance of his beliefs. Their biographic importance—intellectually and spiritually—can scarcely be exaggerated. (*a*), (*b*), (*c*), (*d*) are from the 'Memoirs;' (*e*) is from the local newspaper (Kendal), being for the first time fully reprinted.

VOL. II.

Æsthetical and Literary.

I. *Of Literary Biography and Monuments.*

(*a*) A Letter to a Friend of Robert Burns, 1816.
(*b*) Letter to a Friend on Monuments to Literary Men, 1819.
(*c*) Letter to John Peace, Esq., of Bristol, 1844.

These naturally group themselves together. Of the first (*a*), perhaps it is hardly worth while, and perhaps it is worth while, recalling that William Hazlitt, in his Lectures upon the English Poets, attacked Wordsworth on this Letter with characteristic insolence and uncritical shallowness and haste. Under date Feb. 24th, 1818, Mr. H. Crabb Robinson thus refers to the thing: 'Heard part of a lecture by Hazlitt at the Surrey Institution. He was so contemptuous towards Wordsworth, speaking of his Letter about Burns, that I lost my temper. He imputed to Wordsworth the desire of representing himself as a superior man' (vol. i. p. 311, 3d ed.). The lecture is included in Hazlitt's published Lectures in all its ignorance and wrong-headedness; but it were a pity to lose one's temper over such trash. His eyes were spectacles, not 'seeing eyes,' and jaundice-yellow. (*b*) and (*c*) are sequels to (*a*), and as such accompany it.

II. Upon Epitaphs.

(*a*) From 'The Friend.
(*b* and *c*) From the Author's mss., for the first time.

Of (*a*) Charles Lamb wrote: 'Your Essay on Epitaphs is the only sensible thing which has been written on that subject, and it goes to the bottom' (Talfourd's 'Final Memorials,' vol. i. p. 180). The two additional Papers—only briefly quoted from in the 'Memoirs' (c.

xxx. vol. i.)—were also intended for 'The Friend,' had COLERIDGE succeeded in his announced arrangement of principles. These additional papers are in every respect equal to the first, with Wordsworthian touches and turns in his cunningest faculty. They are faithfully given from the MSS.

III. ESSAYS, LETTERS, AND NOTES ELUCIDATORY AND CONFIRMATORY OF THE POEMS, 1798-1835.

(*a*) Of the Principles of Poetry and the 'Lyrical Ballads' (1798-1802.)

(*b*) Of Poetic Diction.

(*c*) Poetry as a Study (1815).

(*d*) Of Poetry as Observation and Description, and Dedication of 1815.

(*e*) Of 'The Excursion:' Preface.

(*f*) Letters to Sir George and Lady Beaumont and others on the Poems and related Subjects.

(*g*) Letter to Charles Fox with the 'Lyrical Ballads,' and his Answer, &c.

(*h*) Letter on the Principles of Poetry and his own Poems to (afterwards) Professor John Wilson.

(*a*) to (*e*) form appendices to the early and later editions of the Poems, and created an epoch in literary criticism. COLERIDGE put forth his utmost strength on a critical examination of them, oblivious that he had himself impelled, not to say compelled, his friend to write these Prefaces, as WORDSWORTH signifies. It is not meant by this that COLERIDGE was thereby shut out from criticising the definitions and statements to which he objected.

IV. DESCRIPTIVE.

(*a*) A Guide through the District of the Lakes, 1835.

(*b*) Kendal and Windermere Railway: two Letters, &c.

These very much explain themselves; but of the

former it may be of bibliographical interest to state that it formed originally the letterpress and Introduction to 'Select Views in Cumberland, Westmoreland, and Lancashire,' by the Rev. JOSEPH WILKINSON, Rector of East Wrotham, Norfolk, 1810 (folio). It was reprinted in the volume of Sonnets on the River Duddon. The fifth edition (1835) has been selected as the Author's own final text. In Notes and Illustrations in the place, a strangely overlooked early account of the Lake District is pointed out and quoted from. The 'Two Letters' need no vindication at this late day. Ruskin is reiterating their arguments and sentiment eloquently as these pages pass through the press. Apart from deeper reasons, let the fault-finder realise to himself the differentia of general approval of railways, and a railway forced through the 'old churchyard' that holds his mother's grave or the garden of his young prime. It was a merely sordid matter on the part of the promoters. Their professions of care for the poor and interest in the humbler classes getting to the Lakes had a Judas element in them, nothing higher or purer.

VOL. III.

CRITICAL AND ETHICAL.

I. *Notes and Illustrations of the Poems, incorporating:*

(*a*) The Notes originally added to the first and successive editions.
(*b*) The whole of the I.F. MSS.

This division of the Prose has cost the Editor more labour and thought than any other, from the scattered and hitherto unclassified semi-publication of these Notes. Those called 'original' are from the first and successive editions of the Poems, being found in some and absent in other collections. An endeavour has been made to include everything, even the briefest; for judging by himself, the Editor believes that to the reverent and thoughtful student of WORDSWORTH the slightest thing is of interest; *e.g.* one turns to the most commonplace book of topography or contemporary verse in any way noticed by him, just because it is WORDSWORTH who has noticed it, while an old ballad, a legend, a bit of rural usage, takes a light of glory from the page in which it is found. Hence as so much diamond-dust or filings of gold the published Notes are here brought together. Added, and far exceeding in quantity and quality alike, it is the privilege of the Editor to print *completely and in integrity* the I.F. MSS., as written down to the dictation of WORDSWORTH by Miss FENWICK. These have been hitherto given with tantalising and almost provoking fragmentariness in the 'Memoirs' and in the centenary edition of the Poems—again withdrawn in the recent Rossetti edition. In these Notes—many of which in both senses are elaborate and full—are some of the deepest and daintiest-worded things from WORDSWORTH. The I.F. MSS. are delightfully chatty and informal, and ages hence will be treasured and studied in relation to the Poems by the (then) myriad millions of the English-speaking races.

Miss FENWICK, to whom the world is indebted for these MSS., is immortalised in two Sonnets by WORDSWORTH, which surely long ere this ought to have been included in the Poetical Works; and they may fitly reappear here (from the 'Memoirs'):

'*On a Portrait of I. F., painted by Margaret Gillies.*

We gaze—nor grieve to think that we must die,
But that the precious love this friend hath sown
Within our hearts, the love whose flower hath blown
Bright as if heaven were ever in its eye,
Will pass so soon from human memory;
And not by strangers to our blood alone,
But by our best descendants be unknown,
Unthought of—this may surely claim a sigh.
Yet, blessed Art, we yield not to dejection;
Thou against Time so feelingly dost strive:
Where'er, preserved in this most true reflection,
An image of her soul is kept alive,
Some lingering fragrance of the pure affection,
Whose flower with us will vanish, must survive.

William Wordsworth.

Rydal Mount, New Year's Day, 1840.'

'*To I. F.*

The star which comes at close of day to shine
More heavenly bright than when it leads the morn
Is Friendship's emblem, whether the forlorn
She visiteth, or shedding light benign
Through shades that solemnise Life's calm decline,
Doth make the happy happier. This have we
Learnt, Isabel, from thy society,
Which now we too unwillingly resign
Though for brief absence. But farewell! the page
Glimmers before my sight through thankful tears,
Such as start forth, not seldom, to approve
Our truth, when we, old yet unchill'd by age,
Call thee, though known but for a few fleet years,
The heart-affianced sister of our love!

William Wordsworth.

Rydal Mount, Feb. 1840.'

In addition to these Sonnets the beautiful memory of Miss Fenwick has been reilluminated in the 'Memoir and Letters of Sara Coleridge' (2 vols. 1873); *e.g.* 'I take great delight in Miss Fenwick, and in her conversation. Well should I like to have her constantly in the drawing-room, to come down to and from my little study up-stairs—her mind is such a noble compound of heart and intelligence, of spiritual feeling and moral strength, and the most perfect feminineness. She is intellectual, but—what is a great excellence—never talks for effect, never *keeps possession of the floor*, as clever women are so apt to do. She converses for the interchange of thought and feeling, no matter *how*, so she gets at your mind, and lets you into hers. A more generous and a tenderer heart I never knew. I differ from her on many points of religious faith, but on the whole prefer her views to those of most others who differ from her' (ii. 5). Again: 'Miss FENWICK is to me an angel upon earth. Her being near me now has seemed a special providence. God bless her, and spare her to us and her many friends. She is a noble creature, all tenderness and strength. When I first became acquainted with her, I saw at once that her heart was of the very finest, richest quality, and her wisdom and insight are, as ever must be in such a case, exactly correspondent' (ibid. p. 397). Such words from one so penetrative, so indeceivable, so great in the fullest sense as was the daughter of *the* COLERIDGE, makes every one long to have the same service done for Miss FENWICK as has been done for SARA COLERIDGE and Miss HARE, and within these weeks for Mrs. FLETCHER. Her Diaries and Correspondence would be inestimable to lovers of WORDSWORTH; for few or none got so near to him or entered so magnetically into his thinking. The headings and numberings of the successive Notes—lesser and larger—will guide to the respective Poems and places. The numberings accord with ROSSETTI's handy one-volume edition of the Poems, but as a rule will offer no difficulty in any. The I.F. MSS. are marked with an asterisk [*]: They are *for the first time* furnished in their entirety, and accurately.

II. *Letters and Extracts of Letters.*

These are arranged as nearly as possible chronologically from the 'Memoirs,' &c. &c., with the benefit, as before, of collation in many cases of the original MSS., especially in the Sir W. R. HAMILTON letters, and a number are *for the first time printed.* The Editor does not at all like 'Extracts,' and must be permitted to regret that what in his judgment was an antiquated and mistaken idea of biography led the excellent as learned Bishop of Lincoln to abridge and mutilate so very many —the places not always marked. On this and the principle and *motif* which approve and vindicate the publication of the Letters of every really potential intellect such as WORDSWORTH's, the accomplished daughter of SARA COLERIDGE has remarked: 'A book composed of epistolary extracts can never be a wholly satisfactory one, because its contents are not only relative and fragmentary, but unauthorised and unrevised. To arrest the passing utterances of the hour, and reveal to the world that which was spoken either in the innermost circle of home affection, or in the outer (but still guarded) circle of social or friendly intercourse, seems almost like a betrayal of confidence, and is a step which cannot be taken by survivors without some feelings of hesitation and reluctance. That reluctance is only to be overcome by the sense that, however natural, it is partly founded on delusion—a delusion which leads us to personify "the world," to our imagination, as an obtuse and somewhat hostile individual, who is certain to take things by the wrong handle, and cannot be trusted to make the needful allowance, and supply the inevitable omissions. Whereas it is a more reasonable and a more comfortable belief, that the only part of the world which is in the least likely to concern itself with such volumes as these is composed of a number of enlightened and sympathetic persons' (as before, Preface, vii. viii.). The closing consideration ought to overweigh all scruples and reserve.* There *is* the select circle of lovers of WORDSWORTH—yearly widening—and there are the far-off multitudes of the future to whom WILLIAM WORDSWORTH will be the grand name of the 18th-19th century, and all that SHAKESPEARE and MILTON are now; and consequently the letters of one so chary in letter-writing ought to be put beyond the risks of loss, and given to Literature in entirety and trueness. WORDSWORTH had a morbid dislike of writing letters, his weak eyes throughout rendering all penmanship painful; but the present Editor, while conceding that his letters lack the charm of style of COWPER'S, and the vividness and passion of BYRON'S, finds in them, even the hastiest, matter of rarest biographic and interpretative value. He was not a great sentence-

* The charming 'Journal' in full of Miss WORDSWORTH has only within the past year been published. The welcome it has met with—having bounded into a third edition already—is at once proof of the soundness of judgment that at long-last issued it, if it be also accusatory that many have gone who yearned to read it. The Editor ventures to invite special attention to WORDSWORTH'S own express wish that the foreign 'Journals' of Miss WORDSWORTH and Mrs. WORDSWORTH should be published. Surely *his* words ought to be imperative (vol. iii. p. 77)?

maker; in a way prided himself that his letters were so (intentionally) poor as sure to be counted unworthy of publication; and altogether had the prejudices of an earlier day against the giving of letters to the world; but none the less are his letters informed with his intellect and meditative thoughtfulness and exquisiteness of feeling. It is earnestly to be hoped that one of the Family who is admirably qualified for the task of love will address himself to write adequately and confidingly the Life of his immortal relative; and toward this every one possessed of anything in the handwriting or from the mind of Wordsworth may be appealed to for coöperation. The 'Memoirs' of the (now) Bishop of Lincoln, within its own limits, was a great gift; but it is avowedly not a 'Life,' and *the world wants a Life.* Collation of the originals of these letters has restored sentences and words and things of the most characteristic kind. Very gross mistakes have also been corrected.*

III. *Conversations and Personal Reminiscences of Wordsworth.*

From 'Satyrane's Letters;' Klopstock.

Personal Reminiscences of the Hon. Mr. Justice Coleridge.

Recollections of a Tour in Italy with Wordsworth. By H. C. Robinson.

Reminiscences of Lady Richardson and Mrs. Davy.

Conversations recorded by the Bishop of Lincoln.

Reminiscences by the Rev. R. P. Graves, M.A., Dublin; on the Death of Coleridge; and further (hitherto unpublished) Reminiscences.

---

* It may be well to point out here specially a mistake in heading two of the Wordsworth letters to Sir W. R. Hamilton: 'Royal Dublin Society,' instead of 'Royal Irish Academy' (see vol. iii. pp. 350 and 352); also that at p. 394 'of the' has slipped in from the first 'of the,' and so now reads 'Of the Heresiarch of the Church of Rome,' for 'The Heresiarch Church,' as in the body of the letter.

An American's Reminiscences.
Recollections of Aubrey de Vere, Esq., now first published.*
From 'Recollections of the Last Days of Shelley and Byron,' by E. J. Trelawny, Esq.
From Letters of Professor Tayler (1872).
Anecdote of Crabbe and Wordsworth.
Wordsworth's Later Opinion of Lord Brougham.

These are included in the Prose inevitably, inasmuch as they preserve opinions and sentiments, criticisms and sayings, actually spoken by WORDSWORTH, of exactly the type of which Lord COLERIDGE, among other things, wrote the Editor: 'I hope we shall have a transcript from you of the thoughts and opinions of that very great and noble person, of whom (as far as I know them) it is most true that "the very dust of his writings is gold." Any grave and deliberate opinion of his is entitled to weight; and if we have his opinions at all, we should have them whole and entire.'

The Editor has studied to give WORDSWORTH'S own conversations and sayings—not others' concerning him. Hence such eloquent pseudo-enthusiasm as is found in De Quincey's 'Recollections of the Lakes' (Works, vol. ii.) is excluded. He dares to call it pseudo-enthusiasm; for this book of the little, alert, self-conscious creature, with the marvellous brain and more marvellous tongue—a monkey with a man's soul somehow transmigrated into it—opens and shuts without preserving a solitary saying of the man he professes to honour. That is a measure of *his* admiration as of his insight or no insight. There are besides personal impertinencies,

† Will the Reader indulgently correct a most unfortunate oversight of the printers in vol. iii. p. 497, l. 15, where 'no angel smiled' (mis)reads 'no angle smiled'?

declarative of essential vulgarity.* Smaller men have printed their 'Recollections,' or rather retailed their gossip; but they themselves occupy the foreground, much as your chimney-sweep introduces himself prominently in front of his signboard presentment of some many-chimneyed 'noble house.' Even Emerson's 'English Traits' (a most un-English book) belongs to the same underbred category. The new 'Recollections' by AUBREY DE VERE, Esq., it is a privilege to publish—full of reverence and love, and so daintily and musically worded, as they are.

Such is an account of the contents of these volumes; and it may be permitted the Editor to record his hearty thanks to the Sons of the Poet—WILLIAM WORDSWORTH, Esq., Carlisle, and the just dead Rev. JOHN WORDSWORTH, M.A., Brigham—and his nephew Professor WORDSWORTH of Bombay, for their so flattering committal of this trust to him; and especially to the last, for his sympathetic and gladdening counsel throughout—augury of larger service ultimately, it is to be hoped. To the co-executor with WILLIAM WORDSWORTH, Esq.—STRICKLAND COOKSON, Esq.—like acknowledgment is due. He cannot sufficiently thank AUBREY DE VERE, Esq., for his brilliant contribu-

* Possibly indignation roused by the 'Recollections' has provoked too vehement condemnation. Let it therefore be noted that it is the 'Recollections' that are censured. Elsewhere DE QUINCEY certainly shows a glimmering recognition of WORDSWORTH's great qualities, and that before they had been fully admitted; but everywhere there is an impertinence of familiarity and a patronising self-consciousness that is irritating to any one who reverences great genius and high rectitude. It may be conceded that DE QUINCEY, so far as he was capable, did reverence WORDSWORTH; but his exaggerations of awe and delays bear on the face of them unveracity.

tion to the 'Personal Reminiscences.' The Rev. Robert Perceval Graves, M.A., of Dublin (formerly of Windermere), has greatly added to the interest of these volumes by forwarding his further reminiscences of Wordsworth and the Hamilton Letters. Fifteen of these letters of Wordsworth, not yet published, will be given in a Life of the great mathematician of Ireland, Sir W. R. Hamilton, towards whom Wordsworth felt the warmest friendship, and of whose many-sided genius he had the most absolute admiration. Mr. Graves, walking in the footsteps of Fulke Greville, Lord Brooke, who sought that on his tomb should be graven 'Friend of Sir Philip Sidney' (albeit he would modestly disclaim the lofty comparison), regards it as his title to memory that he was called 'my highly esteemed friend' by Wordsworth (vol. iii. p. 27). For the Graveses the Poet had much regard, and it was mutual. A Sonnet addressed to Wordsworth by the (now) Bishop of Limerick was so highly valued by him that it is a pleasure to be able to read it, as thus:

'*To Wordsworth.*

The Sages of old time have pass'd away,
A throng of mighty names. But little power
Have ancient names to rule the present hour:
No Plato to the learners of our day
In grove of Academe reveals the way,
The law, the soul of Nature. Yet a light
Of living wisdom, beaming calm and bright,
Forbids our youth 'mid error's maze to stray.
To thee, with gratitude and reverent love,
O Poet and Philosopher! we turn;
For in thy truth-inspirèd song we learn
Passion and pride to quell—erect to move,
From doubts and fears deliver'd—and conceiving
Pure hopes of heaven, live happy in believing.

August 1833.' C. G.

Lady RICHARDSON has similarly added to the value of her former 'Recollections' for this work. Very special gratitude is due to the Miss QUILLINANS of Loughrigg, Rydal, for the use of the MS. of Miss FENWICK'S Notes—one half in their father's handwriting, and the other half (or thereabout) in that of Mrs. QUILLINAN ('DORA'), who at the end has written:

> 'To dearest Miss Fenwick are we obliged for these Notes, every word of which was taken down by her kind pen from my father's dictation. The former portion was transcribed at Rydal by Mr. Quillinan, the latter by me, and finished at the Vicarage, Brigham, this twenty-fifth day of August 1843.—D. Q.'

The MS., be it repeated, is now printed *in extenso*, nor will the least acceptable be 'DORA'S' own slight pencillings intercalated. The Miss COOKSONS of Grasmere were good enough to present the Editor with a copy of the 'Two Letters to the Freeholders of Westmoreland,' when he had almost despaired of recovering the pamphlet. Thanks are due to several literary friends for aid in the Notes and Illustrations. There must be named Professor DOWDEN and Rev. R. P. GRAVES, M.A.,* Dublin; F. W. COSENS, Esq., and G. A. SIMCOX, Esq., London; W. ALDIS WRIGHT, Esq., M.A., Trinity College, Cambridge.

One point only remains to be noticed. Every one who knows our highest poetical literature knows the

* Mr. Graves has published the following on the Wordsworths: (*a*) 'Recollections of Wordsworth and the Lake Country;' a lecture, and a capital one. (*b*) 'A Good Name and the Day of Death: two Blessings;' a sermon preached in Ambleside Church, January 30, 1859, on occasion of the death of Mrs. Wordsworth—tender and consolatory. (*c*) 'The Ascension of our Lord, and its Lessons for Mourners;' a sermon (1858) finely commemorative of Arnold, the Wordsworths, Mrs. Fletcher, and others.

'Lost Leader' of ROBERT BROWNING, Esq. Many have been the speculations and surmises and assertions and contradictions as to who the 'Lost Leader' was. The verdict of one of the immortals on his fellow-immortal concerns us all. Hence it is with no common thankfulness the Editor of WORDSWORTH's Prose embraces this opportunity of settling the controversy beyond appeal, by giving a letter which Mr. BROWNING has done him the honour to write for publication. It is as follows:

'19 Warwick-crescent, W.
Feb. 24, '75.

DEAR MR. GROSART,

I have been asked the question you now address me with, and as duly answered it, I can't remember how many times: there is no sort of objection to one more assurance, or rather confession, on my part, that I *did* in my hasty youth presume to use the great and venerated personality of WORDSWORTH as a sort of painter's model; one from which this or the other particular feature may be selected and turned to account: had I intended more, above all, such a boldness as portraying the entire man, I should not have talked about "handfuls of silver and bits of ribbon." These never influenced the change of politics in the great poet; whose defection, nevertheless, accompanied as it was by a regular face-about of his special party, was to my juvenile apprehension, and even mature consideration, an event to deplore. But just as in the tapestry on my wall I can recognise figures which have *struck out* a fancy, on occasion, that though truly enough thus derived, yet would be preposterous as a copy, so, though I dare not deny the original of my little poem, I altogether refuse to have it considered as the "very effigies" of such a moral and intellectual superiority.

Faithfully yours,
ROBERT BROWNING.'

The Editor cannot close this Preface without expressing his sense of the greatness of the trust confided to him, and the personal benefit it has been to himself to have been brought so near to WILLIAM WORDSWORTH as he has been in working on this collection of his Prose.

He felt almost awed as he handled the great and good man's MSS., and found himself behind the screen (as it were), seeing what he had seen, touching what he had touched, knowing what he had known, feeling what he had felt. Reverence, even veneration is an empty word to utter the emotion excited in such communion; these certainly, but something tenderer and more human were in head and heart. It was a grand, high-thoughted, pure-lived, unique course that was run in those sequestered vales. The closer one gets to the man, the greater he proves, the truer, the simpler; and it is a benediction to the race, amid so many fragmentary and jagged and imperfect lives, to have one so rounded and completed, so august and so genuine:

'Summon Detraction to object the worst
That may be told, and utter all it can;
It cannot find a blemish to be enforced
Against him, other than he was a man,
And built of flesh and blood, and did live here,
Within the region of infirmity;
Where all perfections never did appear
To meet in any one so really,
But that his frailty ever did bewray
Unto the world that he was set in clay.'

(Funeral Panegyric on the Earl of Devonshire, by Samuel Daniel.)

ALEXANDER B. GROSART.

Park View,
Blackburn, Lancashire.

NOTE.—It is perhaps right to mention, for Editor and present Printers' sake, that WORDSWORTH's own capitals, italics, punctuation, and other somewhat antique characteristics, have been faithfully reproduced. At the dates, capitals, italics, and punctuation were more abundant than at present. G.

CONTENTS OF VOL. I.

*** A star [*] designates publication herein *for the first time*. G.

I. POLITICAL.

I. APOLOGY FOR THE FRENCH REVOLUTION,

1793.

NOTE.

For an account of the manuscript of this 'Apology,' and details on other points, see Preface in the present volume. G.

APOLOGY FOR THE FRENCH REVOLUTION, 1793.

My Lord,

Reputation may not improperly be termed the moral life of man. Alluding to our natural existence, Addison, in a sublime allegory well known to your Lordship, has represented us as crossing an immense bridge, from whose surface from a variety of causes we disappear one after another, and are seen no more. Every one who enters upon public life has such a bridge to pass. Some slip through at the very commencement of their career from thoughtlessness, others pursue their course a little longer, till, misled by the phantoms of avarice and ambition, they fall victims to their delusion. Your Lordship was either seen, or supposed to be seen, continuing your way for a long time unseduced and undismayed; but those who now look for you will look in vain, and it is feared you have at last fallen, through one of the numerous trap-doors, into the tide of contempt, to be swept down to the ocean of oblivion.

It is not my intention to be illiberal; these latter expressions have been forced from me by indignation. Your Lordship has given a proof that even religious controversy may be conducted without asperity; I hope I shall profit by your example. At the same time, with a spirit which you may not approve—for it is a republican spirit—I shall not preclude myself from any truths, however severe, which I may think beneficial to the cause which I have undertaken to defend. You will not, then, be surprised when I inform you that it is only the name of its author which has induced me to notice an Appendix to a Sermon which you have lately given to the world, with a hope that it may have some effect in calming a perturbation which, you say, has been *excited* in the minds of the lower orders of the community. While, with a servility which has prejudiced many people against religion itself, the ministers of the Church of England have appeared as writers upon public measures only to be the advocates of slavery civil and religious, your Lordship stood almost alone as the defender of truth and political charity. The names of levelling prelate, bishop of the Dissenters, which were intended as a dishonour to your character, were looked upon by your friends—perhaps by yourself—as an acknowledgment of your possessing an enlarged and philosophical mind; and, like the generals in a neighbouring country, if it had been equally becoming your profession, you might have adopted, as an honourable title, a denomination intended as a stigma.

On opening your Appendix, your admirers will naturally expect to find an impartial statement of the grievances which harass this Nation, and a sagacious inquiry into the proper modes of redress. They will be disappointed. Sensible how large a portion of mankind receive opinions upon authority, I am apprehensive lest the doctrines which they will there find should derive a weight from your name to which they are by no means intrinsically entitled. I will therefore examine what you have advanced, from a hope of being able to do away any impression left on the minds of such as may be liable to confound with argument a strong prepossession for your Lordship's talents, experience, and virtues.

Before I take notice of what you appear to have laid down as principles, it may not be improper to advert to some incidental opinions found at the commencement of your political confession of faith.

At a period big with the fate of the human race I am sorry that you attach so much importance to the personal sufferings of the late royal martyr, and that an anxiety for the issue of the present convulsions should not have prevented you from joining in the idle cry of modish lamentation which has resounded from the Court to the cottage. You wish it to be supposed you are one of those who are unpersuaded of the guilt of Louis XVI. If you had attended to the history of the French Revolution as minutely as its importance demands, so far from stopping to bewail his death, you would rather have regretted that the blind fondness of his people had placed a human being in that monstrous situation which rendered him unaccountable before a human tribunal. A bishop, a man of philosophy and humanity* as distinguished as your Lordship, declared at the

* M. Gregoire.

opening of the National Convention—and twenty-five millions of men were convinced of the truth of the assertion—that there was not a citizen on the tenth of August who, if he could have dragged before the eyes of Louis the corse of one of his murdered brothers, might not have exclaimed to him: 'Tyran, voilà ton ouvrage.' Think of this, and you will not want consolation under any depression your spirits may feel at the contrast exhibited by Louis on the most splendid throne of the universe, and Louis alone in the tower of the Temple or on the scaffold. But there is a class of men who received the news of the late execution with much more heartfelt sorrow than that which you, among such a multitude, so officiously express. The passion of pity is one of which, above all others, a Christian teacher should be cautious of cherishing the abuse when, under the influence of reason, it is regulated by the disproportion of the pain suffered to the guilt incurred. It is from the passion thus directed that the men of whom I have just spoken are afflicted by the catastrophe of the fallen monarch. They are sorry that the prejudice and weakness of mankind have made it necessary to force an individual into an unnatural situation, which requires more than human talents and human virtues, and at the same time precludes him from attaining even a moderate knowledge of common life, and from feeling a particular share in the interests of mankind. But, above all, these men lament that any combination of circumstances should have rendered it necessary or advisable to veil for a moment the statues of the laws, and that by such emergency the cause of twenty-five millions of people, I may say of the whole human race, should have been so materially injured. Any other sorrow for the death of Louis is irrational and weak.

In France royalty is no more. The person of the last anointed is no more also; and I flatter myself I am not alone, even in this *kingdom*, when I wish that it may please the Almighty neither by the hands of His priests nor His nobles (I allude to a striking passage of Racine) to raise his posterity to the rank of his ancestors, and reillume the torch of extinguished David.*

* See *Athalie*, [act i.] scene 2:

'Il faut que sur le trône un roi soit élevé,
Qui *se souvienne un jour* qu'au rang de ses ancêtres.

You say: 'I fly with terror and abhorrence even from the altar of Liberty, when I see it stained with the blood of the aged, of the innocent, of the defenceless sex, of the ministers of religion, and of the faithful adherents of a fallen monarch.' What! have you so little knowledge of the nature of man as to be ignorant that a time of revolution is not the season of true Liberty? Alas, the obstinacy and perversion of man is such that she is too often obliged to borrow the very arms of Despotism to overthrow him, and, in order to reign in peace, must establish herself by violence. She deplores such stern necessity, but the safety of the people, her supreme law, is her consolation. This apparent contradiction between the principles of liberty and the march of revolutions; this spirit of jealousy, of severity, of disquietude, of vexation, indispensable from a state of war between the oppressors and oppressed, must of necessity confuse the ideas of morality, and contract the benign exertion of the best affections of the human heart. Political virtues are developed at the expense of moral ones; and the sweet emotions of compassion, evidently dangerous when traitors are to be punished, are too often altogether smothered. But is this a sufficient reason to reprobate a convulsion from which is to spring a fairer order of things? It is the province of education to rectify the erroneous notions which a habit of oppression, and even of resistance, may have created, and to soften this ferocity of character, proceeding from a necessary suspension of the mild and social virtues; it belongs to her to create a race of men who, truly free, will look upon their fathers as only enfranchised.

I proceed to the sorrow you express for the fate of the French priesthood. The measure by which that body was immediately stripped of part of its possessions, and a more equal distribution enjoined of the rest, does not meet with your Lordship's approbation. You do not question the right of the Nation over

---

Dieu l'a fait remonter par la main de ses prêtres:
L'a tiré par leurs mains de l'oubli du tombeau,
Et de David éteint rallumé le flambeau.'

The conclusion of the same speech applies so strongly to the present period that I cannot forbear transcribing it:

'Daigne, daigne, mon Dieu, sur Mathan, et sur elle
Répandre *cet esprit d'imprudence et d'erreur,*
De la chute des rois funeste avant-coureur!'

ecclesiastical wealth; you have voluntarily abandoned a ground which you were conscious was altogether untenable. Having allowed this right, can you question the propriety of exerting it at that particular period? The urgencies of the State were such as required the immediate application of a remedy. Even the clergy were conscious of such necessity; and aware, from the immunities they had long enjoyed, that the people would insist upon their bearing some share of the burden, offered of themselves a considerable portion of their superfluities. The Assembly was true to justice, and refused to compromise the interests of the Nation by accepting as a satisfaction the insidious offerings of compulsive charity. They enforced their right. They took from the clergy a large share of their wealth, and applied it to the alleviation of the national misery. Experience shows daily the wise employment of the ample provision which yet remains to them. While you reflect on the vast diminution which some men's fortunes must have undergone, your sorrow for these individuals will be diminished by recollecting the unworthy motives which induced the bulk of them to undertake the office, and the scandalous arts which enabled so many to attain the rank and enormous wealth which it has seemed necessary to annex to the charge of a Christian pastor. You will rather look upon it as a signal act of justice that they should thus unexpectedly be stripped of the rewards of their vices and their crimes. If you should lament the sad reverse by which the hero of the necklace* has been divested of about 1,300,000 livres of annual revenue, you may find some consolation that a part of this prodigious mass of riches is gone to preserve from famine some thousands of curés, who were pining in villages unobserved by Courts.

I now proceed to principles. Your Lordship very properly asserts that 'the liberty of man in a state of society consists in his being subject to no law but the law enacted by the general will of the society to which he belongs.' You approved of the object which the French had in view when, in the infancy of the Revolution, they were attempting to destroy arbitrary power, and to erect a temple to Liberty on its remains. It is with surprise, then, that I find you afterwards presuming to dictate to the world a servile adoption of the British constitution. It is with

* Prince de Rohan.

indignation I perceive you 'reprobate' a people for having imagined happiness and liberty more likely to flourish in the open field of a Republic than under the shade of Monarchy. You are therefore guilty of a most glaring contradiction. Twenty-five millions of Frenchmen have felt that they could have no security for their liberties under any modification of monarchical power. They have in consequence unanimously chosen a Republic. You cannot but observe that they have only exercised that right in which, by your own confession, liberty essentially resides.

As to your arguments, by which you pretend to justify your anathemas of a Republic—if arguments they may be called—they are so concise, that I cannot but transcribe them. 'I dislike a Republic for this reason, because of all forms of government, scarcely excepting the most despotic, I think a Republic the most oppressive to the bulk of the people; they are deceived in it with a show of liberty, but they live in it under the most odious of all tyrannies—the tyranny of their equals.'

This passage is a singular proof of that fatality by which the advocates of error furnish weapons for their own destruction: while it is merely *assertion* in respect to a justification of your aversion to Republicanism, a strong *argument* may be drawn from it in its favour. Mr. Burke, in a philosophic lamentation over the extinction of chivalry, told us that in those times vice lost half its evil by losing all its grossness. Infatuated moralist! Your Lordship excites compassion as labouring under the same delusion. Slavery is a bitter and a poisonous draught. We have but one consolation under it, that a Nation may dash the cup to the ground when she pleases. Do not imagine that by taking from its bitterness you weaken its deadly quality; no, by rendering it more palatable you contribute to its power of destruction. We submit without repining to the chastisements of Providence, aware that we are creatures, that opposition is vain and remonstrance impossible. But when redress is in our own power and resistance is rational, we suffer with the same humility from beings like ourselves, because we are taught from infancy that we were born in a state of inferiority to our oppressors, that they were sent into the world to scourge, and we to be scourged. Accordingly we see the bulk of mankind, actuated by these fatal prejudices, even more ready to lay themselves under the feet of *the great* than the great are to trample upon them.

Now taking for granted, that in Republics men live under the tyranny of what you call their equals, the circumstance of this being the most odious of all tyrannies is what a Republican would boast of; as soon as tyranny becomes odious, the principal step is made towards its destruction. Reflecting on the degraded state of the mass of mankind, a philosopher will lament that oppression is not odious to them, that the iron, while it eats the soul, is not felt to enter into it. 'Tout l'homme né dans l'esclavage naît pour l'esclavage, rien n'est plus certain; les esclaves perdent tout dans leurs fers, jusqu'au désir d'en sortir; ils aiment leur servitude, comme les compagnons d'Ulysse aimaient leur abrutissement.'

I return to the quotation in which you reprobate Republicanism. Relying upon the temper of the times, you have surely thought little argument necessary to content what few will be hardy enough to support; the strongest of auxiliaries, imprisonment and the pillory, has left your arm little to perform. But the happiness of mankind is so closely connected with this subject, that I cannot suffer such considerations to deter me from throwing out a few hints, which may lead to a conclusion that a Republic legitimately constructed contains less of an oppressive principle than any other form of government.

Your Lordship will scarcely question that much of human misery, that the great evils which desolate States, proceed from the governors having an interest distinct from that of the governed. It should seem a natural deduction, that whatever has a tendency to identify the two must also in the same degree promote the general welfare. As the magnitude of almost all States prevents the possibility of their enjoying a pure democracy, philosophers—from a wish, as far as is in their power, to make the governors and the governed one—will turn their thoughts to the system of universal representation, and will annex an equal importance to the suffrage of every individual. Jealous of giving up no more of the authority of the people than is necessary, they will be solicitous of finding out some method by which the office of their delegates may be confined as much as is practicable to the proposing and deliberating upon laws rather than to enacting them; reserving to the people the power of finally inscribing them in the national code. Unless this is attended to, as soon as a people has chosen representatives it no longer has a political existence, except as it is understood to retain the privilege of annihilating the trust when it shall think proper, and of resuming its original power. Sensible that at the moment of election an interest distinct from that of the general body is created, an enlightened legislator will endeavour by every possible method to diminish the operation of such interest. The first and most natural mode that presents itself is that of shortening the regular duration of this trust, in order that the man who has betrayed it may soon be superseded by a more worthy successor. But this is not enough; aware of the possibility of imposition, and of the natural tendency of power to corrupt the heart of man, a sensible Republican will think it essential that the office of legislator be not intrusted to the same man for a succession of years. He will also be induced to this wise restraint by the grand principle of identification; he will be more sure of the virtue of the legislator by knowing that, in the capacity of private citizen, to-morrow he must either smart under the oppression or bless the justice of the law which he has enacted to-day.

Perhaps in the very outset of this inquiry the principle on which I proceed will be questioned, and I shall be told that the people are not the proper judges of their own welfare. But because under every government of modern times, till the foundation of the American Republic, the bulk of mankind have appeared incapable of discerning their true interests, no conclusion can be drawn against my principle. At this moment have we not daily the strongest proofs of the success with which, in what you call the best of all monarchical governments, the popular mind may be debauched? Left to the quiet exercise of their own judgment, do you think that the people would have thought it necessary to set fire to the house of the philosophic Priestley, and to hunt down his life like that of a traitor or a parricide? that, deprived almost of the necessaries of existence by the burden of their taxes, they would cry out, as with one voice, for a war from which not a single ray of consolation can visit them to compensate for the additional keenness with which they are about to smart under the scourge of labour, of cold, and of hunger?

Appearing, as I do, the advocate of Republicanism, let me not be misunderstood. I am well aware, from the abuse of the executive power in States, that there is not a single European nation but what affords a melancholy proof that if, at this moment, the original authority of the people should be restored, all that could be expected from such restoration would in the beginning be but a change of tyranny. Considering the nature of a Republic in reference to the present condition of Europe, your Lordship stops here; but a philosopher will extend his views much farther: having dried up the source from which flows the corruption of the public opinion, he will be sensible that the stream will go on gradually refining itself. I must add also, that the coercive power is of necessity so strong in all the old governments, that a people could not at first make an abuse of that liberty which a legitimate Republic supposes. The animal just released from its stall will exhaust the overflow of its spirits in a round of wanton vagaries; but it will soon return to itself, and enjoy its freedom in moderate and regular delight.

But, to resume the subject of universal representation, I ought to have mentioned before, that in the choice of its representatives a people will not immorally hold out wealth as a criterion of integrity, nor lay down as a fundamental rule, that to be qualified for the trying duties of legislation a citizen should be possessed of a certain fixed property. Virtues, talents, and acquirements are all that it will look for.

Having destroyed every external object of delusion, let us now see what makes the supposition necessary that the people will mislead themselves. Your Lordship respects 'peasants and mechanics when they intrude not themselves into concerns for which their education has not fitted them.'

Setting aside the idea of a peasant or mechanic being a legislator, what vast education is requisite to enable him to judge amongst his neighbours which is most qualified by his industry and integrity to be intrusted with the care of the interests of himself and of his fellow-citizens? But leaving this ground, as governments formed on such a plan proceed in a plain and open manner, their administration would require much less of what is usually called talents and experience, that is, of disciplined treachery and hoary Machiavelism; and at the same time, as it would no longer be their interest to keep the mass of the nation in ignorance, a moderate portion of useful knowledge would be universally disseminated. If your Lordship has travelled in the democratic cantons of Switzerland, you must have seen the herdsman with the staff in one hand and the book in the other. In the constituent Assembly of France was found a peasant whose sagacity was as distinguished as his integrity, whose blunt honesty overawed and baffled the refinements of hypocritical patriots. The people of Paris followed him with acclamations, and the name of Père Gerard will long be mentioned with admiration and respect through the eighty-three departments.

From these hints, if pursued further, might be demonstrated the expediency of the whole people 'intruding themselves' on the office of legislation, and the wisdom of putting into force what they may claim as a right. But government is divided into two parts—the legislative and executive. The executive power you would lodge in the hands of an individual. Before we inquire into the propriety of this measure, it will be necessary to state the proper objects of the executive power in governments where the principle of universal representation is admitted. With regard to that portion of this power which is exerted in the application of the laws, it may be observed that much of it would be superseded. As laws, being but the expression of the general will, would be enacted only from an almost universal conviction of their utility, any resistance to such laws, any desire of eluding them, must proceed from a few refractory individuals. As far, then, as relates to the internal administration of the country, a Republic has a manifest advantage over a Monarchy, inasmuch as less force is requisite to compel obedience to its laws.

From the judicial tribunals of our own country, though we labour under a variety of partial and oppressive laws, we have an evident proof of the nullity of regal interference, as the king's name is confessedly a mere fiction, and justice is known to be most equitably administered when the judges are least dependent on the crown.

I have spoken of laws partial and oppressive; our penal code is so crowded with disproportioned penalties and indiscriminate severity that a conscientious man would sacrifice, in many instances, his respect for the laws to the common feelings of humanity; and there must be a strange vice in that legislation from which can proceed laws in whose execution a man cannot be instrumental without forfeiting his self-esteem and incurring the contempt of his fellow-citizens.

But to return from this digression: with regard to the other branches of the executive government, which relate rather to original measures than to administering the law, it may be observed that the power exercised in conducting them is distinguished by almost imperceptible shades from the legislative, and that all such as admit of open discussion and of the delay attendant on public deliberations are properly the province of the representative assembly. If this observation be duly attended to, it will appear that this part of the executive power will be extremely circumscribed, will be stripped almost entirely of a deliberative capacity, and will be reduced to a mere hand or instrument. As a Republican government would leave this power to a select body destitute of the means of corruption, and whom the people, continually contributing, could at all times bring to account or dismiss, will it not necessarily ensue that a body so selected and supported would perform their simple functions with greater efficacy and fidelity than the complicated concerns of royalty can be expected to meet with in the councils of princes; of men who from their wealth and interest have forced themselves into trust; and of statesmen, whose constant object is to exalt themselves by laying pitfalls for their colleagues and for their country.

I shall pursue this subject no further; but adopting your Lordship's method of argument, instead of continuing to demonstrate the superiority of a Republican executive government, I will repeat some of the objections which have been often made to monarchy, and have not been answered.

My first objection to regal government is its instability, proceeding from a variety of causes. Where monarchy is found in its greatest intensity, as in Morocco and Turkey, this observation is illustrated in a very pointed manner, and indeed is more or less striking as governments are more or less despotic. The reason is obvious: as the monarch is the chooser of his ministers, and as his own passions and caprice are in general the sole guides of his conduct, these ministers, instead of pursuing directly the one grand object of national welfare, will make it their chief study to vary their measures according to his humours. But a minister *may* be refractory: his successor will naturally run headlong into plans totally the reverse of the former system; for if he treads in the same path, he is well aware that a similar fate will attend him. This observation will apply to each succession of kings, who, from vanity and a desire of distinction, will in general studiously avoid any step which may lead to a suspicion that they are so spiritless as to imitate their predecessor. That a similar instability is not incident to Republics is evident from their very constitution.

As from the nature of monarchy, particularly of hereditary monarchy, there must always be a vast disproportion between the duties to be performed and the powers that are to perform them; and as the measures of government, far from gaining additional vigour, are, on the contrary, enfeebled by being intrusted to one hand, what arguments can be used for allowing to the will of a single being a weight which, as history shows, will subvert that of the whole body politic? And this brings me to my grand objection to monarchy, which is drawn from THE ETERNAL NATURE OF MAN. The office of king is a trial to which human virtue is not equal. Pure and universal representation, by which alone liberty can be secured, cannot, I think, exist together with monarchy. It seems madness to expect a manifestation of the *general* will, at the same time that we allow to a *particular* will that weight which it must obtain in all governments that can with any propriety be called monarchical. They must war with each other till one of them is extinguished. It was so in France and * * *

I shall not pursue this topic further, but, as you are a teacher of purity of morals, I cannot but remind you of that atmosphere of corruption without which it should seem that courts cannot exist.

You seem anxious to explain what ought to be understood by the equality of men in a state of civil society; but your Lordship's success has not answered your trouble. If you had looked in the articles of the Rights of Man, you would have found your efforts superseded: 'Equality, without which liberty cannot exist, is to be met with in perfection in that State in which no distinctions are admitted but such as have evidently for their object the general good;' 'The end of government cannot be attained without authorising some members of the society to command, and of course without imposing on the rest the necessity of obedience.'

Here, then, is an inevitable inequality, which may be denominated that of power. In order to render this as small as possible, a legislator will be careful not to give greater force to such authority than is essential to its due execution. Government is at best but a necessary evil. Compelled to place themselves in a state of subordination, men will obviously endeavour to prevent the abuse of that superiority to which they submit; accordingly they will cautiously avoid whatever may lead those in whom it is acknowledged to suppose they hold it as a right. Nothing will more effectually contribute to this than that the person in whom authority has been lodged should occasionally descend to the level of private citizen; he will learn from it a wholesome lesson, and the people will be less liable to confound the person with the power. On this principle hereditary authority will be proscribed; and on another also—that in such a system as that of hereditary authority, no security can be had for talents adequate to the discharge of the office, and consequently the people can only feel the mortification of being humbled without having protected themselves.

Another distinction will arise amongst mankind, which, though it may be easily modified by government, exists independent of it; I mean the distinction of wealth, which always will attend superior talents and industry. It cannot be denied that the security of individual property is one of the strongest and most natural motives to induce men to bow their necks to the yoke of civil government. In order to attain this end of security to property, a legislator will proceed with impartiality. He should not suppose that, when he has insured to their proprietors the possession of lands and movables against the depredation of the necessitous, nothing remains to be done. The history of all ages has demonstrated that wealth not only can secure itself, but includes even an oppressive principle. Aware of this, and that the extremes of poverty and riches have a necessary tendency to corrupt the human heart, he will banish from his code all laws such as the unnatural monster of primogeniture, such as encourage associations against labour in the form of corporate bodies, and indeed all that monopolising system of legislation, whose baleful influence is shown in the depopulation of the country and in the necessity which reduces the sad relicks to owe their very existence to the ostentatious bounty of their oppressors. If it is true in common life, it is still more true in governments, that we should be just before we are generous; but our legislators seem to have forgotten or despised this homely maxim. They have unjustly left unprotected that most important part of property, not less real because it has no material existence, that which ought to enable the labourer to provide food for himself and his family. I appeal to innumerable statutes, whose constant and professed object it is to lower the price of labour, to compel the workman to be *content* with arbitrary wages, evidently too small from the necessity of legal enforcement of the acceptance of them. Even from the astonishing amount of the sums raised for the support of one description of the poor may be concluded the extent and greatness of that oppression, whose effects have rendered it possible for the few to afford so much, and have shown us that such a multitude of our brothers exist in even helpless indigence. Your Lordship tells us that the science of civil government has received all the perfection of which it is capable. For my part, I am more enthusiastic. The sorrow I feel from the contemplation of this melancholy picture is not unconsoled by a comfortable hope that the class of wretches called mendicants will not much longer shock the feelings of humanity; that the miseries entailed upon the marriage of those who are not rich will no longer tempt the bulk of mankind to fly to that promiscuous intercourse to which they are impelled by the instincts of nature, and the dreadful satisfaction of escaping the prospect of infants, sad fruit of such intercourse, whom they are unable to support. If these flattering prospects be ever realised, it must be owing to some wise and salutary regulations counteracting that inequality among mankind which proceeds from the present *fixed* disproportion of their possessions.

I am not an advocate for the agrarian law nor for sumptuary regulations, but I contend that the people amongst whom the law of primogeniture exists, and among whom corporate bodies are encouraged, and immense salaries annexed to useless and indeed hereditary offices, is oppressed by an inequality in the distribution of wealth which does not necessarily attend men in a state of civil society.

Thus far we have considered inequalities inseparable from civil society. But other arbitrary distinctions exist among mankind, either from choice or usurpation. I allude to titles, to stars, ribbons, and garters, and other badges of fictitious superiority. Your Lordship will not question the grand principle on which this inquiry set out; I look upon it, then, as my duty to try the propriety of these distinctions by that criterion, and think it will be no difficult task to prove that these separations among mankind are absurd, impolitic, and immoral. Considering hereditary nobility as a reward for services rendered to the State—and it is to my charity that you owe the permission of taking up the question on this ground—what services can a man render to the State adequate to such a compensation that the making of laws, upon which the happiness of millions is to depend, shall be lodged in him and his posterity, however depraved may be their principles, however contemptible their understandings?

But here I may be accused of sophistry; I ought to subtract every idea of power from such distinction, though from the weakness of mankind it is impossible to disconnect them. What services, then, can a man render to society to compensate for the outrage done to the dignity of our nature when we bind ourselves to address him and his posterity with humiliating circumlocutions, calling him most noble, most honourable, most high, most august, sereno, excellent, eminent, and so forth; when it is more than probable that such unnatural flattery will but generate vices which ought to consign him to neglect and solitude, or make him the perpetual object of the finger of scorn? And does not experience justify the observation, that where titles—a thing very rare—have been conferred as the rewards of merit, those to whom they have descended, far from being thereby animated to imitate their ancestor, have presumed upon that lustre which they supposed thrown round them, and, prodigally relying on such resources, lavished what alone was their own, their personal reputation?

It would be happy if this delusion were confined to themselves; but, alas, the world is weak enough to grant the indulgence which they assume. Vice, which is forgiven in one character, will soon cease to meet with sternness of rebuke when found in others. Even at first she will entreat pardon with confidence, assured that ere long she will be charitably supposed to stand in no need of it.

But let me ask you seriously, from the mode in which these distinctions are originally conferred, is it not almost necessary that, far from being the rewards of services rendered to the State, they should usually be the recompense of an industrious sacrifice of the general welfare to the particular aggrandisement of that power by which they are bestowed? Let us even alter their source, and consider them as proceeding from the Nation itself, and deprived of that hereditary quality; even here I should proscribe them, and for the most evident reason—that a man's past services are no sufficient security for his future character; he who to-day merits the civic wreath may to-morrow deserve the Tarpeian rock. Besides, where respect is not perverted, where the world is not taught to reverence men without regarding their conduct, the esteem of mankind will have a very different value, and, when a proper independence is secured, will be regarded as a sufficient recompense for services however important, and will be a much surer guarantee of the continuance of such virtues as may deserve it.

I have another strong objection to nobility, which is that it has a necessary tendency to dishonour labour, a prejudice which extends far beyond its own circle; that it binds down whole ranks of men to idleness, while it gives the enjoyment of a reward which exceeds the hopes of the most active exertions of human industry. The languid tedium of this noble repose must be dissipated, and gaming, with the tricking manœuvres of the horse-race, afford occupation to hours which it would be happy for mankind had they been totally unemployed.

Reflecting on the corruption of the public manners, does your Lordship shudder at the prostitution which miserably deluges our streets? You may find the cause in our aristocratical prejudices. Are you disgusted with the hypocrisy and sycophancy of our intercourse in private life? You may find the cause in the necessity of dissimulation which we have established by regulations which oblige us to address as our superiors, indeed as our masters, men whom we cannot but internally despise. Do you lament that such large portions of mankind should stoop to occupations unworthy the dignity of their nature? You may find in the pride and luxury thought necessary to nobility how such servile arts are encouraged. Besides, where the most honourable of the Land do not blush to accept such offices as groom of the bedchamber, master of the hounds, lords in waiting, captain of the honourable band of gentlemen-pensioners, is it astonishing that the bulk of the people should not ask of an occupation, what is it? but what may be gained by it?

If the long equestrian train of equipage should make your Lordship sigh for the poor who are pining in hunger, you will find that little is thought of snatching the bread from their mouths to eke out the '*necessary* splendour' of nobility.

I have not time to pursue this subject further, but am so strongly impressed with the baleful influence of aristocracy and nobility upon human happiness and virtue, that if, as I am persuaded, monarchy cannot exist without such supporters, I think that reason sufficient for the preference I have given to the Republican system.

It is with reluctance that I quit the subjects I have just touched upon; but the nature of this Address does not permit me to continue the discussion. I proceed to what more immediately relates to this Kingdom at the present crisis.

You ask with triumphant confidence, to what other law are the people of England subject than the general will of the society to which they belong? Is your Lordship to be told that acquiescence is not choice, and that obedience is not freedom? If there is a single man in Great Britain who has no suffrage in the election of a representative, the will of the society of which he is a member is not generally expressed; he is a Helot in that society. You answer the question, so confidently put, in this singular manner: 'The King, we are all justly persuaded, has not the inclination—and we all know that, if he had the inclination, he has not the power—to substitute his will in the place of law. The House of Lords has no such power. The House of Commons has no such power.' This passage, so artfully and unconstitutionally framed to agree with the delusions of the moment, cannot deceive a thinking reader. The expression of your full persuasion of the upright intentions of the King can only be the language of flattery. You are not to be told that it is constitutionally a maxim not to attribute to the person of the King the measures and misconduct of government. Had you chosen to speak, as you ought to have done, openly and explicitly, you must have expressed your just persuasion and implicit confidence in the integrity, moderation, and wisdom of his

Majesty's ministers. Have you forgot the avowed ministerial maxim of Sir Robert Walpole? Are you ignorant of the overwhelming corruption of the present day?

You seem unconscious of the absurdity of separating what is inseparable even in imagination. Would it have been any consolation to the miserable Romans under the second triumvirate to have been asked insultingly, Is it Octavius, is it Anthony, or is it Lepidus that has caused this bitterness of affliction? and when the answer could not be returned with certainty, to have been reproached that their sufferings were imaginary? The fact is that the King *and* Lords *and* Commons, by what is termed the omnipotence of Parliament, have constitutionally the right of enacting whatever laws they please, in defiance of the petitions or remonstrances of the nation. They have the power of doubling our enormous debt of 240 millions, and *may* pursue measures which could never be supposed the emanation of the general will without concluding the people stripped of reason, of sentiment, and even of that first instinct which prompts them to preserve their own existence.

I congratulate your Lordship upon your enthusiastic fondness for the judicial proceedings of this country. I am happy to find you have passed through life without having your fleece torn from your back in the thorny labyrinth of litigation. But you have not lived always in colleges, and must have passed by some victims, whom it cannot be supposed, without a reflection on your heart, that you have forgotten. Here I am reminded of what I have said on the subject of representation—to be qualified for the office of legislation you should have felt like the bulk of mankind; their sorrows should be familiar to you, of which, if you are ignorant, how can you redress them? As a member of the assembly which, from a confidence in its experience, sagacity, and wisdom, the constitution has invested with the supreme appellant jurisdiction to determine the most doubtful points of an intricate jurisprudence, your Lordship cannot, I presume, be ignorant of the consuming expense of our never-ending process, the verbosity of unintelligible statutes, and the perpetual contrariety in our judicial decisions.

'The greatest freedom that can be enjoyed by man in a state of civil society, the greatest security that can be given with respect to the protection of his character, property, personal liberty, limb, and life, is afforded to every individual by our present constitution.'

'Let it never be forgotten by ourselves, and let us impress the observation upon the hearts of our children, that we are in possession of both (liberty and equality), of as much of both as can be consistent with the end for which civil society was introduced among mankind.'

Many of my readers will hardly believe me when I inform them that these passages are copied verbatim from your Appendix. Mr. Burke roused the indignation of all ranks of men when, by a refinement in cruelty superior to that which in the East yokes the living to the dead, he strove to persuade us that we and our posterity to the end of time were riveted to a constitution by the indissoluble compact of—a dead parchment, and were bound to cherish a corse at the bosom when reason might call aloud that it should be entombed. Your Lordship aims at the same detestable object by means more criminal, because more dangerous and insidious. Attempting to lull the people of England into a belief that any inquiries directed towards the nature of liberty and equality can in no other way lead to their happiness than by convincing them that they have already arrived at perfection in the science of government, what is your object but to exclude them for ever from the most fruitful field of human knowledge? Besides, it is another cause to execrate this doctrine that the consequence of such fatal delusion would be that they must entirely draw off their attention, not only from the government, but from their governors; that the stream of public vigilance, far from clearing and enriching the prospect of society, would by its stagnation consign it to barrenness, and by its putrefaction infect it with death. You have aimed an arrow at liberty and philosophy, the eyes of the human race; why, like the inveterate enemy of Philip, in putting your name to the shaft, did you not declare openly its destination?

As a teacher of religion, your Lordship cannot be ignorant of a class of breaches of duty which may be denominated faults of omission. You profess to give your opinions upon the present turbulent crisis, expressing a wish that they may have some effect in tranquillising the minds of the people. Whence comes it, then, that the two grand causes of this working of the popular mind are passed over in silence? Your Lordship's conduct may bring to mind the story of a company of strolling comedians, who gave out the play of *Hamlet* as the performance of the evening. The audience were not a little surprised to be told, on the drawing up of the curtain, that from circumstances of particular convenience it was hoped they would dispense with the omission of the character of—Hamlet! But to be serious—for the subject is serious in the extreme—from your silence respecting the general call for a PARLIAMENTARY REFORM, supported by your assertion that we at present enjoy as great a portion of liberty and equality as is consistent with civil society, what can be supposed but that you are a determined enemy to the redress of what the people of England call and feel to be grievances?

From your omitting to speak upon the war, and your general disapprobation of French measures and French principles, expressed particularly at this moment, we are necessarily led also to conclude that you have no wish to dispel an infatuation which is now giving up to the sword so large a portion of the poor, and consigning the rest to the more slow and more painful consumption of want. I could excuse your silence on this point, as it would ill become an English bishop at the close of the eighteenth century to make the pulpit the vehicle of exhortations which would have disgraced the incendiary of the Crusades, the hermit Peter. But you have deprived yourself of the plea of decorum by giving no opinion on the REFORM OF THE LEGISLATURE. As undoubtedly you have some secret reason for the reservation of your sentiments on this latter head, I cannot but apply the same reason to the former. Upon what principle is your conduct to be explained? In some parts of England it is quaintly said, when a drunken man is seen reeling towards his home, that he has business on both sides of the road. Observing your Lordship's tortuous path, the spectators will be far from insinuating that you have partaken of Mr. Burke's intoxicating bowl; they will content themselves, shaking their heads as you stagger along, with remarking that you have business on both sides of the road.

The friends of Liberty congratulate themselves upon the odium under which they are at present labouring, as the causes which have produced it have obliged so many of her false adherents to disclaim with officious earnestness any desire to promote her interests; nor are they disheartened by the diminution which their body is supposed already to have sustained. Conscious that an enemy lurking in our ranks is ten times more formidable than when drawn out against us, that the unblushing aristocracy of a Maury or a Cazalès is far less dangerous than the insidious mask of patriotism assumed by a La Fayette or a Mirabeau, we thank you for your desertion. Political convulsions have been said particularly to call forth concealed abilities, but it has been seldom observed how vast is their consumption of them. Reflecting upon the fate of the greatest portion of the members of the constituent and legislative assemblies, we must necessarily be struck with a prodigious annihilation of human talents. Aware that this necessity is attached to a struggle for Liberty, we are the less sorry that we can expect no advantage from the mental endowments of your Lordship.

APPENDIX.

[It is deemed expedient to reprint here the Appendix to Bishop Watson's Sermon, which is animadverted on in the preceding Apology. G.]

The Sermon which is now, for the first time, published, was written many years ago; it may, perhaps, on that account be more worthy of the attention of those for whose benefit it is designed. If it shall have any effect in calming the perturbation which has been lately excited, and which still subsists in the minds of the lower classes of the community, I shall not be ashamed of having given to the world a composition in every other light uninteresting. I will take this opportunity of adding, with the same intention, a few reflections on the present circumstances of our own and of a neighbouring country.

With regard to France—I have no hesitation in declaring, that the object which the French seemed to have in view at the commencement of their revolution had my hearty approbation. The object was to free themselves and their posterity from arbitrary power. I hope there is not a man in Great Britain so little sensible of the blessings of that free constitution under which he has the happiness to live, so entirely dead to the interests of general humanity, as not to wish that a constitution similar to our own might be established, not only in France, but in every despotic state in Europe; not only in Europe, but in every quarter of the globe.

It is one thing to approve of an end, another to approve of the means by which an end is accomplished. I did not approve of the means by which the first revolution was effected in France. I thought that it would have been a wiser measure to have abridged the oppressive privileges, and to have lessened the enormous number of the nobility, than to have abolished the order. I thought that the State ought not in justice to have seized any part of the property of the Church, till it had reverted, as it were, to the community, by the death of its immediate possessors. I thought that the king was not only treated with unmerited indignity, but that too little authority was left him to enable him, as the chief executive magistrate, to be useful to the State. These were some of my reasons for not approving the means by which the first revolution in France was brought about. As to other evils which took place on the occasion, I considered them certainly as evils of importance; but at the same time as evils inseparable from a state of civil commotion, and which I conceived would be more than compensated by the establishment of a limited monarchy.

The French have abandoned the constitution they had at first established, and have changed it for another. No one can reprobate with more truth than I do both the means and the end of this change. The end has been the establishment of a republic. Now a republic is a form of government which, of all others, I most dislike—and I dislike it for this reason; because of all forms of government, scarcely excepting the most despotic, I think a republic the most oppressive to the bulk of the people: they are deceived in it with the show of liberty; but they live in it under the most odious of all tyrannies, the tyranny of their equals. With respect to the means by which this new republic has been erected in France, they have been sanguinary, savage, more than brutal. They not merely fill the heart of every individual with commiseration for the unfortunate sufferers, but they exhibit to the eye of contemplation an humiliating picture of human nature, when its passions are not regulated by religion, or controlled by law. I fly with terror and abhorrence even from the altar of Liberty, when I see it stained with the blood of the aged, of the innocent, of the defenceless sex, of the ministers of religion, and of the faithful adherents of a fallen monarch. My heart sinks within me when I see it streaming with the blood of the monarch himself. Merciful God! strike speedily, we beseech Thee, with deep contrition and sincere remorse, the obdurate hearts of the relentless perpetrators and projectors of these horrid deeds, lest they should suddenly sink into eternal and extreme perdition, loaded with an unutterable weight of unrepented and, except through the blood of Him whose religion they reject, inexpiable sin.

The monarch, you will tell me, was guilty of perfidy and perjury. I know not that he was guilty of either; but admitting that he has been guilty of both, who, alas, of the sons of men is so confident in the strength of his own virtue, so assured of his own integrity and intrepidity of character, as to be certain that, under similar temptations, he would not have been guilty of similar offences? Surely it would have been no diminution of the sternness of new republican virtue, no disgrace to the magnanimity of a great nation, if it had pardoned the perfidy which its own oppression had occasioned, if it had remitted the punishment of the perjury of the king to the tribunal of Him by whom *kings reign and princes decree justice.*

And are there any men in this kingdom, except such as find their account in public confusion, who would hazard the introduction of such scenes of rapine, barbarity, and bloodshed, as have disgraced France and outraged humanity, for the sake of obtaining—what?—Liberty and Equality. I suspect that the meaning of these terms is not clearly and generally understood: it may be of use to explain them.

The liberty of a man in a state of nature consists in his being subject to no law but the law of nature; and the liberty of a man in a state of society consists in his being subject to no law but to the law enacted by the general will of the society to which he belongs. And to what other law is any man in Great Britain subject? The king, we are all justly persuaded, has not the inclination, and we all know that if he had the inclination, he has not the power, to substitute his will in the place of the law. The House of Lords has no such power; the House of Commons has no such power; the Church has no such power; the rich men of the country have no such power. The poorest man amongst us, the beggar at our door, is governed—not by the uncertain, passionate, arbitrary will of an individual—not by the selfish insolence of an aristocratic faction—not by the madness of democratic violence—but by the fixed, impartial, deliberate voice of law, enacted by the general suffrage of a free people. Is your property injured? Law, indeed, does not give you property; but it ascertains it. Property is acquired by industry and probity; by the exercise of talents and ingenuity; and the possession of it is secured by the laws of the community. Against whom think you is it secured? It is secured against thieves and robbers; against idle and profligate men, who, however low your condition may be, would be glad to deprive you of the little you possess. It is secured, not only against such disturbers of the public peace, but against the oppression of the noble, the rapacity of the powerful, and the avarice of the rich. The courts of British justice are impartial and incorrupt; they respect not the persons of men; the poor man's lamb is, in their estimation, as sacred as the monarch's crown; with inflexible integrity they adjudge to every man his own. Your property under their protection is secure. If your personal liberty be unjustly restrained, though but for an hour, and that by the highest servants of the crown, the crown cannot screen them; the throne cannot hide them; the law, with an undaunted arm, seizes them, and drags them with irresistible might to the judgment of whom?—of your equals—of twelve of your neighbours. In such a constitution as this, what is there to complain of on the score of liberty?

The greatest freedom that can be enjoyed by man in a state of civil society, the greatest security that can be given him with respect to the protection of his character, property, personal liberty, limb, and life, is afforded to every individual by our present constitution.

The equality of men in a state of nature does not consist in an equality of bodily strength or intellectual ability, but in their being equally free from the dominion of each other. The equality of men in a state of civil society does not consist in an equality of wisdom, honesty, ingenuity, industry, nor in an equality of property resulting from a due exertion of these talents; but in being equally subject to, equally protected by the same laws. And who knows not that every individual in this great nation is, in this respect, equal to every other? There is not one law for the nobles, another for the commons of the land—one for the clergy, another for the laity—one for the rich, another for the poor. The nobility, it is true, have some privileges annexed to their birth; the judges, and other magistrates, have some annexed to their office; and professional men have some annexed to their professions:—but these privileges are neither injurious to the liberty or property of other men. And you might as reasonably contend, that the bramble ought to be equal to the oak, the lamb to the lion, as that no distinctions should take place between the members of the same society. The burdens of the State are distributed through the whole community, with as much impartiality as the complex nature of taxation will admit; every man sustains a part in proportion to his strength; no order is exempted from the payment of taxes. Nor is any order of men exclusively entitled to the enjoyment of the lucrative offices of the State. All cannot enjoy them, but all enjoy a capacity of acquiring them. The son of the meanest man in the nation may become a general or an admiral, a lord chancellor or an archbishop. If any persons have been so simple as to suppose that even the French ever intended, by the term equality, an equality of property, they have been quite mistaken in their ideas. The French never understood by it anything materially different from what we and our ancestors have been in full possession of for many ages.

Other nations may deluge their land with blood in struggling for liberty and equality; but let it never be forgotten by ourselves, and let us impress the observation upon the hearts of our children, that we are in possession of both, of as much of both as can be consistent with the end for which civil society was introduced amongst mankind.

The provision which is made for the poor in this kingdom is so liberal, as, in the opinion of some, to discourage industry. The rental of the lands in England and Wales does not, I conjecture, amount to more than eighteen millions a year; and the poor rates amount to two millions. The poor then, at present, possess a ninth part of the landed rental of the country; and, reckoning ten pounds for the annual maintenance of each pauper, it may be inferred, that those who are maintained by the community do not constitute a fortieth part of the people. An equal division of land would be to the poor a great misfortune; they would possess far less than by the laws of the land they are at present entitled to. When we add to this consideration an account of the immense sums annually subscribed by the rich for the support of hospitals, infirmaries, dispensaries —for the relief of sufferers by fire, tempests, famine, loss of cattle, great sickness, and other misfortunes, all of which charities must cease were all men on a level, for all men would then be equally poor,—it cannot but excite one's astonishment that so foolish a system should have ever been so much as mentioned by any man of common sense. It is a system not practicable; and was it practicable, it would not be useful; and was it useful, it would not be just.

But some one may think, and, indeed, it has been studiously inculcated into the minds of the multitude, that a monarchy, even a limited one, is a far more expensive mode of civil government than a republic; that a civil-list of a million a year is an enormous sum, which might be saved to the nation. Supposing that every shilling of this sum could be saved, and that every shilling of it was expended in supporting the dignity of the crown—both which suppositions are entirely false—still should I think the liberty, the prosperity, the tranquillity, the happiness of this great nation cheaply purchased by such a sum; still should I think that he would be a madman in politics who would, by a change of the constitution, risk these blessings (and France supplies us with a proof that infinite risk would be run) for a paltry saving of expense. I am not, nor have ever been, the patron of corruption. So far as the civil-list has a tendency to corrupt the judgment of any member of either house of parliament, it has a bad tendency, which I wish it had not; but I cannot wish to see the splendour of the crown reduced to nothing, lest its proper weight in the scale of the constitution should be thereby destroyed. A great portion of this million is expended in paying the salaries of the judges, the interpreters of our law, the guardians of our lives and properties; another portion is expended in maintaining ambassadors at different courts, to protect the general concerns of the nation from foreign aggression; another portion is expended in pensions and donations to men of letters and ingenuity; to men who have, by naval, military, or civil services, just claims to the attention of their country; to persons of respectable families and connections, who have been humbled and broken down by misfortunes. I do not speak with accuracy, nor on such a subject is accuracy requisite; but I am not far wide of truth in saying, that a fifth part of the million is more than sufficient to defray the expenses of the royal household. What a mighty matter is it to complain of, that each individual contributes less than sixpence a year towards the support of the monarchy!

That the constitution of this country is so perfect as neither to require or admit of any improvement, is a proposition to which I never did or ever can assent; but I think it far too excellent to be amended by peasants and mechanics. I do not mean to speak of peasants and mechanics with any degree of disrespect; I am not so ignorant of the importance, either of the natural or social chain by which all the individuals of the human race are connected together, as to think disrespectfully of any link of it. Peasants and mechanics are as useful to the State as any other order of men; but their utility consists in their discharging well the duties of their respective stations; it ceases when they affect to become legislators; when they intrude themselves into concerns for which their education has not fitted them. The liberty of the press is a main support of the liberty of the nation; it is a blessing which it is our duty to transmit to posterity; but a bad use is sometimes made of it: and its use is never more pernicious than when it is employed to infuse into the minds of the lowest orders of the community disparaging ideas concerning the constitution of their country. No danger need be apprehended from a candid examination of our own constitution, or from a display of the advantages of any other; it will bear to be contrasted with the best: but all men are not qualified to make the comparison; and there are so many men, in every community, who wish to have no government at all, that an appeal to them on such a point ought never to be made.

There are, probably, in every government upon earth, circumstances which a man, accustomed to the abstract investigation of truth, may easily prove to be deviations from the rigid rule of strict political justice; but whilst these deviations are either generally not known, or, though known, generally acquiesced in as matters of little moment to the general felicity, I cannot think it to be the part, either of a good man or of a good citizen, to be zealous in recommending such matters to the discussion of ignorant and uneducated men.

I am far from insinuating, that the science of politics is involved in mystery; or that men of plain understandings should be debarred from examining the principles of the government to which they yield obedience. All that I contend for is this—that the foundations of our government ought not to be overturned, nor the edifice erected thereon tumbled into ruins, because an acute politician may pretend that he has discovered a flaw in the building, or that he could have laid the foundation after a better model.

What would you say to a stranger who should desire you to pull down your house, because, forsooth, he had built one in France or America, after what he thought a better plan? You would say to him: No, sir—my ancestors have lived in this mansion comfortably and honourably for many generations; all its walls are strong, and all its timbers sound: if I should observe a decay in any of its parts, I know how to make the reparation without the assistance of strangers; and I know too that the reparation, when made by myself, may be made without injury either to the strength or beauty of the building. It has been buffeted, in the course of ages, by a thousand storms; yet still it stands unshaken as a rock, the wonder of all my neighbours, each of whom sighs for one of a similar construction. Your house may be suited to your climate and temper, this is suited to mine. Permit me, however, to observe to you, that you have not yet lived long enough in your new house to be sensible of all the inconveniences to which it may be liable, nor have you yet had any experience of its strength; it has yet sustained no shocks; the first whirlwind may scatter its component members in the air; the first earthquake may shake its foundation; the first inundation may sweep the superstructure from the surface of the earth. I hope no accident will happen to your house, but I am satisfied with mine own.

Great calamities of every kind attend the breaking up of established governments:—yet there are some forms of government, especially when they happen to be badly administered, so exceedingly destructive of the happiness of mankind, that a change of them is not improvidently purchased at the expense of the mischief accompanying their subversion. Our government is not of that kind; look round the globe, and see if you can discover a single nation on all its surface so powerful, so rich, so beneficent, so free and happy as our own. May Heaven avert from the minds of my countrymen the slightest wish to abolish their constitution!

'Kingdoms,' observes Mr. Locke, 'have been overturned by the pride, ambition, and turbulency of private men; by the people's wantonness and desire to cast off the lawful authority of their rulers, as well as by the rulers' insolence, and endeavours to get and exercise an arbitrary power over the people.' The recent danger to our constitution was in my opinion small; for I considered its excellence to be so obvious to men even of the most unimproved understandings, that I looked upon it as an idle and fruitless effort, either in foreign or domestic incendiaries, to endeavour to persuade the bulk of the people to consent to an alteration of it in favour of a republic. I knew, indeed, that in every country the flagitious dregs of a nation were always ripe for revolutions; but I was sensible, at the same time, that it was the interest, not only of the opulent and powerful, not only of the mercantile and middle classes of life, but even of honest labourers and manufacturers, of every sober and industrious man, to resist the licentious principles of such pestilent members, shall I call them, or outcasts of society. Men better informed and wiser than myself thought that the constitution was in great danger. Whether in fact the danger was great or small, it is not necessary now to inquire; it may be more useful to declare that, in my humble opinion, the danger, of whatever magnitude it may have been, did not originate in any encroachments of either the legislative or executive power on the liberties or properties of the people;

but in the wild fancies and turbulent tempers of discontented or ill-informed individuals. I sincerely rejoice that, through the vigilance of administration, this turbulency has received a check. The hopes of bad men have been disappointed, and the understandings of mistaken men have been enlightened, by the general and unequivocal judgment of a whole nation; a nation not more renowned for its bravery and its humanity, though justly celebrated for both, than for its loyalty to its princes, and, what is perfectly consistent with loyalty, for its love of liberty and attachment to the constitution. Wise men have formed it, brave men have bled for it; it is our part to preserve it.

R. LANDAFF.

London, Jan. 25, 1793.

II. THE CONVENTION OF CINTRA,

1809.

NOTE.

On the 'Convention of Cintra' see Preface in the present volume. G.

CONCERNING

THE RELATIONS

OF

GREAT BRITAIN, SPAIN, AND PORTUGAL,

TO EACH OTHER, AND TO THE COMMON ENEMY,

AT THIS CRISIS;

AND SPECIFICALLY AS AFFECTED BY

THE

CONVENTION OF CINTRA:

The whole brought to the test of those Principles, by which alone the Independence and Freedom of Nations can be Preserved or Recovered.

Qui didicit patriæ quid debeat;—— ——
Quod sit conscripti, quod judicis officium; quæ
Partes in bellum missi ducis.

BY WILLIAM WORDSWORTH.

London:
PRINTED FOR LONGMAN, HURST, REES, AND ORME,
PATERNOSTER-ROW.

1809.

Bitter and earnest writing must not hastily be condemned; for men cannot contend coldly, and without affection, about things which they hold dear and precious. A politic man may write from his brain, without touch and sense of his heart; as in a speculation that appertaineth not unto him;—but a feeling Christian will express, in his words, a character of zeal or love. *Lord Bacon.*

ADVERTISEMENT.

The following pages originated in the opposition which was made by his Majesty's ministers to the expression, in public meetings and otherwise, of the opinions and feelings of the people concerning the Convention of Cintra. For the sake of immediate and general circulation, I determined (when I had made a considerable progress in the manuscript) to print it in different portions in one of the daily newspapers. Accordingly two portions of it (extending to page 25) were printed, in the months of December and January, in the *Courier*,—as being one of the most impartial and extensively circulated journals of the time. The reader is requested to bear in mind this previous publication: otherwise he will be at a loss to account for the arrangement of the matter in one instance in the earlier part of the work. An accidental loss of several sheets of the manuscript delayed the continuance of the publication in that manner, till the close of the Christmas holidays; and—the pressure of public business rendering it then improbable that room could be found, in the columns of the paper, regularly to insert matter extending to such a length —this plan of publication was given up.

It may be proper to state that, in the extracts which have been made from the Spanish Proclamations, I have been obliged to content myself with the translations which appeared in the public journals; having only in one instance had access to the original. This is, in some cases, to be regretted—where the language falls below the dignity of the matter: but in general it is not so; and the feeling has suggested correspondent expressions to the translators; hastily as, no doubt, they must have performed their work.

I must entreat the reader to bear in mind that I began to write upon this subject in November last; and have continued without bringing my work earlier to a conclusion, partly from accident, and partly from a wish to possess additional documents and facts. Passing occurrences have made changes in the situation of certain objects spoken of; but I have not thought it necessary to accommodate what I had previously written to these changes: the whole stands without alteration; except where additions have been made, or errors corrected.

As I have spoken without reserve of things (and of persons as far as it was necessary to illustrate things, but no further); and as this has been uniformly done according to the light of my conscience; I have deemed it right to prefix my name to these pages, in order that this last testimony of a sincere mind might not be wanting.

May 20th, 1809.

CONCERNING THE CONVENTION OF CINTRA.

The Convention, recently concluded by the Generals at the head of the British army in Portugal, is one of the most important events of our time. It would be deemed so in France, if the Ruler of that country could dare to make it public with those merely of its known bearings and dependences with which the English people are acquainted; it has been deemed so in Spain and Portugal as far as the people of those countries have been permitted to gain, or have gained, a knowledge of it; and what this nation has felt and still feels upon the subject is sufficiently manifest. Wherever the tidings were communicated, they carried agitation along with them—a conflict of sensations in which, though sorrow was predominant, yet, through force of scorn, impatience, hope, and indignation, and through the universal participation in passions so complex, and the sense of power which this necessarily included — the whole partook of the energy and activity of congratulation and joy. Not a street, not a public room, not a fire-side in the island which was not disturbed as by a local or private trouble; men of all estates, conditions, and tempers were affected apparently in equal degrees. Yet was the event by none received as an open and measurable affliction: it had indeed features bold and intelligible to every one; but there was an under-expression which was strange, dark, and mysterious—and, accordingly as different notions prevailed, or the object was looked at in different points of view, we were astonished like men who are overwhelmed without forewarning—fearful like men who feel themselves to be helpless, and indignant and angry like men who are betrayed. In a word, it would not be too much to say that the tidings of this event did not spread with the commotion of a storm which sweeps visibly over our heads, but like an earthquake which rocks the ground under our feet.

How was it possible that it could be otherwise? For that army had been sent upon a service which appealed so strongly to all that was human in the heart of this nation—that there was scarcely a gallant father of a family who had not his moments of regret that he was not a soldier by profession, which might have made it his duty to accompany it; every high-minded youth grieved that his first impulses, which would have sent him upon the same errand, were not to be yielded to, and that after-thought did not sanction and confirm the instantaneous dictates or the reiterated persuasions of an heroic spirit. The army took its departure with prayers and blessings which were as widely spread as they were fervent and intense. For it was not doubted that, on this occasion, every person of which it was composed, from the General to the private soldier, would carry both into his conflicts with the enemy in the field, and into his relations of peaceful intercourse with the inhabitants, not only the virtues which might be expected from him as a soldier, but the antipathies and sympathies, the loves and hatreds of a citizen—of a human being—acting, in a manner hitherto unprecedented under the obligation of his human and social nature. If the conduct of the rapacious and merciless adversary rendered it neither easy nor wise—made it, I might say, impossible to give way to that unqualified admiration of courage and skill, made it impossible in relation to him to be exalted by those triumphs of the courteous affections, and to be purified by those refinements of civility which do, more than any thing, reconcile a man of thoughtful mind and humane dispositions to the horrors of ordinary war; it was felt that for such loss the benign and accomplished soldier would upon this mission be abundantly recompensed by the enthusiasm of fraternal love with which his Ally, the oppressed people whom he was going to aid in rescuing themselves, would receive him; and that this, and the virtues which he would witness in them, would furnish his heart with never-failing and far nobler objects of complacency and admiration. The discipline of the army was well known; and as a machine, or a vital organized body, the Nation was assured that it could not but be formidable; but thus to the standing excellence of mechanic or organic power seemed to be superadded, at this time, and for this service, the force of *inspiration:* could any thing therefore be looked for, but a glorious result? The army proved its prowess in the field; and what has been the result is attested, and long will be attested, by the downcast looks—the silence—the passionate exclamations—the sighs and shame of every man who is worthy to breathe the air or to look upon the green-fields of Liberty in this blessed and highly-favoured Island which we inhabit.

If I were speaking of things however weighty, that were long past and dwindled in the memory, I should scarcely venture to use this language; but the feelings are of yesterday—they are of to-day; the flower, a melancholy flower it is! is still in blow, nor will, I trust, its leaves be shed through months that are to come: for I repeat that the heart of the nation is in this struggle. This just and necessary war, as we have been accustomed to hear it styled from the beginning of the contest in the year 1793, had, some time before the Treaty of Amiens, viz. after the subjugation of Switzerland, and not till then, begun to be regarded by the body of the people, as indeed both just and necessary; and this justice and necessity were by none more clearly perceived, or more feelingly bewailed, than by those who had most eagerly opposed the war in its commencement, and who continued most bitterly to regret that this nation had ever borne a part in it. Their conduct was herein consistent: they proved that they kept their eyes steadily fixed upon principles; for, though there was a shifting or transfer of hostility in their minds as far as regarded persons, they only combated the same enemy opposed to them under a different shape; and that enemy was the spirit of selfish tyranny and lawless ambition. This spirit, the class of persons of whom I have been speaking, (and I would now be understood, as associating them with an immense majority of the people of Great Britain, whose affections, notwithstanding all the delusions which had been practised upon them, were, in the former part of the contest, for a long time on the side of their nominal enemies,) this spirit, when it became undeniably embodied in the French government, they wished, in spite of all dangers, should be opposed by war; because peace was not to be procured without submission, which could not but be followed by a communion, of which the word of greeting would be, on the one part, insult,—and, on the other, degradation. The people now wished for war, as their rulers had done before, because open war between nations is a defined and effectual partition, and the sword, in the hands of the good and the virtuous, is the most intelligible symbol of abhorrence. It was in order to be preserved from spirit-breaking submissions —from the guilt of seeming to approve that which they had not the power to prevent, and out of a consciousness of the danger that such guilt would otherwise actually steal upon them, and that thus, by evil communications and participations, would be weakened and finally destroyed, those moral sensibilities and energies, by virtue of which alone, their liberties, and even their lives, could be preserved,—that the people of Great Britain determined to encounter all perils which could follow in the train of open resistance.—There were some, and those deservedly of high character in the country, who exerted their utmost influence to counteract this resolution; nor did they give to it so gentle a name as want of prudence, but they boldly termed it blindness and obstinacy. Let them be judged with charity! But there are promptings of wisdom from the penetralia of human nature, which a people can hear, though the wisest of their practical Statesmen be deaf towards them. This authentic voice, the people of England had heard and obeyed: and, in opposition to French tyranny growing daily more insatiate and implacable, they ranged themselves zealously under their Government; though they neither forgot nor forgave its transgressions, in having first involved them in a war with a people then struggling for its own liberties under a twofold infliction —confounded by inbred faction, and beleagured by a cruel and imperious external foe. But these remembrances did not vent themselves in reproaches, nor hinder us from being reconciled to our Rulers, when a change or rather a revolution in circumstances had imposed new duties: and, in defiance of local and personal clamour, it may be safely said, that the nation united heart and hand with the Government in its resolve to meet the worst, rather than stoop its head to receive that which, it was felt, would not be the garland but the yoke of peace. Yet it was an afflicting alternative; and it is not to be denied, that the effort, if it had the determination, wanted the cheerfulness of duty. Our condition savoured too much of a grinding constraint—too much of the vassalage of necessity;—it had too much of fear, and therefore of selfishness, not to be contemplated in the main with rueful emotion. We desponded though we did not despair. In fact a deliberate and preparatory fortitude—a sedate and stern melancholy, which had no sunshine and was exhilarated only by the lightnings of indignation—this was the highest and best state of moral feeling to which the most noble-minded among us could attain.

But, from the moment of the rising of the people of the Pyrenean peninsula, there was a mighty change; we were instantaneously animated; and, from that moment, the contest assumed the dignity, which it is not in the power of any thing but hope to bestow: and, if I may dare to transfer language, prompted by a revelation of the state of being that admits not of decay or change, to the concerns and interests of our transitory planet, from that moment 'this corruptible put on incorruption, and this mortal put on immortality.' This sudden elevation was on no account more welcome—was by nothing more endeared, than by the returning sense which accompanied it of inward liberty and choice, which gratified our moral yearnings, inasmuch as it would give henceforward to our actions as a people, an origination and direction unquestionably moral—as it was free—as it was manifestly in sympathy with the species—as it admitted therefore of fluctuations of generous feeling—of approbation and of complacency. We were intellectualized also in proportion; we looked backward upon the records of the human race with pride, and, instead of being afraid, we delighted to look forward into futurity. It was imagined that this new-born spirit of resistance, rising from the most sacred feelings of the human heart, would diffuse itself through many countries; and not merely for the distant future, but for the present, hopes were entertained as bold as they were disinterested and generous.

Never, indeed, was the fellowship of our sentient nature more intimately felt—never was the irresistible power of justice more gloriously displayed than when the British and Spanish Nations, with an impulse like that of two ancient heroes throwing down their weapons and reconciled in the field, cast off at once their aversions and enmities, and mutually embraced each other—to solemnize this conversion of love, not by the festivities of peace, but by combating side by side through danger and under affliction in the devotedness of perfect brotherhood. This was a conjunction which excited hope as fervent as it was rational. On the one side was a nation which brought with it sanction and authority, inasmuch as it had tried and approved the blessings for which the other had risen to contend: the one was a people which, by the help of the surrounding ocean and its own virtues, had preserved to itself through ages its liberty, pure and inviolated by a foreign invader; the other a high-minded nation, which a tyrant, presuming on its decrepitude, had, through the real decrepitude of its Government, perfidiously enslaved. What could be more delightful than to think of an intercourse beginning in this manner? On the part of the Spaniards their love towards us was enthusiasm and adoration; the faults of our national character were hidden from them by a veil of splendour; they saw nothing around us but glory and light; and, on our side, we estimated *their* character with partial and indulgent fondness;—thinking on their past greatness, not as the undermined foundation of a magnificent building, but as the root of a majestic tree recovered from a long disease, and beginning again to flourish with promise of wider branches and a deeper shade than it had boasted in the fulness of its strength. If in the sensations with which the Spaniards prostrated themselves before the religion of their country we did not keep pace with them—if even their loyalty was such as, from our mixed constitution of government and from other causes, we could not thoroughly sympathize with,—and if, lastly, their devotion to the person of their Sovereign appeared to us to have too much of the alloy of delusion,—in all these things we judged them gently: and, taught by the reverses of the French revolution, we looked upon these dispositions as more human—more social—and therefore as wiser, and of better omen, than if they had stood forth the zealots of abstract principles, drawn out of the laboratory of unfeeling philosophists. Finally, in this reverence for the past and present, we found an earnest that they were prepared to contend to the death for as much liberty as their habits and their knowledge enabled them to receive. To assist them and their neighbours the Portuguese in the attainment of this end, we sent to them in love and in friendship a powerful army to aid—to invigorate—and to chastise:—they landed; and the first proof they afforded of their being worthy to be sent on such a service—the first pledge of amity given by them was the victory of Vimiera; the second pledge (and this was from the hand of their Generals,) was the Convention of Cintra.——

The reader will by this time have perceived, what thoughts were uppermost in my mind, when I began with asserting, that this Convention is among the most important events of our times:—an assertion, which was made deliberately, and after due allowance for that infirmity which inclines us to magnify things present and passing, at the expence of those which are past. It is my aim to prove, wherein the real importance of this event lies: and, as a necessary preparative for forming a right judgment upon it, I have already given a representation of the sentiments, with which the people of Great Britain and those of Spain looked upon each other. I have indeed spoken rather of the Spaniards than of the Portuguese; but what has been said, will be understood as applying in the main to the whole Peninsula. The wrongs of the two nations have been equal, and their cause is the same: they must stand or fall together. What their wrongs have been, in what degree they considered themselves united, and what their hopes and resolutions were, we have learned from public Papers issued by themselves and by their enemies. These were read by the people of this Country, at the time when they were severally published, with due impression.—Pity, that those impressions could not have been as faithfully retained as they were at first received deeply! Doubtless, there is not a man in these Islands, who is not convinced that the cause of Spain is the most righteous cause in which, since the opposition of the Greek Republics to the Persian Invader at Thermopylæ and Marathon, sword ever was drawn! But this is not enough. We are actors in the struggle; and, in order that we may have steady PRINCIPLES to controul and direct us, (without which we may do much harm, and can do no good,) we ought to make it a duty to revive in the memory those words and facts, which first carried the conviction to our hearts: that, as far as it is possible, we may see as we then saw, and feel as we then felt. Let me therefore entreat the Reader seriously to peruse once more such parts of those Declarations as I shall extract from them. I feel indeed with sorrow, that events are hurrying us forward, as down the Rapid of an American river, and that there is too much danger *before*, to permit the mind easily to turn back upon the course which is past. It is indeed difficult.—But I need not say, that to yield to the difficulty, would be degrading to rational beings. Besides, if from the retrospect, we can either gain strength by which we can overcome, or learn prudence by which we may avoid, such submission is not only degrading, but pernicious. I address these words to those who have feeling, but whose judgment is overpowered by their feelings:—such as have not, and who are mere slaves of curiosity, calling perpetually for something new, and being able to create nothing new for themselves out of old materials, may be left to wander about under the yoke of their own unprofitable appetite.—Yet not so! Even these I would include in my request: and conjure them, as they are men, not to be impatient, while I place before their eyes, a composition made out of fragments of those Declarations from various parts of the Peninsula, which, disposed as it were in a tesselated pavement, shall set forth a story which may be easily understood; which will move and teach, and be consolatory to him who looks upon it. I say, consolatory: and let not the Reader shrink from the word. I am well aware of the burthen which is to be supported, of the discountenance from recent calamity under which every thing, which speaks of hope for the Spanish people, and through *them* for mankind, will be received. But this, far from deterring, ought to be an encouragement; it makes the duty more imperious. Nevertheless, whatever confidence any individual of meditative mind may have in these representations of the principles and feelings of the people of Spain, both as to their sanctity and truth, and as to their competence in ordinary circumstances to make these acknowledged, it would be unjust to recall them to the public mind, stricken as it is by present disaster, without attempting to mitigate the bewildering terror which accompanies these events, and which is caused as much by their nearness to the eye, as by any thing in their own nature. I shall, however, at present confine myself to suggest a few considerations, some of which will be developed hereafter, when I resume the subject.

It appears then, that the Spanish armies have sustained great defeats, and have been compelled to abandon their positions, and that these reverses have been effected by an army greatly superior to the Spanish forces in number, and far excelling them in the art and practice of war. This is the sum of those tidings, which it was natural we should receive with sorrow, but which too many have received with dismay and despair, though surely no events could be more in the course of rational expectation. And what is the amount of the evil?—It is manifest that, though a great army may easily defeat or disperse another *army*, less or greater, yet it is not in a like degree formidable to a determined *people*, nor efficient in a like degree to subdue them, or to keep them in subjugation—much less if this people, like those of Spain in the present instance, be numerous, and, like them, inhabit a territory extensive and strong by nature. For a great army, and even several great armies, cannot accomplish this by marching about the country, unbroken, but each must split itself into many portions, and the several detachments become weak accordingly, not merely as they are small in size, but because the soldiery, acting thus, necessarily relinquish much of that part of their superiority, which lies in what may be called the enginery of war; and far more, because they lose, in proportion as they are broken, the power of profiting by the military skill of the Commanders, or by their own military habits. The experienced soldier is thus brought down nearer to the plain ground of the inexperienced, man to the level of man: and it is then, that the truly brave man rises, the man of good hopes and purposes; and superiority in moral brings with it superiority in physical power. Hence, if the Spanish armies have been defeated, or even dispersed, it not only argues a want of magnanimity, but of sense, to conclude that the cause *therefore* is lost. Supposing that the spirit of the people is not crushed, the war is now brought back to that plan of conducting it, which was recommended by the Junta of Seville in that inestimable paper entitled 'PRECAUTIONS,' which plan ought never to have been departed from, except by compulsion, or with a moral certainty of success; and which the Spaniards will now be constrained to re-adopt, with the advantage, that the lesson, which has been received, will preclude the possibility of their ever committing the same error. In this paper it is said, 'let the first object be to avoid all general actions, and to convince ourselves of the very great hazards without any advantage or the hope of it, to which they would expose us.' The paper then gives directions, how the war ought to be conducted as a war of partizans, and shews the peculiar fitness of the country for it.

Yet, though relying solely on this unambitious mode of warfare, the framers of the paper, which is in every part of it distinguished by wisdom, speak with confident thoughts of success. To this mode of warfare, then, after experience of calamity from not having trusted in it; to this, and to the people in whom the contest originated, and who are its proper depository, that contest is now referred.

Secondly, if the spirits of the Spaniards be not broken by defeat, which is impossible, if the sentiments that have been publicly expressed be fairly characteristic of the nation, and do not belong only to particular spots or to a few individuals of superior mind,—a doubt, which the internal evidence of these publications, sanctioned by the resistance already made, and corroborated by the universal consent with which certain qualities have been attributed to the Spaniards in all ages, encourages us to repel;—then are there mighty resources in the country which have not yet been called forth. For all has hitherto been done by the spontaneous efforts of the people, acting under little or no compulsion of the Government, but with its advice and exhortation. It is an error to suppose, that, in proportion as a people are strong, and act largely for themselves, the Government must therefore be weak. This is not a necessary consequence even in the heat of Revolution, but only when the people are lawless from want of a steady and noble object among themselves for their love, or in the presence of a foreign enemy for their hatred. In the early part of the French Revolution, indeed as long as it was evident that the end was the common safety, the National Assembly had the power to turn the people into any course, to constrain them to any task, while their voluntary efforts, as far as these could be exercised, were not abated in consequence. That which the National Assembly did for France, the Spanish Sovereign's authority acting through those whom the people themselves have deputed to represent him, would, in their present enthusiasm of loyalty, and condition of their general feelings, render practicable and easy for Spain. The Spaniards, it is true, with a thoughtfulness most hopeful for the cause which they have undertaken, have been loth to depart from established laws, forms, and practices. This dignified feeling of self-restraint they would do well to cherish so far as never to depart from it without some reluctance;—but, when old and familiar means are not equal to the exigency, new ones must, without timidity, be resorted to, though by many they may be found harsh and ungracious. Nothing but good would result from such conduct. The well-disposed would rely more confidently upon a Government which thus proved that it had confidence in itself. Men, less zealous, and of less comprehensive minds, would soon be reconciled to measures from which at first they had revolted; the remiss and selfish might be made servants of their country, through the influence of the same passions which had prepared them to become slaves of the Invader; or, should this not be possible, they would appear in their true character, and the main danger to be feared from them would be prevented. The course which ought to be pursued is plain. Either the cause has lost the people's love, or it has not. If it has, let the struggle be abandoned. If it has not, let the Government, in whatever shape it may exist, and however great may be the calamities under which it may labour, act up to the full stretch of its rights, nor doubt that the people will support it to the full extent of their power. If, therefore, the Chiefs of the Spanish Nation be men of wise and strong minds, they will bring both the forces, those of the Government and of the people, into their utmost action; tempering them in such a manner that neither shall impair or obstruct the other, but rather that they shall strengthen and direct each other for all salutary purposes.

Thirdly, it was never dreamt by any thinking man; that the Spaniards were to succeed by their army; if by their *army* be meant any thing but the people. The whole people is their army, and their true army is the people, and nothing else. Five hundred men, who in the early part of the struggle had been taken prisoners,—I think it was at the battle of Rio Seco—were returned by the French General under the title of Galician Peasants, a title, which the Spanish General, Blake, rejected and maintained in his answer that they were genuine soldiers, meaning regular troops. The conduct of the Frenchman was politic, and that of the Spaniard would have been more in the spirit of his cause and of his own noble character, if, waiving on this occasion the plea of any subordinate and formal commission which these men might have, he had rested their claim to the title of soldiers on its true ground, and affirmed that this was no other than the rights of the cause which they maintained, by which rights every Spaniard was a soldier who could appear in arms, and was authorized to take that place, in which it was probable, to those under whom he acted, and on many occasions to himself, that he could most annoy the enemy. But these patriots of Galicia were not clothed alike, nor perhaps armed alike, nor had the outward appearance of those bodies, which are called regular troops; and the Frenchman availed himself of this pretext, to apply to them that insolent language, which might, I think, have been more nobly repelled on a more comprehensive principle. For thus are men of the gravest minds imposed upon by the presumptuous; and through these influences it comes, that the strength of a tyrant is in opinion— not merely in the opinion of those who support him, but alas! even of those who willingly resist, and who would resist effectually, if it were not that their own understandings betray them, being already half enslaved by shews and forms. The whole Spanish nation ought to be encouraged to deem themselves an army, embodied under the authority of their country and of human nature. A military spirit should be there, and a military action, not confined like an ordinary river in one channel, but spreading like the Nile over the whole face of the land. Is this possible? I believe it is: if there be minds among them worthy to lead, and if those leading minds cherish a *civic* spirit by all warrantable aids and appliances, and, above all other means, by combining a reverential memory of their elder ancestors with distinct hopes of solid advantage, from the privileges of freedom, for themselves and their posterity—to which the history and the past state of Spain furnish such enviable facilities; and if they provide for the sustenance of this spirit, by organizing it in its primary sources, not timidly jealous of a people, whose toils and sacrifices have approved them worthy of all love and confidence, and whose failing of excess, if such there exist, is assuredly on the side of loyalty to their Sovereign, and predilection for all established institutions. We affirm, then, that a universal military spirit may be produced; and not only this, but that a much more rare and more admirable phenomenon may be realized—the civic and military spirit united in one people, and in enduring harmony with each other. The people of Spain, with arms in their hands, are already in an elevated mood, to which they have been raised by the indignant passions, and the keen sense of insupportable wrong and insult from the enemy, and its infamous instruments. But they must be taught, not to trust too exclusively to the violent passions, which have already done much of their peculiar task and service. They must seek additional aid from affections, which less imperiously exclude all individual interests, while at the same time they consecrate them to the public good.—But the enemy is in the heart of their Land! We have not forgotten this. We would encourage their military zeal, and all qualities especially military, by all rewards of honourable ambition, and by rank and dignity conferred on the truly worthy, whatever may be their birth or condition, the elevating influence of which would extend from the individual possessor to the class from which he may have sprung. For the necessity of thus raising and upholding the military spirit, we plead: but yet the *professional* excellencies of the soldier must be contemplated according to their due place and relation. Nothing is done, or worse than nothing, unless something higher be taught, *as* higher, something more fundamental, *as* more fundamental. In the moral virtues and qualities of passion which belong to a people, must the ultimate salvation of a people be sought for. Moral qualities of a high order, and vehement passions, and virtuous as vehement, the Spaniards have already displayed; nor is it to be anticipated, that the conduct of their enemies will suffer the heat and glow to remit and languish. These may be trusted to themselves, and to the provocations of the merciless Invader. They must now be taught, that their strength *chiefly* lies in moral qualities, more silent in their operation, more permanent in their nature; in the virtues of perseverance, constancy, fortitude, and watchfulness, in a long memory and a quick feeling, to rise upon a favourable summons, a texture of life which, though cut through (as hath been feigned of the bodies of the Angels) unites again—these are the virtues and qualities on which the Spanish People must be taught *mainly* to depend. These it is not in the power of their Chiefs to create; but they may preserve and procure to them opportunities of unfolding themselves, by guarding the Nation against an intemperate reliance on other qualities and other modes of exertion, to which it could never have resorted in the degree in which it appears to have resorted to them without having been in contradiction to itself, paying at the same time an indirect homage to its enemy. Yet, in hazarding this conditional censure, we are still inclined to believe, that, in spite of our deductions on the score of exaggeration, we have still given too easy credit to the accounts furnished by the enemy, of the rashness with which the Spaniards engaged in pitched battles, and of their dismay after defeat. For the Spaniards have repeatedly proclaimed, and they have inwardly felt, that their strength was from their cause—of course, that it was moral. Why then should they abandon this, and endeavour to prevail by means in which their opponents are confessedly so much superior? Moral strength is their's; but physical power for the purposes of immediate or rapid destruction is on the side of their enemies. This is to them no disgrace, but, as soon as they understand themselves, they will see that they are disgraced by mistrusting their appropriate stay, and throwing themselves upon a power which for them must be weak. Nor will it then appear to them a sufficient excuse, that they were seduced into this by the splendid qualities of courage and enthusiasm, which, being the frequent companions, and, in given circumstances, the necessary agents of virtue, are too often themselves hailed as virtues by their own title. But courage and enthusiasm have equally characterized the best and the worst beings, a Satan, equally with an ABDIEL—a BONAPARTE equally with a LEONIDAS. They are indeed indispensible to the Spanish soldiery, in order that, man to man, they may not be inferior to their enemies in the field of battle. But inferior they are and long must be in warlike skill and coolness; inferior in assembled numbers, and in blind mobility to the preconceived purposes of their leader. If therefore the Spaniards are not superior in some superior quality, their fall may be predicted with the certainty of a mathematical calculation. Nay, it is right to acknowledge, however depressing to false hope the thought may be, that from a people prone and disposed to war, as the French are, through the very absence of those excellencies which give a contra-distinguishing dignity to the Spanish character; that, from an army of men presumptuous by nature, to whose presumption the experience of constant success has given the confidence and stubborn strength of reason, and who balance against the devotion of patriotism the superstition so naturally attached by the sensual and disordinate to the strange fortunes and continual felicity of their Emperor; that, from the armies of such a people a more manageable enthusiasm, a courage less under the influence of accidents, may be expected in the confusion of immediate conflict, than from forces like the Spaniards, united indeed by devotion to a common cause, but not equally united by an equal confidence in each other, resulting from long fellowship and brotherhood in all conceivable incidents of war and battle. Therefore, I do not hesitate to affirm, that even the occasional flight of the Spanish levies, from sudden panic under untried circumstances, would not be so injurious to the Spanish cause; no, nor so dishonourable to the Spanish character, nor so ominous of ultimate failure, as a paramount reliance on superior valour, instead of a principled reposal on superior constancy and immutable resolve. Rather let them have fled once and again, than direct their prime admiration to the blaze and explosion of animal courage, in slight of the vital and sustaining warmth of fortitude; in slight of that moral contempt of death and privation, which does not need the stir and shout of battle to call it forth or support it, which can smile in patience over the stiff and cold wound, as well as rush forward regardless, because half senseless of the fresh and bleeding one. Why did we give our hearts to the present cause of Spain with a fervour and elevation unknown to us in the commencement of the late Austrian or Prussian resistance to France? Because we attributed to the former an heroic temperament which would render their transfer to such domination an evil to human nature itself, and an affrightening perplexity in the dispensations of Providence. But if in oblivion of the prophetic wisdom of their own first leaders in the cause, they are surprised beyond the power of rallying, utterly cast down and manacled by fearful thoughts from the first thunder-storm of defeat in the field, wherein do they differ from the Prussians and Austrians? Wherein are they a PEOPLE, and not a mere army or set of armies? If this be indeed so, what have we to mourn over but our own honourable impetuosity, in hoping where no just ground of hope existed? A nation, without the virtues necessary for the attainment of independence, have failed to attain it. This is all. For little has that man understood the majesty of true national freedom, who believes that a population, like that of Spain, in a country like that of Spain, may want the qualities needful to fight out their independence, and yet possess the excellencies which render men susceptible of true liberty. The Dutch, the Americans, did possess the former; but it is, I fear, more than doubtful whether the one ever did, or the other ever will, evince the nobler morality indispensible to the latter.

It was not my intention that the subject should at present have been pursued so far. But I have been carried forward by a strong wish to be of use in raising and steadying the minds of my countrymen, an end to which every thing that I shall say hereafter (provided it be true) will contribute. For all knowledge of human nature leads ultimately to repose; and I shall write to little purpose if I do not assist some portion of my readers to form an estimate of the grounds of hope and fear in the present effort of liberty against oppression, in the present or any future struggle which justice will have to maintain against might. In fact, this is my main object, 'the sea-mark of my utmost sail:' in order that, understanding the sources of strength and seats of weakness, both in the tyrant and in those who would save or rescue themselves from his grasp, we may act as becomes men who would guard their own liberties, and would draw a good use from the desire which they feel, and the efforts which they are making, to benefit the less favoured part of the family of mankind. With these as my ultimate objects, I have undertaken to examine the Convention of Cintra; and, as an indispensible preparative for forming a right judgment of this event, I have already faithfully exhibited the feelings of the people of Great Britain and of Spain towards each other, and have shewn by what sacred bonds they were united. With the same view, I shall next proceed to shew by what barrier of aversion, scarcely less sacred, the people of the *Peninsula* were divided from their enemies,—their feelings towards them, and their hopes for themselves; trusting, that I have already mitigated the deadening influences of recent calamity, and that the representation I shall frame, in the manner which has been promised, will speak in its true colours and life to the eye and heart of the spectator.

The government of Asturias, which was the first to rise against their oppressors, thus expresses itself in the opening of its Address to the People of that Province. 'Loyal Asturians! beloved Countrymen! your wishes are already fulfilled. The Principality, discharging those duties which are most sacred to men, has already declared war against France. You may perhaps dread this vigorous resolution. But what other measure could or ought we to adopt? Shall there be found one single man among us, who prefers the vile and ignominious death of slaves, to the glory of dying on the field of honour, with arms in his hand, defending our unfortunate monarch, our homes, our children, and our wives? If, in the very moment when those bands of banditti were receiving the kindest offices and favours from the inhabitants of our Capital, they murdered in cold blood upwards of two thousand people, for no other reason than their having defended their insulted brethren, what could we expect from them, had we submitted to their dominion? Their perfidious conduct towards our king and his whole family, whom they deceived and decoyed into France under the promise of an eternal armistice, in order to chain them all, has no precedent in history. Their conduct towards the whole nation is more iniquitous, than we had the right to expect from a horde of Hottentots. They have profaned our temples; they have insulted our religion; they have assailed our wives; in fine, they have broken all their promises, and there exists no right which they have not violated. To arms, Asturians! to arms!' The Supreme Junta of Government, sitting at Seville, introduces its declaration of war in words to the same effect. 'France, under the government of the emperor Napoleon the First, has violated towards Spain the most sacred compacts—has arrested her monarchs—obliged them to a forced and manifestly void abdication and renunciation; has behaved with the same violence towards the Spanish Nobles whom he keeps in his power—has declared that he will elect a king of Spain, the most horrible attempt that is recorded in history—has sent his troops into Spain, seized her fortresses and her Capital, and scattered his troops throughout the country—has committed against Spain all sorts of assassinations, robberies, and unheard-of cruelties; and this he has done with the most enormous ingratitude to the services which the Spanish nation has rendered France, to the friendship it has shewn her, thus treating it with the most dreadful perfidy, fraud, and treachery, such as was never committed against any nation or monarch by the most barbarous or ambitious king or people. He has in fine declared, that he will trample down our monarchy, our fundamental laws, and bring about the ruin of our holy catholic religion.—The only remedy therefore to such grievous ills, which are so manifest to all Europe, is in war, which we declare against him.' The injuries, done to the Portuguese Nation and Government, previous to its declaration of war against the Emperor of the French, are stated at length in the manifesto of the Court of Portugal, dated Rio Janeiro, May 1st, 1808; and to that the reader may be referred: but upon this subject I will beg leave to lay before him, the following extract from the Address of the supreme Junta of Seville to the Portuguese nation, dated May 30th, 1808. 'PORTUGUESE,—Your lot is, perhaps, the hardest ever endured by any people on the earth. Your princes were compelled to fly from you, and the events in Spain have furnished an irrefragable proof of the absolute necessity of that measure.—You were ordered not to defend yourselves, and you did not defend yourselves. Junot offered to make you happy, and your happiness has consisted in being treated with greater cruelty than the most ferocious conquerors inflict on the people whom they have subdued by force of arms and after the most obstinate resistance. You have been despoiled of your princes, your laws, your usages, your customs, your property, your liberty, even your lives, and your holy religion, which your enemies never have respected, however they may, according to their custom, have promised to protect it, and however they may affect and pretend to have any sense of it themselves. Your nobility has been annihilated,—its property confiscated in punishment of its fidelity and loyalty. You have been basely dragged to foreign countries, and compelled to prostrate yourselves at the feet of the man who is the author of all your calamities, and who, by the most horrible perfidy, has usurped your government, and rules you with a sceptre of iron. Even now your troops have left your borders, and are travelling in chains to die in the defence of him who has oppressed you; by which means his deep malignity may accomplish his purpose,—by destroying those who should constitute your strength, and by rendering their lives subservient to his triumphs, and to the savage glory to which he aspires.—Spain beheld your slavery, and the horrible evils which followed it, with mingled sensations of grief and despair. You are her brother, and she panted to fly to your assistance. But certain Chiefs, and a Government either weak or corrupt, kept her in chains, and were preparing the means by which the ruin of our king, our laws, our independence, our liberty, our lives, and even the holy religion in which we are united, might accompany your's,—by which a barbarous people might consummate their own triumph, and accomplish the slavery of every nation in Europe:—our loyalty, our honour, our justice, could not submit to such flagrant atrocity! We have broken our chains,—let us then to action.' But the story of Portuguese sufferings shall be told by Junot himself; who, in his proclamation to the people of Portugal (dated Palace of Lisbon, June 26,) thus speaks to them: 'You have earnestly entreated of him a king, who, aided by the omnipotence of that great monarch, might raise up again your unfortunate Country, and replace her in the rank which belongs to her. Doubtless at this moment your new monarch is on the point of visiting you.—He expects to find faithful Subjects—shall he find only rebels? I expected to have delivered over to him a peaceable kingdom and flourishing cities—shall I be obliged to shew him only ruins and heaps of ashes and dead bodies?—Merit pardon by prompt submission, and a prompt obedience to my orders; if not, think of the punishment which awaits you.—Every city, town, or village, which shall take up arms against my forces, and whose inhabitants shall rise upon the French troops, shall be delivered up to pillage and totally destroyed, and the inhabitants shall be put to the sword—every individual taken in arms shall be instantly shot.' That these were not empty threats, we learn from the bulletins published by authority of the same Junot, which at once shew his cruelty, and that of the persons whom he employed, and the noble resistance of the Portuguese. 'We entered Beia,' says one of those dismal chronicles, 'in the midst of great carnage. The rebels left 1200 dead on the field of battle; all those taken with arms in their hands were put to the sword, and all the houses from which we had been fired upon were burned.' Again in another, 'The spirit of insanity, which had led astray the inhabitants of Beia and rendered necessary the terrible chastisement which they have received, has likewise been exercised in the north of Portugal.' Describing another engagement, it is said, 'the lines endeavoured to make a stand, but they were forced; the massacre was terrible—more than a thousand dead bodies remained on the field of battle, and General Loison, pursuing the remainder of these wretches, entered Guerda with fixed bayonets.' On approaching Alpedrinha, they found the *rebels* posted in a kind of redoubt—'it was forced, the town of Alpedrinha taken, and delivered to the flames:' the whole of this tragedy is thus summed up—'In the engagements fought in these different marches, we lost twenty men killed, and 30 or 40 wounded. The insurgents have left at least 13000 dead in the field, the melancholy consequence of a frenzy which nothing can justify, which forces us to multiply victims, whom we lament and regret, but whom a terrible necessity obliges us to sacrifice.' 'It is thus,' continues the writer, 'that deluded men, ungrateful children as well as culpable citizens, exchange all their claims to the benevolence and protection of Government for misfortune and wretchedness; ruin their families; carry into their habitations desolation, conflagrations, and death; change flourishing cities into heaps of ashes—into vast tombs; and bring on their whole country calamities which they deserve, and from which (feeble victims!) they cannot escape. In fine, it is thus that, covering themselves with opprobrium and ridicule at the same time that they complete their destruction, they have no other resource but the pity of those they have wished to assassinate—a pity which they never have implored in vain, when acknowledging their crime, they have solicited pardon from Frenchmen, who, incapable of departing from their noble character, are ever as generous as they are brave.'—By order of Monseigneur le duc d'Abrantes, Commander in chief.' —Compare this with the Address of Massaredo to the Biscayans, in which there is the like avowal that the Spaniards are to be treated as Rebels. He tells them, that he is commanded by his master, Joseph Bonaparte, to assure them—'that, in case they disapprove of the insurrection in the City of Bilboa, his majesty will consign to oblivion the mistake and error of the Insurgents, and that he will punish only the heads and beginners of the insurrection, with regard to whom *the law must take its course.*'

To be the victim of such bloody-mindedness is a doleful lot for a Nation; and the anguish must have been rendered still more poignant by the scoffs and insults, and by that heinous contempt of the most awful truths, with which the Perpetrator of those cruelties has proclaimed them.—Merciless ferocity is an evil familiar to our thoughts; but these combinations of malevolence historians have not yet been called upon to record; and writers of fiction, if they have ever ventured to create passions resembling them, have confined, out of reverence for the acknowledged constitution of human nature, those passions to reprobate Spirits. Such tyranny is, in the strictest sense, intolerable; not because it aims at the extinction of life, but of every thing which gives life its value—of virtue, of reason, of repose in God, or in truth. With what heart may we suppose that a genuine Spaniard would read the following impious address from the Deputation, as they were falsely called, of his apostate countrymen at Bayonne, seduced or compelled to assemble under the eye of the Tyrant, and speaking as he dictated? 'Dear Spaniards, Beloved Countrymen!—Your habitations, your cities, your power, and your property, are as dear to us as ourselves; and we wish to keep all of you in our eye, that we may be able to establish your security.—We, as well as yourselves, are bound in allegiance to the old dynasty—to her, to whom an end has been put by that God-like Providence which rules all thrones and sceptres. We have seen the greatest states fall under the guidance of this rule, and our land alone has hitherto escaped the same fate. An unavoidable destiny has now overtaken our country, and brought us under the protection of the invincible Emperor of France.—We know that you will regard our present situation with the utmost consideration; and we have accordingly, in this conviction, been uniformly conciliating the friendship to which we are tied by so many obligations. With what admiration must we see the benevolence and humanity of his imperial and royal Majesty outstep our wishes—qualities which are even more to be admired than his great power! He has desired nothing else, than that we should be indebted to him for our welfare. Whenever he gives us a sovereign to reign over us in the person of his magnanimous brother Joseph, he will consummate our prosperity.—As he has been pleased to change our old system of laws, it becomes us to obey, and to live in tranquillity: as he has also promised to re-organize our financial system, we may hope that then our naval and military power will become terrible to our enemies, &c.'—That the Castilians were horror-stricken by the above blasphemies, which are the habitual language of the French Senate and Ministers to their Emperor, is apparent from an address dated Valladolid,—'He (Bonaparte) carries his audacity the length of holding out to us offers of happiness and peace, while he is laying waste our country, pulling down our churches, and slaughtering our brethren. His pride, cherished by a band of villains who are constantly anxious to offer incense on his shrine, and tolerated by numberless victims who pine in his chains, has caused him to conceive the fantastical idea of proclaiming himself Lord and Ruler of the whole world. There is no atrocity which he does not commit to attain that end * * * *. Shall these outrages, these iniquities, remain unpunished while Spaniards—and Castilian Spaniards—yet exist?'

Many passages might be adduced to prove that carnage and devastation spread over their land have not afflicted this noble people so deeply as this more searching warfare against the conscience and the reason. They groan less over the blood which has been shed, than over the arrogant assumptions of beneficence made by him from whose order that blood has flowed. Still to be talking of bestowing and conferring, and to be happy in the sight of nothing but what he thinks he has bestowed or conferred, this, in a man to whom the weakness of his fellows has given great power, is a madness of pride more hideous than cruelty itself. We have heard of Attila and Tamerlane who called themselves the scourges of God, and rejoiced in personating the terrors of Providence; but such monsters do less outrage to the reason than he who arrogates to himself the gentle and gracious attributes of the Deity: for the one acts professedly from the temperance of reason, the other avowedly in the gusts of passion. Through the terrors of the Supreme Ruler of things, as set forth by works of destruction and ruin, we see but darkly; we may reverence the chastisement, may fear it with awe, but it is not natural to incline towards it in love: moreover, devastation passes away—a perishing power among things that perish: whereas to found, and to build, to create and to institute, to bless through blessing, this has to do with objects where we trust we can see clearly,—it reminds us of what we love,—it aims at permanence,—and the sorrow is, (as in the present instance the people of Spain feel) that it may last; that, if the giddy and intoxicated Being who proclaims that he does these things with the eye and through the might of Providence be not overthrown, it will last; that it needs must last:—and therefore would they hate and abhor him and his pride, even if he were not cruel; if he were merely an image of mortal presumption thrust in between them and the piety which is natural to the heart of man; between them and that religious worship which, as authoritatively as his reason forbids idolatry, that same reason commands. Accordingly, labouring under these violations done to their moral nature, they describe themselves, in the anguish of their souls, treated as a people at once dastardly and *insensible*. In the same spirit they make it even matter of complaint, as comparatively a far greater evil, that they have not fallen by the brute violence of open war, but by deceit and perfidy, by a subtle undermining, or contemptuous overthrow of those principles of good faith, through prevalence of which, in some degree, or under some modification or other, families, communities, a people, or any frame of human society, even destroying armies themselves can exist.

But enough of their wrongs; let us now see what were their consolations, their resolves, and their hopes. First, they neither murmur nor repine; but with genuine religion and philosophy they recognize in these dreadful visitations the ways of a benign Providence, and find in them cause for thankfulness. The Council of Castile exhort the people of Madrid 'to cast off their lethargy, and purify their manners, and to acknowledge the calamities which the kingdom and that great capital had endured as a punishment necessary to their correction.' General Morla in his address to the citizens of Cadiz thus speaks to them:—'The commotion, more or less violent, which has taken place in the whole peninsula of Spain, has been of eminent service to rouse us from the state of lethargy in which we indulged, and to make us acquainted with our rights, our glory, and the inviolable duty which we owe to our holy religion and our monarch. We wanted some electric stroke to rouse us from our paralytic state of inactivity; we stood in need of a hurricane to clear the atmosphere of the insalubrious vapours with which it was loaded.'—The unanimity with which the whole people were affected they rightly deem an indication of wisdom, an authority, and a sanction,—and they refer it to its highest source. 'The defence of our country and our king,' (says a manifesto of the Junta of Seville) 'that of our laws, our religion, and of all the rights of man, trodden down and violated in a manner which is without example, by the Emperor of the French, Napoleon I. and by his troops in Spain, compelled the whole nation to take up arms, and choose itself a form of government; and, in the difficulties and dangers into which the French had plunged it, all, or nearly all the provinces, as it were by the inspiration of heaven, and in a manner little short of miraculous, created Supreme Juntas, delivered themselves up to their guidance, and placed in their hands the rights and the ultimate fate of Spain. The effects have hitherto most happily corresponded with the designs of those who formed them.'

With this general confidence, that the highest good may be brought out of the worst calamities, they have combined a solace, which is vouchsafed only to such nations as can recal to memory the illustrious deeds of their ancestors. The names of Pelayo and The Cid are the watch-words of the address to the people of Leon; and they are told that to these two deliverers of their country, and to the sentiments of enthusiasm which they excited in every breast, Spain owes the glory and happiness which she has *so long* enjoyed. The Biscayans are called to cast their eyes upon the ages which are past, and they will see their ancestors at one time repulsing the Carthaginians, at another destroying the hordes of Rome; at one period was granted to them the distinction of serving in the van of the army; at another the privilege of citizens. 'Imitate,' says the address, 'the glorious example of your worthy progenitors.' The Asturians, the Gallicians, and the city of Cordova, are exhorted in the same manner. And surely to a people thus united in their minds with the heroism of years which have been long departed, and living under such obligation of gratitude to their ancestors, it is not difficult, nay it is natural, to take upon themselves the highest obligations of duty to their posterity; to enjoy in the holiness of imagination the happiness of unborn ages to which they shall have eminently contributed; and that each man, fortified by these thoughts, should welcome despair for himself, because it is the assured mother of hope for his country.— 'Life or Death,' says a proclamation affixed in the most public places of Seville, 'is in this crisis indifferent;—ye who shall return shall receive the reward of gratitude in the embraces of your country, which shall proclaim you her deliverers;—ye whom heaven destines to seal with your blood the independence of your nation, the honour of your women, and the purity of the religion which ye profess, do not dread the anguish of the last moments; remember in these moments that there are in our hearts inexhaustible tears of tenderness to shed over your graves, and fervent prayers, to which the Almighty Father of mercies will lend an ear, to grant you a glory superior to that which they who survive you shall enjoy.' And in fact it ought never to be forgotten, that the Spaniards have not wilfully blinded themselves, but have steadily fixed their eyes not only upon danger and upon death, but upon a deplorable issue of the contest. They have contemplated their subjugation as a thing possible. The next extract, from the paper entitled Precautions, (and the same language is holden by many others) will show in what manner alone they reconcile themselves to it. 'Therefore, it is necessary to sacrifice our lives and property in defence of the king, and of the country; and, though our lot (which we hope will never come to pass) should destine us to become slaves, let us become so fighting and dying like gallant men, not giving ourselves up basely to the yoke like sheep, as the late infamous government would have done, and fixing upon Spain and her slavery eternal ignominy and disgrace.'

But let us now hear them, as becomes men with such feelings, express more cheering and bolder hopes rising from a confidence in the supremacy of justice,—hopes which, however the Tyrant from the iron fortresses of his policy may scoff at them and at those who entertained them, will render their memory dear to all good men, when his name will be pronounced with universal abhorrence.

'All Europe,' says the Junta of Seville, 'will applaud our efforts and hasten to our assistance: Italy, Germany, and the whole North, which suffer under the despotism of the French nation, will eagerly avail themselves of the favourable opportunity, held out to them by Spain, to shake off the yoke and recover their liberty, their laws, their monarchs, and all they have been robbed of by that nation. France herself will hasten to erase the stain of infamy, which must cover the tools and instruments of deeds so treacherous and heinous. She will not shed her blood in so vile a cause. She has already suffered too much under the idle pretext of peace and happiness, which never came, and can never be attained, but under the empire of reason, peace, religion, and laws, and in a state where the rights of other nations are respected and preserved.' To this may be added a hope, the fulfilment of which belongs more to themselves, and lies more within their own power, namely, a hope that they shall be able in their progress towards liberty, to inflict condign punishment on their cruel and perfidious enemies. The Junta of Seville, in an Address to the People of Madrid, express themselves thus: 'People of Madrid! Seville has learned, with consternation and surprize, your dreadful catastrophe of the second of May; the weakness of a government which did nothing in our favour,—which ordered arms to be directed against you; and your heroic sacrifices. Blessed be ye, and your memory shall shine immortal in the annals of our nation!—She has seen with horror that the author of all your misfortunes and of our's has published a proclamation, in which he distorted every fact, and pretended that you gave the first provocation, while it was he who provoked you. The government was weak enough to sanction and order that proclamation to be circulated; and saw, with perfect composure, numbers of you put to death for a pretended violation of laws which did not exist. The French were told in that proclamation, that French blood profusely shed was crying out for vengeance! And the Spanish blood, does not *it* cry out for vengeance? That Spanish blood, shed by an army which hesitated not to attack a disarmed and defenceless people, living under their laws and their king, and against whom cruelties were committed, which shake the human frame with horror. We, all Spain, exclaim—the Spanish blood shed in Madrid cries aloud for revenge! Comfort yourselves, we are your brethren: we will fight like you, until we perish in defending our king and country. Assist us with your good wishes, and your continual prayers offered up to the Most High, whom we adore, and who cannot forsake us, because he never forsakes a just cause.' Again, in the conclusion of their address to the People of Portugal, quoted before, 'The universal cry of Spain is, we will die in defence of our country, but we will take care that those infamous enemies shall die with us. Come then, ye generous Portugueze, and unite with us. You have among yourselves the objects of your vengeance—obey not the authors of your misfortunes—attack them—they are but a handful of miserable panic-struck men, humiliated and conquered already by the perfidy and cruelties which they have committed, and which have covered them with disgrace in the eyes of Europe and the world! Rise then in a body, but avoid staining your honourable hands with crimes, for your design is to resist them and to destroy them—our united efforts will do for this perfidious nation; and Portugal, Spain, nay, all Europe, shall breathe or die free like men.'—Such are their hopes; and again see, upon this subject, the paper entitled '*Precautions;*' a contrast this to the impious mockery of Providence, exhibited by the Tyrant in some passages heretofore quoted! 'Care shall be taken to explain to the nation, and to convince them that, when free, as we trust to be, from this civil war, to which the French have forced us, and when placed in a state of tranquillity, our Lord and King, Ferdinand VII, being restored to the throne of Spain, under him and by him, *the Cortes will be assembled, abuses reformed,* and such laws shall be enacted, as the circumstances of the time and experience may dictate for the public good and happiness. Things which we Spaniards know how to do, which we have done as well as other nations, without any necessity that the vile French should come to instruct us, and, according to their custom, under the mask of friendship, should deprive us of our liberty, our laws, &c. &c.'

One extract more and I shall conclude. It is from a proclamation dated Oviedo, July 17th. 'Yes—Spain with the energies of Liberty has to contend with France debilitated by slavery. If she remain firm and constant, Spain will triumph. A whole people is more powerful than disciplined armies. Those, who unite to maintain the independence of their country, must triumph over tyranny. Spain will inevitably conquer, in a cause the most just that has ever raised the deadly weapon of war; for she fights, not for the concerns of a day, but for the security and happiness of ages; not for an insulated privilege, but for the rights of human nature; not for temporal blessings, but for eternal happiness; not for the benefit of one nation, but for all mankind, and even for France herself.'

I will now beg of my reader to pause a moment, and to review in his own mind the whole of what has been laid before him. He has seen of what kind, and how great have been the injuries endured by these two nations; what they have suffered, and what they have to fear; he has seen that they have felt with that unanimity which nothing but the light of truth spread over the inmost concerns of human nature can create; with that simultaneousness which has led Philosophers upon like occasions to assert, that the voice of the people is the voice of God. He has seen that they have submitted as far as human nature could bear; and that at last these millions of suffering people have risen almost like one man, with one hope; for whether they look to triumph or defeat, to victory or death, they are full of hope—despair comes not near them—they will die, they say —each individual knows the danger, and, strong in the magnitude of it, grasps eagerly at the thought that he himself is to perish; and more eagerly, and with higher confidence, does he lay to his heart the faith that the nation will survive and be victorious;—or, at the worst, let the contest terminate how it may as to superiority of outward strength, that the fortitude and the martyrdom, the justice and the blessing, are their's and cannot be relinquished. And not only are they moved by these exalted sentiments of universal morality, and of direct and universal concern to mankind, which have impelled them to resist evil and to endeavour to punish the evil-doer, but also they descend (for even this, great as in itself it is, may be here considered as a descent) to express a rational hope of reforming domestic abuses, and of re-constructing, out of the materials of their ancient institutions, customs, and laws, a better frame of civil government, the same in the great outlines of its architecture, but exhibiting the knowledge, and genius, and the needs of the present race, harmoniously blended with those of their forefathers. Woe, then, to the unworthy who intrude with their help to maintain this most sacred cause! It calls aloud for the aid of intellect, knowledge, and love, and rejects every other. It is in vain to send forth armies if these do not inspire and direct them. The stream is as pure as it is mighty, fed by ten thousand springs in the bounty of untainted nature; any augmentation from the kennels and sewers of guilt and baseness may clog, but cannot strengthen it.—It is not from any thought that I am communicating new information, that I have dwelt thus long upon this subject, but to recall to the reader his own knowledge, and to re-infuse into that knowledge a breath and life of appropriate feeling; because the bare sense of wisdom is nothing without its powers, and it is only in these feelings that the powers of wisdom exist. If then we do not forget that the Spanish and Portugueze Nations stand upon the loftiest ground of principle and passion, and do not suffer on our part those sympathies to languish which a few months since were so strong, and do not negligently or timidly descend from those heights of magnanimity to which as a Nation we were raised, when they first represented to us their wrongs and entreated our assistance, and we devoted ourselves sincerely and earnestly to their service, making with them a common cause under a common hope; if we are true in all this to them and to ourselves, we shall not be at a loss to conceive what actions are entitled to our commendation as being in the spirit of a friendship so nobly begun, and tending assuredly to promote the common welfare; and what are abject, treacherous, and pernicious, and therefore to be condemned and abhorred. Is then, I may now ask, the Convention of Cintra an act of this latter kind? Have the Generals, who signed and ratified that agreement, thereby proved themselves unworthy associates in such a cause? And has the Ministry, by whose appointment these men were enabled to act in this manner, and which sanctioned the Convention by permitting them to carry it into execution, thereby taken to itself a weight of guilt, in which the Nation must feel that it participates, until the transaction shall be solemnly reprobated by the Government, and the remote and immediate authors of it brought to merited punishment? An answer to each of these questions will be implied in the proof which will be given that the condemnation, which the People did with one voice pronounce upon this Convention when it first became known, was just; that the nature of the offence of those who signed it was such, and established by evidence of such a kind, making so imperious an exception to the ordinary course of action, that there was no need to wait here for the decision of a Court of Judicature, but that the People were compelled by a necessity involved in the very constitution of man as a moral Being to pass sentence upon them. And this I shall prove by trying this act of their's by principles of justice which are of universal obligation, and by a reference to those moral sentiments which rise out of that retrospect of things which has been given.

I shall now proceed to facts. The dispatches of Sir Arthur

Wellesley, containing an account of his having defeated the enemy in two several engagements, spread joy through the Nation. The latter action appeared to have been decisive, and the result may be thus briefly reported, in a never to be forgotten sentence of Sir Arthur's second letter. 'In this action,' says he, 'in which the whole of the French force in Portugal was employed, under the command of the Duc D'Abrantes in person, in which the enemy was certainly superior in cavalry and artillery, and in which not more than half of the British army was actually engaged, he sustained a signal defeat, and has lost thirteen pieces of cannon, &c. &c.' In the official communication, made to the public of these dispatches, it was added, that 'a General officer had arrived at the British head-quarters to treat for terms.' This was joyful intelligence! First, an immediate, effectual, and honourable deliverance of Portugal was confidently expected: secondly, the humiliation and captivity of a large French army, and just punishment, from the hands of the Portugueze government, of the most atrocious offenders in that army and among those who, having held civil offices under it, (especially if Portugueze) had, in contempt of all law, civil and military, notoriously abused the power which they had treasonably accepted: thirdly, in this presumed surrender of the army, a diminution of the enemy's military force was looked to, which, after the losses he had already sustained in Spain, would most sensibly weaken it: and lastly, and far above this, there was an anticipation of a shock to his power, where that power is strongest, in the imaginations of men, which are sure to fall under the bondage of long-continued success. The judicious part of the Nation fixed their attention chiefly on these results, and they had good cause to rejoice. They also received with pleasure this additional proof (which indeed with the unthinking many, as after the victory of Maida, weighed too much,) of the superiority in courage and discipline of the British soldiery over the French, and of the certainty of success whenever our army was led on by men of even respectable military talents against any equal or not too greatly disproportionate number of the enemy. But the pleasure was damped in the minds of reflecting persons by several causes. It occasioned regret and perplexity, that they had not heard more of the Portugueze. They knew what that People had suffered, and how they had risen;—remembered the language of the proclamation addressed to them, dated August the 4th, and signed CHARLES COTTON and ARTHUR WELLESLEY, in which they (the Portugueze) were told, that 'The British Army had been sent in consequence of ardent supplications from all parts of Portugal; that the glorious struggle, in which they are engaged, is for all that is dear to man; that the noble struggle against the tyranny and usurpation of France will be *jointly* maintained by Portugal, Spain, and England.' Why then, it was asked, do we not hear more of those who are at least coequals with us, if not principals, in this contest? They appeared to have had little share in either engagement; (*See Appendix A.*) and, while the French were abundantly praised, no word of commendation was found for *them*. Had they deserved to be thus neglected? The body of the People by a general rising had proved their zeal and courage, their animosity towards their enemies, their hatred of them. It was therefore apprehended, from this silence respecting the Portugueze, that their Chiefs might either be distracted by factions, or blinded by selfish interests, or that they mistrusted their Allies. Situated as Portugal then was, it would argue gross ignorance of human nature to have expected that unanimity should prevail among all the several authorities or leading persons, as to the *means* to be employed: it was enough, that they looked with one feeling to the *end*, namely, an honourable deliverance of their country and security for its Independence in conjunction with the liberation and independence of Spain. It was therefore absolutely necessary to make allowance for some division in conduct from difference of opinion. Instead of acquiescing in the first feelings of disappointment, our Commanders ought to have used the best means to win the confidence of the Portugueze Chiefs, and to induce them to regard the British as dispassionate arbiters; they ought to have endeavoured to excite a genuine patriotic spirit where it appeared wanting, and to assist in creating for it an organ by which it might act. Were these things done? or, if such evils existed among the Portugueze, was *any* remedy or alleviation attempted? Sir Arthur Wellesley has told us, before the Board of Inquiry, that he made applications to the Portugueze General, FRERE, for assistance, which were acceded to by General FRERE upon such conditions only as made Sir Arthur deem it more advisable to refuse than accept his co-operation: and it is alleged that, in his general expectations of assistance, he was greatly disappointed. We are not disposed to deny, that such cause for complaint *might* exist; but that it *did*, and upon no provocation on our part, requires confirmation by other testimony. And surely, the Portugueze have a right to be heard in answer to this accusation, before they are condemned. For they have supplied no fact from their own hands, which tends to prove that they were languid in the cause, or that they had unreasonable jealousies of the British Army or Nation, or dispositions towards them which were other than friendly. Now there is a fact, furnished by Sir Arthur Wellesley himself, which may seem to render it in the highest degree probable that, previously to any recorded or palpable act of disregard or disrespect to the situation and feelings of the Portugueze, the general tenour of his bearing towards them might have been such that they could not look favourably upon him; that he was not a man framed to conciliate them, to compose their differences, or to awaken or strengthen their zeal. I allude to the passage in his letter above quoted, where, having occasion to speak of the French General, he has found no name by which to designate him but that of Duc D'Abrantes—words necessarily implying, that Bonaparte, who had taken upon himself to confer upon General Junot this Portugueze title with Portugueze domains to support it, was lawful Sovereign of that Country, and that consequently the Portugueze Nation were rebels, and the British Army, and he himself at the head of it, aiders and abettors of that rebellion. It would be absurd to suppose, that Sir Arthur Wellesley, at the time when he used these words, was aware of the meaning really involved in them: let them be deemed an oversight. But the capability of such an oversight affords too strong suspicion of a deadness to the moral interests of the cause in which he was engaged, and of such a want of sympathy with the just feelings of his injured Ally as could exist only in a mind narrowed by exclusive and overweening attention to the *military* character, led astray by vanity, or hardened by general habits of contemptuousness. These words, 'Duke of Abrantes *in person*,' were indeed words of bad omen: and thinking men trembled for the consequences. They saw plainly, that, in the opinion of the exalted Spaniards—of those assuredly who framed, and of all who had felt, that affecting Proclamation addressed by the Junta of Seville to the Portugueze people, he must appear utterly unworthy of the station in which he had been placed. He had been sent as a deliverer—as an assertor and avenger of the rights of human nature. But these words would carry with them every where the conviction, that Portugal and Spain, yea, all which was good in England, or iniquitous in France or in Frenchmen, was forgotten, and his head full only of himself, miserably conceiting that he swelled the importance of his conquered antagonist by sounding titles and phrases, come from what quarter they might; and that, in proportion as this was done, he magnified himself and his achievements. It was plain, then, that here was a man, who, having not any fellow-feeling with the people whom he had been commissioned to aid, could not know where their strength lay, and therefore could not turn it to account, nor by his example call it forth or cherish it; but that, if his future conduct should be in the same spirit, he must be a blighting wind wherever his influence was carried: for he had neither felt the wrongs of his Allies nor been induced by common worldly prudence to affect to feel them, or at least to disguise his insensibility; and therefore what could follow, but, in despite of victory and outward demonstrations of joy, inward disgust and depression? These reflections interrupted the satisfaction of many; but more from fear of future consequences than for the immediate enterprize, for here success seemed inevitable; and a happy and glorious termination was confidently expected, yet not without that intermixture of apprehension, which was at once an acknowledgment of the general condition of humanity, and a proof of the deep interest attached to the impending event.

Sir Arthur Wellesley's dispatches had appeared in the Gazette on the 2d of September, and on the 16th of the same month suspence was put an end to by the publication of Sir Hew Dalrymple's letter, accompanied with the Armistice and Convention. The night before, by order of ministers, an attempt had been made at rejoicing, and the Park and Tower guns had been fired in sign of good news.—Heaven grant that the ears of that great city may be preserved from such another outrage! As soon as the truth was known, never was there such a burst of rage and indignation—such an overwhelming of stupefaction and sorrow. But I will not, I cannot dwell upon it—it is enough to say, that Sir Hew Dalrymple and Sir Arthur Wellesley must be bold men if they can think of what must have been reported to them, without awe and trembling; the heart of their country was turned against them, and they were execrated in bitterness.

For they had changed all things into their contraries, hope into despair; triumph into defeat; confidence into treachery, which left no place to stand upon; justice into the keenest injury.—Whom had they delivered but the Tyrant in captivity? Whose hands had they bound but those of their Allies, who were able of themselves to have executed their own purposes? Whom had they punished but the innocent sufferer? Whom rewarded but the guiltiest of Oppressors? They had reversed every thing:—favour and honour for their enemies—insult for their friends—and robbery (they had both protected the person of the robber and secured to him his booty) and opprobrium for themselves;—to those over whom they had been masters, who had crouched to them by an open act of submission, they had made themselves servants, turning the British Lion into a beast of burthen, to carry a vanquished enemy, with his load of iniquities, when and whither it had pleased him.

Such issue would have been a heavy calamity at any time; but now, when we ought to have risen above ourselves, and if possible to have been foremost in the strife of honour and magnanimity; now, when a new-born power had been arrayed against the Tyrant, the only one which ever offered a glimpse of hope to a sane mind, the power of popular resistance rising out of universal reason, and from the heart of human nature,—and by a peculiar providence disembarrassed from the imbecility, the cowardice, and the intrigues of a worn-out government—that at this time we, the most favoured Nation upon earth, should have acted as if it had been our aim to level to the ground by one blow this long-wished-for spirit, whose birth we had so joyfully hailed, and by which even our own glory, our safety, our existence, were to be maintained; this was verily a surpassing affliction to every man who had a feeling of life beyond his meanest concerns!

As soon as men had recovered from the shock, and could bear to look somewhat steadily at these documents, it was found that the gross body of the transaction, considered as a military transaction, was this; that the Russian fleet, of nine sail of the line, which had been so long watched, and could not have escaped, was to be delivered up to us; the ships to be detained till six months after the end of the war, and the sailors sent home by us, and to be by us protected in their voyage through the Swedish fleet, and to be at liberty to fight immediately against our ally, the king of Sweden. Secondly, that a French army of more than twenty thousand men, already beaten, and no longer able to appear in the field, cut off from all possibility of receiving reinforcements or supplies, and in the midst of a hostile country loathing and abhorring it, was to be transported with its arms, ammunition, and plunder, at the expence of Great Britain, in British vessels, and landed within a few days march of the Spanish frontier,—there to be at liberty to commence hostilities immediately!

Omitting every characteristic which distinguishes the present contest from others, and looking at this issue merely as an affair between two armies, what stupidity of mind to provoke the accusation of not merely shrinking from future toils and dangers, but of basely shifting the burthen to the shoulders of an ally, already overpressed!—What infatuation, to convey the imprisoned foe to the very spot, whither, if he had had wings, he would have flown! This last was an absurdity as glaring as if, the French having landed on our own island, we had taken them from Yorkshire to be set on shore in Sussex; but ten thousand times worse! from a place where without our interference they had been virtually blockaded, where they were cut off, hopeless, useless, and disgraced, to become an efficient part of a mighty host, carrying the strength of their numbers, and alas! the strength of their glory, (not to mention the sight of their plunder) to animate that host; while the British army, more numerous in the proportion of three to two, with all the population and resources of the peninsula to aid it, within ten days sail of it's own country, and the sea covered with friendly shipping at it's back, was to make a long march to encounter this same enemy, (the British forfeiting instead of gaining by the treaty as to superiority of numbers, for that this would be the case was clearly foreseen) to encounter, in a new condition of strength and pride, those whom, by its deliberate act, it had exalted,—having taken from itself, meanwhile, all which it had conferred, and bearing into the presence of its noble ally an infection of despondency and disgrace. The motive assigned for all this, was the great importance of gaining time; fear of an open beach and of equinoctial gales for the shipping; fear that reinforcements could not be landed; fear of famine;—fear of every thing but dishonour! (*See Appendix B.*)

The nation had expected that the French would surrender immediately at discretion; and, supposing that Sir Arthur Wellesley had told them the whole truth, they had a right to form this expectation. It has since appeared, from the evidence given before the Board of Inquiry, that Sir Arthur Wellesley earnestly exhorted his successor in command (Sir Harry Burrard) to pursue the defeated enemy at the battle of Vimiera; and that, if this had been done, the affair, in Sir Arthur Wellesley's opinion, would have had a much more satisfactory termination. But, waiving any considerations of this advice, or of the fault which might be committed in not following it; and taking up the matter from the time when Sir Hew Dalrymple entered upon the command, and when the two adverse armies were in that condition, relatively to each other, that none of the Generals has pleaded any difference of opinion as to their ability to advance against the enemy, I will ask what confirmation has appeared before the Board of Inquiry, of the reasonableness of the causes, assigned by Sir Hew Dalrymple in his letter, for deeming a Convention adviseable. A want of cavalry, (for which they who occasioned it are heavily censurable,) has indeed been proved; and certain failures of duty in the Commissariat department with respect to horses, &c.; but these deficiencies, though furnishing reasons against advancing upon the enemy in the open field, had ceased to be of moment, when the business was to expel him from the forts to which he might have the power of retreating. It is proved, that, though there are difficulties in landing upon that coast, (and what military or marine operation can be carried on without difficulty?) there was not the slightest reason to apprehend that the army, which was then abundantly supplied, would suffer hereafter from want of provisions; proved also that heavy ordnance, for the purpose of attacking the forts, was ready on ship-board, to be landed when and where it might be needed. Therefore, so far from being exculpated by the facts which have been laid before the

Board of Inquiry, Sir Hew Dalrymple and the other Generals, who deemed *any* Convention necessary or expedient upon the grounds stated in his letter, are more deeply criminated. But grant, (for the sake of looking at a different part of the subject,) grant a case infinitely stronger than Sir Hew Dalrymple has even hinted at;—why was not the taste of some of those evils, in apprehension so terrible, actually tried? It would not have been the first time that Britons had faced hunger and tempests, had endured the worst of such enmity, and upon a call, under an obligation, how faint and feeble, compared with that which the brave men of that army must have felt upon the present occasion! In the proclamation quoted before, addressed to the Portugueze, and signed Charles Cotton and Arthur Wellesley, they were told, that the objects, for which they contended, 'could only be attained by distinguished examples of fortitude and constancy.' Where were the fortitude and constancy of the teachers? When Sir Hew Dalrymple had been so busy in taking the measure of his own weakness, and feeding his own fears, how came it to escape him, that General Junot must also have had *his* weaknesses and *his* fears? Was it nothing to have been defeated in the open field, where he himself had been the assailant? Was it nothing that so proud a man, the servant of so proud a man, had stooped to send a General Officer to treat concerning the evacuation of the country? Was the hatred and abhorrence of the Portugueze and Spanish Nations nothing? the people of a large metropolis under his eye—detesting him, and stung almost to madness, nothing? The composition of his own army made up of men of different nations and languages, and forced into the service,—was there no cause of mistrust in this? And, finally, among the many unsound places which, had his mind been as active in this sort of inquiry as Sir Hew Dalrymple's was, he must have found in his constitution, could a bad cause have been missed—a worse cause than ever confounded the mind of a soldier when boldly pressed upon, or gave courage and animation to a righteous assailant? But alas! in Sir Hew Dalrymple and his brethren, we had Generals who had a power of sight only for the strength of their enemies and their own weakness.

Let me not be misunderstood. While I am thus forced to repeat things, which were uttered or thought of these men in reference to their military conduct, as heads of that army, it is needless to add, that their personal courage is in no wise implicated in the charge brought against them. But, in the name of my countrymen, I do repeat these accusations, and tax them with an utter want of *intellectual* courage—of that higher quality, which is never found without one or other of the three accompaniments, talents, genius, or principle;—talents matured by experience, without which it cannot exist at all; or the rapid insight of peculiar genius, by which the fitness of an act may be instantly determined, and which will supply higher motives than mere talents can furnish for encountering difficulty and danger, and will suggest better resources for diminishing or overcoming them. Thus, through the power of genius, this quality of intellectual courage may exist in an eminent degree, though the moral character be greatly perverted; as in those personages, who are so conspicuous in history, conquerors and usurpers, the Alexanders, the Cæsars, and Cromwells; and in that other class still more perverted, remorseless and energetic minds, the Catilines and Borgias, whom poets have denominated 'bold, bad men.' But, though a course of depravity will neither preclude nor destroy this quality, nay, in certain circumstances will give it a peculiar promptness and hardihood of decision, it is not on this account the less true, that, to *consummate* this species of courage, and to render it equal to all occasions, (especially when a man is not acting for himself, but has an additional claim on his resolution from the circumstance of responsibility to a superior) *Principle* is indispensibly requisite. I mean that fixed and habitual principle, which implies the absence of all selfish anticipations, whether of hope or fear, and the inward disavowal of any tribunal higher and more dreaded than the mind's own judgment upon its own act. The existence of such principle cannot but elevate the most commanding genius, add rapidity to the quickest glance, a wider range to the most ample comprehension; but, without this principle, the man of ordinary powers must, in the trying hour, be found utterly wanting. Neither, without it, can the man of excelling powers be trust-worthy, or have at all times a calm and confident repose in himself. But he, in whom talents, genius, and principle are united, will have a firm mind, in whatever embarrassment he may be placed; will look steadily at the most undefined shapes of difficulty and danger, of possible mistake or mischance; nor will they appear to him more formidable than they really are. For HIS attention is not distracted—he has but one business, and that is with the object before him. Neither in general conduct nor in particular emergencies, are HIS plans subservient to considerations of rewards, estate, or title: these are not to have precedence in his thoughts, to govern his actions, but to follow in the train of his duty. Such men, in ancient times, were Phocion, Epaminondas, and Philopœmen; and such a man was Sir Philip Sidney, of whom it has been said, that he first taught this country *the majesty of honest dealing.* With these may be named, the honour of our own age, Washington, the deliverer of the American Continent; with these, though in many things unlike, Lord Nelson, whom we have lately lost. Lord Peterborough, who fought in Spain a hundred years ago, had the same excellence; with a sense of exalted honour, and a tinge of romantic enthusiasm, well suited to the country which was the scene of his exploits. Would that we had a man, like Peterborough or Nelson, at the head of our army in Spain at this moment! I utter this wish with more earnestness, because it is rumoured, that some of those, who have already called forth such severe reprehension from their countrymen, are to resume a command, which must entrust to them a portion of those sacred hopes in which, not only we, and the people of Spain and Portugal, but the whole human race are so deeply interested. (*See Appendix C.*)

I maintain then that, merely from want of this intellectual courage, of courage as generals or chiefs, (for I will not speak at present of the want of other qualities equally needful upon this service,) grievous errors were committed by Sir Hew Dalrymple and his colleagues in estimating the relative state of the two armies. A precious moment, it is most probable, had been lost after the battle of Vimiera; yet still the inferiority of the enemy had been proved; they themselves had admitted it —not merely by withdrawing from the field, but by proposing terms:—monstrous terms! and how ought they to have been received? Repelled undoubtedly with scorn, as an insult. If our Generals had been men capable of taking the measure of their real strength, either as existing in their own army, or in those principles of liberty and justice which they were commissioned to defend, they must of necessity have acted in this manner;—if they had been men of common sagacity for business, they must have acted in this manner;—nay, if they had been upon a level with an ordinary bargain-maker in a Fair or a market, they could not have acted otherwise.—Strange that they should so far forget the nature of their calling! They were soldiers, and their business was to fight. Sir Arthur Wellesley had fought, and gallantly; it was not becoming his high situation, or that of his successors, to treat, that is, to beat down, to chaffer, or on their part to propose: it does not become any general at the head of a victorious army so to do.* They were to *accept*,—and, if the terms offered were flagrantly presumptuous, our commanders ought to have rejected them with dignified scorn, and to have referred the proposer to the sword for a lesson of decorum and humility. This is the general rule of all high-minded men upon such occasions; and meaner minds copy them, doing in prudence what they do from principle. But it has been urged, before the Board of Inquiry, that the conduct of the French armies upon like occasions, and their known character, rendered it probable that a determined resistance would in the present instance be maintained. We need not fear to say that this conclusion, from reasons which have been adverted to, was erroneous. But, in the mind of him who had admitted it upon whatever ground, whether false or true, surely the first thought which followed, ought to have been, not that we should bend to the enemy, but that, if they were resolute in defence, we should learn from that example to be courageous in attack. The tender feelings, however, are pleaded against this determination; and it is said, that one of the motives for the cessation of hostilities was to prevent the further effusion of human blood.—When, or how? The enemy was delivered over to us; it was not to be hoped that, cut off from all assistance as they were, these, or an equal number of men, could ever be reduced to such straits as would ensure their destruction as an enemy, with so small a sacrifice of life on their part, or on ours. What then was to be gained by this tenderness? The shedding of a few drops of blood is not to be risked in Portugal to-day,

* Those rare cases are of course excepted, in which the superiority on the one side is not only fairly to be presumed but positive—and so prominently obtrusive, that to *propose* terms is to *inflict* terms.

and streams of blood must shortly flow from the same veins in the fields of Spain! And, even if this had not been the assured consequence, let not the consideration, though it be one which no humane man can ever lose sight of, have more than its due weight. For national independence and liberty, and *that* honour by which these and other blessings are to be preserved, honour—which is no other than the most elevated and pure conception of justice which can be formed, these are more precious than life: else why have we already lost so many brave men in this struggle?—Why not submit at once, and let the Tyrant mount upon his throne of universal dominion, while the world lies prostrate at his feet in indifference and apathy, which he will proclaim to it is peace and happiness? But peace and happiness can exist only by knowledge and virtue; slavery has no enduring connection with tranquillity or security—she cannot frame a league with any thing which is desirable—she has no charter even for her own ignoble ease and darling sloth. Yet to this abject condition, mankind, betrayed by an ill-judging tenderness, would surely be led; and in the face of an inevitable contradiction! For neither in this state of things would the shedding of blood be prevented, nor would warfare cease. The only difference would be, that, instead of wars like those which prevail at this moment, presenting a spectacle of such character that, upon one side at least, a superior Being might look down with favour and blessing, there would follow endless commotions and quarrels without the presence of justice any where,—in which the alternations of success would not excite a wish or regret; in which a prayer could not be uttered for a decision either this way or that;—wars from no impulse in either of the combatants, but rival instigations of demoniacal passion. If, therefore, by the faculty of reason we can prophecy concerning the shapes which the future may put on,—if we are under any bond of duty to succeeding generations, there is high cause to guard against a specious sensibility, which may encourage the hoarding up of life for its own sake, seducing us from those considerations by which we might learn when it ought to be resigned. Moreover, disregarding future ages, and confining ourselves to the present state of mankind, it may be safely affirmed that he, who is the most watchful of the honour of his country, most determined to preserve her fair name at all hazards, will be found, in any view of things which looks beyond the passing hour, the best steward of the *lives* of his countrymen. For, by proving that she is of a firm temper, that she will only submit or yield to a point of her own fixing, and that all beyond is immutable resolution, he will save her from being wantonly attacked; and, if attacked, will awe the aggressor into a speedier abandonment of an unjust and hopeless attempt. Thus will he preserve not only that which gives life its value, but life itself; and not for his own country merely, but for that of his enemies, to whom he will have offered an example of magnanimity, which will ensure to them like benefits; an example, the re-action of which will be felt by his own countrymen, and will prevent them from becoming assailants unjustly or rashly. Nations will thus be taught to respect each other, and mutually to abstain from injuries. And hence, by a benign ordinance of our nature, genuine honour is the hand-maid of humanity; the attendant and sustainer—both of the sterner qualities which constitute the appropriate excellence of the male character, and of the gentle and tender virtues which belong more especially to motherliness and womanhood. These general laws, by which mankind is purified and exalted, and by which Nations are preserved, suggest likewise the best rules for the preservation of individual armies, and for the accomplishment of all equitable service upon which they can be sent.

Not therefore rashly and unfeelingly, but from the dictates of thoughtful humanity, did I say that it was the business of our Generals to fight, and to persevere in fighting; and that they did not bear this duty sufficiently in mind; this, almost the sole duty which professional soldiers, till our time, (happily for mankind) used to think of. But the victories of the French have been attended every where by the subversion of Governments; and their generals have accordingly united *political* with military functions: and with what success this has been done by them, the present state of Europe affords melancholy proof. But have they, on this account, ever neglected to calculate upon the advantages which might fairly be anticipated from future warfare? Or, in a treaty of to-day, have they ever forgotten a victory of yesterday? Eager to grasp at the double honour of captain and negociator, have they ever sacrificed the one to the other; or, in the blind effort, lost both? Above all, in their readiness to flourish with the pen, have they ever overlooked the sword, the symbol of their power, and the appropriate instrument of their success and glory? I notice this assumption of a double character on the part of the French, not to lament over it and its consequences, but to render somewhat more intelligible the conduct of our own Generals; and to explain how far men, whom we have no reason to believe other than brave, have, through the influence of such example, lost sight of their primary duties, apeing instead of imitating, and following only to be misled.

It is indeed deplorable, that our Generals, from this infirmity, or from any other cause, did not assume that lofty deportment which the character and relative strength of the two armies authorized them, and the nature of the service upon which they were sent, enjoined them to assume;—that they were in such haste to treat—that, with such an enemy (let me say at once,) and in such circumstances, they should have treated at all. Is it possible that they could ever have asked themselves who that enemy was, how he came into that country, and what he had done there? From the manifesto of the Portugueze government, issued at Rio Janeiro, and from other official papers, they might have learned, what was notorious to all Europe, that this body of men commissioned by Bonaparte, in the time of profound peace, without a declaration of war, had invaded Portugal under the command of Junot, who had perfidiously entered the country, as the General of a friendly and allied Power, assuring the people, as he advanced, that he came to protect their Sovereign against an invasion of the English; and that, when in this manner he had entered a peaceable kingdom, which offered no resistance, and had expelled its lawful Sovereign, he wrung from it unheard-of contributions, ravaged it, cursed it with domestic pillage and open sacrilege; and that, when this unoffending people, unable to endure any longer, rose up against the tyrant, he had given their towns and villages to the flames, and put the whole country, thus resisting, under military execution.—Setting aside all natural sympathy with the Portugueze and Spanish nations, and all prudential considerations of regard or respect for *their feelings* towards these men, and for *their expectations* concerning the manner in which they ought to be dealt with, it is plain that the French had forfeited by their crimes all right to those privileges, or to those modes of intercourse, which one army may demand from another according to the laws of war. They were not soldiers in any thing but the power of soldiers, and the outward frame of an army. During their occupation of Portugal, the laws and customs of war had never been referred to by them, but as a plea for some enormity, to the aggravated oppression of that unhappy country! Pillage, sacrilege, and murder—sweeping murder and individual assassination, had been proved against them by voices from every quarter. They had outlawed themselves by their offences from membership in the community of war, and from every species of community acknowledged by reason. But even, should any one be so insensible as to question this, he will not at all events deny, that the French ought to have been dealt with as having put on a double character. For surely they never considered themselves merely as an army. They had dissolved the established authorities of Portugal, and had usurped the civil power of the government; and it was in this compound capacity, under this two-fold monstrous shape, that they had exercised, over the religion and property of the country, the most grievous oppressions. What then remained to protect them but their power? —Right they had none,—and power! it is a mortifying consideration, but I will ask if Bonaparte, (nor do I mean in the question to imply any thing to his honour,) had been in the place of Sir Hew Dalrymple, what would he have thought of their power?—Yet before this shadow the solid substance of *justice* melted away.

And this leads me from the contemplation of their errors in the estimate and application of means, to the contemplation of their heavier errors and worse blindness in regard to ends. The British Generals acted as if they had no purpose but that the enemy should be removed from the country in which they were, upon *any* terms. Now the evacuation of Portugal was not the prime object, but the manner in which that event was to be brought about; this ought to have been deemed first both in order and importance;—the French were to be subdued, their ferocious warfare and heinous policy to be confounded; and in this way, and no other, was the deliverance of that country to be accomplished. It was not for the soil, or for the cities and forts, that Portugal was valued, but for the human feeling which was there; for the rights of human nature which might be there conspicuously asserted; for a triumph over injustice and oppression there to be achieved, which could neither be concealed nor disguised, and which should penetrate the darkest corner of the dark Continent of Europe by its splendour. We combated for victory in the empire of reason, for strongholds in the imagination. Lisbon and Portugal, as city and soil, were chiefly prized by us as a *language;* but our Generals mistook the counters of the game for the stake played for. The nation required that the French should surrender at discretion;—grant that the victory of Vimiera had excited some unreasonable impatience—we were not so overweening as to demand that the enemy should surrender within a given time, but that they should surrender. Every thing, short of this, was felt to be below the duties of the occasion; not only no service, but a grievous injury. Only as far as there was a prospect of forcing the enemy to an unconditional submission, did the British Nation deem that they had a right to interfere;—if that prospect failed, they expected that their army would know that it became it to retire, and take care of itself. But our Generals have told us, that the Convention would not have been admitted, if they had not judged it right to effect, even upon these terms, the evacuation of Portugal—as ministerial to their future services in Spain. If this had been a common war between two established governments measuring with each other their regular resources, there might have been some appearance of force in this plea. But who does not cry out at once, that the affections and opinions, that is, the souls of the people of Spain and Portugal, must be the inspiration and the power, if this labour is to be brought to a happy end? Therefore it was worse than folly to think of supporting Spain by physical strength, at the expence of moral. Besides, she was strong in men; she never earnestly solicited troops from us; some of the Provinces had even refused them when offered,—and all had been lukewarm in the acceptance of them. The Spaniards could not *ultimately* be benefited but by Allies acting under the same impulses of honour, roused by a sense of their wrongs, and sharing their loves and hatreds—above all, their *passion* for justice. They had themselves given an example, at Baylen, proclaiming to all the world what ought to be aimed at by those who would uphold their cause, and be associated in arms with them. And was the law of justice, which Spaniards, Spanish peasantry, I might almost say, would not relax in favour of Dupont, to be relaxed by a British army in favour of Junot? Had the French commander at Lisbon, or his army, proved themselves less perfidious, less cruel, or less rapacious than the other? Nay, did not the pride and crimes of Junot call for humiliation and punishment far more importunately, inasmuch as his power to do harm, and therefore his will, keeping pace with it, had been greater? Yet, in the noble letter of the Governor of Cadiz to Dupont, he expressly tells him, that his conduct, and that of his army, had been such, that they owed their lives only to that honour which forbad the Spanish army to become executioners. The Portugueze also, as appears from various letters produced before the Board of Inquiry, have shewn to our Generals, as boldly as their respect for the British Nation would permit them to do, what *they* expected. A Portugueze General, who was also a member of the regency appointed by the Prince Regent, says, in a protest addressed to Sir Hew Dalrymple, that he had been able to drive the French out of the provinces of Algarve and Alentejo; and therefore he could not be convinced, that such a Convention was necessary. What was this but implying that it was dishonourable, and that it would frustrate the efforts which his country was making, and destroy the hopes which it had built upon its own power? Another letter from a magistrate inveighs against the Convention, as leaving the crimes of the French in Portugal unpunished; as giving no indemnification for all the murders, robberies, and atrocities which had been committed by them. But I feel that I shall be wanting in respect to my countrymen if I pursue this argument further. I blush that it should be necessary to speak upon the subject at all. And these are men and things, which we have been reproved for condemning, because evidence was wanting both as to fact and person! If there ever was a case, which could not, in any rational sense of the word, be prejudged, this is one. As to the fact—it appears, and sheds from its own body, like the sun in heaven, the light by which it is seen; as to the person—each has written down with his own hand, *I am the man.* Condemnation of actions and men like these is not, in the minds of a people, (thanks to the divine Being and to human nature!) a matter of choice; it is like a physical necessity, as the hand must be burned which is thrust into the furnace—the body chilled which stands naked in the freezing north-wind. I am entitled to make this assertion here, when the *moral* depravity of the Convention, of which I shall have to speak hereafter, has not even been touched upon. Nor let it be blamed in any man, though his station be in private life, that upon this occasion he speaks publicly, and gives a decisive opinion concerning that part of this public event, and those measures, which are more especially military. All have a right to speak, and to make their voices heard, as far as they have power. For these are times, in which the conduct of military men concerns us, perhaps, more intimately than that of any other class; when the business of arms comes unhappily too near to the fire-side; when the character and duties of a soldier ought to be understood by every one who values his liberty, and bears in mind how soon he may have to fight for it. Men will and ought to speak upon things in which they are so deeply interested; how else are right notions to spread, or is error to be destroyed? These are times also in which, if we may judge from the proceedings and result of the Court of Inquiry, the heads of the army, more than at any other period, stand in need of being taught wisdom by the voice of the people. It is their own interest, both as men and as soldiers, that the people should speak fervently and fearlessly of their actions:—from no other quarter can they be so powerfully reminded of the duties which they owe to themselves, to their country, and to human nature. Let any one read the evidence given before that Court, and he will there see, how much the intellectual and moral constitution of many of our military officers, has suffered by a profession, which, if not counteracted by admonitions willingly listened to, and by habits of meditation, does, more than any other, denaturalize—and therefore degrade the human being;—he will note with sorrow, how faint are their sympathies with the best feelings, and how dim their apprehension of some of the most awful truths, relating to the happiness and dignity of man in society. But on this I do not mean to insist at present; it is too weighty a subject to be treated incidentally: and my purpose is—not to invalidate the authority of military men, *positively* considered, upon a military question, but *com-*

paratively;—to maintain that there are military transactions upon which the people have a right to be heard, and upon which their authority is entitled to far more respect than any man or number of men can lay claim to, who speak merely with the ordinary professional views of soldiership;—that there are such military transactions;—and that *this* is one of them.

The condemnation, which the people of these islands pronounced upon the Convention of Cintra considered as to its main *military* results, that is, as a treaty by which it was established that the Russian fleet should be surrendered on the terms specified; and by which, not only the obligation of forcing the French army to an unconditional surrender was abandoned, but its restoration in freedom and triumph to its own country was secured;—the condemnation, pronounced by the people upon a treaty, by virtue of which these things were to be done, I have recorded—accounted for—and thereby justified.—I will now proceed to another division of the subject, on which I feel a still more earnest wish to speak; because, though in itself of the highest importance, it has been comparatively neglected;—I mean the political injustice and moral depravity which are stamped upon the front of this agreement, and pervade every regulation which it contains. I shall shew that our Generals (and with them our Ministers, as far as they might have either given directions to this effect, or have countenanced what has been done)—when it was their paramount duty to maintain at all hazards the noblest principles in unsuspected integrity; because, upon the summons of these, and in defence of them, their Allies had risen, and by these alone could stand—not only did not perform this duty, but descended as far below the level of ordinary principles as they ought to have mounted above it;—imitating not the majesty of the oak with which it lifts its branches towards the heavens, but the vigour with which, in the language of the poet, it strikes its roots downwards towards hell:—

Radice in Tartara tendit.

The Armistice is the basis of the Convention; and in the first article we find it agreed, 'That there shall be a suspension of hostilities between the forces of his Britannic Majesty, and those of his Imperial and Royal Majesty, Napoleon I.' I will ask if it be the practice of military officers, in instruments of this kind, to acknowledge, in the person of the head of the government with which they are at war, titles which their own government—for which they are acting—has not acknowledged. If this be the practice, which I will not stop to determine, it is grossly improper; and ought to be abolished. Our Generals, however, had entered Portugal as Allies of a Government by which this title had been acknowledged; and they might have pleaded this circumstance in mitigation of their offence; but surely not in an instrument, where we not only look in vain for the name of the Portugueze Sovereign, or of the Government which he appointed, or of any heads or representatives of the Portugueze armies or people as a party in the contract,—but where it is stipulated (in the 4th article) that the British General shall engage to include the Portugueze armies in this Convention. What an outrage!—We enter the Portugueze territory as Allies; and, without their consent—or even consulting them, we proceed to form the basis of an agreement, relating—not to the safety or interests of our own army—but to Portugueze territory, Portugueze persons, liberties, and rights,—and engage, out of our own will and power, to include the Portugueze army, they or their Government willing or not, within the obligation of this agreement. I place these things in contrast, viz. the acknowledgement of Bonaparte as emperor and king, and the utter neglect of the Portugueze Sovereign and Portugueze authorities, to shew in what spirit and temper these agreements were entered upon. I will not here insist upon what was our duty, on this occasion, to the Portugueze—as dictated by those sublime precepts of justice which it has been proved that they and the Spaniards had risen to defend,—and without feeling the force and sanctity of which, they neither could have risen, nor can oppose to their enemy resistance which has any hope in it; but I will ask, of any man who is not dead to the common feelings of his social nature—and besotted in understanding, if this be not a cruel mockery, and which must have been felt, unless it were repelled with hatred and scorn, as a heart-breaking insult. Moreover, this conduct acknowledges, by implication, that principle which by his actions the enemy has for a long time covertly maintained, and now openly and insolently avows in his words—that power is the measure of right;—and it is in a steady adherence to this abominable doctrine that his strength mainly lies.

I do maintain then that, as far as the conduct of our Generals in framing these instruments tends to reconcile men to this course of action, and to sanction this principle, they are virtually his Allies: their weapons may be against him, but he will laugh at their weapons,—for he knows, though they themselves do not, that their souls are for him. Look at the preamble to the Armistice! In what is omitted and what is inserted, the French Ruler could not have fashioned it more for his own purpose if he had traced it with his own hand. We have then trampled upon a fundamental principle of justice, and countenanced a prime maxim of iniquity; thus adding, in an unexampled degree, the foolishness of impolicy to the heinousness of guilt. A conduct thus grossly unjust and impolitic, without having the hatred which it inspires neutralised by the contempt, is made contemptible by utterly wanting that colour of right which authority and power, put forth in defence of our Allies—in asserting their just claims and avenging their injuries, might have given. But we, instead of triumphantly displaying our power towards our enemies, have ostentatiously exercised it upon our friends; reversing here, as every where, the practice of sense and reason;—conciliatory even to abject submission where we ought to have been haughty and commanding,—and repulsive and tyrannical where we ought to have been gracious and kind. Even a common law of good breeding would have served us here, had we known how to apply it. We ought to have endeavoured to raise the Portugueze in their own estimation by concealing our power in comparison with theirs; dealing with them in the spirit of those mild and humane delusions, which spread such a genial grace over the intercourse, and add so much to the influence of love in the concerns of private life. It is a common saying, presume that a man is dishonest, and that is the readiest way to make him so: in like manner it may be said, presume that a nation is weak, and that is the surest course to bring it to weakness,—if it be not rouzed to prove its strength by applying it to the humiliation of your pride. The Portugueze had been weak; and, in connection with their Allies the Spaniards, they were prepared to become strong. It was, therefore, doubly incumbent upon us to foster and encourage them—to look favourably upon their efforts—generously to give them credit upon their promises—to hope with them and for them; and, thus anticipating and foreseeing, we should, by a natural operation of love, have contributed to create the merits which were anticipated and foreseen. I apply these rules, taken from the intercourse between individuals, to the conduct of large bodies of men, or of nations towards each other, because these are nothing but aggregates of individuals; and because the maxims of all just law, and the measures of all sane practice, are only an enlarged or modified application of those dispositions of love and those principles of reason, by which the welfare of individuals, in their connection with each other, is promoted. There was also here a still more urgent call for these courteous and humane principles as guides of conduct; because, in exact proportion to the physical weakness of Governments, and to the distraction and confusion which cannot but prevail, when a people is struggling for independence and liberty, are the well-intentioned and the wise among them remitted for their support to those benign elementary feelings of society, for the preservation and cherishing of which, among other important objects, government was from the beginning ordained.

Therefore, by the strongest obligations, we were bound to be studious of a delicate and respectful bearing towards those ill-fated nations, our Allies: and consequently, if the government of the Portugueze, though weak in power, possessed their affections, and was strong in right, it was incumbent upon us to turn our first thoughts to that government,—to look for it if it were hidden—to call it forth,—and, by our power combined with that of the people, to assert its rights. Or, if the government were dissolved and had no existence, it was our duty, in such an emergency, to have resorted to the nation, expressing its will through the most respectable and conspicuous authority, through that which seemed to have the best right to stand forth as its representative. In whatever circumstances Portugal had been placed, the paramount right of the Portugueze nation, or government, to appear not merely as a party but a principal, ought to have been established as a primary position, without the admission of which, all proposals to treat would be peremptorily rejected. But the Portugueze *had* a government; they had a lawful prince in Brazil; and a regency, appointed by him, at home; and generals, at the head of considerable bodies of troops, appointed also by the regency or the prince. Well then might one of those generals enter a formal protest against the treaty, on account of its being 'totally void of that deference due to the prince regent, or the government that represents him; as being hostile to the sovereign authority and independence of that government; and as being against the honour, safety, and independence of the nation.' I have already reminded the reader, of the benign and happy influences which might have attended upon a different conduct; how much good we might have added to that already in existence; how far we might have assisted in strengthening, among our Allies, those powers, and in developing those virtues, which were producing themselves by a natural process, and to which these breathings of insult must have been a deadly check and interruption. Nor would the evil be merely negative; for the interference of professed friends, acting in this manner, must have superinduced dispositions and passions, which were alien to the condition of the Portugueze;—scattered weeds which could not have been found upon the soil, if our ignorant hands had not sown them. Of this I will not now speak, for I have already detained the reader too long at the threshold;—but I have put the master key into his possession; and every chamber which he opens will be found loathsome as the one which he last quitted. Let us then proceed.

By the first article of the Convention it is covenanted, that all the places and forts in the kingdom of Portugal, occupied by the French troops, shall be delivered to the British army. Articles IV. and XII. are to the same effect—determining the surrender of Portugueze fortified places, stores, and ships, to the English forces; but not a word of their being to be holden in trust for the prince regent, or his government, to whom they belonged! The same neglect or contempt of justice and decency is shewn here, as in the preamble to these instruments. It was further shewn afterwards, by the act of hoisting the British flag instead of the Portugueze upon these forts, when they were first taken possession of by the British forces. It is no excuse to say that this was not intended. Such inattentions are among the most grievous faults which can be committed; and are *impossible*, when the affections and understandings of men are of that quality, and in that state, which are required for a service in which there is any thing noble or virtuous. Again, suppose that it was the purpose of the generals, who signed and ratified a Convention containing the articles in question, that the forts and ships, &c. should be delivered immediately to the Portugueze government,—would the delivering up of them wipe away the affront? Would it not rather appear, after the omission to recognize the right, that we had ostentatiously taken upon us to bestow—as a boon—that which they felt to be their own?

Passing by, as already deliberated and decided upon, those conditions, (Articles II. and III.) by which it is stipulated, that the French army shall not be considered as prisoners of war, shall be conveyed with arms, &c. to some port between Rochefort and L'Orient, and be at liberty to serve; I come to that memorable condition, (Article V.) 'that the French army shall carry with it all its equipments, that is to say, its military chests and carriages, attached to the field commissariat and field hospitals, or shall be allowed to dispose of such part, as the Commander in Chief may judge it unnecessary to embark. In like manner all individuals of the army shall be at liberty to dispose of *their private property* of *every* description, with full security hereafter for the purchasers.' This is expressed still more pointedly in the Armistice,—though the meaning, implied in the two articles, is precisely the same. For, in the fifth article of the Armistice, it is agreed provisionally, 'that all those, of whom the French army consists, shall be conveyed to France with arms and baggage, *and* all their private property of every description, no part of which shall be wrested from them.' In the Convention it is only expressed, that they shall be at liberty to depart, (Article II.) with arms and baggage, and (Article V.) to dispose of their private property of every description. But, if they had a right to dispose of it, *this* would include a right to carry it away—which was undoubtedly understood by the French general. And in the Armistice it is expressly said, that their private property of every description shall be conveyed to France along with their persons. What then are we to understand by the words, *their private property of every description?* Equipments of the army in general, and baggage of individuals, had been stipulated for before: now we all know that the lawful professional gains and earnings of a soldier must be small; that he is not in the habit of carrying about him, during actual warfare, any accumulation of these or other property; and that the ordinary private property, which he can be supposed to have a *just* title to, is included under the name of his *baggage*;—therefore this was something more; and what it was—is apparent. No part of their property, says the Armistice, shall be *wrested from them*. Who does not see in these words the consciousness of guilt, an indirect self-betraying admission that they had in their hands treasures which might be lawfully taken from them, and an anxiety to prevent that act of justice by a positive stipulation? Who does not see, on what sort of property the Frenchman had his eye; that it was not property by right, but their *possessions*—their plunder—every thing, by what means soever acquired, that the French army, or any individual in it, was possessed of? But it has been urged, that the monstrousness of such a supposition precludes this interpretation, renders it impossible that it could either be intended by the one party, or so understood by the other. What right they who signed, and he who ratified this Convention, have to shelter themselves under this plea—will appear from the 16th and 17th articles. In these it is stipulated, 'that all subjects of France, or of Powers in alliance with France, domiciliated in Portugal, or accidentally in the country, shall have their property of every kind—moveable and immoveable—guaranteed to them, with liberty of retaining or disposing of it, and passing the produce into France:' the same is stipulated, (Article XVII.) for such natives of Portugal as have sided with the French, or occupied situations under *the French Government*. Here then is a direct avowal, still more monstrous, that every Frenchman, or native of a country in alliance with France, however obnoxious his crimes may have made him, and every traitorous Portugueze, shall have his property guaranteed to him (both previously to and after the reinstatement of the Portugueze government) by the British army! Now let us ask, what sense the word property must have had fastened to it in *these* cases. Must it not necessarily have included all the rewards which the Frenchman had received for his iniquity, and the traitorous Portugueze for his treason? (for no man would bear a part in such oppressions, or would be a traitor for nothing; and, moreover, all the rewards, which the French could bestow, must have been taken from the Portugueze, extorted from the honest and loyal, to be given to the wicked and disloyal.) These rewards of iniquity must necessarily have been included; for, on our side, no attempt is made at a distinction;

and, on the side of the French, the word *immoveable* is manifestly intended to preclude such a distinction, where alone it could have been effectual. Property, then, here means—possessions thus infamously acquired; and, in the instance of the Portugueze, the fundamental notion of the word is subverted; for a traitor can have no property, till the government of his own country has remitted the punishment due to his crimes. And these wages of guilt, which the master by such exactions was enabled to pay, and which the servant thus earned, are to be guaranteed to him by a British *army!* Where does there exist a power on earth that could confer this right? If the Portugueze government itself had acted in this manner, it would have been guilty of wilful suicide; and the nation, if it had acted so, of high treason against itself. Let it not, then, be said, that the monstrousness of covenanting to convey, along with the persons of the French, their plunder, secures the article from the interpretation which the people of Great Britain gave, and which, I have now proved, they were bound to give to it.—But, conceding for a moment, that it was not intended that the words should bear this sense, and that, neither in a fair grammatical construction, nor as illustrated by other passages or by the general tenour of the document, they actually did bear it, had not unquestionable voices proclaimed the cruelty and rapacity—the acts of sacrilege, assassination, and robbery, by which these treasures had been amassed? Was not the perfidy of the French army, and its contempt of moral obligation, both as a body and as to the individuals which composed it, infamous through Europe?—Therefore, the concession would signify nothing: for our Generals, by allowing an army of this character to depart with its equipments, waggons, military chest, and baggage, had provided abundant means to enable it to carry off whatsoever it desired, and thus to elude and frustrate any stipulations which might have been made for compelling it to restore that which had been so iniquitously seized. And here are we brought back to the fountain-head of all this baseness; to that apathy and deadness to the principle of justice, through the influence of which, this army, outlawed by its crimes, was suffered to depart from the Land, over which it had so long tyrannized—other than as a band of disarmed prisoners.—I maintain, therefore, that permission to carry off the booty was distinctly expressed; and, if it had not been so, that the principle of justice could not here be preserved; as a violation of it must necessarily have followed from other conditions of the treaty. Sir Hew Dalrymple himself, before the Court of Inquiry, has told us, in two letters (to Generals Beresford and Friere,) that 'such part of the plunder as was in money, it would be difficult, if not impossible, to identify;' and, consequently, the French could not be prevented from carrying it away with them. From the same letters we learn, that 'the French were intending to carry off a considerable part of their plunder, by calling it public money, and saying that it belonged to the military chest; and that their evasions of the article were most shameful, and evinced a want of probity and honour, which was most disgraceful to them.' If the French had given no other proofs of their want of such virtues, than those furnished by this occasion, neither the Portugueze, nor Spanish, nor British nations would condemn them, nor hate them as they now do; nor would this article of the Convention have excited such indignation. For the French, by so acting, could not deem themselves breaking an engagement; no doubt they looked upon themselves as injured,—that the failure in good faith was on the part of the British; and that it was in the lawlessness of power, and by a mere quibble, that this construction was afterwards put upon the article in question.

Widely different from the conduct of the British was that of the Spaniards in a like case:—with high feeling did they, abating not a jot or a tittle, enforce the principle of justice. 'How,' says the governor of Cadiz to General Dupont in the same noble letter before alluded to, 'how,' says he, after enumerating the afflictions which his army, and the tyrant who had sent it, had unjustly brought upon the Spanish nation, (for of these, in *their* dealings with the French, they never for a moment lost sight,) 'how,' asks he, 'could you expect, that your army should carry off from Spain the fruit of its rapacity, cruelty, and impiety? how could you conceive this possible, or that we should be so stupid or senseless?' And this conduct is as wise in reason as it is true to nature. The Spanish people could have had no confidence in their government, if it had not acted thus. These are the sympathies which prove that a government is paternal,—that it makes one family with the people:

besides, it is only by such adherence to justice, that, in times of like commotion, popular excesses can either be mitigated or prevented. If we would be efficient allies of Spain, nay, if we would not run the risk of doing infinite harm, these sentiments must not only be ours as a nation, but they must pervade the hearts of our ministers and our generals—our agents and our ambassadors. If it be not so, they, who are sent abroad, must either be conscious how unworthy they are, and with what unworthy commissions they appear, or not: if they do feel this, then they must hang their heads, and blush for their country and themselves; if they do not, the Spaniards must blush for them and revolt from them; or, what would be ten thousand times more deplorable, they must purchase a reconcilement and a communion by a sacrifice of all that is excellent in themselves. Spain must either break down her lofty spirit, her animation and fiery courage, to run side by side in the same trammels with Great Britain; or she must start off from her intended yoke-fellow with contempt and aversion. This is the alternative, and there is no avoiding it.

I have yet to speak of the influence of such concessions upon the French Ruler and his army. With what Satanic pride must he have contemplated the devotion of his servants and adherents to *their* law, the steadiness and zeal of their perverse loyalty, and the faithfulness with which they stand by him and each other! How must his heart have distended with false glory, while he contrasted these qualities of his subjects with the insensibility and slackness of his British enemies! This notice has, however, no especial propriety in this place; for, as far as concerns Bonaparte, his pride and depraved confidence may be equally fed by almost all the conditions of this instrument. But, as to his army, it is plain that the permission (whether it be considered as by an express article formally granted, or only involved in the general conditions of the treaty), to bear away in triumph the harvest of its crimes, must not only have emboldened and exalted it with arrogance, and whetted its rapacity; but that hereby every soldier, of which this army was composed, must, upon his arrival in his own country, have been a seed which would give back plenteously in its kind. The French are at present a needy people, without commerce or manufactures,—unsettled in their minds and debased in their morals by revolutionary practices and habits of warfare; and the youth of the country are rendered desperate by oppression, which, leaving no choice in their occupation, discharges them from all responsibility to their own consciences. How powerful then must have been the action of such incitements upon a people so circumstanced! The actual sight, and, far more, the imaginary sight and handling of these treasures, magnified by the romantic tales which must have been spread about them, would carry into every town and village an antidote for the terrors of conscription; and would rouze men, like the dreams imported from the new world when the first discoverers and adventurers returned, with their ingots and their gold dust—their stories and their promises, to inflame and madden the avarice of the old. 'What an effect,' says the Governor of Cadiz, 'must it have upon the people,' (he means the Spanish people,) 'to know that a single soldier was carrying away 2580 livres tournois!' What an effect, (he might have said also,) must it have upon the French!—I direct the reader's attention to this, because it seems to have been overlooked; and because some of the public journals, speaking of the Convention, (and, no doubt, uttering the sentiments of several of their readers,)—say 'that they are disgusted with the transaction, not because the French have been permitted to carry off a few diamonds, or some ingots of silver; but because we confessed, by consenting to the treaty, that an army of 35,000 British troops, aided by the Portugueze nation, was not able to compel 20,000 French to surrender at discretion.' This is indeed the root of the evil, as hath been shewn; and it is the curse of this treaty, that the several parts of it are of such enormity as singly to occupy the attention and to destroy comparison and coexistence. But the people of Great Britain are disgusted both with the one and the other. They bewail the violation of the principle: if the value of the things carried off had been in itself trifling, their grief and their indignation would have been scarcely less. But it is manifest, from what has been said, that it was not trifling; and that therefore, (upon that account as well as upon others,) this permission was no less impolitic than it was unjust and dishonourable.

In illustrating these articles of the Armistice and Convention, by which the French were both expressly permitted and indirectly enabled to carry off their booty, we have already seen, that a concession was made which is still more enormous; viz. that all subjects of France, or of powers in alliance with France, domiciliated in Portugal or resident there, and all natives of Portugal who have accepted situations under *the French government*, &c., shall have their *property* of every kind guaranteed to them by the British army. By articles 16th and 17th, their *persons* are placed under the like protection. 'The French' (Article XVI.) 'shall be at liberty either to accompany the French army, or to remain in Portugal;' 'And the Portugueze' (Article XVII.) 'shall not be rendered accountable for their political conduct during the period of the occupation of the country by the French army: they all are placed under the protection of the British commanders, and shall sustain no injury in their property or persons.'

I have animadverted, heretofore, upon the unprofessional eagerness of our Generals to appear in the character of negotiators when the sword would have done them more service than the pen. But, if they had confined themselves to mere military regulations, they might indeed with justice have been grievously censured as injudicious commanders, whose notion of the honour of armies was of a low pitch, and who had no conception of the peculiar nature of the service in which they were engaged: but the censure must have stopped here. Whereas, by these provisions, they have shewn that they have never reflected upon the nature of military authority as contra-distinguished from civil. French example had so far dazzled and blinded them, that the French army is suffered to denominate itself '*the French government*;' and, from the whole tenour of these instruments, (from the preamble, and these articles especially,) it should seem that our Generals fancied themselves and their army to be *the British government*. For these regulations, emanating from a mere military authority, are purely civil; but of such a kind, that no power on earth could confer a right to establish them. And this trampling upon the most sacred rights—this sacrifice of the consciousness of a self-preserving principle, without which neither societies nor governments can exist, is not made by our generals in relation to subjects of their own sovereign, but to an independent nation, our ally, into whose territories we could not have entered but from its confidence in our friendship and good faith. Surely the persons, who (under the countenance of too high authority) have talked so loudly of prejudging this question, entirely overlooked or utterly forgot this part of it. What have these monstrous provisions to do with the relative strength of the two armies, or with any point admitting a doubt? What need here of a Court of Judicature to settle who were the persons (their names are subscribed by their own hands), and to determine the quality of the thing? Actions and agents like these, exhibited in this connection with each other, must of necessity be condemned the moment they are known: and to assert the contrary, is to maintain that man is a being without understanding, and that morality is an empty dream. And, if this condemnation must after this manner follow, to utter it is less a duty than a further inevitable consequence from the constitution of human nature. They, who hold that the formal sanction of a Court of Judicature is in this case required before a people has a right to pass sentence, know not to what degree they are enemies to that people and to mankind; to what degree selfishness, whether arising from their peculiar situation or from other causes, has in them prevailed over those faculties which are our common inheritance, and cut them off from fellowship with the species. Most deplorable would be the result, if it were possible that the injunctions of these men could be obeyed, or their remonstrances acknowledged to be just. For, (not to mention that, if it were not for such prompt decisions of the public voice, misdemeanours of men high in office would rarely be accounted for at all,) we must bear in mind, at this crisis, that the adversary of all good is hourly and daily extending his ravages; and, according to such notions of fitness, our indignation, our sorrow, our shame, our sense of right and wrong, and all those moral affections, and powers of the understanding, by which alone he can be effectually opposed, are to enter upon a long vacation; their motion is to be suspended—a thing impossible; if it could, it would be destroyed.

Let us now see what language the Portugueze speak upon that part of the treaty which has incited me to give vent to these feelings, and to assert these truths. 'I protest,' says General Friere, 'against Article XVII., one of the two now under examination, because it attempts to tie down the government of this kingdom not to bring to justice and condign punishment those persons, who have been notoriously and scandalously disloyal to their prince and the country by joining and serving the French party: and, even if the English army should be allowed to screen them from the punishment they have deserved, still it should not prevent their expulsion—whereby this country would no longer have to fear being again betrayed by the same men.' Yet, while the partizans of the French are thus guarded, not a word is said to protect the loyal Portugueze, whose fidelity to their country and their prince must have rendered them obnoxious to the French army; and who in Lisbon and the environs, were left at its mercy from the day when the Convention was signed, till the departure of the French. Couple also with this the first additional article, by which it is agreed, 'that the individuals in the civil employment of the army,' (including all the agitators, spies, informers, all the jackals of the ravenous lion,) 'made prisoners either by the British troops or the Portugueze in any part of Portugal, will be restored (*as is customary*) without exchange.' That is, no stipulations being made for reciprocal conditions! In fact, through the whole course of this strange interference of a military power with the administration of civil justice in the country of an Ally, there is only one article (the 15th) which bears the least shew of attention to Portugueze interests. By this it is stipulated, 'That, from the date of the ratification of the Convention, all arrears of contributions, requisitions, or claims whatever of the French Government against subjects of Portugal, or any other individuals residing in this country, founded on the occupation of Portugal by the French troops in the month of December 1807, which may not have been paid up, are cancelled: and all sequestrations, laid upon their property moveable or immoveable, are removed; and the free disposal of the same is restored to the proper owners.' Which amounts to this. The French are called upon formally to relinquish, in favour of the Portugueze, that to which they never had any right; to abandon false claims, which they either had a power to enforce, or they had not: if they departed immediately and had *not* power, the article was nugatory; if they remained a day longer and *had* power, there was no security that they would abide by it. Accordingly, loud complaints were made that, after the date of the Convention, all kinds of ravages were committed by the French upon Lisbon and its neighbourhood: and what did it matter whether these were upon the plea of old debts and requisitions; or new debts were created more greedily than ever—from the consciousness that the time for collecting them was so short? This article, then, the only one which is even in shew favourable to the Portugueze, is, in substance, nothing: inasmuch as, in what it is silent upon, (viz. that the People of Lisbon and its neighbourhood shall not be vexed and oppressed by the French, during their stay, with new claims and robberies,) it is grossly cruel or negligent; and, in that for which it actually stipulates, wholly delusive. It is in fact insulting; for the very admission of a formal renunciation of these claims does to a certain degree acknowledge their justice. The only decent manner of introducing matter to this effect would have been by placing it as a bye clause of a provision that secured the Portugueze from further molestations, and merely alluding to it as a thing understood of course. Yet, from the place which this specious article occupies, (preceding immediately the 16th and 17th which we have been last considering,) it is clear that it must have been intended by the French General as honey smeared upon the edge of the cup—to make the poison, contained in those two, more palateable.

Thus much for the Portugueze, and their particular interests. In one instance, a concern of the Spanish Nation comes directly under notice; and that Nation also is treated without delicacy or feeling. For by the 18th article it is agreed, 'that the Spaniards, (4000 in number) who had been disarmed, and were confined on ship-board in the port of Lisbon by the French, should be liberated.' And upon what consideration? Not upon their *right* to be free, as having been treacherously and cruelly dealt with by men who were part of a Power that was labouring to subjugate their country, and in this attempt had committed inhuman crimes against it;—not even exchanged as soldiers against soldiers:—but the condition of their emancipation is, that the British General engages 'to obtain of the Spaniards to restore such French subjects, either military or civil, as have been detained in Spain, without having been taken in battle or in consequence of military operations, but on account of the *occurrences* of the 29th of last May and the days immediately following. '*Occurrences!*' I know not what are exactly the features of the face for which this word serves as a veil: I have no register at hand to inform me what these events precisely were: but there can be no doubt that it was a time of triumph for liberty and humanity; and that the persons, for whom those noble-minded Spaniards were to be exchanged, were no other than a horde from among the most abject of the French Nation; probably those wretches, who, having never faced either the dangers or the fatigues of war, had been most busy in secret preparations or were most conspicuous in open acts of massacre, when the streets of Madrid, a few weeks before, had been drenched with the blood of two thousand of her bravest citizens. Yet the liberation of these Spaniards, upon these terms, is recorded (in the report of the Court of Enquiry) 'as one of the advantages which, in the contemplation of the Generals, would result from the Convention!'

Finally, 'If there shall be any doubt (Article XIV.) as to the meaning of any article, it shall be explained favourably to the French Army; and Hostages (Article XX.) of the rank of Field Officers, on the part of the British Army and Navy, shall be furnished for the guarantee of the present Convention.'

I have now gone through the painful task of examining the most material conditions of the CONVENTION of CINTRA:—the whole number of the articles is twenty-two, with three additional ones—a long ladder into a deep abyss of infamy!—

Need it be said that neglects—injuries—and insults—like these which we have been contemplating, come from what quarter they may, let them be exhibited towards whom they will, must produce not merely mistrust and jealousy, but alienation and hatred. The passions and feelings may be quieted or diverted for a short time; but, though out of sight or seemingly asleep, they must exist; and the life which they have received cannot, but by a long course of justice and kindness, be overcome and destroyed. But why talk of a long course of justice and kindness, when the immediate result must have been so deplorable? Relying upon our humanity, our fellow-feeling, and our justice, upon these instant and urgent claims, sanctioned by the more mild one of ancient alliance, the Portugueze People by voices from every part of their land entreated our succour; the arrival of a British Army upon their coasts was joyfully hailed; and the people of the country zealously assisted in landing the troops; without which help, as a British General has informed us, that landing could not have been effected. And it is in this manner that they are repaid! Scarcely have we set foot upon their country before we sting them into self-reproaches, and act in every thing as if it were our wish to make them ashamed of their generous confidence as of a foolish simplicity—proclaiming to them that they have escaped from one thraldom only to fall into another. If the French had any traitorous partizans in Portugal, (and we have seen that such there were; and that nothing was left undone on our part, which could be done, to keep them there, and to strengthen them) what answer could have been given to one of these, if (with this treaty in his hand) he had said, 'The French have dealt hardly with us, I allow; but we have gained nothing: the change is not for the better, but for the worse: for the appetite of their tyranny was palled; but this, being new to its food, is keen and vigorous. If you have only a choice between two masters, (such an advocate might have argued) chuse always the stronger: for he, after his evil passions have had their first harvest, confident in his strength, will not torment you wantonly in order to prove it. Besides, the property which he has in you he can maintain; and there will be no risk of your being torn in pieces—the unsettled prey of two rival claimants. You will thus have the advantage of a fixed and assured object of your hatred: and your fear, being stripped of doubt, will lose its motion and its edge: both passions will relax and grow mild; and, though they may not turn into reconcilement and love, though you may not be independent nor be free, yet you will at least exist in tranquillity,—and possess, if not the activity of hope, the security of despair.' No effectual answer, I say, could have been given to a man pleading thus in such circumstances. So much for the choice of evils. But, for the hope of good!—what is to become of the efforts and high resolutions of the Portugueze and Spanish Nations, manifested by their own hand in the manner which we have seen? They may live indeed and prosper; but not by us, but in despite of us.

Whatever may be the character of the Portugueze Nation; be it true or not, that they had a becoming sense of the injuries which they had received from the French Invader, and were rouzed to throw off oppression by a universal effort, and to form a living barrier against it;—certain it is that, betrayed and trampled upon as they had been, they held unprecedented claims upon humanity to secure them from further outrages.—Moreover, our conduct towards them was grossly inconsistent. For we entered their country upon the supposition that they had such sensibility and virtue; we announced to them publickly and solemnly our belief in this: and indeed to have landed a force in the Peninsula upon any other inducement would have been the excess of folly and madness. But the Portugueze *are* a brave people—a people of great courage and worth! Conclusions, drawn from intercourse with certain classes of the depraved inhabitants of Lisbon only, and which are true only with respect to them, have been hastily extended to the whole Nation, which has thus unjustly suffered both in our esteem and in that of all Europe. In common with their neighbours the Spaniards, they *were* making a universal, zealous, and fearless effort; and, whatever may be the final issue, the very act of having risen under the pressure and in the face of the most tremendous military power which the earth has ever seen—is itself evidence in their favour, the strongest and most comprehensive which can be given; a transcendent glory! which, let it be remembered, no subsequent failures in duty on their part can forfeit. This they must have felt—that they had furnished an illustrious example; and that nothing can abolish their claim upon the good wishes and upon the gratitude of mankind, which is—and will be through all ages their due. At such a time, then, injuries and insults from any quarter would have been deplorable; but, proceeding from us, the evil must have been aggravated beyond calculation. For we have, throughout Europe, the character of a sage and meditative people. Our history has been read by the degraded Nations of the Continent with admiration, and some portions of it with awe; with a recognition of superiority and distance, which was honourable to us—salutary for those to whose hearts, in their depressed state, it could find entrance—and promising for the future condition of the human race. We have been looked up to as a people who have acted nobly; whom their constitution of government has enabled to speak and write freely, and who therefore have thought comprehensively; as a people among whom philosophers and poets, by their surpassing genius—their wisdom—and knowledge of human nature, have circulated—and made familiar—divinely-tempered sentiments and the purest notions concerning the duties and true dignity of individual and social man in all situations and under all trials. By so readily acceding to the prayers with which the Spaniards and Portugueze entreated our assistance, we had proved to them that we were not wanting in fellow-feeling. Therefore might we be admitted to be judges between them and their enemies—unexceptionable judges—more competent even than a dispassionate posterity, which, from the very want comparatively of interest and passion, might be in its examination remiss and negligent, and therefore in its decision erroneous. We, their contemporaries, were drawn towards them as suffering beings; but still their sufferings were not ours, nor could be; and we seemed to stand at that due point of distance from which right and wrong might be fairly looked at and seen in their just proportions. Every thing conspired to prepossess the Spaniards and Portugueze in our favour, and to give the judgment of the British Nation authority in their eyes. Strange, then, would be their first sensations, when, upon further trial, instead of a growing sympathy, they met with demonstrations of a state of sentiment and opinion abhorrent from their own. A shock must have followed upon this discovery, a shock to their confidence—not perhaps at first in us, but in themselves: for, like all men under the agitation of extreme passion, no doubt they had before experienced occasional misgivings that they were subject to error and distraction from afflictions pressing too violently upon them. These flying apprehensions would now take a fixed place; and that moment would be most painful. If they continued to respect our opinion, so far must they have mistrusted themselves: fatal mistrust at such a crisis! Their passion of just vengeance, their indignation, their aspiring hopes, every thing that elevated and cheared, must have departed from them. But this bad influence, the *excess* of the outrage would mitigate or prevent; and we may be assured that they rather recoiled from Allies who had thus by their actions discountenanced and condemned efforts, which the most solemn testimony of conscience had avouched to them were just;—that they recoiled from us with that loathing and contempt which unexpected, determined, and absolute hostility, upon points of dearest interest will for ever create.

Again: independence and liberty were the blessings for which the people of the Peninsula were contending—immediate independence, which was not to be gained but by modes of exertion from which liberty must ensue. Now, liberty—healthy, matured, time-honoured liberty—this is the growth and peculiar boast of Britain; and Nature herself, by encircling with the ocean the country which we inhabit, has proclaimed that this mighty Nation is for ever to be her own ruler, and that the land is set apart for the home of immortal independence. Judging then from these first fruits of British Friendship, what bewildering and depressing and hollow thoughts must the Spaniards and Portugueze have entertained concerning the real value of these blessings, if the people who have possessed them longest, and who ought to understand them best, could send forth an army capable of enacting the oppression and baseness of the Convention of Cintra; if the government of that people could sanction this treaty; and if, lastly, this distinguished and favoured people themselves could suffer it to be held forth to the eyes of men as expressing the sense of their hearts—as an image of their understandings.

But it did not speak their sense—it was not endured—it was not submitted to in their hearts. Bitter was the sorrow of the people of Great Britain when the tidings first came to their ears, when they first fixed their eyes upon this covenant—overwhelming was their astonishment, tormenting their shame; their indignation was tumultuous; and the burthen of the past would have been insupportable, if it had not involved in its very nature a sustaining hope for the future. Among many alleviations, there was one, which, (not wisely, but overcome by circumstances) all were willing to admit;—that the event was so strange and uncouth, exhibiting such discordant characteristics of innocent fatuity and enormous guilt, that it could not without violence be thought of as indicative of a general constitution of things, either in the country or the government; but that it was a kind of *lusus naturæ* in the moral world—a solitary straggler out of the circumference of Nature's law—a monster which could not propagate, and had no birthright in futurity. Accordingly, the first expectation was that the government would deem itself under the necessity of disanulling the Convention; a necessity which, though in itself a great evil, appeared small in the eyes of judicious men, compared with the consequences of admitting that such a contract could be binding. For they, who had signed and ratified it, had not only glaringly exceeded all power which could be supposed to be vested in them as holding a military office; but, in the exercise of political functions, they had framed ordinances which neither the government, nor the Nation, nor any Power on earth, could confer upon them a right to frame: therefore the contract was self-destroying from the beginning. It is a wretched oversight, or a wilful abuse of terms still more wretched, to speak of the good faith of a Nation as being pledged to an act which was not a shattering of the edifice of justice, but a subversion of its foundations. One man cannot sign away the faculty of reason in another; much less can one or two individuals do this for a whole people. Therefore the contract was void, both from its injustice and its absurdity; and the party, with whom it was made, must have known it to be so. It could not then but be expected by many that the government would reject it. Moreover, extraordinary outrages against reason and virtue demand that extraordinary sacrifices of atonement should be made upon their altars; and some were encouraged to think that a government might upon this impulse rise above itself, and turn an exceeding disgrace into true glory, by a public profession of shame and repentance for having appointed such unworthy instruments; that, this being acknowledged, it would clear itself from all imputation of having any further connection with what had been done, and would provide that the Nation should as speedily as possible, be purified from all suspicion of looking upon it with other feelings than those of abhorrence. The people knew what had been their own wishes when the army was sent in aid of their Allies; and they clung to the faith, that their wishes and the aims of the Government must have been in unison; and that the guilt would soon be judicially fastened upon those who stood forth as principals, and who (it was hoped) would be found to have fulfilled only their own will and pleasure,—to have had no explicit commission or implied encouragement for what they had done, —no accessaries in their crime. The punishment of these persons was anticipated, not to satisfy any cravings of vindictive justice (for these, if they could have existed in such a case, had been thoroughly appeased already: for what punishment could be greater than to have brought upon themselves the sentence passed upon them by the voice of their countrymen?); but for this reason—that a judicial condemnation of the men, who were openly the proximate cause, and who were forgetfully considered as the single and sole originating source, would make our detestation of the effect more signally manifest.

These thoughts, if not welcomed without scruple and relied upon without fear, were at least encouraged; till it was recollected that the persons at the head of government had ordered that the event should be communicated to the inhabitants of the metropolis with signs of national rejoicing. No wonder if, when these rejoicings were called to mind, it was impossible to entertain the faith which would have been most consolatory. The evil appeared no longer as the forlorn monster which I have described. It put on another shape and was endued with a more formidable life—with power to generate and transmit after its kind. A new and alarming import was added to the event by this open testimony of gladness and approbation; which intimated—which declared—that the spirit, which swayed the individuals who were the ostensible and immediate authors of the Convention, was not confined to them; but that it was widely prevalent: else it could not have been found in the very council-seat; there, where if wisdom and virtue have not some influence, what is to become of the Nation in these times of peril? rather say, into what an abyss is it already fallen!

His Majesty's ministers, by this mode of communicating the tidings, indiscreet as it was unfeeling, had committed themselves. Yet still they might have recovered from the lapse, have awakened after a little time. And accordingly, notwithstanding an annunciation so ominous, it was matter of surprise and sorrow to many, that the ministry appeared to deem the Convention binding, and that its terms were to be fulfilled. There had indeed been only a choice of evils: but, of the two the worse—ten thousand times the worse—was fixed upon. The ministers, having thus officially applauded the treaty,—and, by suffering it to be carried into execution, made themselves a party to the transaction,—drew upon themselves those suspicions which will ever pursue the steps of public men who abandon the direct road which leads to the welfare of their country. It was suspected that they had taken this part against the dictates of conscience, and from selfishness and cowardice; that, from the first, they reasoned thus within themselves:—'If the act be indeed so criminal as there is cause to believe that the public will pronounce it to be; and if it shall continue to be regarded as such; great odium must sooner or later fall upon those who have appointed the agents: and this odium, which will be from the first considerable, in spite of the astonishment and indignation of which the framers of the Convention may be the immediate object, will, when the astonishment has relaxed, and the angry passions have died away, settle (for many causes) more heavily upon those who, by placing such men in the command, are the original source of the guilt and the dishonour. How then is this most effectually to be prevented? By endeavouring to prevent or to destroy, as far as may be, the odium attached to the act itself.' For which purpose it was suspected that the rejoicings had been ordered; and that afterwards (when the people had declared themselves so loudly),—partly upon the plea of the good faith of the Nation being pledged, and partly from a false estimate of the comparative force of the two obligations,—the Convention, in the same selfish spirit, was carried into effect: and that the ministry took upon itself a final responsibility, with a vain hope that, by so doing and incorporating its own credit with the transaction, it might bear down the censures of the people, and overrule their judgment to the superinducing of a belief, that the treaty was not so unjust and inexpedient: and thus would be included—in one sweeping exculpation—the misdeeds of the servant and the master.

But,—whether these suspicions were reasonable or not, whatever motives produced a determination that the Convention should be acted upon,—there can be no doubt of the manner in which the ministry wished that the people should appreciate it; when the same persons, who had ordered that it should at first be received with rejoicing, availed themselves of his Majesty's high authority to give a harsh reproof to the City of London for having prayed 'that an enquiry might be instituted into this dishonourable and unprecedented transaction.' In their petition they styled it also 'an afflicting event—humiliating and degrading to the country, and injurious to his Majesty's Allies.' And for this, to the astonishment and grief of all sound minds, the petitioners were severely reprimanded; and told, among other admonitions, 'that it was inconsistent with the principles of British jurisprudence to pronounce judgement without previous investigation.'

Upon this charge, as re-echoed in its general import by persons who have been over-awed or deceived, and by others who have been wilful deceivers, I have already incidentally animadverted; and repelled it, I trust, with becoming indignation. I shall now meet the charge for the last time formally and directly; on account of considerations applicable to all times; and because the whole course of domestic proceedings relating to the Convention of Cintra, combined with menaces which have been recently thrown out in the lower House of Parliament, renders it too probable that a league has been framed for the purpose of laying further restraints upon freedom of speech and of the press; and that the reprimand to the City of London was devised by ministers as a preparatory overt act of this scheme; to the great abuse of the Sovereign's Authority, and in contempt of the rights of the Nation. In meeting this charge, I shall shew to what desperate issues men are brought, and in what woeful labyrinths they are entangled, when, under the pretext of defending instituted law, they violate the laws of reason and nature for their own unhallowed purposes.

If the persons, who signed this petition, acted inconsistently with the principles of British jurisprudence; the offence must have been committed by giving an answer, before adequate and lawful evidence had entitled them so to do, to one or other of these questions:—'What is the act? and who is the agent?'—or to both conjointly. Now the petition gives no opinion upon the agent; it pronounces only upon the act, and that some one must be guilty; but *who*—it does not take upon itself to say. It condemns the act; and calls for punishment upon the authors, whosoever they may be found to be; and does no more. After the analysis which has been made of the Convention, I may ask if there be any thing in this which deserves reproof; and reproof from an authority which ought to be most enlightened and most dispassionate,—as it is, next to the legislative, the most solemn authority in the Land.

It is known to every one that the privilege of complaint and petition, in cases where the Nation feels itself aggrieved, *itself* being the judge, (and who else ought to be, or can be?)—a privilege, the exercise of which implies condemnation of something complained of, followed by a prayer for its removal or correction—not only is established by the most grave and authentic charters of Englishmen, who have been taught by their wisest statesmen and legislators to be jealous over its preservation, and to call it into practice upon every reasonable occasion; but also that this privilege is an indispensable condition of all civil liberty. Nay, of such paramount interest is it to mankind, existing under any frame of Government whatsoever; that, either by law or custom, it has universally prevailed under all governments—from the Grecian and Swiss Democracies to the Despotisms of Imperial Rome, of Turkey, and of France under her present ruler. It must then be a high principle which could exact obeisance from governments at the two extremes of polity, and from all modes of government inclusively; from the best and from the worst; from magistrates acting under obedience to the stedfast law which expresses the general will; and from depraved and licentious tyrants, whose habit it is—to express, and to act upon, their own individual will. Tyrants have seemed to feel that, if this principle were acknowledged, the subject ought to be reconciled to any thing; that, by permitting the free exercise of this right alone, an adequate price was paid down for all abuses; that a standing pardon was included in it for the past, and a daily renewed indulgence for every future enormity. It is then melancholy to think that the time is come when an attempt has been made to tear, out of the venerable crown of the Sovereign of Great Britain, a gem which is in the very front of the turban of the Emperor of Morocco.—(*See Appendix D.*)

To enter upon this argument is indeed both astounding and humiliating: for the adversary in the present case is bound to contend that we cannot pronounce upon evil or good, either in the actions of our own or in past times, unless the decision of a Court of Judicature has empowered us so to do. Why then have historians written? and why do we yield to the impulses of our nature, hating or loving—approving or condemning according to the appearances which their records present to our eyes? But the doctrine is as nefarious as it is absurd. For those public events in which men are most interested, namely, the crimes of rulers and of persons in high authority, for the most part are such as either have never been brought before tribunals at all, or before unjust ones: for, though offenders may be in hostility with each other, yet the kingdom of guilt is not wholly divided against itself; its subjects are united by a general interest to elude or overcome that law which would bring them to condign punishment. Therefore to make a verdict of a Court of Judicature a necessary condition for enabling men to determine the quality of an act, when the 'head and front'—the life and soul of the offence may have been, that it eludes or rises above the reach of all judicature, is a contradiction which would be too gross to merit notice, were it not that men willingly suffer their understandings to stagnate. And hence this rotten bog, rotten and unstable as the crude consistence of Milton's Chaos, 'smitten' (for I will continue to use the language of the poet) 'by the petrific mace—and bound with Gorgonian rigour by the look'—of despotism, is transmuted; and becomes a high-way of adamant for the sorrowful steps of generation after generation.

Again: in cases where judicial inquiries can be and are instituted, and are equitably conducted, this suspension of judgment, with respect to act or agent, is only supposed necessarily to exist in the Court itself; not in the witnesses, the plaintiffs or accusers, or in the minds even of the people who may be present. If the contrary supposition were realized, how could the arraigned person ever have been brought into Court? What would become of the indignation, the hope, the sorrow, or the sense of justice, by which the prosecutors, or the people of the country who pursued or apprehended the presumed criminal, or they who appear in evidence against him, are actuated? If then this suspension of judgment, by a law of human nature and a requisite of society, is not supposed *necessarily* to exist—except in the minds of the Court; if this be undeniable in cases where the eye and ear-witnesses are few;—how much more so in a case like the present; where all, that constitutes the essence of the act, is avowed by the agents themselves, and lies bare to the notice of the whole world?—Now it was in the character of complainants and denunciators, that the petitioners of the City of London appeared before his Majesty's throne; and they have been reproached by his Majesty's ministers under the cover of a sophism, which, if our anxiety to interpret favourably words sanctioned by the First Magistrate—makes us unwilling to think it a deliberate artifice meant for the delusion of the people, must however (on the most charitable comment) be pronounced an evidence of no little heedlessness and self-delusion on the part of those who framed it.

To sum up the matter—the right of petition (which, we have shewn as a general proposition, supposes a right to condemn, and is in itself an act of qualified condemnation) may in too many instances take the ground of absolute condemnation, both with respect to the crime and the criminal. It was confined, in this case, to the crime; but, if the City of London had proceeded farther, they would have been justifiable; because the delinquents had set their hands to their own delinquency. The petitioners, then, are not only clear of all blame; but are entitled to high praise: and we have seen whither the doctrines lead, upon which they were condemned.—And now, mark the discord which will ever be found in the actions of men, where there is no inward harmony of reason or virtue to regulate the outward conduct.

Those ministers, who advised their Sovereign to reprove the City of London for uttering prematurely, upon a measure, an opinion in which they were supported by the unanimous voice of the nation, had themselves before publickly prejudged the question by ordering that the tidings should be communicated with rejoicings. One of their body has since attempted to wipe away this stigma by representing that these orders were given out of a just tenderness for the reputation of the generals, who would otherwise have appeared to be condemned without trial. But did these rejoicings leave the matter indifferent? Was not the *positive* fact of thus expressing an opinion (above all in a case like this, in which surely no man could ever dream that there were any features of splendour) far stronger language of approbation, than the *negative* fact could be of disapprobation? For these same ministers who had called upon the people of Great Britain to rejoice over the Armistice and Convention, and who reproved and discountenanced and suppressed to the utmost of their power every attempt at petitioning for redress of the injury caused by those treaties, have now made publick a document from which it appears that, 'when the instruments were first laid before his Majesty, the king felt himself compelled *at once*'

(i. e. previously to all investigation) 'to express his disapprobation of those articles, in which stipulations were made directly affecting the interests or feelings of the Spanish and Portugueze nations.'

And was it possible that a Sovereign of a free country could be otherwise affected? It is indeed to be regretted that his Majesty's censure was not, upon this occasion, radical—and pronounced in a sterner tone; that a Council was not in existence sufficiently intelligent and virtuous to advise the king to give full expression to the sentiments of his own mind; which, we may reasonably conclude, were in sympathy with those of a brave and loyal people. Never surely was there a public event more fitted to reduce men, in all ranks of society, under the supremacy of their common nature; to impress upon them one belief; to infuse into them one spirit. For it was not done in a remote corner by persons of obscure rank; but in the eyes of Europe and of all mankind; by the leading authorities, military and civil, of a mighty empire. It did not relate to a petty immunity, or a local and insulated privilege—but to the highest feelings of honour to which a Nation may either be calmly and gradually raised by a long course of independence, liberty, and glory; or to the level of which it may be lifted up at once, from a fallen state, by a sudden and extreme pressure of violence and tyranny. It not only related to these high feelings of honour; but to the fundamental principles of justice, by which life and property, that is the means of living, are secured.

A people, whose government had been dissolved by foreign tyranny, and which had been left to work out its salvation by its own virtues, prayed for our help. And whence were we to learn how that help could be most effectually given, how they were even to be preserved from receiving injuries instead of benefits at our hands,—whence were we to learn this but from their language and from our own hearts? They had spoken of unrelenting and inhuman wrongs; of patience wearied out; of the agonizing yoke cast off; of the blessed service of freedom chosen; of heroic aspirations; of constancy, and fortitude, and perseverance; of resolution even to the death; of gladness in the embrace of death; of weeping over the graves of the slain, by those who had not been so happy as to die; of resignation under the worst final doom; of glory, and triumph, and punishment.

This was the language which we heard—this was the devout hymn that was chaunted; and the responses, with which our country bore a part in the solemn service, were from her soul and from the depths of her soul.

O sorrow! O misery for England, the Land of liberty and courage and peace; the Land trustworthy and long approved; the home of lofty example and benign precept; the central orb to which, as to a fountain, the nations of the earth 'ought to repair, and in their golden urns draw light;'—O sorrow and shame for our country; for the grass which is upon her fields, and the dust which is in her graves;—for her good men who now look upon the day;—and her long train of deliverers and defenders, her Alfred, her Sidneys, and her Milton; whose voice yet speaketh for our reproach; and whose actions survive in memory to confound us, or to redeem!

For what hath been done? look at it: we have looked at it: we have handled it: we have pondered it steadily: we have tried it by the principles of absolute and eternal justice; by the sentiments of high-minded honour, both with reference to their general nature, and to their especial exaltation under present circumstances; by the rules of expedience; by the maxims of prudence, civil and military: we have weighed it in the balance of all these, and found it wanting; in that, which is most excellent, most wanting.

Our country placed herself by the side of Spain, and her fellow Nation; she sent an honourable portion of her sons to aid a suffering people to subjugate or destroy an army—but I degrade the word—a banded multitude of perfidious oppressors, of robbers and assassins, who had outlawed themselves from society in the wantonness of power; who were abominable for their own crimes, and on account of the crimes of him whom they served—to subjugate or destroy these; not exacting that it should be done within a limited time; admitting even that they might effect their purpose or not; she could have borne either issue, she was prepared for either; but she was not prepared for such a deliverance as hath been accomplished; not a deliverance of Portugal from French oppression, but of the oppressor from the anger and power (at least from the animating efforts) of the Peninsula: she was not prepared to stand between her Allies, and their worthiest hopes: that, when chastisement could not be inflicted, honour—as much as bad men could receive—should be conferred: that them, whom her own hands had humbled, the same hands and no other should exalt: that finally the sovereign of this horde of devastators, himself the destroyer of the hopes of good men, should have to say, through the mouth of his minister, and for the hearing of all Europe, that his army of Portugal had 'DICTATED THE TERMS OF ITS GLORIOUS RETREAT.'

I have to defend my countrymen: and, if their feelings deserve reverence, if there be any stirrings of wisdom in the motions of their souls, my task is accomplished. For here were no factions to blind; no dissolution of established authorities to confound; no ferments to distemper; no narrow selfish interests to delude. The object was at a distance; and it rebounded upon us, as with force collected from a mighty distance; we were calm till the very moment of transition; and all the people were moved—and felt as with one heart, and spake as with one voice. Every human being in these islands was unsettled; the most slavish broke loose as from fetters; and there was not an individual—it need not be said of heroic virtue, but of ingenuous life and sound discretion—who, if his father, his son, or his brother, or if the flower of his house had been in that army, would not rather that they had perished, and the whole body of their countrymen, their companions in arms, had perished to a man, than that a treaty should have been submitted to upon such conditions. This was the feeling of the people; an awful feeling: and it is from these oracles that rulers are to learn wisdom.

For, when the people speaks loudly, it is from being strongly possessed either by the Godhead or the Demon; and he, who cannot discover the true spirit from the false, hath no ear for profitable communion. But in all that regarded the destinies of Spain, and her own as connected with them, the voice of Britain had the unquestionable sound of inspiration. If the gentle passions of pity, love, and gratitude, be porches of the temple; if the sentiments of admiration and rivalry be pillars upon which the structure is sustained; if, lastly, hatred, and anger, and vengeance, be steps which, by a mystery of nature, lead to the House of Sanctity;—then was it manifest to what power the edifice was consecrated; and that the voice within was of Holiness and Truth.

Spain had risen not merely to be delivered and saved;—deliverance and safety were but intermediate objects;—regeneration and liberty were the end, and the means by which this end was to be attained; had their own high value; were determined and precious; and could no more admit of being departed from, than the end of being forgotten.—She had risen—not merely to be free; but, in the act and process of acquiring that freedom, to recompense herself, as it were in a moment, for all which she had suffered through ages; to levy, upon the false fame of a cruel Tyrant, large contributions of true glory; to lift herself, by the conflict, as high in honour—as the disgrace was deep to which her own weakness and vices, and the violence and perfidy of her enemies, had subjected her.

Let us suppose that our own Land had been so outraged; could we have been content that the enemy should be wafted from our shores as lightly as he came,—much less that he should depart illustrated in his own eyes and glorified, singing songs of savage triumph and wicked gaiety?—No.—Should we not have felt that a high trespass—a grievous offence had been committed; and that to demand satisfaction was our first and indispensable duty? Would we not have rendered their bodies back upon our guardian ocean which had borne them hither; or have insisted that their haughty weapons should submissively kiss the soil which they had polluted? We should have been resolute in a defence that would strike awe and terror: this for our dignity:—moreover, if safety and deliverance are to be so fondly prized for their own sakes, what security otherwise could they have? Would it not be certain that the work, which had been so ill done to-day, we should be called upon to execute still more imperfectly and ingloriously to-morrow; that we should be summoned to an attempt that would be vain?

In like manner were the wise and heroic Spaniards moved. If an Angel from heaven had come with power to take the enemy from their grasp (I do not fear to say this, in spite of the dominion which is now re-extended over so large a portion of their Land), they would have been sad; they would have looked round them; their souls would have turned inward; and they would have stood like men defrauded and betrayed.

For not presumptuously had they taken upon themselves the work of chastisement. They did not wander madly about the world—like the Tamerlanes, or the Chengiz Khans, or the present barbarian Ravager of Europe—under a mock title of Delegates of the Almighty, acting upon self-assumed authority. Their commission had been thrust upon them. They had been trampled upon, tormented, wronged—bitterly, wantonly wronged, if ever a people on the earth was wronged. And this it was which legitimately incorporated their law with the supreme conscience, and gave to them the deep faith which they have expressed—that their power was favoured and assisted by the Almighty.—These words are not uttered without a due sense of their awful import: but the Spirit of evil is strong: and the subject requires the highest mode of thinking and feeling of which human nature is capable.—Nor in this can they be deceived; for, whatever be the immediate issue for themselves, the final issue for their Country and Mankind must be good;—they are instruments of benefit and glory for the human race; and the Deity therefore is with them.

From these impulses, then, our brethren of the Peninsula had risen; they could have risen from no other. By these energies, and by such others as (under judicious encouragement) would naturally grow out of and unite with these, the multitudes, who have risen, stand; and, if they desert them, must fall.—Riddance, mere riddance—safety, mere safety—are objects far too defined, too inert and passive in their own nature, to have ability either to rouze or to sustain. They win not the mind by any attraction of grandeur or sublime delight, either in effort or in endurance: for the mind gains consciousness of its strength to undergo only by exercise among materials which admit the impression of its power,—which grow under it, which bend under it,—which resist,—which change under its influence,—which alter either through its might or in its presence, by it or before it. These, during times of tranquillity, are the objects with which, in the studious walks of sequestered life, Genius most loves to hold intercourse; by which it is reared and supported;—these are the qualities in action and in object, in image, in thought, and in feeling, from communion with which proceeds originally all that is creative in art and science, and all that is magnanimous in virtue. —Despair thinks of *safety*, and hath no purpose; fear thinks of safety; despondency looks the same way:—but these passions are far too selfish, and therefore too blind, to reach the thing at which they aim; even when there is in them sufficient dignity to have an aim.—All courage is a projection from ourselves; however short-lived, it is a motion of hope. But these thoughts bind too closely to something inward,—to the present and to the past,—that is, to the self which is or has been. Whereas the vigour of the human soul is from without and from futurity, —in breaking down limit, and losing and forgetting herself in the sensation and image of Country and of the human race; and, when she returns and is most restricted and confined, her dignity consists in the contemplation of a better and more exalted being, which, though proceeding from herself, she loves and is devoted to as to another.

In following the stream of these thoughts, I have not wandered from my course: I have drawn out to open day the truth from its recesses in the minds of my countrymen.—Something more perhaps may have been done: a shape hath perhaps been given to that which was before a stirring spirit. I have shewn in what manner it was their wish that the struggle with the adversary of all that is good should be maintained—by pure passions and high actions. They forbid that their noble aim should be frustrated by measuring against each other things which are incommensurate—mechanic against moral power—body against soul. They will not suffer, without expressing their sorrow, that purblind calculation should wither the purest hopes in the face of all-seeing justice. These are times of strong appeal—of deep-searching visitation; when the best abstractions of the prudential understanding give way, and are included and absorbed in a supreme comprehensiveness of intellect and passion; which is the perfection and the very being of humanity.

How base! how puny! how inefficient for all good purposes are the tools and implements of policy, compared with these mighty engines of Nature!—There is no middle course: two masters cannot be served:—Justice must either be enthroned above might, and the moral law take place of the edicts of selfish passion; or the heart of the people, which alone can sustain the efforts of the people, will languish: their desires will not spread beyond the plough and the loom, the field and the fireside: the sword will appear to them an emblem of no promise; an instrument of no hope; an object of indifference, of disgust, or fear. Was there ever—since the earliest actions of men which have been transmitted by affectionate tradition or recorded by faithful history, or sung to the impassioned harp of poetry—was there ever a people who presented themselves to the reason and the imagination, as under more holy influences than the dwellers upon the Southern Peninsula; as rouzed more instantaneously from a deadly sleep to a more hopeful wakefulness; as a mass fluctuating with one motion under the breath of a mightier wind; as breaking themselves up, and settling into several bodies, in more harmonious order; as reunited and embattled under a standard which was reared to the sun with more authentic assurance of final victory?—The superstition (I do not dread the word), which prevailed in these nations, may have checked many of my countrymen who would otherwise have exultingly accompanied me in the challenge which, under the shape of a question, I have been confidently uttering; as I know that this stain (so the same persons termed it) did, from the beginning, discourage their hopes for the cause. Short-sighted despondency! Whatever mixture of superstition there might be in the religious faith or devotional practices of the Spaniards; this must have necessarily been transmuted by that triumphant power, wherever that power was felt, which grows out of intense moral suffering—from the moment in which it coalesces with fervent hope. The chains of bigotry, which enthralled the mind, must have been turned into armour to defend and weapons to annoy. Wherever the heaving and effort of freedom was spread, purification must have followed it. And the types and ancient instruments of error, where emancipated men shewed their foreheads to the day, must have become a language and a ceremony of imagination; expressing, consecrating, and invigorating, the most pure deductions of Reason and the holiest feelings of universal Nature.

When the Boy of Saragossa (as we have been told), too immature in growth and unconfirmed in strength to be admitted by his Fellow-citizens into their ranks, too tender of age for them to bear the sight of him in arms—when this Boy, forgetful or unmindful of the restrictions which had been put upon him, rushed into the field where his Countrymen were engaged in battle, and, fighting with the sinew and courage of an unripe Hero, won a standard from the enemy, and bore his acquisition to the Church, and laid it with his own hands upon the Altar of the Virgin;—surely there was not less to be hoped for his Country from this act, than if the banner, taken from his grasp, had, without any such intermediation, been hung up in the place of worship—a direct offering to the incorporeal and supreme Being. Surely there is here an object which the most meditative and most elevated minds may contemplate with absolute delight; a well-adapted outlet for the dearest sentiments; an organ by which they may act; a function by which they may be sustained.—Who does not recognise in this presentation a visible affinity with deliverance, with patriotism, with hatred of oppression, and with human means put forth to the height for accomplishing, under divine countenance, the worthiest ends?

Such is the burst and growth of power and virtue which may rise out of excessive national afflictions from tyranny and oppression;—such is the hallowing influence, and thus mighty is the sway, of the spirit of moral justice in the heart of the individual and over the wide world of humanity. Even the very faith in present miraculous interposition, which is so dire a weakness and cause of weakness in tranquil times when the listless Being turns to it as a cheap and ready substitute upon every occasion, where the man sleeps, and the Saint, or the image of the Saint, is to perform his work, and to give effect to his wishes;—even this infirm faith, in a state of incitement from extreme passion sanctioned by a paramount sense of moral justice; having for its object a power which is no longer sole nor principal, but secondary and ministerial; a power added to a power; a breeze which springs up unthought-of to assist the strenuous oarsman;—even this faith is subjugated in order to be exalted; and—instead of operating as a temptation to relax or to be remiss, as an encouragement to indolence or cowardice; instead of being a false stay, a necessary and definite dependence which may fail—it passes into a habit of obscure and infinite confidence of the mind in its own energies, in the cause from its own sanctity, and in the ever-present invisible aid or momentary conspicuous approbation of the supreme Disposer of things.

Let the fire, which is never wholly to be extinguished, break out afresh; let but the human creature be rouzed; whether he have lain heedless and torpid in religious or civil slavery—have languished under a thraldom, domestic or foreign, or under both these alternately—or have drifted about a helpless member of a clan of disjointed and feeble barbarians; let him rise and act; —and his domineering imagination, by which from childhood he has been betrayed, and the debasing affections, which it has imposed upon him, will from that moment participate the dignity of the newly ennobled being whom they will now acknowledge for their master; and will further him in his progress, whatever be the object at which he aims. Still more inevitable and momentous are the results, when the individual knows that the fire, which is reanimated in him, is not less lively in the breasts of his associates; and sees the signs and testimonies of his own power, incorporated with those of a growing multitude and not to be distinguished from them, accompany him wherever he moves.—Hence those marvellous achievements which were performed by the first enthusiastic followers of Mohammed; and by other conquerors, who with their armies have swept large portions of the earth like a transitory wind, or have founded new religions or empires.—But, if the object contended for be worthy and truly great (as, in the instance of the Spaniards, we have seen that it is); if cruelties have been committed upon an ancient and venerable people, which 'shake the human frame with horror;' if not alone the life which is sustained by the bread of the mouth, but that—without which there is no life—the life in the soul, has been directly and mortally warred against; if reason has had abominations to endure in her inmost sanctuary;—then does intense passion, consecrated by a sudden revelation of justice, give birth to those higher and better wonders which I have described; and exhibit true miracles to the eyes of men, and the noblest which can be seen. It may be added that,—as this union brings back to the right road the faculty of imagination, where it is prone to err, and has gone farthest astray; as it corrects those qualities which (being in their essence indifferent), and cleanses those affections which (not being inherent in the constitution of man, nor necessarily determined to their object) are more immediately dependent upon the imagination, and which may have received from it a thorough taint of dishonour;—so the domestic loves and sanctities which are in their nature less liable to be stained,—so these, wherever they have flowed with a pure and placid stream, do instantly, under the same influence, put forth their strength as in a flood; and, without being sullied or polluted, pursue—exultingly and with song—a course which leads the contemplative reason to the ocean of eternal love.

I feel that I have been speaking in a strain which it is difficult to harmonize with the petty irritations, the doubts and fears, and the familiar (and therefore frequently undignified) exterior of present and passing events. But the theme is justice: and my voice is raised for mankind; for us who are alive, and for all posterity:—justice and passion; clear-sighted aspiring justice, and passion sacred as vehement. These, like twin-born Deities delighting in each other's presence, have wrought marvels in the inward mind through the whole region of the Pyrenëan Peninsula. I have shewn by what process these united powers sublimated the objects of outward sense in such rites—practices—and ordinances of Religion—as deviate from simplicity and wholesome piety; how they converted them to instruments of nobler use; and raised them to a conformity with things truly divine. The same reasoning might have been carried into the customs of civil life and their accompanying imagery, wherever these also were inconsistent with the dignity of man; and like effects of exaltation and purification have been shewn.

But a more urgent service calls me to point to further works of these united powers, more obvious and obtrusive—works and appearances, such as were hailed by the citizen of Seville when returning from Madrid;——'where' (to use the words of his own public declaration) 'he had left his countrymen groaning in the chains which perfidy had thrown round them, and doomed at every step to the insult of being eyed with the disdain of the conqueror to the conquered; from Madrid threatened, harrassed, and vexed; where mistrust reigned in every heart, and the smallest noise made the citizens tremble in the bosom of their families; where the enemy, from time to time, ran to arms to sustain the impression of terror by which the inhabitants had been stricken through the recent massacre; from Madrid a prison, where the gaolers took pleasure in terrifying the prisoners by alarms to keep them quiet; from Madrid thus tortured and troubled by a relentless Tyrant, to fit it for the slow and interminable evils of Slavery;'——when he returned, and was able to compare the oppressed and degraded state of the inhabitants of that metropolis with the noble attitude of defence in which Andalusia stood. 'A month ago,' says he, 'the Spaniards had lost their country;—Seville has restored it to life more glorious than ever; and those fields, which for so many years have seen no steel but that of the plough-share, are going amid the splendour of arms to prove the new cradle of their adored country.'—'I could not,' he adds, 'refrain from tears of joy on viewing the city in which I first drew breath—and to see it in a situation so glorious!'

We might have trusted, but for late disgraces, that there is not a man in these islands whose heart would not, at such a spectacle, have beat in sympathy with that of this fervent Patriot—whose voice would not be in true accord with his in the prayer (which, if he has not already perished for the service of his dear country, he is perhaps uttering at this moment) that Andalusia and the city of Seville may preserve the noble attitude in which they then stood, and are yet standing; or, if they be doomed to fall, that their dying efforts may not be unworthy of their first promises; that the evening—the closing hour of their freedom may display a brightness not less splendid, though more aweful, than the dawn; so that the names of Seville and Andalusia may be consecrated among men, and be words of life to endless generations.

Saragossa!—She also has given bond, by her past actions, that she cannot forget her duty and will not shrink from it.* Valencia is under the seal of the same obligation. The multitudes of men who were arrayed in the fields of Baylen, and upon the mountains of the North; the peasants of Asturias, and the students of Salamanca; and many a solitary and untold-of hand, which, quitting for a moment the plough or the spade, has discharged a more pressing debt to the country by levelling with the dust at least one insolent and murderous Invader;—these have attested the efficacy of the passions which we have been contemplating—that the will of good men is not a vain impulse, heroic desires a delusive prop;—have proved that the condition of human affairs is not so forlorn and desperate, but that there are golden opportunities when the dictates of justice may be unrelentingly enforced, and the beauty of the inner mind substantiated in the outward act;—for a visible standard to look

* Written in February.

back upon; for a point of realized excellence at which to aspire; a monument to record;—for a charter to fasten down; and, as far as it is possible, to preserve.

Yes! there was an annunciation which the good received with gladness; a bright appearance which emboldened the wise to say—We trust that Regeneration is at hand; these are works of recovered innocence and wisdom:

> Magnus ab integro seclorum nascitur ordo;
> *Jam* redit et Virgo, redeunt Saturnia regna;
> *Jam* nova progenies cœlo demittitur alto.

The spirits of the generous, of the brave, of the meditative, of the youthful and undefiled—who, upon the strongest wing of human nature, have accompanied me in this journey into a fair region—must descend: and, sorrowful to think! it is at the name and remembrance of Britain that we are to stoop from the balmy air of this pure element. Our country did not create, but there was created for her, one of those golden opportunities over which we have been rejoicing: an invitation was offered—a summons sent to her ear, as if from heaven, to go forth also and exhibit on her part, in entire coincidence and perfect harmony, the beneficent action with the benevolent will; to advance in the career of renovation upon which the Spaniards had so gloriously entered; and to solemnize yet another marriage between Victory and Justice. How she acquitted herself of this duty, we have already seen and lamented: yet on this—and on this duty only—ought the mind of that army and of the government to have been fixed. Every thing was smoothed before their feet;—Providence, it might almost be said, held forth to the men of authority in this country a gracious temptation to deceive them into the path of the new virtues which were stirring;—the enemy was delivered over to them; and they were unable to close their infantine fingers upon the gift.—The helplessness of infancy was their's—oh! could I but add, the innocence of infancy!

Reflect upon what was the temper and condition of the Southern Peninsula of Europe—the noble temper of the people of this mighty island sovereigns of the all-embracing ocean; think also of the condition of so vast a region in the Western continent and its islands; and we shall have cause to fear that ages may pass away before a conjunction of things, so marvellously adapted to ensure prosperity to virtue, shall present itself again. It could scarcely be spoken of as being to the wishes of men,—it was so far beyond their hopes.—The government which had been exercised under the name of the old Monarchy of Spain—this government, imbecile even to dotage, whose very selfishness was destitute of vigour, had been removed; taken laboriously and foolishly by the plotting Corsican to his own bosom; in order that the world might see, more triumphantly set forth than since the beginning of things had ever been seen before, to what degree a man of bad principles is despicable—though of great power—working blindly against his own purposes. It was a high satisfaction to behold demonstrated, in this manner, to what a narrow domain of knowledge the intellect of a Tyrant must be confined; that if the gate by which wisdom enters has never been opened, that of policy will surely find moments when it will shut itself against its pretended master imperiously and obstinately. To the eyes of the very peasant in the field, this sublime truth was laid open—not only that a Tyrant's domain of knowledge is narrow, but melancholy as narrow; inasmuch as—from all that is lovely, dignified, or exhilarating in the prospect of human nature—he is inexorably cut off; and therefore he is inwardly helpless and forlorn.

Was not their hope in this—twofold hope; from the weakness of him who had thus counteracted himself; and a hope, still more cheering, from the strength of those who had been disburthened of a cleaving curse by an ordinance of Providence—employing their most wilful and determined enemy to perform for them the best service which man could perform? The work of liberation was virtually accomplished—we might almost say, established. The interests of the people were taken from a government whose sole aim it had been to prop up the last remains of its own decrepitude by betraying those whom it was its duty to protect;—withdrawn from such hands, to be committed to those of the people; at a time when the double affliction which Spain had endured, and the return of affliction with which she was threatened, made it impossible that the emancipated Nation could abuse its new-born strength to any substantial injury to itself.—Infinitely less favourable to all good ends was the condition of the French people when, a few years past, a Revolution made them, for a season, their own masters,—rid them from the incumbrance of superannuated institutions—the galling pressure of so many unjust laws—and the tyranny of bad customs. The Spaniards became their own masters: and the blessing lay in this, that they became so at once: there had not been time for them to court their power: their fancies had not been fed to wantonness by ever-changing temptations: obstinacy in them would not have leagued itself with trivial opinions: petty hatreds had not accumulated to masses of strength conflicting perniciously with each other: vanity with them had not found leisure to flourish—nor presumption: they did not assume their authority,—it was given them,—it was thrust upon them. The perfidy and tyranny of Napoleon '*compelled,*' says the Junta of Seville in words before quoted, 'the whole Nation to take up arms and *to choose itself a form of government*; and, in the difficulties and dangers into which the French had plunged it, all—or nearly all—the provinces, as it were *by the inspiration of Heaven* and *in a manner little short of miraculous*, created Supreme Juntas—delivered themselves up to their guidance—and placed in their hands the rights and the ultimate fate of Spain.'—Governments, thus newly issued from the people, could not but act from the spirit of the people—be organs of their life. And, though misery (by which I mean pain of mind not without some consciousness of guilt) naturally disorders the understanding and perverts the moral sense,—calamity (that is suffering, individual or national, when it has been inflicted by one to whom no injury has been done or provocation given) ever brings wisdom along with it; and, whatever outward agitation it may cause, does inwardly rectify the will.

But more was required; not merely judicious desires; not alone an eye from which the scales had dropped off—which could see widely and clearly; but a mighty hand was wanting. The government had been formed; and it could not but recollect that the condition of Spain did not exact from her children, as a *first* requisite, virtues like those due and familiar impulses of Spring-time by which things are revived and carried forward in accustomed health according to established order—not power so much for a renewal as for a birth—labour by throes and violence;—a chaos was to be conquered—a work of creation begun and consummated;—and afterwards the seasons were to advance, and continue their gracious revolutions. The powers, which were needful for the people to enter upon and assist in this work, had been given; we have seen that they had been bountifully conferred. The Nation had been thrown into—rather, lifted up to—that state when conscience, for the body of the people, is not merely an infallible monitor (which may be heard and disregarded); but, by combining—with the attributes of insight to perceive, and of inevitable presence to admonish and enjoin—the attribute of passion to enforce, it was truly an all-powerful deity in the soul.

Oh! let but any man, who has a care for the progressive happiness of the species, peruse merely that epitome of Spanish wisdom and benevolence and 'amplitude of mind for highest deeds' which, in the former part of this investigation, I have laid before the reader: let him listen to the reports—which they, who really have had means of knowledge, and who are worthy to speak upon the subject, will give to him—of the things done or endured in every corner of Spain; and he will see what emancipation had there been effected in the mind;—how far the perceptions—the impulses—and the actions also—had outstripped the habit and the character, and consequently were in a process of permanently elevating both; and how much farther (alas! by infinite degrees) the principles and practice of a people, with great objects before them to concentrate their love and their hatred, transcend the principles and practice of governments; not excepting those which, in their constitution and ordinary conduct, furnish the least matter for complaint.

Then it was—when the people of Spain were thus rouzed; after this manner released from the natal burthen of that government which had bowed them to the ground; in the free use of their understandings, and in the play and 'noble rage' of their passions; while yet the new authorities, which they had generated, were truly living members of their body, and (as I have said) organs of their life: when that numerous people were in a stage of their journey which could not be accomplished without the spirit which was then prevalent in them, and which (as might be feared) would too soon abate of itself;—then it was that we—not we, but the heads of the British army and Nation—when, if they could not breathe a favouring breath, they ought at least to have stood at an awful distance—stepped in with their forms, their impediments, their rotten customs and precedents, their narrow desires, their busy and purblind fears; and called out to those aspiring travellers to halt—'For ye are in a dream;' confounded them (for it was the voice of a seeming friend that spoke); and spell-bound them, as far as was possible, by an instrument framed 'in the eclipse' and sealed 'with curses dark.'—In a word, we had the power to act up to the most sacred letter of justice—and this at a time when the mandates of justice were of an affecting obligation such as had never before been witnessed; and we plunged into the lowest depths of injustice:—We had power to give a brotherly aid to our Allies in supporting the mighty world which their shoulders had undertaken to uphold; and, while they were expecting from us this aid, we undermined—without forewarning them—the ground upon which they stood. The evil is incalculable; and the stain will cleave to the British name as long as the story of this island shall endure.

Did we not (if, from this comprehensive feeling of sorrow, I may for a moment descend to particulars)—did we not send forth a general, one whom, since his return, Court, and Parliament, and Army, have been at strife with each other which shall most caress and applaud—a general, who, in defending the armistice which he himself had signed, said in open Court that he deemed that the French army was *entitled* to such terms. The people of Spain had, through the Supreme Junta of Seville, thus spoken of this same army: 'Ye have, among yourselves, the objects of your vengeance;—attack them;—they are but a handful of miserable panic-struck men, humiliated and conquered already by their perfidy and cruelties;—resist and destroy them: our united efforts will extirpate this perfidious nation.' The same Spaniards had said (speaking officially of the state of the whole Peninsula, and no doubt with their eye especially upon this army in Portugal)—'Our enemies have taken up exactly those positions in which they may most easily be destroyed'—Where then did the British General find this right and title of the French army in Portugal? 'Because,' says he in military language, 'it was not broken.'—Of the Man, and of the understanding and heart of the man—of the Citizen, who could think and feel after this manner in such circumstances, it is needless to speak; but to the General I will say, This is most pitiable pedantry. If the instinctive wisdom of your Ally could not be understood, you might at least have remembered the resolute policy of your enemy. The French army was not broken? Break it then—wither it—pursue it with unrelenting warfare—hunt it out of its holds;—if impetuosity be not justifiable, have recourse to patience—to watchfulness—to obstinacy: at all events, never for a moment forget who the foe is—and that he is in your power. This is the example which the French Ruler and his Generals have given you at Ulm—at Lubeck—in Switzerland—over the whole plain of Prussia—every where;—and this for the worst deeds of darkness; while your's was the noblest service of light.

This remonstrance has been forced from me by indignation:—let me explain in what sense I propose, with calmer thought, that the example of our enemy should be imitated.—The laws and customs of war, and the maxims of policy, have all had their foundation in reason and humanity; and their object has been the attainment or security of some real or supposed—some positive or relative—good. They are established among men as ready guides for the understanding, and authorities to which the passions are taught to pay deference. But the relations of things to each other are perpetually changing; and in course of time many of these leaders and masters, by losing part of their power to do service and sometimes the whole, forfeit in proportion their right to obedience. Accordingly they are disregarded in some instances, and sink insensibly into neglect with the general improvement of society. But they often survive when they have become an oppression and a hindrance which cannot be cast off decisively, but by an impulse—rising either from the absolute knowledge of good and great men,—or from the partial insight which is given to superior minds, though of a vitiated moral constitution,—or lastly from that blind energy and those habits of daring which are often found in men who, checked by no restraint of morality, suffer their evil passions to gain extraordinary strength in extraordinary circumstances. By any of these forces may the tyranny be broken through. We have seen, in the conduct of our Countrymen, to what degree it tempts to weak actions,—and furnishes excuse for them, admitted by those who sit as judges. I wish then that we could so far imitate our enemies as, like them, to shake off these bonds; but not, like them, from the worst—but from the worthiest impulse. If this were done, we should have learned how much of their practice would harmonize with justice; have learned to distinguish between those rules which ought to be wholly abandoned, and those which deserve to be retained; and should have known when, and to what point, they ought to be trusted.—But how is this to be? Power of mind is wanting, where there is power of place. Even we cannot, as a beginning of a new journey, force or win our way into the current of success, the flattering motion of which would awaken intellectual courage—the only substitute which is able to perform any arduous part of the secondary work of 'heroic wisdom;'—I mean, execute happily any of its prudential regulations. In the person of our enemy and his chieftains we have living example how wicked men of ordinary talents are emboldened by success. There is a kindliness, as they feel, in the nature of advancement; and prosperity is their Genius. But let us know and remember that this prosperity, with all the terrible features which it has gradually assumed, is a child of noble parents—Liberty and Philanthropic Love. Perverted as the creature is which it has grown up to (rather, into which it has passed),—from no inferior stock could it have issued. It is the Fallen Spirit, triumphant in misdeeds, which was formerly a blessed Angel.

If then (to return to ourselves) there be such strong obstacles in the way of our drawing benefit either from the maxims of policy or the principles of justice: what hope remains that the British Nation should repair, by its future conduct, the injury which has been done?——We cannot advance a step towards a rational answer to this question—without previously adverting to the original sources of our miscarriages; which are these:—First; a want, in the minds of the members of government and public functionaries, of knowledge indispensible for this service; and, secondly, a want of power, in the same persons acting in their corporate capacities, to give effect to the knowledge which individually they possess.—Of the latter source of weakness,—this inability as caused by decay in the machine of government, and by illegitimate forces which are checking and controuling its constitutional motions,—I have not spoken, nor shall I now speak: for I have judged it best to suspend my task for a while: and this subject, being in its nature delicate, ought not to be lightly or transiently touched. Besides, no *immediate* effect can be expected from the soundest and most unexceptionable doctrines which might be laid down for the correcting of this evil. —The former source of weakness,—namely, the want of appropriate and indispensible knowledge,—has, in the past investigation, been reached, and shall be further laid open; not without a hope of some result of *immediate* good by a direct application to the mind; and in full confidence that the best and surest way to render operative that knowledge which is already possessed—is to increase the stock of knowledge.

Here let me avow that I undertook this present labour as a serious duty; rather, that it was forced (and has been unremittingly pressed) upon me by a perception of justice united with strength of feeling;—in a word, by that power of conscience, calm or impassioned, to which throughout I have done reverence as the animating spirit of the cause. My work was begun and prosecuted under this controul:—and with the accompanying satisfaction that no charge of presumption could, by a thinking mind, be brought against me: though I had taken upon myself to offer instruction to men who, if they possess not talents and acquirements, have no title to the high stations which they hold; who also, by holding those stations, are understood to obtain certain benefit of experience and of knowledge not otherwise to be gained; and who have a further claim to deference—founded upon reputation, even when it is spurious (as much of the reputation of men high in power must necessarily be; their errors being veiled and palliated by the authority attached to their office; while that same authority gives more than due weight and effect to their wiser opinions). Yet, notwithstanding all this, I did not fear the censure of having unbecomingly obtruded counsels or remonstrances. For there can be no presumption, upon a call so affecting as the present, in an attempt to assert the sanctity and to display the efficacy of principles and passions which are the natural birth-right of man; to some share of which all are born; but an inheritance which may be alienated or consumed; and by none more readily and assuredly than by those who are most eager for the praise of policy, of prudence, of sagacity, and of all those qualities which are the darling virtues of the worldly-wise. Moreover; the evidence to which I have made appeal, in order to establish the truth, is not locked up in cabinets; but is accessible to all; as it exists in the bosoms of men—in the appearances and intercourse of daily life—in the details of passing events—and in general history. And more especially is its right import within the reach of him who—taking no part in public measures, and having no concern in the changes of things but as they affect what is most precious in his country and humanity—will doubtless be more alive to those genuine sensations which are the materials of sound judgment. Nor is it to be overlooked that such a man may have more leisure (and probably will have a stronger inclination) to communicate with the records of past ages.

Deeming myself justified then in what has been said,—I will continue to lay open (and, in some degree, to account for) those privations in the materials of judgment, and those delusions of opinion, and infirmities of mind, to which practical Statesmen, and particularly such as are high in office, are more than other men subject;—as containing an answer to that question, so interesting at this juncture,—How far is it in our power to make amends for the harm done?

After the view of things which has been taken,—we may confidently affirm that nothing but a knowledge of human nature directing the operations of our government, can give it a right to an intimate association with a cause which is that of human nature. I say, an intimate association founded on the right of thorough knowledge;—to contradistinguish this best mode of exertion from another which might found *its* right upon a vast and commanding military power put forth with manifestation of sincere intentions to benefit our Allies—from a conviction merely of policy that their liberty, independence, and honour, are our genuine gain;—to distinguish the pure brotherly connection from this other (in its appearance at least more magisterial) which such a power, guided by such intention uniformly displayed, might authorize. But of the former connection (which supposes the main military effort to be made, even at present, by the people of the Peninsula on whom the moral interest more closely presses), and of the knowledge which it demands, I have hitherto spoken—and have further to speak.

It is plain *à priori* that the minds of Statesmen and Courtiers are unfavourable to the growth of this knowledge. For they are in a situation exclusive and artificial; which has the further disadvantage, that it does not separate men from men by collateral partitions which leave, along with difference, a sense of equality—that they, who are divided, are yet upon the same level; but by a degree of superiority which can scarcely fail to be accompanied with more or less of pride. This situation therefore must be eminently unfavourable for the reception and establishment of that knowledge which is founded not upon things but upon sensations;—sensations which are general, and under general influences (and this it is which makes them what they are, and gives them their importance);—not upon things which may be *brought;* but upon sensations which must be *met.* Passing by the kindred and usually accompanying influence of birth in a certain rank—and, where education has been pre-defined from childhood for the express purpose of future political power, the tendency of such education to warp (and therefore weaken) the intellect;—we may join at once, with the privation which I have been noticing, a delusion equally common. It is this: that practical Statesmen assume too much credit to themselves for their ability to see into the motives and manage the selfish passions of their immediate agents and dependants; and for the skill with which they baffle or resist the aims of their opponents. A promptness in looking through the most superficial part of the characters of those men—who, by the very circumstance of their contending ambitiously for the rewards and honours of government, are separated from the mass of the society to which they belong—is mistaken for a knowledge of human kind. Hence, where higher knowledge is a prime requisite, they not only are unfurnished, but, being unconscious that they are so, they look down contemptuously upon those who endeavour to supply (in some degree) their want.—The instincts of natural and social man; the deeper emotions; the simpler feelings; the spacious range of the disinterested imagination; the pride in country for country's sake, when to serve has not been a formal profession—and the mind is therefore left in a state of dignity only to be surpassed by having served nobly and generously; the instantaneous accomplishment in which they start up who, upon a searching call, stir for the Land which they love—not from personal motives, but for a reward which is undefined and cannot be missed; the solemn fraternity which a great Nation composes—gathered together, in a stormy season, under the shade of ancestral feeling;

the delicacy of moral honour which pervades the minds of a people, when despair has been suddenly thrown off and expectations are lofty; the apprehensiveness to a touch unkindly or irreverent, where sympathy is at once exacted as a tribute and welcomed as a gift; the power of injustice and inordinate calamity to transmute, to invigorate, and to govern—to sweep away the barriers of opinion—to reduce under submission passions purely evil—to exalt the nature of indifferent qualities, and to render them fit companions for the absolute virtues with which they are summoned to associate—to consecrate passions which, if not bad in themselves, are of such temper that, in the calm of ordinary life, they are rightly deemed so—to correct and embody these passions—and, without weakening them (nay, with tenfold addition to their strength), to make them worthy of taking their place as the advanced guard of hope, when a sublime movement of deliverance is to be originated;—these arrangements and resources of nature, these ways and means of society, have so little connection with those others upon which a ruling minister of a long-established government is accustomed to depend; these—elements as it were of a universe, functions of a living body—are so opposite, in their mode of action, to the formal machine which it has been his pride to manage;—that he has but a faint perception of their immediate efficacy; knows not the facility with which they assimilate with other powers; nor the property by which such of them—as, from necessity of nature, must change or pass away—will, under wise and fearless management, surely generate lawful successors to fill their place when their appropriate work is performed. Nay, of the majority of men, who are usually found in high stations under old governments, it may without injustice be said; that, when they look about them in times (alas! too rare) which present the glorious product of such agency to their eyes, they have not a right to say—with a dejected man in the midst of the woods, the rivers, the mountains, the sunshine, and shadows of some transcendant landscape—

'I see, not feel, how beautiful they are:'

These spectators neither see nor feel. And it is from the blindness and insensibility of these, and the train whom they draw along with them, that the throes of nations have been so ill recompensed by the births which have followed; and that revolutions, after passing from crime to crime and from sorrow to sorrow, have often ended in throwing back such heavy reproaches of delusiveness upon their first promises.

I am satisfied that no enlightened Patriot will impute to me a wish to disparage the characters of men high in authority, or to detract from the estimation which is fairly due to them. My purpose is to guard against unreasonable expectations. That specific knowledge,—the paramount importance of which, in the present condition of Europe, I am insisting upon,—they, who usually fill places of high trust in old governments, neither do—nor, for the most part, can—possess: nor is it necessary, for the administration of affairs in ordinary circumstances, that they should.—The progress of their own country, and of the other nations of the world, in civilization, in true refinement, in science, in religion, in morals, and in all the real wealth of humanity, might indeed be quicker, and might correspond more happily with the wishes of the benevolent,—if Governors better understood the rudiments of nature as studied in the walks of common life; if they were men who had themselves felt every strong emotion 'inspired by nature and by fortune taught;' and could calculate upon the force of the grander passions. Yet, at the same time, there is temptation in this. To know may seduce; and to have been agitated may compel. Arduous cares are attractive for their own sakes. Great talents are naturally driven towards hazard and difficulty; as it is there that they are most sure to find their exercise, and their evidence, and joy in anticipated triumph—the liveliest of all sensations. Moreover; magnificent desires, when least under the bias of personal feeling, dispose the mind—more than itself is conscious of—to regard commotion with complacency, and to watch the aggravations of distress with welcoming; from an immoderate confidence that, when the appointed day shall come, it will be in the power of intellect to relieve. There is danger in being a zealot in any cause—not excepting that of humanity. Nor is it to be forgotten that the incapacity and ignorance of the regular agents of long-established governments do not prevent some progress in the dearest concerns of men; and that society may owe to these very deficiencies, and to the tame and unenterprizing course which they necessitate, much security and tranquil enjoyment.

Nor, on the other hand, (for reasons which may be added to

those already given) is it so desirable as might at first sight be imagined, much less is it desirable as an absolute good, that men of comprehensive sensibility and tutored genius—either for the interests of mankind or for their own—should, in ordinary times, have vested in them political power. The Empire, which they hold, is more independent: its constituent parts are sustained by a stricter connection: the dominion is purer and of higher origin; as mind is more excellent than body—the search of truth an employment more inherently dignified than the application of force—the determinations of nature more venerable than the accidents of human institution. Chance and disorder, vexation and disappointment, malignity and perverseness within or without the mind, are a sad exchange for the steady and genial processes of reason. Moreover; worldly distinctions and offices of command do not lie in the path—nor are they any part of the appropriate retinue—of Philosophy and Virtue. Nothing, but a strong spirit of love, can counteract the consciousness of pre-eminence which ever attends pre-eminent intellectual power with correspondent attainments: and this spirit of love is best encouraged by humility and simplicity in mind, manners, and conduct of life; virtues, to which wisdom leads. But,—though these be virtues in a Man, a Citizen, or a Sage,—they cannot be recommended to the especial culture of the Political or Military Functionary; and still less of the Civil Magistrate. Him, in the exercise of his functions, it will often become to carry himself highly and with state; in order that evil may be suppressed, and authority respected by those who have not understanding. The power also of office, whether the duties be discharged well or ill, will ensure a never-failing supply of flattery and praise: and of these—a man (becoming at once double-dealer and dupe) may, without impeachment of his modesty, receive as much as his weakness inclines him to; under the shew that the homage is not offered up to himself, but to that portion of the public dignity which is lodged in his person. But, whatever may be the cause, the fact is certain—that there is an unconquerable tendency in all power, save that of knowledge acting by and through knowledge, to injure the mind of him who exercises that power; so much so, that best natures cannot escape the evil of such alliance. Nor is it less certain that things of soundest quality, issuing through a medium to which they have only an arbitrary relation, are vitiated: and it is inevitable that there should be a reäscent of unkindly influence to the heart of him from whom the gift, thus unfairly dealt with, proceeded.——In illustration of these remarks, as connected with the management of States, we need only refer to the Empire of China—where superior endowments of mind and acquisitions of learning are the sole acknowledged title to offices of great trust; and yet in no country is the government more bigotted or intolerant, or society less progressive.

To prevent misconception; and to silence (at least to throw discredit upon) the clamours of ignorance;—I have thought proper thus, in some sort, to strike a balance between the claims of men of routine—and men of original and accomplished minds—to the management of State affairs in ordinary circumstances. But ours is not an age of this character: and,—after having seen such a long series of misconduct, so many unjustifiable attempts made and sometimes carried into effect, good endeavours frustrated, disinterested wishes thwarted, and benevolent hopes disappointed,—it is reasonable that we should endeavour to ascertain to what cause these evils are to be ascribed. I have directed the attention of the Reader to one primary cause: and can he doubt of its existence, and of the operation which I have attributed to it?

In the course of the last thirty years we have seen two wars waged against Liberty—the American war, and the war against the French People in the early stages of their Revolution. In the latter instance the Emigrants and the Continental Powers and the British did, in all their expectations and in every movement of their efforts, manifest a common ignorance—originating in the same source. And, for what more especially belongs to ourselves at this time, we may affirm—that the same presumptuous irreverence of the principles of justice, and blank insensibility to the affections of human nature, which determined the conduct of our government in those two wars *against* liberty, have continued to accompany its exertions in the present struggle *for* liberty,—and have rendered them fruitless. The British government deems (no doubt), on its own part, that its intentions are good. It must not deceive itself: nor must we deceive ourselves. Intentions—thoroughly good—could not mingle with the unblessed actions which we have witnessed. A disinterested and pure intention is a light that guides as well as cheers, and renders desperate lapses impossible.

Our duty is—our aim ought to be—to employ the true means of liberty and virtue for the ends of liberty and virtue. In such policy, thoroughly understood, there is fitness and concord and rational subordination; it deserves a higher name—organization, health, and grandeur. Contrast, in a single instance, the two processes; and the qualifications which they require. The ministers of that period found it an easy task to hire a band of Hessians, and to send it across the Atlantic, that they might assist *in bringing the Americans* (according to the phrase then prevalent) *to reason*. The force, with which these troops would attack, was gross,—tangible,—and might be calculated; but the spirit of resistance, which their presence would create, was subtle—ethereal—mighty—and incalculable. Accordingly, from the moment when these foreigners landed—men who had no interest, no business, in the quarrel, but what the wages of their master bound him to, and he imposed upon his miserable slaves;—nay, from the first rumour of their destination, the success of the British was (as hath since been affirmed by judicious Americans) impossible.

The British government of the present day have been seduced, as we have seen, by the same common-place facilities on the one side; and have been equally blind on the other. A physical auxiliar force of thirty-five thousand men is to be added to the army of Spain: but the moral energy, which thereby *might* be taken away from the principal, is overlooked or slighted; the material being too fine for their calculation. What does it avail to graft a bough upon a tree; if this be done so ignorantly and rashly that the trunk, which can alone supply the sap by which the whole must flourish, receives a deadly wound? Palpable effects of the Convention of Cintra, and self-contradicting consequences even in the matter especially aimed at, may be seen in the necessity which it entailed of leaving 8,000 British troops to protect Portuguese traitors from punishment by the laws of their country. A still more serious and fatal contradiction lies in this—that the English army was made an instrument of injustice, and was dishonoured, in order that it might be hurried forward to uphold a cause which could have no life but by justice and honour. The Nation knows how that army languished in the heart of Spain: that it accomplished nothing except its retreat, is sure: what great service it might have performed, if it had moved from a different impulse, we have shown.

It surely then behoves those who are in authority—to look to the state of their own minds. There is indeed an inherent impossibility that they should be equal to the arduous duties which have devolved upon them: but it is not unreasonable to hope that something higher might be aimed at; and that the People might see, upon great occasions,—in the practice of its Rulers—a more adequate reflection of its own wisdom and virtue. Our Rulers, I repeat, must begin with their own minds. This is a precept of immediate urgency; and, if attended to, might be productive of immediate good. I will follow it with further conclusions directly referring to future conduct.

I will not suppose that any ministry of this country can be so abject, so insensible, and unwise, as to abandon the Spaniards and Portuguese while there is a Patriot in arms; or, if the people should for a time be subjugated, to deny them assistance the moment they rise to require it again. I cannot think so unfavourably of my country as to suppose this possible. Let men in power, however, take care (and let the nation be equally careful) not to receive any reports from our army—of the disposition of the Spanish people—without mistrust. The British generals, who were in Portugal (the whole body of them,* according to the statement of Sir Hew Dalrymple), approved of the Convention of Cintra; and have thereby shewn that *their* communications are not to be relied upon in this case. And indeed there is not any information, which we can receive upon this subject, that is so little trust-worthy as that which comes from our army—or from any part of it. The opportunities of notice, afforded to soldiers in actual service, must necessarily be very limited; and a thousand things stand in the way of their power to make a right use of these. But a retreating army, in the country of an Ally;——harrassed and dissatisfied; willing to find a reason for its failures in any thing but itself, and actually not without much solid ground for complaint; re-

* From this number, however, must be excepted the gallant and patriotic General Ferguson. For that officer has had the virtue publicly and in the most emphatic manner, upon two occasions, to reprobate the whole transaction.

treating; sometimes, perhaps, fugitive; and, in its disorder, tempted (and even forced) to commit offences upon the people of the district through which it passes; while they, in their turn, are filled with fear and inconsiderate anger;——an army, in such a condition, must needs be incapable of seeing objects as they really are; and, at the same time, all things must change in its presence, and put on their most unfavourable appearances.

Deeming it then not to be doubted that the British government will continue its endeavours to support its Allies; one or other of two maxims of policy follows obviously from the painful truths which we have been considering:—Either, first, that we should put forth to the utmost our strength as a military power—strain it to the very last point, and prepare (no erect mind will start at the proposition) to pour into the Peninsula a force of two hundred thousand men or more,—and make ourselves for a time, upon Spanish ground, principals in the contest; or, secondly, that we should direct our attention to giving support rather in *Things* than in Men.

The former plan, though requiring a great effort and many sacrifices, is (I have no doubt) practicable: its difficulties would yield to a bold and energetic Ministry, in despite of the present constitution of Parliament. The Militia, if they had been called upon at the beginning of the rising in the Peninsula, would (I believe)—almost to a man—have offered their services: so would many of the Volunteers in their individual capacity. They would do so still. The advantages of this plan would be—that the power, which would attend it, must (if judiciously directed) insure unity of effort; taming down, by its dignity, the discords which usually prevail among allied armies; and subordinating to itself the affections of the Spanish and Portuguese by the palpable service which it was rendering to their Country. A further encouragement for adopting this plan he will find, who perceives that the military power of our Enemy is not in substance so formidable, by many—many degrees of terror, as outwardly it appears to be. The last campaign has not been wholly without advantage: since it has proved that the French troops are indebted, for their victories, to the imbecility of their opponents far more than to their own discipline or courage—or even to the skill and talents of their Generals. There is a superstition hanging over us which the efforts of our army (not to speak of the Spaniards) have, I hope, removed.—But their mighty numbers!—In that is a delusion of another kind. In the former instance, year after year we imagined things to be what they were not: and in this, by a more fatal and more common delusion, the thought of what things really are—precludes the thought of what in a moment they may become: the mind, overlaid by the present, cannot lift itself to attain a glimpse of the future.

All—which is comparatively inherent, or can lay claim to any degree of permanence, in the tyranny which the French Nation maintains over Europe—rests upon two foundations:—First; Upon the despotic rule which has been established in France over a powerful People who have lately passed from a state of revolution, in which they supported a struggle begun for domestic liberty, and long continued for liberty and national independence:—and, secondly, upon the personal character of the Man by whom that rule is exercised.

As to the former; every one knows that Despotism, in a general sense, is but another word for weakness. Let one generation disappear; and a people over whom such rule has been extended, if it have not virtue to free itself, is condemned to embarrassment in the operations of its government, and to perpetual languor; with no better hope than that which may spring from the diseased activity of some particular Prince on whom the authority may happen to devolve. This, if it takes a regular hereditary course: but,—if the succession be interrupted, and the supreme power frequently usurped or given by election,—worse evils follow. Science and Art must dwindle, whether the power be hereditary or not: and the virtues of a Trajan or an Antonine are a hollow support for the feeling of contentment and happiness in the hearts of their subjects: such virtues are even a painful mockery;—something that is, and may vanish in a moment, and leave the monstrous crimes of a Caracalla or a Domitian in its place,—men, who are probably leaders of a long procession of their kind. The feebleness of despotic power we have had before our eyes in the late condition of Spain and Prussia; and in that of France before the Revolution; and in the present condition of Austria and Russia. But, in a *new-born* arbitrary and military Government (especially if, like that of France, it have been immediately preceded by a popular Constitution), not only this weakness is not found; but it possesses, for the purposes of external annoyance, a preternatural vigour. Many causes contribute to this: we need only mention that, fitness—real or supposed—being necessarily the chief (and almost sole) recommendation to offices of trust, it is clear that such offices will in general be ably filled; and their duties, comparatively, well executed: and that, from the conjunction of absolute civil and military authority in a single Person, there naturally follows promptness of decision; concentration of effort; rapidity of motion; and confidence that the movements made will be regularly supported. This is all which need now be said upon the subject of this first basis of French Tyranny.

For the second—namely, the personal character of the Chief; I shall at present content myself with noting (to prevent misconception) that this basis is not laid in any superiority of talents in him, but in his utter rejection of the restraints of morality—in wickedness which acknowledges no limit but the extent of its own power. Let any one reflect a moment; and he will feel that a new world of forces is opened to a Being who has made this desperate leap. It is a tremendous principle to be adopted, and steadily adhered to, by a man in the station which Buonaparte occupies; and he has taken the full benefit of it. What there is in this principle of weak, perilous, and self-destructive—I may find a grateful employment in endeavouring to shew upon some future occasion. But it is a duty which we owe to the present moment to proclaim—in vindication of the dignity of human nature, and for an admonition to men of prostrate spirit—that the dominion, which this Enemy of mankind holds, has neither been acquired nor is sustained by endowments of intellect which are rarely bestowed, or by uncommon accumulations of knowledge; but that it has risen from circumstances over which he had no influence; circumstances which, with the power they conferred, have stimulated passions whose natural food hath been and is ignorance; from the barbarian impotence and insolence of a mind—originally of ordinary constitution—lagging, in moral sentiment and knowledge, three hundred years behind the age in which it acts. In such manner did the power originate; and, by the forces which I have described, is it maintained. This should be declared:

and it should be added—that the crimes of Buonaparte are more to be abhorred than those of other denaturalized creatures whose actions are painted in History; because the Author of those crimes is guilty with less temptation, and sins in the presence of a clearer light.

No doubt in the command of almost the whole military force of Europe (the subject which called upon me to make these distinctions) he has, *at this moment*, a third source of power which may be added to these two. He himself rates this last so high —either is, or affects to be, so persuaded of its pre-eminence— that he boldly announces to the world that it is madness, and even impiety, to resist him. And sorry may we be to remember that there are British Senators, who (if a judgement may be formed from the language which they speak) are inclined to accompany him far in this opinion. But the enormity of this power has in it nothing *inherent* or *permanent*. Two signal overthrows in pitched battles would, I believe, go far to destroy it. Germans, Dutch, Italians, Swiss, Poles, would desert the army of Buonaparte, and flock to the standard of his Adversaries, from the moment they could look towards it with that confidence which one or two conspicuous victories would inspire. A regiment of 900 Swiss joined the British army in Portugal; and, if the French had been compelled to surrender as Prisoners of War, we should have seen that all those troops, who were not native Frenchmen, would (if encouragement had been given) have joined the British: and the opportunity that was lost of demonstrating this fact—was not among the least of the mischiefs which attended the termination of the campaign.—In a word; the vastness of Buonaparte's military power is formidable—not because it is impossible to break it; but because it has not yet been penetrated. In this respect it may not inaptly be compared to a huge pine-forest (such as are found in the Northern parts of this Island), whose ability to resist the storms is in its skirts: let but the blast once make an inroad; and it levels the forest, and sweeps it away at pleasure. A hundred thousand men, such as fought at Vimiera and Corunna, would accomplish three such victories as I have been anticipating. This Nation *might* command a military force which would drive the French out of the Peninsula: I do not say that we could sustain there a military force which would prevent their re-entering; but that we could transplant thither, by a great effort, one which would expel them:—*This* I maintain: and it is matter of thought in which infirm minds may find both reproach and instruction. The Spaniards could then take possession of their own fortresses; and have leisure to give themselves a blended civil and military organization, complete and animated by liberty; which, if once accomplished, they would be able to protect themselves. The oppressed Continental Powers also, seeing such unquestionable proof that Great Britain was sincere and earnest, would lift their heads again; and, by so doing, would lighten the burthen of war which might remain for the Spaniards.

In treating of this plan—I have presumed that a General might be placed at the head of this great military power who would not sign a Treaty like that of the Convention of Cintra, and say (look at the proceedings of the Board of Inquiry) that he was determined to this by 'British interests;' or frame *any* Treaty in the country of an Ally (save one purely military for the honourable preservation, if necessary, of his own army or part of it) to which the sole, or even the main, inducement was—our interests contradistinguished from those of that Ally; —a General and a Ministry whose policy would be comprehensive enough to perceive that the true welfare of Britain is best promoted by the independence, freedom, and honour of other Nations; and that it is only by the diffusion and prevalence of these virtues that French Tyranny can be ultimately reduced; or the influence of France over the rest of Europe brought within its natural and reasonable limits.

If this attempt be 'above the strain and temper' of the country, there remains only a plan laid down upon the other principles; namely, service (as far as is required) in *things* rather than in men; that is, men being secondary to things. It is not, I fear, possible that the moral sentiments of the British Army or Government should accord with those of Spain in her present condition. Commmanding power indeed (as hath been said), put forth in the repulse of the common enemy, would tend, more effectually than any thing save the prevalence of true wisdom, to prevent disagreement, and to obviate any temporary injury which the moral spirit of the Spaniards might receive from us: at all events—such power, should there ensue any injury, would bring a solid compensation. But from a middle course—an association sufficiently intimate and wide to scatter every where unkindly passions, and yet unable to attain the salutary point of decisive power—no good is to be expected. Great would be the evil, at this momentous period, if the hatred of the Spaniards should look two ways. Let it be as steadily fixed upon the French, as the Pilot's eye upon his mark. Military stores and arms should be furnished with unfailing liberality: let Troops also be supplied; but let these act separately, —taking strong positions upon the coast, if such can be found, to employ twice their numbers of the Enemy; and, above all, let there be floating Armies—keeping the Enemy in constant uncertainty where he is to be attacked. The peninsula frame of Spain and Portugal lays that region open to the full shock of British warfare. Our Fleet and Army should act, wherever it is possible, as parts of one body—a right hand and a left; and the Enemy ought to be made to feel the force of both.

But—whatever plans be adopted—there can be no success, unless the execution be entrusted to Generals of competent judgement. That the British Army swarms with those who are incompetent—is too plain from successive proofs in the transactions at Buenos Ayres, at Cintra, and in the result of the Board of Inquiry.—Nor must we see a General appointed to command—and required, at the same time, to frame his operations according to the opinion of an inferior Officer: an injunction (for a recommendation, from such a quarter, amounts to an injunction) implying that a man had been appointed to a high station—of which the very persons, who had appointed him, deemed him unworthy; else they must have known that he would endeavour to profit by the experience of any of his inferior officers, from the suggestions of his own understanding: at the same time—by denying to the General-in-Chief the free use of his own judgement, and by the act of announcing this presumption of his incompetence to the man himself—such an indignity is put upon him, that his passions must of necessity be rouzed; so as to leave it scarcely possible that he could draw any benefit, which he might otherwise have drawn, from the local knowledge or talents of the individual to whom he was referred: and, lastly, this injunction virtually involves a subversion of all military subordination. In the better times of the

House of Commons—a minister, who had presumed to write such a letter as that to which I allude, would have been impeached.

The Debates in Parliament, and measures of Government, every day furnish new proofs of the truths which I have been attempting to establish—of the utter want of general principles; — new and lamentable proofs! This moment (while I am drawing towards a conclusion) I learn, from the newspaper reports, that the House of Commons has refused to declare that the Convention of Cintra *disappointed the hopes and expectations of the Nation.*

The motion, according to the letter of it, was ill-framed; for the Convention might have been a very good one, and still have disappointed the hopes and expectations of the Nation—as those might have been unwise: at all events, the words ought to have stood — the *just* and *reasonable* hopes of the Nation. But the hacknied phrase of '*disappointed hopes and expectations*'—should not have been used at all: it is a centre round which much delusion has gathered. The Convention not only did not satisfy the Nation's hopes of good; but sunk it into a pitfall of unimagined and unimaginable evil. The hearts and understandings of the People tell them that the language of a proposed parliamentary resolution, upon this occasion, ought—not only to have been different in the letter—but also widely different in the spirit: and the reader of these pages will have deduced, that no terms of reprobation could in severity exceed the offences involved in—and connected with—that instrument. But, while the grand keep of the castle of iniquity was to be stormed, we have seen nothing but a puny assault upon heaps of the scattered rubbish of the fortress; nay, for the most part, on some accidental mole-hills at its base. I do not speak thus in disrespect to the Right Hon. Gentleman who headed this attack. His mind, left to itself, would (I doubt not) have prompted something worthier and higher: but he moves in the phalanx of Party;—a spiritual Body; in which (by strange inconsistency) the hampering, weakening, and destroying, of every individual mind of which it is composed—is the law which must constitute the strength of the whole. The question was—whether principles, affecting the very existence of Society, had not been violated; and an arm lifted, and let fall, which struck at the root of Honour; with the aggravation of the crime having been committed at this momentous period. But what relation is there between these principles and actions, and being in Place or out of it? If the People would constitutionally and resolutely assert their rights, their Representatives would be taught another lesson; and for their own profit. Their understandings would be enriched accordingly: for it is there—there where least suspected—that the want, from which this country suffers, chiefly lies. They err, who suppose that venality and corruption (though now spreading more and more) are the master-evils of this day: neither these nor immoderate craving for power are so much to be deprecated, as the non-existence of a widely-ranging intellect; of an intellect which, if not efficacious to infuse truth as a vital fluid into the heart, might at least make it a powerful tool in the hand. Outward profession,—which, for practical purposes, is an act of most desirable subservience,—would then wait upon those objects to which inward reverence, though not felt, was known to be due. Schemes of ample reach and true benefit would also promise best to insure the rewards coveted by personal ambition: and men of baser passions, finding it their interest, would naturally combine to perform useful service under the direction of strong minds: while men of good intentions would have their own pure satisfaction; and would exert themselves with more upright—I mean, more hopeful—cheerfulness, and more successfully. It is not therefore inordinate desire of wealth or power which is so injurious—as the means which are and must be employed, in the present intellectual condition of the Legislature, to sustain and secure that power: these are at once an effect of barrenness, and a cause; acting, and mutually re-acting, incessantly. An enlightened Friend has, in conversation, observed to the Author of these pages—that formerly the principles of men were better than they who held them; but that now (a far worse evil!) men are better than their principles. I believe it:—of the deplorable quality and state of principles, the public proceedings in our Country furnish daily new proof. It is however some consolation, at this present crisis, to find—that, of the thoughts and feelings uttered during the two debates which led me to these painful declarations, such—as approach towards truth which has any dignity in it—come from the side of his

Majesty's Ministers.—But note again those contradictions to which I have so often been obliged to advert. The Ministers advise his Majesty publicly to express sentiments of disapprobation upon the Convention of Cintra; and, when the question of the merits or demerits of this instrument comes before them in Parliament, the same persons—who, as advisers of the crown, lately condemned the treaty—now, in their character of representatives of the people, by the manner in which they received this motion, have pronounced an encomium upon it. For, though (as I have said) the motion was inaccurately and inadequately worded, it was not set aside upon this ground. And the Parliament has therefore persisted in withholding, from the insulted and injured People and from their Allies, the only reparation which perhaps it may be in its power to grant; has refused to signify its repentance and sorrow for what hath been done; without which, as a previous step, there can be no proof --no gratifying intimation, even to this Country or to its Allies, that the future efforts of the British Parliament are in a sincere spirit. The guilt of the transaction therefore being neither repented of, nor atoned for; the course of evil is, by necessity, persevered in.———But let us turn to a brighter region.

The events of the last year, gloriously destroying many frail fears, have placed—in the rank of serene and immortal truths—a proposition which, as an object of belief, hath in all ages been fondly cherished; namely—That a numerous Nation, determined to be free, may effect its purpose in despite of the mightiest power which a foreign Invader can bring against it. These events also have pointed out how, in the ways of Nature and under the guidance of Society, this happy end is to be attained: in other words, they have shewn that the cause of the People, in dangers and difficulties issuing from this quarter of oppression, is safe while it remains not only in the bosom but in the hands of the People; or (what amounts to the same thing) in those of a government which, being truly *from* the People, is faithfully *for* them. While the power remained with the provincial Juntas, that is, with the body natural of the community (for those authorities, newly generated in such adversity, were truly living members of that body); every thing prospered in Spain. Hopes of the best kind were opened out and encouraged; liberal opinions countenanced; and wise measures arranged: and last, and (except as proceeding from these) least of all,—victories in the field, in the streets of the city, and upon the walls of the fortress.

I have heretofore styled it a blessing that the Spanish People became their own masters at once. It *was* a blessing; but not without much alloy: as the same disinterested generous passions, which preserved (and would for a season still have preserved) them from a bad exercise of their power, impelled them to part with it too soon; before labours, hitherto neither tried nor thought-of, had created throughout the country the minor excellences indispensible for the performance of those labours; before powerful minds, not hitherto of general note, had found time to shew themselves; and before men, who were previously known, had undergone the proof of new situations. Much therefore was wanting to direct the general judgement in the choice of persons, when the second delegation took place; which was a removal (the first, we have seen, had not been so) of the power from the People. But, when a common centre became absolutely necessary, the power ought to have passed from the provincial Assemblies into the hands of the Cortes; and into none else. A pernicious Oligarchy crept into the place of this comprehensive—this constitutional—this saving and majestic Assembly. Far be it from me to speak of the Supreme Junta with ill-advised condemnation: every man must feel for the distressful trials to which that Body has been exposed. But eighty men or a hundred, with a king at their head veiled under a cloud of fiction (we might say, with reference to the difficulties of this moment, begotten upon a cloud of fiction), could not be an image of a Nation like that of Spain, or an adequate instrument of their power for their ends. The Assembly, from the smallness of its numbers, must have wanted breadth of wing to extend itself and brood over Spain with a quickening touch of warmth every where. If also, as hath been mentioned, there was a want of experience to determine the judgment in choice of persons; this same smallness of numbers must have unnecessarily increased the evil—by excluding many men of worth and talents which were so far known and allowed as that they would surely have been deputed to an Assembly upon a larger scale. Gratitude, habit, and numerous other causes must have given an undue preponderance to birth, station, rank, and fortune; and have fixed the election, more than was reasonable, upon those who were most conspicuous for these distinctions; —men whose very virtue would incline them superstitiously to respect established things, and to mistrust the People—towards whom not only a frank confidence but a forward generosity was the first of duties. I speak not of the vices to which such men would be liable, brought up under the discipline of a government administered like the old Monarchy of Spain: the matter is both ungracious and too obvious.

But I began with hope; and hope has inwardly accompanied me to the end. The whole course of the campaign, rightly interpreted, has justified my hope. In Madrid, in Ferrol, in Corunna, in every considerable place, and in every part of the country over which the French have re-extended their dominion, —we learn, from their own reports, that the body of the People have shewed against them, to the last, the most determined hostility. Hence it is clear that the lure, which the invading Usurper found himself constrained lately to hold out to the inferior orders of society in the shape of various immunities, has totally failed: and therefore he turns for support to another quarter, and now attempts to cajole the wealthy and the privileged. But this class has been taught, by late Decrees, what it has to expect from him; and how far he is to be confided-in for its especial interests. Many individuals, no doubt, he will seduce; but the bulk of the class, even if they could be insensible to more liberal feelings, cannot but be his enemies. This change, therefore, is not merely shifting ground; but retiring to a position which he himself has previously undermined. Here is confusion; and a power warring against itself.

So will it ever fare with foreign Tyrants when (in spite of domestic abuses) a People, which has lived long, feels that it has a Country to love; and where the heart of that People is sound. Between the native inhabitants of France and Spain there has existed from the earliest period, and still does exist, an universal and utter dissimilitude in laws, actions, deportment, gait, manners, customs: join with this the difference in the language, and the barrier of the Pyrenees; a separation and an opposition in great things, and an antipathy in small. Ignorant then must he be of history and of the reports of travellers and residents in the two countries, or strangely inattentive to the constitution of human nature, who (this being true) can admit the belief that the Spaniards, numerous and powerful as they are, will live under Frenchmen as their lords and masters. Let there be added to this inherent mutual repulsiveness—those recent indignities and horrible outrages; and we need not fear to say that such reconcilement is impossible; even without that further insuperable obstacle which we hope will exist, an establishment of a free Constitution in Spain.—The intoxicated setter-up of Kings may fill his diary with pompous stories of the acclamations with which his solemn puppets are received; he may stuff their mouths with impious asseverations; and hire knees to bend before them, and lips to answer with honied greetings of gratitude and love: these cannot remove the old heart, and put a new one into the bosom of the spectators. The whole is a pageant seen for a day among men in its passage to that 'Limbo large and broad' whither, as to their proper home, fleet

> All the unaccomplish'd works of Nature's hand,
> Abortive, monstrous, or unkindly mix'd,
> *Dissolv'd on earth.*

Talk not of the perishable nature of enthusiasm; and rise above a craving for perpetual manifestations of things. He is to be pitied whose eye can only be pierced by the light of a meridian sun, whose frame can only be warmed by the heat of midsummer. Let us hear no more of the little dependence to be had in war upon voluntary service. The things, with which we are primarily and mainly concerned, are inward passions; and not outward arrangements. These latter may be given at any time; when the parts, to be put together, are in readiness. Hatred and love, and each in its intensity, and pride (passions which, existing in the heart of a Nation, are inseparable from hope)—these elements being in constant preparation—enthusiasm will break out from them, or coalesce with them, upon the summons of a moment. And these passions are scarcely less than inextinguishable. The truth of this is recorded in the manners and hearts of North and South Britons, of Englishmen and Welshmen, on either border of the Tweed and of the Esk, on both sides of the Severn and the Dee; an inscription legible, and in strong characters, which the tread of many and great blessings, continued through hundreds of years, has been unable to efface. The Sicilian Vespers are to this day a familiar game among the boys of the villages on the sides of Mount Etna, and through every corner of the Island; and 'Exterminate the French!' is the action in their arms, and the word of triumph upon their tongues. He then is a sorry Statist, who desponds or despairs (nor is he less so who is too much elevated) from any considerations connected with the quality of enthusiasm. Nothing is so easy as to sustain it by partial and gradual changes of its object; and by placing it in the way of receiving new interpositions according to the need. The difficulty lies—not in kindling, feeding, or fanning the flame; but in continuing so to regulate the relations of things—that the fanning breeze and the feeding fuel shall come from no unworthy quarter, and shall neither of them be wanting in appropriate consecration. The Spaniards have as great helps towards ensuring this, as ever were vouchsafed to a People.

What then is to be desired? Nothing but that the Government and the higher orders of society should deal sincerely towards the middle class and the lower: I mean, that the general temper should be sincere.—It is not required that every one should be disinterested, or zealous, or of one mind with his fellows. Selfishness or slackness in individuals, and in certain bodies of men also (and at times perhaps in all), have their use: else why should they exist? Due circumspection and necessary activity, in those who are sound, could not otherwise maintain themselves. The deficiencies in one quarter are more than made up by consequent overflowings in another. 'If my Neighbour fails,' says the true Patriot, 'more devolves upon me.' Discord and even treason are not, in a country situated as Spain is, the pure evils which, upon a superficial view, they appear to be. Never are a people so livelily admonished of the love they bear their country, and of the pride which they have in their common parent, as when they hear of some parricidal attempt of a false brother. For this cause chiefly, in times of national danger, are their fancies so busy in suspicion; which under such shape, though oftentimes producing dire and pitiable effects, is notwithstanding in its general character no other than that habit which has grown out of the instinct of self-preservation—elevated into a wakeful and affectionate apprehension for the whole, and ennobling its private and baser ways by the generous use to which they are converted. Nor ever has a good and loyal man such a swell of mind, such a clear insight into the constitution of virtue, and such a sublime sense of its power, as at the first tidings of some atrocious act of perfidy; when, having taken the alarm for human nature, a second thought recovers him; and his faith returns—gladsome from what has been revealed within himself, and awful from participation of the secrets in the profaner grove of humanity which that momentary blast laid open to his view.

Of the ultimate independence of the Spanish Nation there is no reason to doubt: and for the immediate furtherance of the good cause, and a throwing-off of the yoke upon the first favourable opportunity by the different tracts of the country upon which it has been re-imposed, nothing is wanting but sincerity on the part of the government towards the provinces which are yet free. The first end to be secured by Spain is riddance of the enemy: the second, permanent independence: and the third, a free constitution of government; which will give their main (though far from sole) value to the other two; and without which little more than a formal independence, and perhaps scarcely that, can be secured. Humanity and honour, and justice, and all the sacred feelings connected with atonement, retribution, and satisfaction; shame that will not sleep, and the sting of unperformed duty; and all the powers of the mind, the memory that broods over the dead and turns to the living, the understanding, the imagination, and the reason;—demand and enjoin that the wanton oppressor should be driven, with confusion and dismay, from the country which he has so heinously abused.

This cannot be accomplished (scarcely can it be aimed at) without an accompanying and an inseparable resolution, in the souls of the Spaniards, to be and remain their own masters; that is, to preserve themselves in the rank of Men; and not become as the Brute that is driven to the pasture, and cares not who owns him. It is a common saying among those who profess to be lovers of civil liberty, and give themselves some credit for understanding it,—that, if a Nation be not free, it is mere dust in the balance whether the slavery be bred at home, or comes from abroad; be of their own suffering, or of a stranger's imposing. They see little of the under-ground part of the tree of liberty, and know less of the nature of man, who can think thus. Where indeed there is an indisputable and immeasurable superiority in one nation over another; to be conquered may, in course of time, be a benefit to the inferior nation: and, upon this principle, some of the conquests of the Greeks and Romans may be justified. But in what of really useful or honourable are the French superior to their Neighbours? Never far advanced, and, now barbarizing apace, they may carry—amongst the sober and dignified Nations which surround them—much to be avoided, but little to be imitated.

There is yet another case in which a People may be benefited by resignation or forfeiture of their rights as a separate independent State; I mean, where—of two contiguous or neighbouring countries, both included by nature under one conspicuously defined limit—the weaker is united with, or absorbed into, the more powerful; and one and the same Government is extended over both. This, with due patience and foresight, may (for the most part) be amicably effected, without the intervention of conquest; but—even should a violent course have been resorted to, and have proved successful—the result will be matter of congratulation rather than of regret, if the countries have been incorporated with an equitable participation of natural advantages and civil privileges. Who does not rejoice that former partitions have disappeared,—and that England, Scotland, and Wales, are under one legislative and executive authority; and that Ireland (would that she had been more justly dealt with!) follows the same destiny? The large and numerous Fiefs, which interfered injuriously with the grand demarcation assigned by nature to France, have long since been united and consolidated. The several independent Sovereignties of Italy (a country, the boundary of which is still more expressly traced out by nature; and which has no less the further definition and cement of country which Language prepares) have yet this good to aim at: and it will be a happy day for Europe, when the natives of Italy and the natives of Germany (whose duty is, in like manner, indicated to them) shall each dissolve the pernicious barriers which divide them, and form themselves into a mighty People. But Spain, excepting a free union with Portugal, has no benefit of this kind to look for: she has long since attained it. The Pyrenees on the one side, and the Sea on every other; the vast extent and great resources of the territory; a population numerous enough to defend itself against the whole world, and capable of great increase; language; and long duration of independence;—point out and command that the two nations of the Peninsula should be united in friendship and strict alliance; and, as soon as it may be effected without injustice, form one independent and indissoluble sovereignty. The Peninsula cannot be protected but by itself: it is too large a tree to be framed by nature for a station among underwoods; it must have power to toss its branches in the wind, and lift a bold forehead to the sun.

Allowing that the 'regni novitas' should either compel or tempt the Usurper to do away some ancient abuses, and to accord certain insignificant privileges to the People upon the purlieus of the forest of Freedom (for assuredly he will never suffer them to enter the body of it); allowing this, and much more; that the mass of the Population would be placed in a condition outwardly more thriving—would be *better off* (as the phrase in conversation is); it is still true that—in the act and consciousness of submission to an imposed lord and master, to a will not growing out of themselves, to the edicts of another People their triumphant enemy—there would be the loss of a sensation within for which nothing external, even though it should come close to the garden and the field—to the door and the fire-side, can make amends. The Artisan and the Merchant (men of classes perhaps least attached to their native soil) would not be insensible to this loss; and the Mariner, in his thoughtful mood, would sadden under it upon the wide ocean. The central or cardinal feeling of these thoughts may, at a future time, furnish fit matter for the genius of some patriotic Spaniard to express in his own noble language—as an inscription for the Sword of Francis the First; if that Sword, which was so ingloriously and perfidiously surrendered, should ever, by the energies of Liberty, be recovered, and deposited in its ancient habitation in the Escurial. The Patriot will recollect that,—if the memorial, then given up by the hand of the Government, had also been abandoned by the heart of the People, and that indignity patiently subscribed to, —his country would have been lost for ever.

There are multitudes by whom, I know, these sentiments will not be languidly received at this day; and sure I am—that, a hundred and fifty years ago, they would have been ardently welcomed by all. But, in many parts of Europe (and especially in our own country), men have been pressing forward, for some time, in a path which has betrayed by its fruitfulness; furnishing them constant employment for picking up things about their feet, when thoughts were perishing in their minds. While Mechanic Arts, Manufactures, Agriculture, Commerce, and all those products of knowledge which are confined to gross—definite—and tangible objects, have, with the aid of Experimental Philosophy, been every day putting on more brilliant colours; the splendour of the Imagination has been fading: Sensibility, which was formerly a generous nursling of rude Nature, has been chased from its ancient range in the wide domain of patriotism and religion with the weapons of derision by a shadow calling itself Good Sense: calculations of presumptuous Expediency—groping its way among partial and temporary consequences—have been substituted for the dictates of paramount and infallible Conscience, the supreme embracer of consequences: lifeless and circumspect Decencies have banished the graceful negligence and unsuspicious dignity of Virtue.

The progress of these arts also, by furnishing such attractive stores of outward accommodation, has misled the higher orders of society in their more disinterested exertions for the service of the lower. Animal comforts have been rejoiced over, as if they were the end of being. A neater and more fertile garden; a greener field; implements and utensils more apt; a dwelling more commodious and better furnished;—let these be attained, say the actively benevolent, and we are sure not only of being in the right road, but of having successfully terminated our journey. Now a country may advance, for some time, in this course with apparent profit: these accommodations, by zealous encouragement, may be attained: and still the Peasant or Artisan, their master, be a slave in mind; a slave rendered even more abject by the very tenure under which these possessions are held: and—if they veil from us this fact, or reconcile us to it—they are worse than worthless. The springs of emotion may be relaxed or destroyed within him; he may have little thought of the past, and less interest in the future.—The great end and difficulty of life for men of all classes, and especially difficult for those who live by manual labour, is a union of peace with innocent and laudable animation. Not by bread alone is the life of Man sustained; not by raiment alone is he warmed;—but by the genial and vernal inmate of the breast, which at once pushes forth and cherishes; by self-support and self-sufficing endeavours; by anticipations, apprehensions, and active remembrances; by elasticity under insult, and firm resistance to injury; by joy, and by love; by pride which his imagination gathers in from afar; by patience, because life wants not promises; by admiration; by gratitude which—debasing him not when his fellow-being is its object—habitually expands itself, for his elevation, in complacency towards his Creator.

Now, to the existence of these blessings, national independence is indispensible; and many of them it will itself produce and maintain. For it is some consolation to those who look back upon the history of the world to know—that, even without civil liberty, society may possess—diffused through its inner recesses in the minds even of its humblest members—something of dignified enjoyment. But, without national independence, this is impossible. The difference, between inbred oppression and that which is from without, is *essential;* inasmuch as the former does not exclude, from the minds of a people, the feeling of being self-governed; does not imply (as the latter does, when patiently submitted to) an abandonment of the first duty imposed by the faculty of reason. In reality: where this feeling has no place, a people are not a society, but a herd; man being indeed distinguished among them from the brute; but only to his disgrace. I am aware that there are too many who think that, to the bulk of the community, this independence is of no value; that it is a refinement with which they feel they have no concern; inasmuch as, under the best frame of Government, there is an inevitable dependence of the poor upon the rich—of the many upon the few—so unrelenting and imperious as to reduce this other, by comparison, into a force which has small influence, and is entitled to no regard. Superadd civil liberty to national independence; and this position is overthrown at once: for there is no more certain mark of a sound frame of polity than this; that, in all individual instances (and it is upon these generalized that this position is laid down), the dependence is in reality far more strict on the side of the wealthy; and the labouring man leans less upon others than any man in the community.—But the case before us is of a country not internally free, yet supposed capable of repelling an external enemy who attempts its subjugation. If a country have put on chains of its own forging; in the name of virtue, let it be conscious that to itself it is accountable: let it not have cause to look beyond its own limits for reproof: and,—in the name of humanity,—if it be self-depressed, let it have its pride and some hope within itself. The poorest Peasant, in an unsubdued land, feels this pride. I do not appeal to the example of Britain or of Switzerland, for the one is free, and the other lately was free (and, I trust, will ere long be so again): but talk with the Swede; and you will see the joy he finds in these sensations. With him animal courage (the substitute for many and the friend of all the manly virtues) has space to move in; and is at once elevated by his imagination, and softened by his affections: it is invigorated also; for the whole courage of his Country is in his breast.

In fact: the Peasant, and he who lives by the fair reward of his manual labour, has ordinarily a larger proportion of his gratifications dependent upon these thoughts—than, for the most part, men in other classes have. For he is in his person attached, by stronger roots, to the soil of which he is the growth: his intellectual notices are generally confined within narrower bounds: in him no partial or antipatriotic interests counteract the force of those nobler sympathies and antipathies which he has in right of his Country; and lastly the belt or girdle of his mind has never been stretched to utter relaxation by false philosophy, under a conceit of making it sit more easily and gracefully. These sensations are a social inheritance to him: more important, as he is precluded from luxurious—and those which are usually called refined—enjoyments.

Love and admiration must push themselves out towards some quarter: otherwise the moral man is killed. Collaterally they advance with great vigour to a certain extent—and they are checked: in that direction, limits hard to pass are perpetually encountered: but upwards and downwards, to ancestry and to posterity, they meet with gladsome help and no obstacles; the tract is interminable.—Perdition to the Tyrant who would wantonly cut off an independent Nation from its inheritance in past ages; turning the tombs and burial-places of the Forefathers into dreaded objects of sorrow, or of shame and reproach, for the Children! Look upon Scotland and Wales: though, by the union of these with England under the same Government (which was effected without conquest in one instance), ferocious and desolating wars, and more injurious intrigues, and sapping and disgraceful corruptions, have been prevented; and tranquillity, security, and prosperity, and a thousand interchanges of amity, not otherwise attainable, have followed;—yet the flashing eye, and the agitated voice, and all the tender recollections, with which the names of Prince Llewellin and William Wallace are to this day pronounced by the fire-side and on the public road, attest that these substantial blessings have not been purchased without the relinquishment of something most salutary to the moral nature of Man: else the remembrances would not cleave so faithfully to their abiding-place in the human heart. But, if these affections be of general interest, they are of especial interest to Spain; whose history, written and traditional, is pre-eminently stored with the sustaining food of such affections: and in no country are they more justly and generally prized, or more feelingly cherished.

In the conduct of this argument I am not speaking *to* the humbler ranks of society: it is unnecessary: *they* trust in nature, and are safe. The People of Madrid, and Corunna, and Ferrol, resisted to the last; from an impulse which, in their hearts, was its own justification. The failure was with those who stood higher in the scale. In fact; the universal rising of the Peninsula, under the pressure and in the face of the most tremendous military power which ever existed, is evidence which cannot be too much insisted upon; and is decisive upon this subject, as involving a question of virtue and moral sentiment. All ranks were penetrated with one feeling: instantaneous and universal was the acknowledgement. If there have been since individual fallings-off; those have been caused by that kind of after-thoughts which are the bastard offspring of selfishness. The matter was brought home to Spain; and no Spaniard has offended herein with a still conscience.—It is to the worldlings of our own country, and to those who think without carrying their thoughts far enough, that I address myself. Let them know, there is no true wisdom without imagination; no genuine sense;—that the man, who in this age feels no regret for the ruined honour of other Nations, must be poor in sympathy for the honour of his own Country; and that, if he be wanting here towards that which circumscribes the whole, he neither has—nor can have—a social regard for the lesser communities which Country includes. Contract the circle, and bring him to his family; such a man cannot protect *that* with dignified loves. Reduce his thoughts to his own person; he may defend himself,—what *he* deems his honour; but it is the *action* of a brave man from the impulse of the brute, or the motive of a coward.

But it is time to recollect that this vindication of human feeling began from an *hypothesis*,—that the *outward* state of the mass of the Spanish people would be improved by the French usurpation. To this I now give an unqualified denial. Let me also observe to those men, for whose infirmity this hypothesis was tolerated,—that the true point of comparison does not lie between what the Spaniards have been under a government of their own, and what they may become under French domination; but between what the Spaniards may do (and, in all likelihood, will do) for themselves, and what Frenchmen would do for them. But,—waiving this,—the sweeping away of the most splendid monuments of art, and rifling of the public treasuries in the conquered countries, are an apt prologue to the tragedy which is to ensue. Strange that there are men who can be so besotted as to see, in the decrees of the Usurper concerning feudal tenures and a worn-out Inquisition, any other evidence than that of insidiousness and of a constrained acknowledgement of the strength which he felt he had to overcome. What avail the lessons of history, if men can be duped thus? Boons and promises of this kind rank, in trustworthiness, many degrees lower than amnesties after expelled kings have recovered their thrones. The fate of subjugated Spain may be expressed in these words,—pillage—depression—and helotism—for the supposed aggrandizement of the imaginary freeman its master. There would indeed be attempts at encouragement, that there might be a supply of something to pillage: studied depression there would be, that there might arise no power of resistance: and lastly helotism;—but of what kind? that a vain and impious Nation might have slaves, worthier than itself, for work which its own hands would reject with scorn.

What good can the present arbitrary power confer upon France itself? Let that point be first settled by those who are inclined to look farther. The earlier proceedings of the French

Revolution no doubt infused health into the country; something of which survives to this day: but let not the now-existing Tyranny have the credit of it. France neither owes, nor can owe, to this any rational obligation. She has seen decrees without end for the increase of commerce and manufactures; pompous stories without number of harbours, canals, warehouses, and bridges: but there is no worse sign in the management of affairs than when that, which ought to follow as an effect, goes before under a vain notion that it will be a cause.—Let us attend to the springs of action, and we shall not be deceived. The works of peace cannot flourish in a country governed by an intoxicated Despot; the motions of whose distorted benevolence must be still more pernicious than those of his cruelty. '*I have bestowed; I have created; I have regenerated; I have been pleased to organize;*'—this is the language perpetually upon his lips, when his ill-fated activities turn that way. Now commerce, manufactures, agriculture, and all the peaceful arts, are of the nature of virtues or intellectual powers: they cannot be given; they cannot be stuck in here and there; they must spring up; they must grow of themselves: they may be encouraged; they thrive better with encouragement, and delight in it; but the obligation must have bounds nicely defined; for they are delicate, proud, and independent. But a Tyrant has no joy in any thing which is endued with such excellence: he sickens at the sight of it: he turns away from it, as an insult to his own attributes. We have seen the present ruler of France publicly addressed as a Providence upon earth; styled, among innumerable other blasphemies, the supreme Ruler of things; and heard him say, in his answers, that he approved of the language of those who thus saluted him. (*See Appendix E.*)—Oh folly to think that plans of reason can prosper under such countenance! If this be the doom of France, what a monster would be the double-headed tyranny of Spain!

It is immutably ordained that power, taken and exercised in contempt of right, never can bring forth good. Wicked actions indeed have oftentimes happy issues: the benevolent œconomy of nature counter-working and diverting evil; and educing finally benefits from injuries, and turning curses to blessings. But I am speaking of good in a direct course. All good in this order—all moral good—begins and ends in reverence of right. The whole Spanish People are to be treated not as a mighty multitude with feeling, will, and judgment; not as rational creatures;—but as objects without reason; in the language of human law, insuperably laid down not as Persons but as Things. Can good come from this beginning; which, in matter of civil government, is the fountain-head and the main feeder of all the pure evil upon earth? Look at the past history of our sister Island for the quality of foreign oppression: turn where you will, it is miserable at best; but, in the case of Spain!—it might be said, engraven upon the rocks of her own Pyrenees,

> Per me si va nella città dolente;
> Per me si va nell' eterno dolore;
> Per me si va tra la perduta gente.

So much I have thought it necessary to speak upon this subject; with a desire to enlarge the views of the short-sighted, to chear the desponding, and stimulate the remiss. I have been treating of duties which the People of Spain feel to be solemn and imperious; and have referred to springs of action (in the sensations of love and hatred, of hope and fear),—for promoting the fulfilment of these duties,—which cannot fail. The People of Spain, thus animated, will move now; and will be prepared to move, upon a favourable summons, for ages. And it is consolatory to think that,—even if many of the leading persons of that country, in their resistance to France, should not look beyond the two first objects (viz. riddance of the enemy, and security of national independence);—it is, I say, consolatory to think that the conduct, which can alone secure either of these ends, leads directly to a free internal Government. We have therefore both the passions and the reason of these men on our side in two stages of the common journey: and, when this is the case, surely we are justified in expecting some further companionship and support from their reason—acting independent of their partial interests, or in opposition to them. It is obvious that, to the narrow policy of this class (men loyal to the Nation and to the King, yet jealous of the People), the most dangerous failures, which have hitherto taken place, are to be attributed: for, though from acts of open treason Spain may suffer and has suffered much, these (as I have proved) can never affect the vitals of the cause. But the march of Liberty has begun; and they, who will not lead, may be borne along.—At all events, the road is plain. Let members for the Cortes be assembled from those Provinces which are not in the possession of the Invader: or at least (if circumstances render this impossible at present) let it be announced that such is the intention, to be realized the first moment when it shall become possible. In the mean while speak boldly to the People: and let the People write and speak boldly. Let the expectation be familiar to them of open and manly institutions of law and liberty according to knowledge. Let them be universally trained to military exercises, and accustomed to military discipline: let them be drawn together in civic and religious assemblies; and a general communication of those assemblies with each other be established through the country: so that there may be one zeal and one life in every part of it.

With great profit might the Chiefs of the Spanish Nation look back upon the earlier part of the French Revolution. Much, in the outward manner, might there be found worthy of qualified imitation: and, where there is a difference in the inner spirit (and there is a mighty difference!), the advantage is wholly on the side of the Spaniards.—Why should the People of Spain be dreaded by their leaders? I do not mean the profligate and flagitious leaders; but those who are well-intentioned, yet timid. That there are numbers of this class who have excellent intentions, and are willing to make large personal sacrifices, is clear; for they have put every thing to risk—all their privileges, their honours, and possessions—by their resistance to the Invader. Why then should they have fears from a quarter—whence their safety must come, if it come at all?—Spain has nothing to dread from Jacobinism. Manufactures and Commerce have there in far less degree than elsewhere—by unnaturally clustering the people together—enfeebled their bodies, inflamed their passions by intemperance, vitiated from childhood their moral affections, and destroyed their imaginations. Madrid is no enormous city, like Paris; over-grown, and disproportionate; sickening and bowing down, by its corrupt humours, the frame of the body politic. Nor has the pestilential philosophism of France made any progress in Spain. No flight of infidel harpies has alighted upon their ground. A Spanish understanding is a hold too strong to give way to the meagre tactics of the 'Systême de la Nature;' or to the pellets of logic which Condillac has cast in the foundry of national vanity, and tosses about at hap-hazard —self-persuaded that he is proceeding according to art. The Spaniards are a people with imagination: and the paradoxical reveries of Rousseau, and the flippancies of Voltaire, are plants which will not naturalise in the country of Calderon and Cervantes. Though bigotry among the Spaniards leaves much to be lamented; I have proved that the religious habits of the nation must, in a contest of this kind, be of inestimable service.

Yet further: contrasting the present condition of Spain with that of France at the commencement of her revolution, we must not overlook one characteristic; the Spaniards have no division among themselves by and through themselves; no numerous Priesthood—no Nobility—no large body of powerful Burghers —from passion, interest, and conscience—opposing the end which is known and felt to be the duty and only honest and true interest of all. Hostility, wherever it is found, must proceed from the seductions of the Invader: and these depend solely upon his power: let that be shattered; and they vanish.

And this once again leads us directly to that immense military force which the Spaniards have to combat; and which, many think, more than counterbalances every internal advantage. It is indeed formidable: as revolutionary appetites and energies must needs be; when, among a people numerous as the people of France, they have ceased to spend themselves in conflicting factions within the country for objects perpetually changing shape; and are carried out of it under the strong controul of an absolute despotism, as opportunity invites, for a definite object —plunder and conquest. It is, I allow, a frightful spectacle— to see the prime of a vast nation propelled out of their territory with the rapid sweep of a horde of Tartars; moving from the impulse of like savage instincts; and furnished, at the same time, with those implements of physical destruction which have been produced by science and civilization. Such are the motions of the French armies; unchecked by any thought which philosophy and the spirit of society, progressively humanizing, have called forth—to determine or regulate the application of the murderous and desolating apparatus with which by philosophy and science they have been provided. With a like perversion of things, and the same mischievous reconcilement of forces in their nature adverse, these revolutionary impulses and these appetites of barbarous (nay, what is far worse, of barbarized) men are embodied in a new frame of polity; which possesses the consistency of an ancient Government, without its embarrassments and weaknesses. And at the head of all is the mind of one man who acts avowedly upon the principle that every thing, which can be done safely by the supreme power of a State, may be done (*See Appendix F.*); and who has, at his command, the greatest part of the continent of Europe—to fulfil what yet remains unaccomplished of his nefarious purposes.

Now it must be obvious to a reflecting mind that every thing which is desperately immoral, being in its constitution monstrous, is of itself perishable: decay it cannot escape; and, further, it is liable to sudden dissolution: time would evince this in the instance before us; though not, perhaps, until infinite and irreparable harm had been done. But, even at present, each of the sources of this preternatural strength (as far as it is formidable to Europe) has its corresponding seat of weakness; which, were it fairly touched, would manifest itself immediately. —The power is indeed a Colossus: but, if the trunk be of molten-brass, the members are of clay; and would fall to pieces upon a shock which need not be violent. Great Britain, if her energies were properly called forth and directed, might (as we have already maintained) give this shock. 'Magna parvis obscurantur' was the appropriate motto (the device a Sun Eclipsed) when Lord Peterborough, with a handful of men opposed to fortified cities and large armies, brought a great part of Spain to acknowledge a sovereign of the House of Austria. We have *now* a vast military force; and,—even without a Peterborough or a Marlborough,—at this precious opportunity (when, as is daily more probable, a large portion of the French force must march northwards to combat Austria) we might easily, by expelling the French from the Peninsula, secure an immediate footing there for liberty; and the Pyrenees would then be shut against them for ever. The disciplined troops of Great Britain might overthrow the enemy in the field; while the Patriots of Spain, under wise management, would be able to consume him slowly but surely.

For present annoyance his power is, no doubt, mighty: but liberty—in which it originated, and of which it is a depravation—is far mightier; and the good in human nature is stronger than the evil. The events of our age indeed have brought this truth into doubt with some persons: and scrupulous observers have been astonished and have repined at the sight of enthusiasm, courage, perseverance, and fidelity, put forth seemingly to their height,—and all engaged in the furtherance of wrong. But the minds of men are not always devoted to this bad service as strenuously as they appear to be. I have personal knowledge that, when the attack was made which ended in the subjugation of Switzerland, the injustice of the undertaking was grievously oppressive to many officers of the French army; and damped their exertions. Besides, were it otherwise, there is no just cause for despondency in the perverted alliance of these qualities with oppression. The intrinsic superiority of virtue and liberty, even for politic ends, is not affected by it. If the tide of success were, by any effort, fairly turned;—not only a general desertion, as we have the best reason to believe, would follow among the troops of the enslaved nations; but a moral change would also take place in the minds of the native French soldiery. Occasion would be given for the discontented to break out; and, above all, for the triumph of human nature. It would *then* be seen whether men fighting in a bad cause,—men without magnanimity, honour, or justice,—could recover; and stand up against champions who by these virtues were carried forward in good fortune, as by these virtues in adversity they had been sustained. As long as guilty actions thrive, guilt is strong: it has a giddiness and transport of its own; a hardihood not without superstition, as if Providence were a party to its success. But there is no independent spring at the heart of the machine which can be relied upon for a support of these motions in a change of circumstances. Disaster opens the eyes of conscience; and, in the minds of men who have been employed in bad actions, defeat and a feeling of punishment are inseparable.

On the other hand; the power of an unblemished heart and a brave spirit is shewn, in the events of war, not only among unpractised citizens and peasants; but among troops in the most perfect discipline. Large bodies of the British army have been several times broken—that is, technically vanquished—in Egypt, and elsewhere. Yet they, who were conquered as formal soldiers, stood their ground and became conquerors as men. This paramount efficacy of moral causes is not willingly admitted by persons high in the profession of arms; because it seems to diminish their value in society—by taking from the importance of their art: but the truth is indisputable: and those Generals are as blind to their own interests as to the interests of their country, who, by submitting to inglorious treaties or by other misconduct, hazard the breaking down of those personal virtues in the men under their command—to which they themselves, as leaders, are mainly indebted for the fame which they acquire.

Combine, with this moral superiority inherent in the cause of Freedom, the endless resources open to a nation which shews constancy in defensive war; resources which, after a lapse of time, leave the strongest invading army comparatively helpless. Before six cities, resisting as Saragossa hath resisted during her two sieges, the whole of the military power of the adversary would melt away. Without any advantages of natural situation; without fortifications; without even a ditch to protect them; with nothing better than a mud wall; with not more than two hundred regular troops; with a slender stock of arms and ammunition; with a leader inexperienced in war;—the Citizens of Saragossa began the contest. Enough of what was needful—was produced and created; and—by courage, fortitude, and skill rapidly matured—they baffled for sixty days, and finally repulsed, a large French army with all its equipments. In the first siege the natural and moral victory were both on their side; nor less so virtually (though the termination was different) in the second. For, after another resistance of nearly three months, they have given the enemy cause feelingly to say, with Pyrrhus of old,—'A little more of such conquest, and I am destroyed.'

If evidence were wanting of the efficacy of the principles which throughout this Treatise have been maintained,—it has been furnished in overflowing measure. A private individual, I had written; and knew not in what manner tens of thousands were enacting, day after day, the truths which, in the solitude of a peaceful vale, I was meditating. Most gloriously have the Citizens of Saragossa proved that the true army of Spain, in a contest of this nature, is the whole people. The same city has also exemplified a melancholy—yea a dismal truth; yet consolatory, and full of joy; that,—when a people are called suddenly to fight for their liberty, and are sorely pressed upon,—their best field of battle is the floors upon which their children have played; the chambers where the family of each man has slept (his own or his neighbours'); upon or under the roofs by which they have been sheltered; in the gardens of their recreation; in the street, or in the market-place; before the Altars of their Temples; and among their congregated dwellings—blazing, or up-rooted.

The Government of Spain must never forget Saragossa for a moment. Nothing is wanting, to produce the same effects every where, but a leading mind such as that city was blessed with. In the latter contest this has been proved; for Saragossa contained, at that time, bodies of men from almost all parts of Spain. The narrative of those two sieges should be the manual of every Spaniard: he may add to it the ancient stories of Numantia and Saguntum: let him sleep upon the book as a pillow; and, if he be a devout adherent to the religion of his country, let him wear it in his bosom for his crucifix to rest upon.

Beginning from these invincible feelings, and the principles of justice which are involved in them; let nothing be neglected, which policy and prudence dictate, for rendering subservient to the same end those qualities in human nature which are indifferent or even morally bad; and for making the selfish propensities contribute to the support of wise arrangements, civil and military.—Perhaps there never appeared in the field more steady soldiers—troops which it would have been more difficult to conquer with such knowledge of the art of war as then existed—than those commanded by Fairfax and Cromwell: let us see from what root these armies grew. 'Cromwell,' says Sir Philip Warwick, 'made use of the zeal and credulity of these persons' (that is—such of the people as had, in the author's language, the fanatic humour); 'teaching them (as they too readily taught themselves) that they engaged for God, when he led them against his vicegerent the King. And, where this opinion met with a natural courage, it made them bolder—and too often crueller; and, where natural courage wanted, zeal supplied its place. And at first they chose rather to die than flee; and custom removed fear of danger:' and afterwards—

finding the sweet of good pay, and of opulent plunder, and of preferment suitable to activity and merit—the lucrative part made gain seem to them a natural member of godliness. And I cannot here omit' (continues the author) 'a character of this army which General Fairfax gave unto myself; when, complimenting him with the regularity and temperance of his army, he told me, The best common soldiers he had—came out of our army and from the garrisons he had taken in. So (says he) I found you had made them good soldiers; and I have made them good men. But, upon this whole matter, it may appear' (concludes the author) 'that the spirit of discipline of warr may beget that spirit of discipline which even Solomon describes as the spirit of wisdom and obedience.' Apply this process to the growth and maturity of an armed force in Spain. In making a comparison of the two cases; to the sense of the insults and injuries which, as Spaniards and as human Beings, they have received and have to dread,—and to the sanctity which an honourable resistance has already conferred upon their misfortunes,—add the devotion of that people to their religion as Catholics;—and it will not be doubted that the superiority of the radical feeling is, on their side, immeasurable. There is (I cannot refrain from observing) in the Catholic religion, and in the character of its Priesthood especially, a source of animation and fortitude in desperate struggles—which may be relied upon as one of the best hopes of the cause. The narrative of the first siege of Zaragoza, lately published in this country, and which I earnestly recommend to the reader's perusal, informs us that,—'In every part of the town where the danger was most imminent, and the French the most numerous,—was Padre St. Iago Sass, curate of a parish in Zaragoza. As General Palafox made his rounds through the city, he often beheld Sass alternately playing the part of a Priest and a Soldier; sometimes administering the sacrament to the dying; and, at others, fighting in the most determined manner against the enemies of his country.—He was found so serviceable in inspiring the people with religious sentiments, and in leading them on to danger, that the General has placed him in a situation where both his piety and courage may continue to be as useful as before; and he is now both Captain in the army, and Chaplain to the commander-in-chief.'

The reader will have been reminded, by the passage above cited from Sir Philip Warwick's memoirs, of the details given, in the earlier part of this tract, concerning the course which (as it appeared to me) might with advantage be pursued in Spain: I must request him to combine those details with such others as have since been given: the whole would have been further illustrated, if I could sooner have returned to the subject; but it was first necessary to examine the grounds of hope in the grand and disinterested passions, and in the laws of universal morality. My attention has therefore been chiefly directed to these laws and passions; in order to elevate, in some degree, the conceptions of my readers; and with a wish to rectify and fix, in this fundamental point, their judgements. The truth of the general reasoning will, I have no doubt, be acknowledged by men of uncorrupted natures and practised understandings; and the conclusion, which I have repeatedly drawn, will be acceded to; namely, that no resistance can be prosperous which does not look, for its chief support, to these principles and feelings. If, however, there should be men who still fear (as I have been speaking of things under combinations which are transitory) that the action of these powers cannot be sustained; to such I answer that,—if there be a necessity that it should be sustained at the point to which it first ascended, or should recover that height if there have been a fall,—Nature will provide for that necessity. The cause is in Tyranny: and that will again call forth the effect out of its holy retirements. Oppression, its own blind and predestined enemy, has poured this of blessedness upon Spain,—that the enormity of the outrages, of which she has been the victim, has created an object of love and of hatred—of apprehensions and of wishes—adequate (if that be possible) to the utmost demands of the human spirit. The heart that serves in this cause, if it languish, must languish from its own constitutional weakness; and not through want of nourishment from without. But it is a belief propagated in books, and which passes currently among talking men as part of their familiar wisdom, that the hearts of the many *are* constitutionally weak; that they *do* languish; and are slow to answer to the requisitions of things. I entreat those, who are in this delusion, to look behind them and about them for the evidence of experience. Now this, rightly understood, not only gives no support to any such belief; but proves that the truth is in direct opposition to it. The history of all ages; tumults after tumults; wars, foreign or civil, with short or with no breathing-spaces, from generation to generation; wars—why and wherefore? yet with courage, with perseverance, with self-sacrifice, with enthusiasm—with cruelty driving forward the cruel man from its own terrible nakedness, and attracting the more benign by the accompaniment of some shadow which seems to sanctify it; the senseless weaving and interweaving of factions—vanishing and reviving and piercing each other like the Northern Lights; public commotions, and those in the bosom of the individual; the long calenture to which the Lover is subject; the blast, like the blast of the desart, which sweeps perennially through a frightful solitude of its own making in the mind of the Gamester; the slowly quickening but ever quickening descent of appetite down which the Miser is propelled; the agony and cleaving oppression of grief; the ghost-like hauntings of shame; the incubus of revenge; the life-distemper of ambition;—these inward existences, and the visible and familiar occurrences of daily life in every town and village; the patient curiosity and contagious acclamations of the multitude in the streets of the city and within the walls of the theatre; a procession, or a rural dance; a hunting, or a horse-race; a flood, or a fire; rejoicing and ringing of bells for an unexpected gift of good fortune, or the coming of a foolish heir to his estate;——these demonstrate incontestibly that the passions of men (I mean, the soul of sensibility in the heart of man)—in all quarrels, in all contests, in all quests, in all delights, in all employments which are either sought by men or thrust upon them—do immeasurably transcend their objects. The true sorrow of humanity consists in this;—not that the mind of man fails; but that the course and demands of action and of life so rarely correspond with the dignity and intensity of human desires: and hence that, which is slow to languish, is too easily turned aside and abused. But—with the remembrance of what has been done, and in the face of the interminable evils which are threatened—a Spaniard can never have cause to complain of this, while a follower of the tyrant remains in arms upon the Peninsula.

Here then they, with whom I *hope*, take their stand. There

is a spiritual community binding together the living and the dead; the good, the brave, and the wise, of all ages. We would not be rejected from this community: and therefore do we hope. We look forward with erect mind, thinking and feeling: it is an obligation of duty: take away the sense of it, and the moral being would die within us.—Among the most illustrious of that fraternity, whose encouragement we participate, is an Englishman who sacrificed his life in devotion to a cause bearing a stronger likeness to this than any recorded in history. It is the elder Sidney—a deliverer and defender, whose name I have before uttered with reverence; who, treating of the war in the Netherlands against Philip the Second, thus writes: 'If her Majesty,' says he, 'were the fountain; I wold fear, considering what I daily find, that we shold wax dry. But she is but a means whom God useth. And I know not whether I am deceaved; but I am fully persuaded, that, if she shold withdraw herself, other springs wold rise to help this action. For, methinks, I see the great work indeed in hand against the abuses of the world; wherein it is no greater fault to have confidence in man's power, than it is too hastily to despair of God's work.'

The pen, which I am guiding, has stopped in my hand; and I have scarcely power to proceed.—I will lay down one principle; and then shall contentedly withdraw from the sanctuary.

When wickedness acknowledges no limit but the extent of her power, and advances with aggravated impatience like a devouring fire; the only worthy or adequate opposition is—that of virtue submitting to no circumscription of her endeavours save that of her rights, and aspiring from the impulse of her own ethereal zeal. The Christian exhortation for the individual is here the precept for nations—'Be ye therefore perfect; even as your Father, which is in Heaven, is perfect.'

Upon a future occasion (if what has been now said meets with attention) I shall point out the steps by which the practice of life may be lifted up towards these high precepts. I shall have to speak of the child as well as the man; for with the child, or the youth, may we begin with more hope: but I am not in despair even for the man; and chiefly from the inordinate evils of our time. There are (as I shall attempt to shew) tender and subtile ties by which these principles, that love to soar in the pure region, are connected with the ground-nest in which they were fostered and from which they take their flight.

The outermost and all-embracing circle of benevolence has inward concentric circles which, like those of the spider's web, are bound together by links, and rest upon each other; making one frame, and capable of one tremor; circles narrower and narrower, closer and closer, as they lie more near to the centre of self from which they proceeded, and which sustains the whole. The order of life does not require that the sublime and disinterested feelings should have to trust long to their own unassisted power. Nor would the attempt consist either with their dignity or their humility. They condescend, and they adopt: they know the time of their repose; and the qualities which are worthy of being admitted into their service—of being their inmates, their companions, or their substitutes. I shall strive to shew that these principles and movements of wisdom—so far from towering above the support of prudence, or rejecting the rules of experience, for the better conduct of those multifarious actions which are alike necessary to the attainment of ends good or bad—do instinctively prompt the sole prudence which cannot fail. The higher mode of being does not exclude, but necessarily includes, the lower; the intellectual does not exclude, but necessarily includes, the sentient; the sentient, the animal; and the animal, the vital—to its lowest degrees. Wisdom is the hidden root which thrusts forth the stalk of prudence; and these uniting feed and uphold 'the bright consummate flower'—National Happiness—the end, the conspicuous crown, and ornament of the whole.

I have announced the feelings of those who hope: yet one word more to those who despond. And first; *he* stands upon a hideous precipice (and it will be the same with all who may succeed to him and his iron sceptre)—he who has outlawed himself from society by proclaiming, with act and deed, that he acknowledges no mastery but power. This truth must be evident to all who breathe—from the dawn of childhood, till the last gleam of twilight is lost in the darkness of dotage. But take the tyrant as he is, in the plenitude of his supposed strength. The vast country of Germany, in spite of the rusty but too strong fetters of corrupt princedoms and degenerate nobility,—Germany—with its citizens, its peasants, and its philosophers—will not lie quiet under the weight of injuries which has been heaped upon it. There is a sleep, but no death, among the mountains of Switzerland. Florence, and Venice, and Genoa, and Rome,—have their own poignant recollections, and a majestic train of glory in past ages. The stir of emancipation may again be felt at the mouths as well as at the sources of the Rhine. Poland perhaps will not be insensible; Kosciusko and his compeers may not have bled in vain. Nor is Hungarian loyalty to be overlooked. And, for Spain itself, the territory is wide: let it be overrun: the torrent will weaken as the water spreads. And, should all resistance disappear, be not daunted: extremes meet: and how often do hope and despair almost touch each other—though unconscious of their neighbourhood, because their faces are turned different ways! yet, in a moment, the one shall vanish; and the other begin a career in the fulness of her joy.

But we may turn from these thoughts: for the present juncture is most auspicious. Upon liberty, and upon liberty alone, can there be permanent dependence; but a temporary relief will be given by the share which Austria is about to take in the war. Now is the time for a great and decisive effort; and, if Britain does not avail herself of it, her disgrace will be indelible, and the loss infinite. If there be ground of hope in the crimes and errors of the enemy, he has furnished enough of both: but imbecility in his opponents (above all, the imbecility of the British) has hitherto preserved him from the natural consequences of his ignorance, his meanness of mind, his transports of infirm fancy, and his guilt. Let us hasten to redeem ourselves. The field is open for a commanding British military force to clear the Peninsula of the enemy, while the better half of his power is occupied with Austria. For the South of Spain, where the first effort of regeneration was made, is yet free. Saragossa (which, by a truly efficient British army, might have been relieved) has indeed fallen; but leaves little to regret; for consummate have been her fortitude and valour. The citizens and soldiers of Saragossa are to be envied: for they have completed the circle of their duty; they have done all that could be wished—all that could be prayed for. And, though the cowardly malice of the enemy gives too much reason to fear that their leader Palafox (with the fate of Toussaint) will soon be among the dead, it is the high privilege of men who have performed what he has performed—that they cannot be missed; and, in moments of weakness only, can they be lamented: their actions represent them every where and for ever. Palafox has taken his place as parent and ancestor of innumerable heroes.

Oh! that the surviving chiefs of the Spanish people may prove worthy of their situation! With such materials,—their labour would be pleasant, and their success certain. But—though heads of a nation venerable for antiquity, and having good cause to preserve with reverence the institutions of their elder forefathers—they must not be indiscriminately afraid of new things. It is their duty to restore the good which has fallen into disuse; and also to create, and to adopt. Young scions of polity must be engrafted on the time-worn trunk: a new fortress must be reared upon the ancient and living rock of justice. Then would it be seen, while the superstructure stands inwardly immoveable, in how short a space of time the ivy and wild plant would climb up from the base, and clasp the naked walls; the storms, which could not shake, would weather-stain; and the edifice, in the day of its youth, would appear to be one with the rock upon which it was planted, and to grow out of it.

But let us look to ourselves. Our offences are unexpiated: and, wanting light, we want strength. With reference to this guilt and to this deficiency, and to my own humble efforts towards removing both, I shall conclude with the words of a man of disciplined spirit, who withdrew from the too busy world—not out of indifference to its welfare, or to forget its concerns—but retired for wider compass of eye-sight, that he might comprehend and see in just proportions and relations; knowing above all that he, who hath not first made himself master of the horizon of his own mind, must look beyond it only to be deceived. It is Petrarch who thus writes: 'Haec dicerem, et quicquid in rem praesentem et indignatio dolorque dictarent; nisi obtorpuisse animos, actumque de rebus nostris, crederem. Nempe, qui aliis iter rectum ostendere solebamus, nunc (quod exitio proximum est) coeci coecis ducibus per abrupta rapimur; alienoque circumvolvimur exemplo; quid velimus, nescii. Nam (ut cœptum exequar) totum hoc malum, seu nostrum proprium seu potius omnium gentium commune, Ignoratio Finis facit.

Nesciunt inconsulti homines quid agant: ideo quicquid agunt, mox ut cœperint, vergit in nauseam. Hinc ille discursus sine termino; hinc, medio calle, discordiae; et, ante exitum, DAMNATA PRINCIPIA; et expletè nihil.'

As an act of respect to the English reader—I shall add, to the same purpose, the words of our own Milton; who, contemplating our ancestors in his day, thus speaks of them and their errors:—'Valiant, indeed, and prosperous to win a field; but, to know the end and reason of winning, injudicious and unwise. Hence did their victories prove as fruitless, as their losses dangerous; and left them still languishing under the same grievances that men suffer conquered. Which was indeed unlikely to go otherwise; unless men more than vulgar bred up in the knowledge of ancient and illustrious deeds, invincible against many and vain titles, impartial to friendships and relations, had conducted their affairs.'

THE END.

APPENDIX.

A (*page* 67).

When this passage was written, there had appeared only unauthorized accounts of the Board of Inquiry's proceedings. Neither from these however, nor from the official report of the Board (which has been since published), is any satisfactory explanation to be gained on this question—or indeed on any other question of importance. All, which is to be collected from them, is this: the Portuguese General, it appears, offered to unite his whole force with the British on the single condition that they should be provisioned from the British stores; and, accordingly, rests his excuse for not co-operating on the refusal of Sir Arthur Wellesley to comply with this condition. Sir A. W. denies the validity of his excuse; and, more than once, calls it a *pretence;* declaring that, in his belief, Gen. Freire's real motive for not joining was—a mistrust in the competence of the British to appear in the field against the French. This however is mere surmise; and therefore cannot have much weight with those who sincerely sought for satisfaction on this point: moreover, it is a surmise of the individual whose justification rests on making it appear that the difficulty did not arise with himself; and it is right to add, that the only *fact* produced goes to discredit this surmise; viz. that Gen. Friere did, without any delay, furnish the whole number of troops which Sir Arthur engaged to feed. However the Board exhibited so little anxiety to be satisfied on this point, that no positive information was gained.

A reference being here first made to the official report of the Board of Inquiry; I shall make use of the opportunity which it offers to lay before the reader an outline of that Board's proceedings; from which it will appear how far the opinion—pronounced, by the national voice, upon the transactions in Portugal—ought, in sound logic, to be modified by any part of those proceedings.

We find in the warrant under which the Board of Inquiry was to act, and which defined its powers, that an inquiry was to be made into the conditions of the 'armistice and convention; and into all the causes and circumstances, whether arising from the operations of the British army, or otherwise, which led to them.'

Whether answers to the charges of the people of England were made possible by the provisions of this warrant—and, secondly, whether even these provisions have been satisfied by the Board of Inquiry—will best appear by involving those charges in four questions, according to the following scale, which supposes a series of concessions impossible to those who think the nation justified in the language held on the transactions in Portugal.

1. Considering the perfidy with which the French army had entered Portugal; the enormities committed by it during its occupation of that country; the vast military power of which that army was a part, and the use made of that power by its master; the then existing spirit of the Spanish, Portuguese, and British nations; in a word, considering the especial nature of the service, and the individual character of this war;—was it lawful for the British army, under any conceivable circumstances, so long as it had the liberty of re-embarking, to make *any conceivable* convention? i. e. Was the negative evil of a total failure in every object for which it had been sent to Portugal of worse tendency than the positive evil of acknowledging in the French army a fair title to the privileges of an honourable enemy by consenting to a mode of treaty which (in its very name, implying a reciprocation of concession and respect) must be under any limitations as much more indulgent than an ordinary capitulation, as that again must (in its severest form) be more indulgent than the only favour which the French marauders could presume upon obtaining—viz. permission to surrender at discretion?

To this question the reader need not be told that these pages give a naked unqualified denial; and that to establish the reasonableness of that denial is one of their main purposes: but, for the benefit of the men accused, let it be supposed granted; and then the second question will be

2. Was it lawful for the English army, in the case of its being reduced to the supposed dilemma of either re-embarking or making *some* convention, to make *that specifical* convention which it did make at Cintra?

This is of necessity and *à fortiori* denied; and it has been proved that neither to this, nor any other army, could it be lawful to make such a convention—not merely under the actual but under any conceivable circumstances; let however this too, on behalf of the parties accused, be granted; and then the third question will be

3. Was the English Army reduced to that dilemma?

4. Finally, this also being conceded (which not even the Generals have dared to say), it remains to ask by whose and by what misconduct did an army—confessedly the arbiter of its own movements and plans at the opening of the campaign—forfeit that free agency—either to the extent of the extremity supposed, or of any approximation to that extremity?

Now of these four possible questions in the minds of all those who condemn the convention of Cintra, it is obvious that the King's warrant supposes only the three latter to exist (since, though it allows inquiry to be made into the individual convention, it no where questions the tolerability of a convention *in genere*); and it is no less obvious that the Board, acting under that warrant, has noticed only the last—i. e. by what series of military movements the army was brought into a state of difficulty which justified *a* convention (the Board taking for granted throughout—1st, That such a state could exist; 2ndly, That it actually did exist; and 3rdly, That—if it existed, and accordingly justified *some imaginable* convention—it must therefore of necessity justify *this* convention).

Having thus shewn that it is on the last question only that the nation could, in deference to the Board of Inquiry, surrender or qualify any opinion which it had previously given—let us ask what answer is gained, from the proceedings of that Board, to the charge involved even in this last question (premising however—first—that this charge was never explicitly made by the public, or at least was ennunciated only in the form of a conjecture—and 2ndly that the answer to it is collected chiefly from the depositions of the parties accused)? Now the whole sum of their answer amounts to no more than this—that, in the opinion of some part of the English staff, an opportunity was lost on the 21st of exchanging the comparatively slow process of reducing the French army by siege for the brilliant and summary one of a *coup-de-main.*

This opportunity, be it observed, was offered only by Gen. Junot's presumption in quitting his defensive positions, and coming out to meet the English army in the field; so that it was an advantage so much over and above what might fairly have been calculated upon: at any rate, if *this* might have been looked for, still the accident of battle, by which a large part of the French army was left in a situation to be cut off, (to the loss of which advantage Sir A. Wellesley ascribes the necessity of a convention) could surely never have been anticipated; and therefore the British army was, even after that loss, in as prosperous a state as it had from the first any right to expect. Hence it is to be inferred, that Sir A. W. must have entered on this campaign with a predetermination to grant a convention in any case, excepting in one single case which he knew to be in the gift of only very extraordinary good fortune. With respect to him, therefore, the charges—pronounced by the national voice —are not only confirmed, but greatly aggravated. Further, with respect to the General who superseded him, all those—who think that such an opportunity of terminating the campaign was really offered, and, through his refusal to take advantage of it, lost—are compelled to suspect in him a want of military skill, or a wilful sacrifice of his duty to the influence of personal rivalry, accordingly as they shall interpret his motives.

The whole which we gain therefore from the Board of Inquiry is—that what we barely suspected is ripened into certainty—and that on all, which we assuredly knew and declared without needing that any tribunal should lend us its sanction, no effort has been made at denial, or disguise, or palliation.

Thus much for the proceedings of the Board of Inquiry, upon which their decision was to be grounded. As to the decision itself, it declares that no further military proceedings are necessary; 'because' (say the members of the Board), 'however some of us may differ in our sentiments respecting the fitness of the convention in the relative situation of the two armies, it is our unanimous declaration that unquestionable zeal and firmness appear throughout to have been exhibited by Generals Sir H. Dalrymple, Sir H. Burrard, and Sir A. Wellesley.' In consequence of this decision, the Commander-in-Chief addressed a letter to the Board—reminding them that, though the words of his Majesty's warrant expressly enjoin that the *conditions* of the Armistice and Convention should be strictly examined and reported upon, they have altogether neglected to give any opinion upon those conditions. They were therefore called upon then to declare their opinion, whether an armistice was adviseable; and (if so) whether the terms of *that* armistice were such as ought to be agreed upon;—and to declare, in like manner, whether a convention was adviseable; and (if so) whether the terms of *that* convention were such as ought to have been agreed upon.

To two of these questions—viz. those which relate to the particular armistice and convention made by the British Generals—the members of the Board (still persevering in their blindness to the other two which express doubt as to the lawfulness of *any* armistice or convention) severally return answers which convey an approbation of the armistice and convention by four members, a disapprobation of the convention by the remaining three, and further a disapprobation of the armistice by one of those three.

Now it may be observed—first—that, even if the investigation had not been a public one, it might have reasonably been concluded, from the circumstance of the Board having omitted to report any opinion concerning the terms of the armistice and the convention, that those terms had not occupied enough of its attention to justify the Board in giving any opinion upon them—whether of approbation or disapprobation; and, secondly,—this conclusion, which might have been made *à priori*, is confirmed by the actual fact that no examination or inquiry of this kind appears throughout the report of its proceedings: and therefore any opinion subsequently given, in consequence of the requisition of the Commander-in-Chief, can lay claim to no more authority upon these points—than the opinion of the same men, if they had never sat in a public Court upon this question. In this condition are all the members, whether they approve or disapprove of the convention. And with respect to the three who disapprove of the convention,—over and above the general impropriety of having, under these circumstances, pronounced a verdict at all in the character of members of that Board—they are subject to an especial charge of inconsistency in having given such an opinion, in their second report, as renders nugatory that which they first pronounced. For the reason—assigned, in their first report, for deeming no further military proceedings necessary—is because it appears that unquestionable *zeal and firmness* were exhibited throughout by the several General Officers; and the reason—assigned by those three who condemn the convention—is that the Generals did not insist upon the terms to which they were entitled; that is (in direct opposition to their former opinions), the Generals shewed a want of firmness and zeal. If then the Generals were acquitted, in the first case, solely upon the ground of having displayed firmness and zeal; a confessed want of firmness and zeal, in the second case, implies conversely a ground of censure—rendering (in the opinions of these three members) further military proceedings absolutely necessary. They,—who are most aware of the unconstitutional frame of this Court or Board, and of the perplexing situation in which its members must have found themselves placed,—will have the least difficulty in excusing this inconsistency: it is however to be regretted; particularly in the instance of the Earl of Moira;—who, disapproving both of the Convention and Armistice, has assigned for that disapprobation unanswerable reasons drawn—not from hidden sources, unapproachable except by judicial investigation—but from facts known to all the world.

—The reader will excuse this long note; to which however I must add one word:—Is it not strange that, in the general decision of the Board, zeal and firmness—nakedly considered, and without question of their union with judgment and such other qualities as can alone give them any value —should be assumed as sufficient grounds on which to rest the acquittal of men lying under a charge of military delinquency?

B (*page* 72).

It is not necessary to add, that one of these fears was removed by the actual landing of ten thousand men, under Sir J. Moore, pending the negociation: and yet no change in the terms took place in consequence. This was an important circumstance; and, of itself, determined two of the members of the Board of Inquiry to disapprove of the convention: such an accession entitling Sir H. Dalrymple (and, of course, making it his duty) to insist on more favourable terms. But the argument is complete without it.

C (*page* 75).

I was unwilling to interrupt the reader upon a slight occasion; but I cannot refrain from adding here a word or two by way of comment.—I have said at page 71, speaking of Junot's army, that the British were to encounter the same men, &c. Sir Arthur Wellesley, before the Board of Inquiry, disallowed this supposition; affirming that Junot's army had not then reached Spain, nor could be there for some time. Grant this: was it not stipulated that a messenger should be sent off, immediately after the conclusion of the treaty, to Buonaparte—apprising him of its terms, and when he might expect his troops; and would not this enable him to hurry forward forces to the Spanish frontiers, and to bring them into action—knowing that these troops of Junot's would be ready to support him? What did it matter whether the British were again to measure swords with these identical men; whether these men were even to appear again upon Spanish ground? It was enough, that, if these did not, others would—who could not have been brought to that service, but that these had been released and were doing elsewhere some other service for their master; enough that every thing was provided by the British to land them as near the Spanish frontier (and as speedily) as they could desire.

D (*page* 108).

This attempt, the reader will recollect, is not new to our country;—it was accomplished, at one æra of our history, in that memorable act of an English Parliament, which made it unlawful for any man to ask his neighbour to join him in a petition for redress of grievances; and which thus denied the people 'the benefit of tears and prayers to their own infamous deputies!' For the deplorable state of England and Scotland at that time—see the annals of Charles the Second, and his successor.—We must not forget however that to this state of things, as the cause of those measures which the nation afterwards resorted to, we are originally indebted for the blessing of the Bill of Rights.

E (*page* 159).

I allude here more especially to an address presented to Buonaparte (October 27th, 1808) by the deputies of the new departments of the kingdom of Italy; from which address, as given in the English journals, the following passages are extracted:—

'In the necessity, in which you are to overthrow—to destroy—to disperse your enemies as the wind dissipates the dust, you are not an exterminating angel; but you are the being that extends his thoughts—that measures the face of the earth—to re-establish universal happiness upon better and surer bases.'

* * * * * * * *

'We are the interpreters of a million of souls at the extremity of your kingdom of Italy.'——'Deign, *Sovereign Master of all Things*, to hear (as we doubt not you will)' &c.

The answer begins thus:—

'I *applaud* the sentiments you express in the name of my people of Musora, Metauro, and Tronto.'

F (*page* 163).

This principle, involved in so many of his actions, Buonaparte has of late explicitly avowed: the instances are numerous: it will be sufficient, in this place, to allege one—furnished by his answer to the address cited in the last note:—

'I am particularly attached to your Archbishop of Urbino: that prelate, animated with the true faith, repelled with indignation the advice—and braved the menaces—of those who wished to confound the affairs of Heaven, which never change, with the affairs of this world, which are modified according to circumstances of *force* and policy.'

SUSPENSION OF ARMS

Agreed upon between Lieutenant-General Sir Arthur Wellesley, K.B. *on the one part, and the General-of-Division* Kellermann *on the other part; each having powers from the respective Generals of the French and English Armies.*

Head-Quarters of the English Army, August 22, 1808.

Article I. There shall be, from this date, a Suspension of Arms between the armies of his Britannic Majesty, and his Imperial and Royal Majesty, Napoleon I. for the purpose of negociating a Convention for the evacuation of Portugal by the French army.

Art. II. The Generals-in-Chief of the two armies, and the Commander-in-Chief of the British fleet at the entrance of the Tagus, will appoint a day to assemble, on such part of the coast as shall be judged convenient, to negociate and conclude the said Convention.

Art. III. The river of Sirandre shall form the line of demarkation to be established between the two armies; Torres Vedras shall not be occupied by either.

Art. IV. The General-in-Chief of the English army undertakes to include the Portuguese armies in this suspension of arms: and for them the line of demarkation shall be established from Leyria to Thomar.

Art. V. It is agreed provisionally that the French army shall not, in any case, be considered as prisoners of war; that all the individuals who compose it shall be transported to France with their arms and baggage, and the whole of their private property, from which nothing shall be exempted.

Art. VI. No individual, whether Portuguese, or of a nation allied to France, or French, shall be called to account for his political conduct; their respective property shall be protected; and they shall be at liberty to withdraw from Portugal, within a limited time, with their property.

Art. VII. The neutrality of the port of Lisbon shall be recognised for the Russian fleet: that is to say, that, when the English army or fleet shall be in possession of the city and port, the said Russian fleet shall not be disturbed during its stay; nor stopped when it wishes to sail; nor pursued, when it shall sail, until after the time fixed by the maritime law.

Art. VIII. All the artillery of French calibre, and also the horses of the cavalry, shall be transported to France.

Art. IX. This suspension of arms shall not be broken without forty-eight hours' previous notice.

Done and agreed upon between the above-named Generals, the day and year above-mentioned.

(Signed) Arthur Wellesley.
Kellermann, General-of-Division.

Additional Article.

The garrisons of the places occupied by the French army shall be included in the present Convention, if they have not capitulated before the 25th instant.

(Signed) Arthur Wellesley.
Kellermann, General-of-Division.

(A true Copy.)
A. J. Dalrymple, Captain, Military Secretary.

DEFINITIVE CONVENTION FOR THE EVACUATION OF PORTUGAL BY THE FRENCH ARMY.

The Generals commanding in chief the British and French armies in Portugal, having determined to negociate and conclude a treaty for the evacuation of Portugal by the French troops, on the basis of the agreement entered into on the 22d instant for a suspension of hostilities, have appointed the under-mentioned officers to negociate the same in their names;

viz.—on the part of the General-in-Chief of the British army, Lieutenant-Colonel MURRAY, Quarter-Master-General; and, on the part of the General-in-Chief of the French army, Monsieur KELLERMANN, General-of-Division; to whom they have given authority to negociate and conclude a Convention to that effect, subject to their ratification respectively, and to that of the Admiral commanding the British fleet at the entrance of the Tagus.

Those two officers, after exchanging their full powers, have agreed upon the articles which follow:

ARTICLE I. All the places and forts in the kingdom of Portugal, occupied by the French troops, shall be delivered up to the British army in the state in which they are at the period of the signature of the present Convention.

ART. II. The French troops shall evacuate Portugal with their arms and baggage; they shall not be considered as prisoners of war; and, on their arrival in France, they shall be at liberty to serve.

ART. III. The English Government shall furnish the means of conveyance for the French army; which shall be disembarked in any of the ports of France between Rochefort and L'Orient, inclusively.

ART. IV. The French army shall carry with it all its artillery, of French calibre, with the horses belonging to it, and the tumbrils supplied with sixty rounds per gun. All other artillery, arms, and ammunition, as also the military and naval arsenals, shall be given up to the British army and navy in the state in which they may be at the period of the ratification of the Convention.

ART. V. The French army shall carry with it all its equipments, and all that is comprehended under the name of property of the army; that is to say, its military chest, and carriages attached to the Field Commissariat and Field Hospitals; or shall be allowed to dispose of such part of the same, on its account, as the Commander-in-Chief may judge it unnecessary to embark. In like manner, all individuals of the army shall be at liberty to dispose of their private property of every description; with full security hereafter for the purchasers.

ART. VI. The cavalry are to embark their horses; as also the Generals and other officers of all ranks. It is, however, fully understood, that the means of conveyance for horses, at the disposal of the British Commanders, are very limited; some additional conveyance may be procured in the port of Lisbon; the number of horses to be embarked by the troops shall not exceed six hundred; and the number embarked by the Staff shall not exceed two hundred. At all events every facility will be given to the French army to dispose of the horses, belonging to it, which cannot be embarked.

ART. VII. In order to facilitate the embarkation, it shall take place in three divisions; the last of which will be principally composed of the garrisons of the places, of the cavalry, the artillery, the sick, and the equipment of the army. The first division shall embark within seven days of the date of the ratification; or sooner, if possible.

ART. VIII. The garrison of Elvas and its forts, and of Peniche and Palmela, will be embarked at Lisbon; that of Almaida at Oporto, or the nearest harbour. They will be accompanied on their march by British Commissaries, charged with providing for their subsistence and accommodation.

Art. IX. All the sick and wounded, who cannot be embarked with the troops, are entrusted to the British army. They are to be taken care of, whilst they remain in this country, at the expence of the British Government; under the condition of the same being reimbursed by France when the final evacuation is effected. The English government will provide for their return to France; which shall take place by detachments of about one hundred and fifty (or two hundred) men at a time. A sufficient number of French medical officers shall be left behind to attend them.

Art. X. As soon as the vessels employed to carry the army to France shall have disembarked it in the harbours specified, or in any other of the ports of France to which stress of weather may force them, every facility shall be given them to return to England without delay; and security against capture until their arrival in a friendly port.

Art. XI. The French army shall be concentrated in Lisbon, and within a distance of about two leagues from it. The English army will approach within three leagues of the capital; and will be so placed as to leave about one league between the two armies.

Art. XII. The forts of St. Julien, the Bugio, and Cascais, shall be occupied by the British troops on the ratification of the Convention. Lisbon and its citadel, together with the forts and batteries, as far as the Lazaretto or Tarfuria on one side, and fort St. Joseph on the other, inclusively, shall be given up on the embarkation of the second division; as shall also the harbour; and all armed vessels in it of every description, with their rigging, sails, stores, and ammunition. The fortresses of Elvas, Almaida, Peniche, and Palmela, shall be given up as soon as the British troops can arrive to occupy them. In the mean time, the General-in-Chief of the British army will give notice of the present Convention to the garrisons of those places, as also to the troops before them, in order to put a stop to all further hostilities.

Art. XIII. Commissioners shall be named, on both sides, to regulate and accelerate the execution of the arrangements agreed upon.

Art. XIV. Should there arise doubts as to the meaning of any article, it will be explained favourably to the French army.

Art. XV. From the date of the ratification of the present Convention, all arrears of contributions, requisitions, or claims whatever, of the French Government, against the subjects of Portugal, or any other individuals residing in this country, founded on the occupation of Portugal by the French troops in the month of December 1807, which may not have been paid up, are cancelled; and all sequestrations laid upon their property, moveable or immoveable, are removed; and the free disposal of the same is restored to the proper owners.

Art. XVI. All subjects of France, or of powers in friendship or alliance with France, domiciliated in Portugal, or accidentally in this country, shall be protected: their property of every kind, moveable and immoveable, shall be respected: and they shall be at liberty either to accompany the French army, or to remain in Portugal. In either case their property is guaranteed to them; with the liberty of retaining or of disposing of it, and passing the produce of the sale thereof into France, or any other country where they may fix their residence; the space of one year being allowed them for that purpose.

It is fully understood, that the shipping is excepted from this arrangement; only, however, in so far as regards leaving the Port; and that none of the stipulations above-mentioned can be made the pretext of any commercial speculation.

Art. XVII. No native of Portugal shall be rendered accountable for his political conduct during the period of the occupation of this country by the French army; and all those who have continued in the exercise of their employments, or who have accepted situations under the French Government, are placed under the protection of the British Commanders: they shall sustain no injury in their persons or property; it not having been at their option to be obedient, or not, to the French Government: they are also at liberty to avail themselves of the stipulations of the 16th Article.

Art. XVIII. The Spanish troops detained on board ship in the Port of Lisbon shall be given up to the Commander-in-Chief of the British army; who engages to obtain of the Spaniards to restore such French subjects, either military or civil, as may have been detained in Spain, without being taken in battle, or in consequence of military operations, but on occasion of the occurrences of the 29th of last May, and the days immediately following.

Art. XIX. There shall be an immediate exchange established for all ranks of prisoners made in Portugal since the commencement of the present hostilities.

Art. XX. Hostages of the rank of field-officers shall be mutually furnished on the part of the British army and navy, and on that of the French army, for the reciprocal guarantee of the present Convention. The officer of the British army shall be restored on the completion of the articles which concern the army; and the officer of the navy on the disembarkation of the French troops in their own country. The like is to take place on the part of the French army.

Art. XXI. It shall be allowed to the General-in-Chief of the French army to send an officer to France with intelligence of the present Convention. A vessel will be furnished by the British Admiral to convey him to Bourdeaux or Rochefort.

Art. XXII. The British Admiral will be invited to accommodate His Excellency the Commander-in-Chief, and the other principal officers of the French army, on board of ships of war.

Done and concluded at Lisbon this 30th day of August, 1808.

(Signed) George Murray, Quarter-Master-General.
Kellermann, Le Général de Division.

We, the Duke of Abrantes, General-in-Chief of the French army, have ratified and do ratify the present Definitive Convention in all its articles, to be executed according to its form and tenor.

(Signed) The Duke of Abrantes.

Head-Quarters—Lisbon, 30*th August*, 1808.

Additional Articles to the Convention of the 30*th of August*, 1808.

Art. I. The individuals in the civil employment of the army made prisoners, either by the British troops, or by the Portuguese, in any part of Portugal, will be restored, as is customary, without exchange.

Art. II. The French army shall be subsisted from its own magazines up to the day of embarkation; the garrisons up to the day of the evacuation of the fortresses.

The remainder of the magazines shall be delivered over, in the usual form, to the British Government; which charges itself with the subsistence of the men and horses of the army from the above-mentioned periods till they arrive in France; under the condition of their being reimbursed by the French Government for the excess of the expense beyond the estimates, to be made by both parties, of the value of the magazines delivered up to the British army.

The provisions on board the ships of war, in possession of the French army, will be taken in account by the British Government in like manner with the magazines in the fortresses.

Art. III. The General commanding the British troops will take the necessary measures for re-establishing the free circulation of the means of subsistence between the country and the capital.

Done and concluded at Lisbon this 30th day of August, 1808.

(Signed) George Murray, Quarter-Master-General.
Kellermann, Le Général de Division.

We, Duke of Abrantes, General-in-Chief of the French army, have ratified and do ratify the additional articles of the Convention, to be executed according to their form and tenor.

The Duke of Abrantes.

(A true Copy.)
A. J. Dalrymple, Captain, Military Secretary.

Articles of a Convention entered into between Vice-Admiral Seniavin, *Knight of the Order of St. Alexander and other Russian Orders, and Admiral Sir* Charles Cotton, *Bart. for the Surrender of the Russian Fleet, now anchored in the River Tagus.*

Art. I. The ships of war of the Emperor of Russia, now in the Tagus (as specified in the annexed list), shall be delivered up to Admiral Sir Charles Cotton, immediately, with all their stores as they now are; to be sent to England, and there held as a deposit by his Britannic Majesty, to be restored to His Imperial Majesty within six months after the conclusion of a peace between His Britannic Majesty and His Imperial Majesty the Emperor of all the Russias.

Art. II. Vice-Admiral Seniavin, with the officers, sailors, and marines, under his command, to return to Russia, without any condition or stipulation respecting their future services; to be conveyed thither in men of war, or proper vessels, at the expence of His Britannic Majesty.

Done and concluded on board the ship Twerday, in the Tagus, and on board His Britannic Majesty's ship Hibernia, off the mouth of that river, the 3d day of September 1808.

(Signed) De Seniavin.
(Signed) Charles Cotton.
(Counter-signed) By command of the Admiral,
L. Sass, Assesseur de Collège.
(Counter-signed) By command of the Admiral,
James Kennedy, Secretary.

POSTSCRIPT

ON SIR JOHN MOORE'S LETTERS.

Whilst the latter sheets of this work were passing through the press, there was laid before Parliament a series of correspondence between the English Government and its servants in Spain; amongst which were the letters of Sir John Moore. That these letters, even with minds the least vigilant to detect contradictions and to make a commentary from the past actions of the Spaniards, should have had power to alienate them from the Spanish cause—could never have been looked for; except indeed by those who saw, in the party spirit on this question, a promise that more than ordinary pains would be taken to misrepresent their contents and to abuse the public judgment. But however it was at any rate to have been expected—both from the place which Sir J. Moore held in the Nation's esteem previously to his Spanish campaign, and also especially from that which (by his death in battle) he had so lately taken in its affections—that they would weigh a good deal in depressing the general sympathy with Spain: and therefore the Author of this work was desirous that all which these letters themselves, or other sources of information, furnished to mitigate and contradict Sir J. M.'s opinions—should be laid before the public: but—being himself at a great distance from London, and not having within his reach all the documents necessary for this purpose—he has honoured the friend, who corrects the press errors, by making over that task to him; and the reader is therefore apprised, that the Author is not responsible for any thing which follows.

* * * * * * * *

Those, who have not examined these letters for themselves, will have collected enough of their general import, from conversation and the public prints, to know that they pronounce an opinion unfavourable to the Spaniards. They will perhaps have yet to learn that this opinion is not supported by any body of *facts* (for of facts only three are given; and those, as we shall see, misrepresented); but solely by the weight of Sir John Moore's personal authority. This being the case, it becomes the more important to assign the value of that authority, by making such deductions from the present public estimate of it, as are either fairly to be presumed from his profession and office, or directly inferred from the letters under consideration.

As reasons for questioning *à priori* the impartiality of these letters,—it might be suggested (in reference to what they would be likely to *omit*)—first—that they are the letters of a *soldier;* that is, of a man trained (by the prejudices of his profession) to despise, or at least to rate as secondary, those resources which for Spain must be looked to as supreme;—and, secondly, that they are the letters of a *general;* that is, of a soldier removed by his rank from the possibility of any extensive intercourse with the lower classes; concerning whom the question chiefly was. But it is more important to remark (in reference to what they would be likely to *mis-state*)—thirdly—that they are the letters of a *commander-in-chief;* standing—from the very day when he took the field—in a dilemma which compelled him to risk the safety of his army by advancing, or its honour by retreating; and having to make out an apology, for either issue, to the very persons who had imposed this dilemma upon him.—The reader is requested to attend to this. Sir John Moore found himself in Leon with a force 'which, if united,' (to quote his own words) 'would not exceed 26,000 men.' Such a force, after the defeat of the advanced armies,—he was sure—could effect nothing; the best result he could anticipate was an inglorious retreat. That he should be in this situation at the very opening of the campaign, he saw, would declare to all Europe that somewhere there must be blame: but where? with himself he knew that there was none: the English Government (with whom he must have seen that at least a part of the blame lay—for sending him so late, and with a force so lamentably incommensurate to the demands of the service) it was not for him—holding the situation that he did—openly to accuse (though, by implication, he often does accuse them); and therefore it became his business to look to the Spaniards; and, in their conduct, to search for palliations of that inefficiency on his part—which else the persons, to whom he was writing, would understand as charged upon themselves. Writing with such a purpose—and under a double fettering of his faculties; first from anxious forebodings of calamity or dishonour; and secondly from the pain he must have felt at not being free to censure those with whom he could not but be aware that the embarrassments of his situation had, at least in part, originated—we might expect that it would not be difficult for him to find, in the early events of the campaign, all which he sought; and to deceive himself into a belief, that, in stating these events without any commentary or even hints as to the relative circumstances under which they took place (which only could give to the naked facts their value and due meaning), he was making no misrepresentations,—and doing the Spaniards no injustice.

These suggestions are made with the greater earnestness, as it is probable that the honourable death of Sir John Moore will have given so much more weight to his opinion on any subject—as, if these suggestions be warranted, it is entitled on this subject to less weight—than the opinion of any other individual equally intelligent, and not liable (from high office and perplexity of situation) to the same influences of disgust or prejudice.

That these letters *were* written under some such influences, is plain throughout: we find, in them, reports of the four first events in the campaign; and, in justice to the Spaniards, it must be said that all are virtually mis-statements. Take two instances:

1. The main strength and efforts of the French were, at the opening of the campaign, directed against the army of Gen. Blake. The issue is thus given by Sir J. M.:—'Gen. Blake's army in Biscay has been defeated—dispersed; and its officers and men are flying in every direction.' Could it be supposed that the army, whose matchless exertions and endurances are all merged in this over-charged (and almost insulting) statement of their result, was, 'mere peasantry' (Sir J. M.'s own words) and opposed to greatly superior numbers of veteran troops? Confront with this account the description given by an eye-witness (Major-Gen. Leith) of their constancy and the trials of their constancy; remembering that, for ten successive days, they were engaged (under the pressure of similar hardships, with the addition of one not mentioned here, viz.—a want of clothing) in continued actions with the French:—'Here I shall take occasion to state another instance of the patience (and, I will add, the chearfulness) of the Spanish soldiers under the greatest privations.—After the action of Soronosa on the 31st ult., it was deemed expedient by Gen. Blake, for the purpose of forming a junction with the second division and the army of Asturias, that the army should make long, rapid, and continued marches through a country at any time incapable of feeding so numerous an army, and at present almost totally drained of provisions. From the 30th of October to the present day (Nov. 6), with the exception of a small and partial issue of bread at Bilboa on the morning of the 1st of November, this army has been totally destitute of bread, wine, or spirits; and has literally lived on the scanty supply of beef and sheep which those mountains afford. Yet never was there a symptom of complaint or murmur; the soldiers' minds appearing to be entirely occupied with the idea of being led against the enemy at Bilboa.'—'It is impossible for me to do justice to the gallantry and energy of the divisions engaged this day. The army are loud in expressing their desires to be led against the enemy at Bilboa; the universal exclamation is—The bayonet! the bayonet! lead us back to Soronosa.'

2. On the 10th of November the Estramaduran advanced guard, of about 12,000 men, was defeated at Burgos by a division of the French army *selected* for the service—and having a vast superiority in cavalry and artillery. This event, with the same neglect of circumstances as in the former instance, Sir J. M. thus reports:—'The French, after beating the army of Estramadura, are advanced at Burgos.' Now surely to any unprejudiced mind the bare fact of 12,000 men (chiefly raw levies) having gone forward to meet and to find out the main French army—under all the oppression which, to the ignorant of the upper and lower classes throughout Europe, there is in the name of Bonaparte—must appear, under any issue, a title to the highest admiration, such as would have made this slight and incidental mention of it impossible.

The two next events—viz. the forcing of the pass at Somosierra by the Polish horse, and the partial defeat of Castanos—are, as might be shewn even from the French bulletins, no less misrepresented. With respect to the first,—Sir J. Moore, over-looking the whole drama of that noble defence, gives only the catastrophe; and his account of the second will appear, from any report, to be an exaggeration.

It may be objected that—since Sir J. M. no where alleges these events as proving any thing against the Spaniards, but simply as accounting for his own plans (in which view, howsoever effected, whether with or without due resistance, they were entitled to the same value)—it is unfair to say that, by giving them uncircumstantially, he has misrepresented them. But it must be answered, that, in letters containing elsewhere (though not immediately in connexion with these statements) opinions unfavourable to the Spaniards, to omit any thing making *for* them—*is* to misrepresent in effect. And, further, it shall now be shown that even those three charges —which Sir J. M. *does* allege in proof of his opinions—are as glaringly mis-stated.

The first of those charges is the most important: I give it to the reader in the words of Sir John Moore:—'The French cavalry from Burgos, in small detachments, are over-running the province of Leon; raising contributions; to which the inhabitants submit without the least resistance.' Now here it cannot be meant that no efforts at resistance were made by individuals or small parties; because this would not only contradict the universal laws of human nature,—but would also be at utter variance with Sir J. M.'s repeated complaints that he could gain no information of what was passing in his neighbourhood. It is meant therefore that there was no regular organised resistance; no resistance such as might be made the subject of an official report. Now we all know that the Spaniards have every where suffered deplorably from a want of cavalry; and, in the absence of that, hear from a military man (Major-Gen. Brodrick) *why* there was no resistance: '—At that time I was not aware how remarkably the plains of Leon and Castille differ from any other I have seen; nor how strongly the circumstances, which constitute that difference, enforce the opinion I venture to express.' (He means the necessity of cavalry reinforcements from England.) 'My road from Astorga lay through a vast open space, extending from 5 to 20 or more miles on every side; without a single accident of ground which could enable a body of infantry to check a pursuing enemy, or to cover its own retreat. In such ground, any corps of infantry might be insulted, to the very gates of the town it occupied, by cavalry far inferior in numbers; *contributions raised under their eyes*, and the whole neighbourhood exhausted of its resources, *without the possibility of their opposing any resistance to such incursions.*'

The second charge is made on the retreat to Corunna: 'the Gallicians, though armed,' Sir J. M. says, 'made no attempt to stop the passage of the French through the mountains.' That they were armed—is a proof that they had an *intention* to do so (as one of our journals observed): but what encouragement had they in that intention from the sight of a regular force—more than 30,000 strong—abandoning, without a struggle, passes where (as an English general asserts) 'a body of a thousand men might stop an army of twenty times the number?'

The third charge relates to the same Province: it is a complaint that 'the people run away; the villages are deserted;' and again, in his last letter,—'They abandoned their dwellings at our approach; drove away their carts, oxen, and every thing which could be of the smallest aid to the army.' To this charge, in so far as it may be thought to criminate the Spaniards, a full answer is furnished by their accuser himself in the following memorable sentence in another part of the very same letter:—'I am sorry to say that the army, whose conduct I had such reason to extol in its march through Portugal and on its arrival in Spain, has totally changed its character since it began to retreat.' What do we collect from this passage? Assuredly that the army ill-treated the Gallicians; for there is no other way in which an army, as a body, can offend—excepting by an indisposition to fight; and that interpretation (besides that we are all sure that no English army could *so* offend) Sir J. Moore expressly guards against in the next sentence.

The English army then treated its Ally as an enemy: and,—though there are alleviations of its conduct in its great sufferings,—yet it must be remembered that these sufferings were due—not to the Gallicians—but to circumstances over which they had no controul—to the precipitancy of the retreat, the inclemency of the weather, and the poverty of the country; and that (knowing this) they must have had a double sense of injustice in any outrages of an English army, from contrasting them with the professed objects of that army in entering Spain.—It is to be observed that the answer to the second charge would singly have been some answer to this; and, reciprocally, that the answer to this is a full answer to the second.

Having thus shewn that, in Sir J. Moore's very inaccurate statements of facts, we have some further reasons for a previous distrust of any opinion which is supported by those statements,—it is now time to make the reader acquainted with the real terms and extent of that opinion. For it is far less to be feared that, from his just respect for him who gave it, he should allow it an undue weight in his judgment—than that, reposing on the faithfulness of the abstracts and reports of these letters, he should really be still ignorant of its exact tenor.

The whole amount then of what Sir John Moore has alleged against the Spaniards, in any place but one, is comprised in this sentence:—'The enthusiasm, of which we have heard so much, no where appears; whatever good-will there is (and I believe amongst the lower orders there is a great deal) is taken no advantage of.' It is true that, in that one place (viz. in his last letter written at Corunna), he charges the Spaniards with 'apathy and indifference:' but, as this cannot be reconciled with his concession of *a great deal of good-will*, we are bound to take that as his real and deliberate opinion which he gave under circumstances that allowed him most coolness and freedom of judgment.—The Spaniards then were wanting in enthusiasm. Now what is meant by enthusiasm? Does it mean want of ardour and zeal in battle? This Sir J. Moore no where asserts; and, even without a direct acknowledgement of their good conduct in the field (of which he had indeed no better means of judging than we in England), there is involved in his statement of the relative numbers of the French and Spaniards—combined with our knowledge of the time during which they maintained their struggle—a sufficient testimony to that; even if the events of the first campaign had not made it superfluous. Does it mean then a want of good-will to the cause? So far from this, we have seen that Sir J. M. admits that there was, in that class where it was most wanted, 'a great deal' of good-will. And, in the present condition of Spain, let it be recollected what it is that this implies. We see, in the intercepted letter to Marshal Soult (transmitted by Sir J. M.), that the French keep accurate registers of the behaviour of the different towns; and this was, no doubt, well known throughout Spain. Therefore to shew any signs of good-will—much more to give a kind welcome to the English (as had been done at Badajoz and Salamanca)—was, they knew, a pledge of certain punishment on any visit from the French. So that good-will, manifested in these circumstances, was nothing less than a testimony of devotion to the cause.

Here then, the reader will say, I find granted—in the courage and the good-will of the Spaniards—all the elements of an enthusiastic resistance; and cannot therefore imagine what more could be sought for except the throwing out and making palpable of their enthusiasm to the careless eye in some signal outward manifestations. In this accordingly we learn what interpretation we are to give to Sir J. M.'s charge:—there were no tumults on his entrance into Spain; no insurrections; they did not, as he says, 'rally round' the English army. But, to determine how far this disappointment of his expectations tells against the Spaniards, we must first know how far those expectations were reasonable. Let the reader consider, then,

First; what army was this round which the Spaniards were to rally? If it was known by the victory of Vimiera, it was known also to many by the Convention of Cintra; for, though the government had never ventured to communicate that affair officially to the nation, dark and perplexing whispers were however circulated about it throughout Spain. Moreover, it must surely demand some superstition in behalf of regular troops—to see, in an army of 26,000 men, a dignity adequate to the office here claimed for it of awakening a new vigour and enthusiasm in such a nation as Spain; not to mention that an English army, however numerous, had no right to consider itself as other than a tributary force—as itself tending to a centre—and attracted rather than attracting.

Secondly; it appears that Sir J. M. has overlooked one most important circumstance;—viz. that the harvest, in these provinces, had been already reaped; the English army could be viewed only as gleaners. Thus, as we have already seen, Estramadura had furnished an army which had marched before his arrival; from Salamanca also—the very place in which he makes his complaint—there had gone out a battalion to Biscay which Gen. Blake had held up, for its romantic gallantry, to the admiration of his whole army.

Yet, thirdly, it is not meant by any means to assert that Spain has put forth an energy adequate to the service—or in any tolerable proportion to her own strength. Far from it! But upon whom does the blame rest? Not surely upon the people—who, as long as they continued to have confidence in their rulers, could not be expected (after the early fervours of their revolution had subsided) much to overstep the measure of exertion prescribed to them—but solely upon the government. Up to the time when Sir J. M. died, the Supreme Junta had adopted no one grand and comprehensive measure for calling out the strength of the nation;—scarcely any of such ordinary vigour as, in some countries, would have been adopted to meet local disturbances among the people. From their jealousy of popular feeling,—they had never taken any steps, by books or civic assemblies, to make the general enthusiasm in the cause available by bringing it within the general consciousness; and thus to create the nation into an organic whole. Sir J. M. was fully aware of this:—'The Spanish Government,' he says, 'do not seem ever to have contemplated the possibility of a second attack:' and accordingly, whenever he is at leisure to make distinctions, he does the people the justice to say—that the failure was with those who should have 'taken advantage' of their good will. With the people therefore will for ever remain the glory of having resisted heroically with means utterly inadequate; and with the government the whole burthen of the disgrace that the means were thus inadequate.

But, further,—even though it should still be thought that, in the three Provinces which Sir J. Moore saw, there may have been some failures with the people,—it is to be remembered that these were the very three which had never been the theatre of French outrages; which therefore had neither such a vivid sense of the evils which they had to fear, nor so strong an animation in the recollection of past triumphs: we might accordingly have predicted that, if any provinces should prove slack in their exertions, it would be these three. So that, after all, (a candid inquirer into this matter will say) admitting Sir J. M.'s description to be faithful with respect to what he saw, I can never allow that the conduct of these three provinces shall be held forth as an exponent of the general temper and condition of Spain. For that therefore I must look to other authorities.

Such an inquirer we might then refer to the testimonies of Gen. Leith and of Capt. Pasley for Biscay and Asturias; of Mr. Vaughan (as cited by Lord Castlereagh) for the whole East and South; of Lord Cochrane (himself a most gallant man, and giving *his* testimony under a trying comparison of the Spaniards with English Sailors) for Catalonia in particular; of Lord W. Bentinck for the central provinces; and, for all Spain, we might appeal even to the Spanish military reports—which, by the discrimination of their praises (sometimes giving severe rebukes to particular regiments, &c.), authenticate themselves.

But, finally, we are entitled—after the *actions* of the Spaniards—to dispense with such appeals. Spain might justly deem it a high injury and affront, to suppose that (after her deeds performed under the condition of her means) she could require any other testimony to justify her before all posterity. What those deeds have been, it cannot surely now be necessary to inform the reader: and therefore the remainder of this note shall be employed in placing before him the present posture of Spain—under two aspects which may possibly have escaped his notice.

First, Let him look to that part of Spain which is now in the possession of the enemy;—let him bear in mind that the present campaign opened at the latter end of last October; that the French were then masters of the country up to the Ebro; that the contest has since lain between a veteran army (rated, on the lowest estimate, at 113,000 men—with a prodigious superiority in cavalry, artillery, &c.) opposed (as to all *regular* opposition) by unpractised Spaniards, split into three distinct armies, having no communication with each other, making a total of not more than 80,000 men;—and then let him inquire what progress, in this time and with these advantages, the French have been able to make (comparing it, at the same time, with that heretofore made in Prussia, and elsewhere): the answer shall be given from the *Times* newspaper of April 8th—'It appears that, at the date of our last accounts from France as well as Spain, about one half of the Peninsula was still unsubdued by the French arms. The Provinces, which retain their independence, form a sort of irregular or broken crescent; of which one horn consists in parts of Catalonia and Valencia, and the other horn includes Asturias (perhaps we may soon add Gallicia). The broader surface contains the four kingdoms of Andalusia (Seville, Grenada, Cordova, and Murcia), and considerable parts of Estramadura, and La Mancha; besides Portugal.'—The writer might have added that even the Provinces, occupied by the French, cannot yet be counted substantially as conquests: since they have a military representation in the south; large proportions of the defeated armies having retreated thither.

Secondly, Let him look to that part of Spain which yet remains unsubdued.—It was thought no slight proof of heroism in the people of Madrid, that they prepared for their defence—not as the foremost champions of Spain (in which character they might have gained an adventitious support from the splendour of their post; and, at any rate, would have been free from the depression of preceding disasters)—but under a full knowledge of recent and successive overthrows; their advanced armies had been defeated; and their last stay, at Somosierra, had been driven in upon them. But the Provinces in the South have many more causes for dejection: they have heard, since these disasters, that this heroic city of Madrid has fallen; that their forts in Catalonia have been wrested from them; that an English army just moved upon the horizon of Spain—to draw upon itself the gaze and expectations of the people, and then to vanish like an apparition; and, finally, they have heard of the desolation of Saragossa. Under all this accumulation of calamity, what has been their conduct? In Valencia redoubled preparations of defence; in Seville a decree for such energetic retaliation on the enemy,—as places its authors, in the event of his success, beyond the hopes of mercy; in Cadiz—on a suspicion that a compromise was concerted with their enemy—tumults and clamours of the people for instant vengeance; every where, in their uttermost distress, the same stern and unfaultering attitude of defiance as at the glorious birth of their resistance.

In this statement, then, of the past efforts of Spain—and of her present preparations for further efforts—will be found a full answer to all the charges alleged, by Sir John Moore in his letters, against the people of Spain, even if we did not find sufficient ground for rejecting them in an examination of these letters themselves.

* * * * * * * *

The Author of the above note—having, in justice to the Spaniards, spoken with great plainness and freedom—feels it necessary to add a few words, that it may not thence be concluded that he is insensible to Sir J. Moore's claims upon his respect. Perhaps—if Sir J. M. could himself have given us his commentary upon these letters, and have restricted the extension of such passages as (from want of vigilance in making distinctions or laxity of language) are at variance with concessions made elsewhere—they would have been found not more to differ from the reports of other intelligent and less prejudiced observers, than we might have expected from the circumstances under which they were written. Sir J. M. has himself told us (in a letter published since the above note was written) that he thinks the Spaniards 'a fine people;' and that acknowledgement, from a soldier, cannot be supposed to exclude courage; nor, from a Briton, some zeal for national independence. We are therefore to conclude that, when Sir J. M. pronounces opinions on 'the Spaniards' not to be reconciled with this and other passages, he speaks—not of the Spanish people—but of the Spanish government. And, even for what may still remain charged uncandidly upon the people, the writer does not forget that there are infinite apologies to be found in Sir J. Moore's situation: the earliest of these letters were written under great anxiety and disturbance of mind from the anticipation of calamity;—and the latter (which are the most severe) under the actual pressure of calamity; and calamity of that sort which would be the most painful to the feelings of a gallant soldier, and most likely to vitiate his judgment with respect to those who had in part (however innocently) occasioned it. There may be pleaded also for him—that want of leisure which would make it difficult to compare the different accounts he received, and to draw the right inferences from them. But then these apologies for his want of fidelity—are also reasons before-hand for suspecting it: and there are now (May 18th) to be added to these reasons, and their confirmations in the letters themselves, fresh proofs in the present state of Gallicia, as manifested by the late re-capture of Vigo, and the movements of the Marquis de la Romana; all which, from Sir J. Moore's account of the temper in that province, we might have confidently pronounced impossible. We must therefore remember that what in him were simply mis-statements—are now, when repeated with our better information, calumnies; and calumnies so much the less to be excused in us, as we have already (in our conduct towards Spain) given her other and no light matter of complaint against ourselves.

END OF THE APPENDIX.

III. VINDICATION OF OPINIONS IN THE TREATISE ON THE 'CONVENTION OF CINTRA:'

VIZ.

(a) LETTER TO MAJOR-GENERAL SIR CHARLES W. PASLEY, K.C.B., ON HIS 'MILITARY POLICY AND INSTITUTIONS OF THE BRITISH EMPIRE,' 1811.

(b) LETTER ENCLOSING THE PRECEDING TO A FRIEND UN-NAMED.

NOTE.

These two Letters—the latter for the first time printed—form a fitting sequel to the 'Convention of Cintra.' See Preface in the present volume for more on them. G.

TO CAPTAIN PASLEY, ROYAL ENGINEERS.

Grasmere, March 28, 1811.

MY DEAR SIR,

I address this to the publishers of your 'Essay,' not knowing where to find you. Before I speak of the instruction and pleasure which I have derived from your work, let me say a word or two in apology for my own apparent *neglect* of the letter with which you honoured me some time ago. In fact, I was thoroughly sensible of the value of your correspondence, and of your kindness in writing to me, and took up the pen to tell you so. I wrote half of a pretty long letter to you, but I was so disgusted with the imperfect and feeble expression which I had given to some not uninteresting ideas, that I threw away the unfinished sheet, and could not find resolution to resume what had been so inauspiciously begun. I am ashamed to say, that I write so few letters, and employ my pen so little in any way, that I feel both a lack of words (such words I mean as I wish for) and of mechanical skill, extremely discouraging to me. I do not plead these disabilities on my part as an excuse, but I wish you to know that they have been the sole cause of my silence, and not a want of sense of the honour done me by your correspondence, or an ignorance of what good breeding required of me. But enough of my trespasses! Let me only add, that I addressed a letter of some length to you when you were lying ill at Middleburgh; this probably you never received. Now for your book. I had expected it with great impatience, and desired a friend to send it down to me immediately on its appearance, which he neglected to do. On this account, I did not see it till a few days ago. I have read it through twice, with great care, and many parts three or four times over. From this, you will conclude that I must have been much interested; and I assure you that I deem myself also in a high degree instructed. It would be a most pleasing employment to me to dwell, in this letter, upon those points in which I agree with you, and to acknowledge my obligations for the clearer views you have given of truths which I before perceived, though not with that distinctness in which they now stand before my eyes. But I could wish this letter to be of some use to you; and that end is more likely to be attained if I advert to those points in which I think you are mistaken. These are chiefly such as though very material in themselves, are not at all so to the main object you have in view, viz. that of proving that the military power of France may by us be successfully resisted, and even overthrown. In the first place, then, I think that there are great errors in the survey of the comparative strength of the two empires, with which you begin your book, and on which the first 160 pages are chiefly employed. You seem to wish to frighten the people into exertion; and in your ardour to attain your object, that of rousing our countrymen by any means, I think you have caught far too eagerly at every circumstance with respect to revenue, navy, &c. that appears to make for the French. This I think was unnecessary. The people are convinced that the power of France is dangerous, and that it is our duty to resist it to the utmost. I think you might have commenced from this acknowledged fact; and, at all events, I cannot help saying, that the first 100 pages or so of your book, contrasted with the brilliant prospects towards the conclusion, have impressed me with a notion that you have written too much under the influence of feelings similar to those of a poet or novelist, who deepens the distress in the earlier part of his work, in order that the happy catastrophe which he has prepared for his hero and heroine may be more keenly relished. Your object is to conduct us to Elysium, and, lest we should not be able to enjoy that pure air and purpurial sunshine, you have taken a peep at Tartarus on the road. Now I am of your mind, that we ought not to make peace with France, on any account, till she is humiliated, and her power brought within reasonable bounds. It is our duty and our interest to be at war with her; but I do not think with you, that a state of peace would give to France that superiority which you seem so clearly to foresee. In estimating the resources of the two empires, as to revenue, you appear to make little or no allowance for what I deem of prime and paramount importance, the characters of the two nations, and of the two governments. Was there ever an instance, since the world began, of the peaceful arts thriving under a despotism so oppressive as that of France is and must continue to be, and among a people so unsettled, so depraved, and so undisciplined in civil arts and habits as the French nation must now be? It is difficult to come at the real revenue of the French empire; but it appears to me certain, absolutely certain, that it must diminish rapidly every year. The armies have hitherto been maintained chiefly from the contributions raised upon the conquered countries, and from the plunder which the soldiers have been able to find. But that harvest is over. Austria, and particularly Hungary, may have yet something to supply; but the French Ruler will scarcely quarrel with them for a few years at least. But from Denmark, and Sweden, and Russia, there is not much to be gained. In the mean while, wherever his iron yoke is fixed, the spirits of the people are broken; and it is in vain to attempt to extort money which they do not possess, and cannot procure. Their bodies he may command, but their bodies he cannot move without the inspiration of *wealth*, somewhere or other; by wealth I mean superfluous produce, something arising from the labour of the inhabitants of countries beyond what is necessary to their support. What will avail him the command of the whole population of the Continent, unless there be a security for capital somewhere existing, so that the mechanic arts and inventions may thereby be applied in such a manner as that an overplus may arise from the labour of the country which shall find its way into the pocket of the State for the purpose of supporting its military and civil establishments? Now, when I look at the condition of our country, and compare it with that of France, and reflect upon the length of the time, and the infinite combination of favourable circumstances which have been necessary to produce the laws, the regulations, the customs, the moral character, and the physical enginery of all sorts, through means, and by aid of which, labour is carried on in this happy Land; and when I think of the wealth and population (concentrated too in so small a space) which we must have at command for military purposes, I confess I have not much dread, looking either at war or peace, of any power which France, with respect to us, is likely to attain for years, I may say for generations. Whatever may be the form of a government, its spirit, at least, must be mild and free before agriculture, trade, commerce, and manufactures can thrive under it; and if these do not prosper in a State, it may extend its empire to right and to left, and it will only carry poverty and desolation along with it, without being itself permanently enriched. You seem to take for granted, that because the French revenue amounts to so much at present it must continue to keep up to that height. This, I conceive impossible, unless the spirit of the government alters, which is not likely for many years. How comes it that we are enabled to keep, by sea and land, so many men in arms? Not by our foreign commerce, but by our domestic ingenuity, by our home labour, which, with the aid of capital and the mechanic arts and establishments, has enabled a few to produce so much as will maintain themselves, and the hundreds of thousands of their countrymen whom they support in arms. If our foreign trade were utterly destroyed, I am told, that not more than one-sixth of our trade would perish. The spirit of Buonaparte's government is, and must continue to be, like that of the first conquerors of the New World who went raving about for gold—gold! and for whose rapacious appetites the slow but mighty and sure returns of any other produce could have no charms. I cannot but think that generations must pass away before France, or any of the countries under its thraldom, can attain those habits, and that character, and those establishments which must be attained before it can wield its population in a manner that will ensure our overthrow. This (if we conduct the war upon principles of common sense) seems to me impossible, while we continue at war; and should a peace take place (which, however, I passionately deprecate), France will long be compelled to pay tribute to us, on account of our being so far before her in the race of genuine practical philosophy and true liberty. I mean that the *mind* of this country is so far before that of France, and that *that* mind has empowered the *hands* of the country to raise so much national wealth, that France must condescend to accept from us what she will be unable herself to produce. Is it likely that any of our manufacturing capitalists, in case of a peace, would trust themselves to an arbitrary government like that of France, which, without a moment's warning, might go to war with us and seize their persons and their property; nay, if they should be so foolish as to trust themselves to its discretion, would be base enough to pick a quarrel with us for the very purpose of a pretext to strip them of all they possessed? Or is it likely, if the native French manufacturers and traders were capable of rivalling us in point of skill, that any Frenchman would venture upon that ostentatious display of wealth which a large cotton-mill, for instance, requires, when he knows that by so doing he would only draw upon himself a glance of the greedy eye of government, soon to be followed by a squeeze from its rapacious hand? But I have dwelt too long upon this. The sum of what I think, by conversation, I could convince you of is, that your comparative estimate is erroneous, and materially so, inasmuch as it makes no allowance for the increasing superiority which a State, supposed to be independent and equitable in its dealings to its subjects, must have over an oppressive government; and none for the time which is necessary to give prosperity to peaceful arts, even if the government should improve. Our country has a mighty and daily growing forest of this sort of wealth; whereas, in France, the trees are not yet put into the ground. For my own part, I do not think it possible that France, with all her command of territory and coast, can outstrip us in naval power, unless she could previously, by her land power, cut us off from timber and naval stores, necessary for the building and equipment of our fleet. In that intellectual superiority which, as I have mentioned, we possess over her, we should find means to build as many ships as she could build, and also could procure sailors to man them. The same energy would furnish means for maintaining the men; and if they could be fed and maintained, they would surely be produced. Why then am I for *war* with France? 1st. Because I think our naval superiority may be more cheaply maintained, and more easily, by war than by peace; and because I think, that if the war were conducted upon those principles of martial policy which you so admirably and nobly enforce, united with (or rather bottomed upon) those notions of justice and right, and that knowledge of and reverence for the moral sentiments of mankind, which, in my Tract, I attempted to portray and illustrate, the tide of military success would immediately turn in our favour; and we should find no more difficulty in reducing the French power than Gustavus Adolphus did in reducing that of the German Empire in his day. And here let me express my zealous thanks for the spirit and beauty with which you have pursued, through all its details, the course of martial policy which you recommend. Too much praise cannot be given to this which is the great body of your work. I hope that it will not be lost upon your countrymen. But (as I said before) I rather wish to dwell upon those points in which I am dissatisfied with your 'Essay.' Let me then come at once to a fundamental principle. You maintain, that as the military power of France is in progress, ours must be so also, or we must perish. In this I agree with you. Yet you contend also, that this increase or progress can only be brought about by conquests permanently established upon the Continent; and, calling in the doctrines of the writers upon the Law of Nations to your aid, you are for beginning with the conquest of Sicily, and so on, through Italy, Switzerland, &c. &c. Now it does not appear to me, though I should rejoice heartily to see a British army march from Calabria, triumphantly, to the heart of the Alps, and from Holland to the centre of Germany,—yet it does not appear to me that the conquest and permanent possession of these countries is necessary either to produce those resources of men or money which the security and prosperity of our country requires. All that is absolutely needful, for either the one or the other, is a large, experienced, and seasoned *army*, which we cannot possess without a field to fight in, and that field must be somewhere upon the Continent. Therefore, as far as concerns ourselves and our security, I do not think that so wide a space of conquered country is desirable; and, as a patriot, I have no wish for it. If I desire it, it is not for our sakes directly, but for the benefit of those unhappy nations whom we should rescue, and whose prosperity would be reflected back upon ourselves. Holding these notions, it is natural, highly as I rate the importance of military power, and deeply as I feel its necessity for the protection of every excellence and virtue, that I should rest my hopes with respect to the emancipation of Europe more upon moral influence, and the wishes and opinions of the people of the respective nations, than you appear to do. As I have written in my pamphlet, 'on the moral qualities of a people must its salvation ultimately depend. Something higher than military excellence must be taught *as* higher; something more fundamental, *as* more fundamental.' Adopting the opinion of the writers upon the laws of Nations, you treat of *conquest* as if *conquest* could in itself, nakedly and abstractedly considered, confer rights. If we once admit this proposition, all morality is driven out of the world. We conquer Italy—that is, we raise the British standard in Italy,—and, by the aid of the inhabitants, we expel the French from the country, and have a right to keep it for ourselves. This, if I am not mistaken, is not only implied, but explicitly maintained in your book. Undoubtedly, if it be clear that the possession of Italy is necessary for our security, we have a right to keep possession of it, if we should ever be able to master it by the sword. But not because we have gained it by conquest, therefore may we keep it; no; the sword, as the sword, can give no rights; but because a great and noble Nation, like ours, cannot prosper or exist without such possession. If the fact *were* so, we should then have a right to keep possession of what by our valour we had acquired—not otherwise. If these things were matter of mere speculation, they would not be worth talking about; but they are not so. The spirit of conquest, and the ambition of the sword, never can confer true glory and happiness upon a nation that has attained power sufficient to protect itself. Your favourites, the Romans, though no doubt having the fear of the Carthaginians before their eyes, yet were impelled to carry their arms out of Italy by ambition far more than by a rational apprehension of the danger of their condition. And how did they enter upon their career? By an act of atrocious injustice. You are too well read in history for me to remind you what that act was. The same disregard of morality followed too closely their steps everywhere. Their ruling passion, and sole steady guide, was the glory of the Roman name, and the wish to spread the Roman power. No wonder, then, if their armies and military leaders, as soon as they had destroyed all foreign enemies from whom anything was to be dreaded, turned their swords upon each other. The ferocious cruelties of Sylla and Marius, of Catiline, and of Antony and Octavius, and the despotism of the empire, were the necessary consequences of a long course of action pursued upon such blind and selfish principles. Therefore, admiring as I do your scheme of martial policy, and agreeing with you that a British military power may, and that the *present* state of the world requires that it *ought* to be, predominant in Italy, and Germany, and Spain; yet still, I am afraid that you look with too much complacency upon conquest by British arms, and upon British military influence upon the Continent, for *its own sake.* Accordingly, you seem to regard Italy with more satisfaction than Spain. I mean you contemplate our possible exertions in Italy with more pleasure, merely because its dismembered state would probably keep it more under our sway—in other words, more at our mercy. Now, I think there is nothing more unfortunate for Europe than the condition of Germany and Italy in these respects. Could the barriers be dissolved which have divided the one nation into Neapolitans, Tuscans, Venetians, &c., and the other into Prussians, Hanoverians, &c., and could they once be taught to feel their strength, the French would be driven back into their own Land immediately. I wish to see Spain, Italy, France, Germany, formed into independent nations; nor have I any desire to reduce the power of France further than may be necessary for that end. Woe be to that country whose military power is irresistible! I deprecate such an event for Great Britain scarcely less than for any other Land. Scipio foresaw the evils with which Rome would be visited when no Carthage should be in existence for her to contend with. If a nation have nothing to oppose or to fear without, it cannot escape decay and concussion within. Universal triumph and absolute security soon betray a State into abandonment of that discipline, civil and military, by which its victories were secured. If the time should ever come when this island shall have no more formidable enemies by land than it has at this moment by sea, the extinction of all that it previously contained of good and great would soon follow. Indefinite progress, undoubtedly, there ought to be somewhere; but let that be in knowledge, in science, in civilization, in the increase of the numbers of the people, and in the augmentation of their virtue and happiness. But progress in conquest cannot be indefinite; and for that very reason, if for no other, it cannot be a fit object for the exertions of a people, I mean beyond certain limits, which, of course, will vary with circumstances. My prayer, as a patriot, is, that we may always have, somewhere or other, enemies capable of resisting us, and keeping us at arm's length. Do I, then, object that our arms shall be carried into every part of the Continent? No: such is the present condition of Europe, that I earnestly pray for what I deem would be a mighty blessing. France has already destroyed, in almost every part of the Continent, the detestable governments with which the nations have been afflicted; she has extinguished one sort of tyranny, but only to substitute another. Thus, then, have the countries of Europe been taught, that domestic oppression, if not manfully and zealously repelled, must sooner or later be succeeded by subjugation from without; they have tasted the bitterness of both cups, have drunk deeply of both. Their spirits are prepared for resistance to the foreign tyrant, and with our help I think they may shake him off, and, under our countenance, and following (as far as they are capable) our example, they may fashion to themselves, making use of what is best in their own ancient laws and institutions, new forms of government, which may secure posterity from a repetition of such calamities as the present age has brought forth. The materials of a new balance of power exist in the language, and name, and territory of Spain, in those of France, and those of Italy, Germany, Russia, and the British Isles. The smaller States must disappear, and merge in the large nations and wide-spread languages. The possibility of this remodelling of Europe I see clearly; earnestly do I pray for it; and I have in my mind a strong conviction that your invaluable work will be a powerful instrument in preparing the way for that happy issue. Yet, still, we must go deeper than the nature of your labour requires you to penetrate. Military policy merely will not perform all that is needful, nor mere military virtues. If the Roman State was saved from overthrow, by the attack of the slaves and of the gladiators, through the excellence of its armies, yet this was not without great difficulty;* and Rome would have been destroyed by Carthage, had she not been preserved by a civic fortitude in which she surpassed all the nations of the earth. The reception which the Senate gave to Terentius Varro, after the battle of Cannae, is the sublimest event in human history. What a contrast to the wretched conduct of the Austrian government after the battle at Wagram! England requires, as you have shown so eloquently and ably, a new system of martial policy; but England, as well as the rest of Europe, requires what is more difficult to give it,—a new course of education, a higher tone of moral feeling, more of the grandeur of the imaginative faculties, and less of the petty processes of the unfeeling and purblind

* 'Totis imperii viribus consurgitur,' says the historian, speaking of the war of the gladiators.

understanding, that would manage the concerns of nations in the same calculating spirit with which it would set about building a house. Now a State ought to be governed (at least in these times), the labours of the statesman ought to advance, upon calculations and from impulses similar to those which give motion to the hand of a great artist when he is preparing a picture, or of a mighty poet when he is determining the proportions and march of a poem;—much is to be done by rule; the great outline is previously to be conceived in distinctness, but the consummation of the work must be trusted to resources that are not tangible, though known to exist. Much as I admire the political sagacity displayed in your work, I respect you still more for the lofty spirit that supports it; for the animation and courage with which it is replete; for the contempt, in a just cause, of death and danger by which it is ennobled; for its heroic confidence in the valour of your countrymen; and the absolute determination which it everywhere expresses to maintain in all points the honour of the soldier's profession, and that of the noble Nation of which you are a member—of the Land in which you were born. No insults, no indignities, no vile stooping, will your politics admit of; and therefore, more than for any other cause, do I congratulate my country on the appearance of a book which, resting in this point our national safety upon the purity of our national character, will, I trust, lead naturally to make us, at the same time, a more powerful and a highminded nation.

Affectionately yours,

W. Wordsworth.*

Letter enclosing the Preceding to a Friend un-named.

My dear Sir,

I have taken the Liberty of addressing the enclosed to you, with a wish that you would be so kind as to send it by the twopenny Post. The Letter, though to a personal Acquaintance and to some degree a friend, is upon a kind of Public occasion, and consists of Comments upon Captain Pasley's lately published Essay on the Military Policy of Great Britain; a work which if you have not seen I earnestly recommend to your

* *Memoirs*, vol. i. pp. 406-20.

careful Perusal. I have sent my Letter unsealed in order that if you think it worth while you may read it, which would oblige me. You may begin with those words in the 1st Page, 'Now for your Book:' which you will see are legible, being transcribed by a Friend. The rest, in my own hand, is only an Apology for not writing sooner; save that there are two Sonnets which if you like you may glance your eye over. Do not forget to put a wafer on the Letter after you have done with it.

Will you excuse me if I find myself unable to forbear saying, upon this occasion, a few words concerning the conduct pursued with respect to foreign affairs by the Party with whom you act? I learn from a private quarter of unquestionable Authority, that it was Lord Grenville's intention, had he come into power as he lately expected, to have recalled the army from Portugal. In the name of my Country, of our virtuous and suffering Allies, and of Human Nature itself, I give thanks to Providence who has restored the King's health so far as to prevent this intention being put into practice hitherto. The transgressions of the present ministry are grievous; but excepting only a deliberate and direct attack upon the civil liberty of our own Country, there cannot be any thing in a Minister worse than a desponding spirit and the lack of confidence in a good cause. If Lord G. and Mr. Ponsonby think that the privilege allowed to opposition-manœuvering justifies them in speaking as they do, they are sadly mistaken and do not discern what is becoming the times; but if they sincerely believe in the omnipotence of Buonaparte upon the Continent, they are the dupes of their own fears and the slaves of their own ignorance. Do not deem me presumptuous when I say that it is pitiable to hear Lord Grenville talking as he did in the late debate of the inability of Great Britain to take a commanding station as a military Power, and maintaining that our efforts must be essentially, he means exclusively, naval. We have destroyed our enemies upon the Sea, and are equally capable of destroying him upon land. Rich in soldiers and revenues as we are, we are capable, availing ourselves of the present disposition of the Continent, to erect there under our countenance, and by a wise application of our resources, a military Power, which the tyrannical and immoral Government of Buonaparte could not prevail against, and if he could not overthrow it, he must himself perish. Lord G. grudges two millions in aid of Portugal, which has eighty thousand men in arms, and what they can perform has been proved. Yet Lord G. does not object to our granting aid to a great Military Power on the Continent if such could be found, nay he begs of us to wait till that fortunate period arrives. Whence does Lord G., from what quarter does he expect it? from Austria, from the Prussian monarchy, brought to life again, from Russia, or lastly from the Confederacy of the Rhine turning against their Creator and Fashioner? Is the expectation of the Jews for their Messiah or of the Portuguese for St. Sebastian more extravagant? But Lord G. ought to know that such a military POWER does already exist upon the Peninsula, formless indeed compared with what under our plastic hands it may become, yet which has proved itself capable of its giving employment during the course of three years to at least five hundred thousand of the enemy's best troops. An important fact has been proved, that the enemy cannot *drive* us from the Peninsula. We have the point to stand upon which Archimedes wished for, and we may move the Continent if we persevere. Let us prepare to exercise in Spain a military influence like that which we already possess in Portugal, and our affairs must improve daily and rapidly. Whatever money we advance for Portugal and Spain, we can direct the management of it, an inestimable advantage which, with relation to Prussia, Russia or Austria, we never possessed. Besides, how could we govern the purposes of those States, when that inherent imbecility and cowardice leave them no purpose or aim to which they can steadily adhere of themselves for six weeks together? Military Powers! So these States have been called. A strange Misnomer! they are Weaknesses—a true though ill-sounding Title!—and not Powers! Polybius tells us that Hannibal entered into Italy with twenty thousand men, and that the aggregate forces of Italy at that time amounted to seven hundred and sixty thousand foot and horse, with the Roman discipline and power to head that mighty force. Gustavus Adolphus invaded Germany with thirteen thousand men; the Emperor at that time having between two and three hundred thousand warlike and experienced Troops commanded by able Generals, to oppose to him. Let these facts and numerous others which history supplies of the same kind, be thought of; and let us hear no more of the impossibility of Great Britain girt round and defended by the Sea and an invincible Navy, becoming a military Power; Great Britain whose troops surpass in valour those of all the world, and who has an army and a militia of upwards of three hundred thousand men! Do reflect my dear Sir, upon the materials which are now in preparation upon the Continent. Hannibal expected to be joined by a parcel of the contented barbarian Gauls in the north of Italy. Gustavus stood forth as the Champion of the Protestant interest: how feeble and limited each of these auxiliary sentiments and powers, compared with what the state of knowledge, the oppressions of their domestic governments, and the insults and injuries and hostile cruelties inflicted by the French upon the continental nations, must have exerted to second our arms whenever we shall appear in that Force which we can assume, and with that boldness which would become us, and which justice and human nature and Patriotism call upon us to put forth. Farewell, most truly yours,

W. Wordsworth.

Shall we see you this Summer? I hope so.

IV. TWO ADDRESSES TO THE FREEHOLDERS OF WESTMORELAND.

1818.

NOTE.

On the occasion of these 'Two Addresses,' and other related matters, see Preface in the present volume. G.

TWO
ADDRESSES
TO THE
FREEHOLDERS
OF
WESTMORLAND.

Kendal:
PRINTED BY AIREY AND BELLINGHAM.

1818.

ADVERTISEMENT.

THE Author thinks it proper to advise his Reader, that he alone is responsible for the sentiments and opinions expressed in these sheets. Gladly would he have availed himself of the judgment of others, if that benefit could have been had without subjecting the Persons consulted to the possibility of blame, for having sanctioned any view of the topics under consideration, which, either from its erroneousness might deserve, or from Party feelings or other causes might incur, censure.

The matter comprised in these pages was intended to compose a succession of Addresses to be printed in the *Kendal Chronicle*, and a part of the first was published through that channel. The intention was dropped for reasons well known. It is now mentioned in order to account for the disproportion in the length of the two Addresses, and an arrangement of matter, in some places, different from what would otherwise have been chosen. A portion also has appeared in the *Carlisle Patriot*.

It is of little importance to add, that this Publication has been delayed by unavoidable engagements of the Printer.

March 26, 1818.

TO THE READER.

THE new Candidate has appeared amongst us, and concluded, for the present, his labours in the County. They require no further notice here than an expression of thanks for the success with which he has co-operated with the Author of these pages to demonstrate, by the whole of his itinerant proceedings, that the vital principle of the Opposition ostensibly headed by him, is at enmity with the bonds by which society is held together, and Government maintained.

April 4, 1818.

TO THE FREEHOLDERS, &c.

GENTLEMEN,

Two Months have elapsed since warning was given of an intention to oppose the present Representatives of the County of Westmorland, at the ensuing Election; yet, till so late a period as the 26th of January, no avowal of such intention appeared from any quarter entitling it to consideration. For, as to the Body of Men, calling itself the London Committee, there is not, up to this hour I believe, any public evidence even of its existence, except certain notices signed by two obscure individuals. But, in the minds of those naturally interested in the welfare of the County, a ferment was excited by various devices; inflammatory addresses were busily circulated; men, laying claim to the flattering character of Reformers of abuses, became active; and, as this stir did not die away, they who foresaw its bearings and tendencies, were desirous that, if there were any just grounds for discontent, the same should be openly declared, by persons whose characters and situations in life would be a pledge for their having proceeded upon mature deliberation. At length, a set of resolutions have appeared, from a Meeting of dissatisfied Freeholders, holden in a Town, which, if not the principal in point of rank, is the most populous, opulent, and weighty, in the County. Among those who composed this Meeting, the first visible authentic Body which the Opposition has produced, are to be found persons answering to the description above given—men from whom might have been expected, in the exposition of their complaints, sound sense as to the nature of the grievances, and rational views as to the mode of removing them—Have such expectations, if entertained, been fulfilled?

The first Resolution unanimously agreed upon by this Meeting, is couched in these words: 'It is impossible for us, as Freeholders, to submit any longer to a single Family, however respectable, naming both Members for the County.' What if this leading article had been thus expressed? 'That it is injurious to the interests, and derogatory to the dignity, of the County of Westmorland, that both its Representatives should be brought into Parliament, by the influence of one Family.' Words to this effect would surely have given the sense of the Resolution, as proceeding from men of cool reflection; and offered nakedly to the consideration of minds which, it was desired, should be kept in a similar state. But we cannot '*submit* any longer'—if the intention was to mislead and irritate, such language was well adapted for the purpose; but it ill accords with the spirit of the next Resolution, which affirms, that the Meeting is wholly unconnected with any political Party; and, thus disclaiming indirectly those passions and prejudices that are apt to fasten upon political partisans, implicitly promises, that the opinions of the Meeting shall be conveyed in terms suitable to such disavowal. Did the persons in question imagine themselves in a state of degradation? On their own word we must believe they did; and no one could object to their employing, among each other, such language as gave vent to feelings proceeding from that impression, in a way that gratified themselves. But, by *publishing* their Resolutions, they shew that they are not communing for the sake of mutual sympathy, but to induce others to participate a sentiment which probably they are strangers to. We *submit* to the law, and to those who are placed in authority over us, while in the legitimate exercise of their functions—we *submit* to the decrees of Providence, because they are not to be resisted—a coward *submits* to be insulted—a pusillanimous wretch to be despised—and a knave, if detected, must submit to be scouted—a slave submits to his Taskmaster; but, the Freeholders of Westmorland, cannot, *in reason*, be said to submit to the House of Lowther naming their Representatives, unless it can be proved that those Representatives have been thrust upon them by an unjustifiable agency; and that they owe their seats, not to the free suffrages and frank consent of their Constituents, but to unfair means, whether in the shape of seduction or threat. If there be an indignity on one side, there must have been a wrong done on the other; and, to make out this point, it ought to have been shewn, that some other Person, qualified by his property, his education, his rank, and character, had stood forth and offered himself to represent you, Freeholders of Westmorland, in Parliament; and that, in this attempt, he had been crushed by the power of a single Family, careless of the mode in which that power was exercised. I appeal to those who have had an opportunity of being acquainted with the Noble Lord who is at the head of that Family, whether they are of opinion, that any consideration of his own interest or importance in the State, would have induced him to oppose *such* a Candidate, provided there was reason for believing that the unabused sense of the County was with him. If indeed a Candidate supposed to be so favoured by the County, had declared himself an enemy to the general measures of Administration for some years past, those measures have depended on principles of conduct of such vast importance, that the Noble Lord must needs have endeavoured, as far as prudence authorised, to frustrate an attempt, which, in conscience, he could not approve.

I affirm, then, that, as there was no wrong, there is no indignity—the present Members owe their high situation to circumstances, local and national. They are there *because no one else has presented himself*, or, for some years back, has been likely to present himself, with pretensions, the reasonableness of which could enter into competition with their's. This is, in some points of view, a misfortune, but it is the fact; and no class of men regret it more than the independent and judicious adherents of the House of Lowther: Men who are happy and proud to rally round the Nobleman who is the head of that House, in defence of rational liberty: Men who know that he has proved himself a faithful guardian to the several orders of the State—that he is a tried enemy to dangerous innovations—a condemner of fantastic theories—one who understands mankind, and knows the heights and levels of human nature, by which the course of the streams of social action is determined—a Lover of the People, but one who despises, as far as relates to his own practice; and deplores, in respect to that of others, the shows, and pretences, and all the false arts by which the plaudits of the multitude are won, and the people flattered to the common ruin of themselves and their deceivers.

But after all, let us soberly enquire to what extent it is really an evil that two persons, so nearly connected in blood, should represent this County. And first looking at the matter *locally*, what *is* that portion of England known by the name of the County of Westmorland? A County which indeed the natives of it love, and are justly proud of; a region famous for the production of shrewd, intelligent, brave, active, honest, enterprising men:—but it covers no very large space on the map; the soil is in general barren, the country poor accordingly, and of necessity thinly inhabited. There are in England single Towns, even of a third or fourth rate importance, that contain a larger population than is included within the limits of Westmorland, from the foot of Wrynose to the sides of Stainmoor, and from the banks of the Kent to those of the Emont. Is it, then, to be wondered at, considering the antiquity of the House of Lowther, that circumstances should have raised it to the elevation which it holds in a district so thinly peopled, neither rich in the products of Agriculture, nor in the materials of Commerce, and where it is impossible that any considerable number of Country Gentlemen of large, or as our ancestors expressed themselves of notable estate, can co-exist. It must unavoidably happen therefore that, at all times, there will be few persons, in such a County, furnished with the stable requisites of property, rank, family, and personal fitness, that shall point them out for such an office, and *dispose them to covet it*, by insuring that degree of public confidence which will make them independent, comfortable, and happy, in discharging the duties which it imposes. This small number will, at particular periods, be liable to be reduced; that this *has* been the case is apparent upon retrospect; and that the number is not large at present, may be inferred from the difficulty with which a third Candidate has been found; and from the insignificant station which the Individual, who has at length obeyed the call of the discontented, holds in the County.

With these local circumstances *general* considerations have powerfully co-operated, to place the representation of Westmorland where it now is; and to this second division of the subject I particularly request your attention, Gentlemen, as reflecting Patriots.

Looking up to the government with respectful attachment, we all acknowledge that power must be controlled and checked, or it will be abused; hence the desirableness of a vigorous opposition in the House of Commons; and hence a wish, grounded upon a conviction of general expediency, that the opposition to ministry, whose head and chief seat of action are in Parliament, should be efficaciously diffused through all parts of the Country. On this principle the two grand divisions of Party, under our free government, are founded. Conscience regulated by expediency, is the basis; honour, binding men to each other in spite of temptation, is the corner-stone; and the superstructure is friendship, protecting kindness, gratitude, and all the moral sentiments by which self-interest is liberalized. Such is Party, looked at on the favourable side. Cogent *moral* inducements, therefore, exist for the prevalence of two powerful bodies in the practice of the State, spreading their influence and interests throughout the country; and, on *political* considerations, it is desirable that the strength of each should bear such proportion to that of the other, that, while Ministry are able to carry into effect measures not palpably injurious, the vigilance of Opposition may turn to account, being backed by power at all times sufficient to awe, but never, (were that possible) except when supported by manifest reason, to intimidate.

Such apportioning of the strength of the two Parties *has* existed; such a degree of power the Opposition formerly possessed; and if they have lost that salutary power, if they are dwindled and divided, they must ascribe it to their own errors. They are weak because they have been unwise: they are brought low, because when they had solid and high ground to stand upon, they took a flight into the air. To have hoped too ardently of human nature, as they did at the commencement of the French Revolution, was no dishonour to them as men; but *politicians* cannot be allowed to plead temptations of fancy, or impulses of feeling, in exculpation of mistakes in judgement. Grant, however, to the enthusiasm of Philanthropy as much indulgence as it may call for, it is still extraordinary that, in the minds of English Statesmen and Legislators, the naked absurdity of the means did not raise a doubt as to the attainableness of the end. Mr. Fox, captivated by the vanities of a system founded upon abstract rights, chaunted his expectations in the House of Parliament; and too many of his Friends partook of the illusion. The most sagacious Politician of his age broke out in an opposite strain. Time has verified his predictions; the books remain in which his principles of foreknowledge were laid down; but, as the Author became afterwards a Pensioner of State, thousands, in this country of free opinions, persist in asserting that his divination was guess-work, and that conscience had no part in urging him to speak. That warning voice proved vain; the Party from whom he separated, proceeded—confiding in splendid oratorical talents and ardent feelings rashly wedded to novel expectations, when common sense, uninquisitive experience, and a modest reliance on old habits of judgement, when either these, or a philosophic penetration, were the only qualities that could have served them.

How many private Individuals, at that period, were kept in a rational course by circumstances, supplying restraints which their own understandings would not have furnished! Through what fatality it happens, that Bodies of Men are so slow to profit, in a similar way, by circumstances affecting their prosperity, the Opposition seem never to have enquired. They could not avoid observing, that the Holders of Property throughout the country, being mostly panic-stricken by the proceedings in France, turned instinctively against the admirers of the new system;—and, as security for property is the very basis of civil society, how was it possible but that reflecting men, who perceived this truth, should mistrust those Representatives of the People, who could not have acted less prudently, had they been utterly unconscious of it! But they had committed themselves and did not retract; either from unabating devotion to their cause, or from false honour, and that self-injuring consistency, the favourite sister of obstinacy, which the mixed conscience of mankind is but too apt to produce. Meanwhile the tactics of Parliament must continue in exercise on some system or other; their adversaries were to be annoyed at any rate; and so intent were they upon this, that, in proportion as the entrenchments of Ministry strengthened, the assaults of Opposition became more careless and desperate.

While the war of words and opinions was going forward in this country, Europe was deluged with blood. They in whose hands power was vested among us, in course of time, lost ground in public opinion, through the failure of their efforts. Parties were broken and re-composed; but Men who are brought together less by principle than by events, cannot cordially co-operate, or remain long united. The opponents of the war, in this middle stage and desponding state of it, were not popular; and afterwards, when the success of the enemy made the majority of the Nation feel, that Peace dictated by him could not be lasting, and they were bent on persevering in the struggle, the Party of Opposition persisted in a course of action which, as their countenance of the doctrine of the rights of man, had brought their understandings into disrepute, cast suspicion on the soundness of their patriotic affections. Their passions made them blind to the differences between a state of peace and war, (above all such a war!) as prescribing rules for their own conduct. They were ignorant, or never bore in mind, that a species of hostility which, had there been no foreign enemy to resist, might have proved useful and honourable, became equally pernicious and disgraceful, when a formidable foe threatened us with destruction.

I appeal to impartial recollection, whether, during the course of the late awful struggle, and in the latter stages of it especially, the antagonists of Ministers, in the two Houses of Parliament, did not, for the most part, conduct themselves more like allies to a military despot, who was attempting to enslave the world, and to whom their own country was an object of paramount hatred, than like honest Englishmen, who had breathed the air of liberty from their cradles. If any state of things could supply them with motives for acting in that manner, they must abide by the consequences. They must reconcile themselves as well as they can to dislike and to disesteem, the unavoidable results of behaviour so unnatural. Peace has indeed come; but do they who deprecated the continuance of the war, and clamoured for its close, on any terms, rejoice heartily in a triumph by which their prophecies were belied? Did they lend their voices to swell the hymn of transport, that resounded through our Land, when the arch-enemy was overthrown? Are they pleased that inheritances have been restored, and that legitimate governments have been re-established, on the Continent? And do they grieve when those re-established governments act unworthily of the favour which Providence has shown them? Do not too many rather secretly congratulate themselves on every proof of imbecility or misconduct there exhibited; and endeavour that attention shall be exclusively fixed on those melancholy facts, as if they were the only fruits of a triumph, to which we Britons owe, that we are a fearless, undishonoured, and rapidly improving people, and the nations of the Continent owe their very existence as self-governed communities?

The Party of Opposition, or what remains of it, has much to repent of; many humiliating reflections must pass through the minds of those who compose it, and they must learn the hard lesson to be thankful for them as a discipline indispensible to their amendment. Thus only can they furnish a sufficient nucleus for the formation of a new Body; nor can there be any hope of such Body being adequate to its appropriate service, and of its possessing that portion of good opinion which shall entitle it to the respect of its antagonists, unless it live and act, for a length of time, under a distinct conception of the kind and degree of hostility to the executive government, which is fairly warrantable. The Party must cease indiscriminately to court the discontented, and to league itself with Men who are athirst for innovation, to a point which leaves it doubtful, whether an Opposition, that is willing to co-operate with such Agitators, loves as it ought to do, and becomingly venerates, the happy and glorious Constitution, in Church and State, which we have inherited from our Ancestors.

Till not a doubt can be left that this indispensible change has been effected, Freeholders of Westmorland! you will remain—but to *exhort* is not my present business—I was retracing the history of the influence of one Family, and have shewn that much of it depends upon that steady support given by them to government, during a long and arduous struggle, and upon the general course of their public conduct, which has secured your approbation and won for them your confidence. Let us now candidly ask what practical evil has arisen from this preponderance. Is it not obvious, that it is justified by the causes that have produced it? As far as it concerns the general well-being of the Kingdom, it would be easy to shew, that if the democratic activities of the great Towns and of the manufacturing Districts, were not counteracted by the sedentary power of large estates, continued from generation to generation in particular families, it would be scarcely possible that the Laws and Constitution of the Country could sustain the shocks which they would be subject to. And as to our own County, *that* Man must be strangely prejudiced, who does not perceive how desireable it is, that some powerful Individual should be attached to it; who, by his influence with Government, may facilitate the execution of any plan tending, with due concern for *general* welfare, to the especial benefit of Westmorland. The influence of the House of Lowther is, we acknowledge, great; but has a case been made out, that this influence has been abused? The voice of gratitude is not loud, out of delicacy to the Benefactor; but, if all who know were at liberty to speak, to the measure of their wishes, the services which have been rendered by the House of Lowther to Westmorland, its Natives, and Inhabitants, would be proclaimed in a manner that would confound detraction.—Yet the Kendal Committee of the 26th of January—without troubling themselves to inquire how far this preponderance is a reasonable thing, and what have been its real and practical effects—are indignant; their blood is roused; 'and they are determined to address their Brother Freeholders, and call upon them to recover the exercise of the elective Franchise, which has been withheld from them for half a century.'—*Withheld* from them! Suppose these Champions, in this their first declaration of hostility, had said, 'to recover the elective Franchise *which we have suffered to lie dormant*.' But no!—Who would take blame to himself, when, by so doing, he is likely to break the force of the indignation, which, whether deserved or not, he hopes to heap upon his adversary? This is politic—but does it become professing men? Does it suit those who set forward with a proclamation, that they are select spirits, free from Party ties; and, of course, superior to those artifices and misrepresentations —to those groundless or immoderate aversions—which men who act in parties find it so difficult to keep clear of?

What degree of discernment and consistency, an assembly of persons, who begin their labours with such professions and publish such intentions, have shewn, by making choice of the Individual whom they have recommended, as eminently entitled to their confidence and qualified to assist them in attaining their end, may become the fit subject of a future enquiry.

SECOND ADDRESS.

Gentlemen,

Much of my former Address, originated in deference to that sense of right, which is inseparable from the minds of enlightened Patriots. Passing from local considerations, I wrote under a belief that, whatever personal or family leanings might prevail among you, you would be moved by a wish to see the supporters of his Majesty's Ministers and their opponents—possessed, relatively to each other, of that degree of strength which might render both parties, in their several capacities, most serviceable to the State. I noticed, that this just proportion of strength no longer remained; and shewed, that the Opposition had caused it to be destroyed by holding, from the beginning of the French Revolution, such a course as introduced in Parliament, discord among themselves; deprived them, in that House and elsewhere, of the respect which from their Adversaries they had been accustomed to command; turned indifferent persons into enemies; and alienated, throughout the Island, the affections of thousands who had been proud to unite with them. This weakness and degradation, deplored by all true Friends of the Commonweal, was sufficiently accounted for, without even adverting to the fact that—when the disasters of the war had induced the Country to forgive, and, in some degree, to forget, the alarming attachment of that Party to French theories: and power, heightened by the popularity of hope and expectation, was thrown into their hands—they disgusted even bigotted adherents, by the rapacious use they made of that power;—stooping to so many offensive compromises, and committing so many faults in every department, that, a Government of Talents, if such be the fruits of talent, was proved to be the most mischievous sort of government which England had ever been troubled with. So that, whether in or out of place, an evil genius seemed to attend them!

How could all this happen? For the fundamental reason, that neither the religion, the laws, the morals, the manners, nor the literature of the country, especially as contrasted with those of France, were prized by the Leaders of the Party as they deserved. It is a notorious fact that, among their personal Friends, was scarcely to be found a single Clergyman of distinction;—so that, how to dispose of their ecclesiastical patronage in a manner that might do them credit, they were almost as ignorant as strangers landed, for the first time, in a foreign Country. This is not to be accounted for on any supposition (since the education of men of rank naturally devolves on those members of our Universities, who choose the Church for their profession) but that of a repugnance on their part to associate with persons of grave character and decorous manners. Is the distracted remnant of the Party, now surviving, improved in that respect? The dazzling talents with which it was once distinguished have passed away; pleasure and dissipation are no longer, in that quarter, exhibited to the world in such reconcilement with business as excited dispositions to forgive what could not be approved, and a species of wonder, not sufficiently kept apart from envy, at the extraordinary gifts and powers by which the union was accomplished. This injurious conjunction no longer exists, so as to attract the eyes of the Nation. But we look in vain for signs that the opinions, habits, and feelings of the Party are tending towards a restoration of that genuine English character, by which alone the confidence of the sound part of the People can be recovered.

The public life of the Candidate who now, for the first time, solicits your suffrages, my Brother Freeholders, cannot, however, without injustice to that Party, be deemed a fair exponent of its political opinions. It has, indeed, been too tolerant with Mr. Brougham, while he was labouring to ingraft certain sour cuttings from the wild wood of ultra reform on the reverend, though somewhat decayed, stock of that tree of Whiggism, which flourished proudly under the cultivation of our Ancestors. This indulgence, and others like it, will embolden him to aim at passing himself off as the Delegate of Opposition, and the authorized pleader of their cause. But Time, that Judge from whom none but triflers appeal to conjecture, has decided upon leading principles and main events, and given the verdict against his clients. While, with a ready tongue, the Advocate of a disappointed party is filling one scale, do you, with a clear memory and apt judgment, silently throw in what of right belongs to the other; and the result will be, that no sensible man among you, who has supported the present Members on account of their steady adherence to Ministers, can be induced to change his conduct, or be persuaded that the hour is either come, or approaching, when, for the sake of bringing the power of Opposition in this County nearer to an equality with that of Ministers, it will be his duty to vote against those Representatives in whom he has hitherto confided. No, if Mr. Brougham had not individually passed far beyond the line of that Party—if his conduct had been such that even they themselves would admit that he truly belonged to them—the exception would still lie against the general rule; and will remain till the character of men and measures materially changes, for the better, assuredly, on the one side, if not for the worse on the other. Remember what England might have been with an Administration countenancing French Doctrines at the dawn of the French Revolution, and suffering them, as it advanced, to be sown with every wind that came across the Channel! Think what was the state of Europe before the French Emperor, the apparent, and in too many respects the real, Idol of Opposition, was overthrown!

Numbers, I am aware, do not cease vehemently to maintain, that the late war was neither just nor necessary; that the ostensible and real causes of it were widely different; that it was not begun, and persisted in, for the purpose of withstanding foreign aggression, and in defence of social order: but from unprincipled ambition in the Powers of Europe, eager to seize that opportunity of augmenting their territories at the expence of distracted and enfeebled France.—Events ever-to-be-lamented do, I grant, give too much colour to those affirmations. But this was a war upon a large scale, wherein many Belligerents took part; and no one who distinctly remembers the state of Europe at its commencement will be inclined any more to question that the alleged motives had a solid foundation, because then, or afterwards, others might mix with them, than he would doubt that the maintenance of Christianity and the reduction of the power of the Infidels were the principal motives of the Crusades, because roving Adventurers, joining in those expeditions, turned them to their own profit. Traders and hypocrites may make part of a Caravan bound to Mecca; but it does not follow that a religious observance is not the prime object of the Pilgrimage. The political fanaticism (it deserves no milder name) that pervaded the Manifesto issued by the Duke of Brunswick, on his entry into France, proves, that he and the Power whose organ he was, were swayed on their march by an ambition very different from that of territorial aggrandizement;—at least, if such ambition existed, it is plain that feelings of another kind blinded them to the means of gratifying it. Nevertheless, we must acknowledge the passion soon manifested itself, and in a quarter where it was least excusable. The seizure of Valenciennes, in the name of the Emperor of Germany, was an act of such glaring rapacity, and gave the lie so unfeelingly to all that had been professed, that the then Ministers of Great Britain, doubtless, opposed the intention with a strong remonstrance. But the dictates of magnanimity (which in such cases is but another word for high and sage policy) would have been—'this unjust act must either be abandoned, or Great Britain shall retire from a contest which, if such principles are to govern, or interfere with, the conduct of it, cannot but be calamitous.' A threat to this purpose was either not given or not acted upon. *Hinc illæ clades!* From that moment the alliance of the French Loyalists with the coalesced Powers seemed to have no ground of rational patriotism to stand upon. Their professed helpers became their worst enemies; and numbers among them not only began to wish for the defeat of their false friends, but joined themselves to their fellow-countrymen, of all parties, who were labouring to effect it.—But the military successes of the French, arising mainly from this want of principle in the Confederate Powers, in course of time placed the policy and justice of the war upon a new footing. However men might differ about the necessity or reasonableness of resorting to arms in the first instance, things were brought to such a state that, among the disinterested and dispassionate, there could be but one opinion (even if nothing higher than security was aimed at) on the demand for the utmost strength of the nation being put forth in the prosecution of the war, till it should assume a more hopeful aspect.—And now it was that Ministers made ample amends for past subserviency to selfish coadjutors, and proved themselves worthy of being entrusted with the fate of Europe. While the Opposition were taking counsel from their fears, and recommending despair—while they continued to magnify without scruple the strength of the Enemy, and to expose, misrepresent, and therefore increase the weaknesses of their country, his

Majesty's Ministers were not daunted, though often discouraged: they struggled up against adversity with fortitude, and persevered heroically; throwing themselves upon the honour and wisdom of the Country, and trusting for the issue to the decrees of a just Providence:—and for this determination everlasting gratitude will attend them!

From the internal situation of France, produced by the Revolution, War with the contiguous Powers was inevitable; sooner or later the evil must have been encountered; and it was of little importance whether England took a share in it somewhat earlier than, by fallible judgments, might be deemed necessary, or not. The frankness with which the faults that were committed have been acknowledged entitles the writer to some regard, when, speaking from an intimate knowledge of the internal state of France at that time, he affirms, that the war waged against her was, in a liberal interpretation of the words, *just and necessary*. At all events our Nation viewed it in this light. A large majority of the Inhabitants of Great Britain called for the war; and they who *will* the end *will* the means: the war being deemed necessary, taxes became indispensible for its support. Some might prefer one mode of raising them—some another; but these are minor considerations. Public men, united in bodies, must act on great principles. Mutual deference is a fundamental requisite for the composition and efficiency of a Party: for, if individual judgment is to be obtruded and insisted upon in subordinate concerns, the march of business will be perpetually obstructed. The leaders will not know whom they can depend upon, and therefore will be at a loss what to recommend, and how to act. If a public man differs from his Party in essentials, Conscience and Honour demand that he should withdraw; but if there be no such difference, it is incumbent upon him to submit his personal opinion to the general sense. He, therefore, who thought the prosecution of the war necessary, could not condemn the public Imposts; on this consequence the steady adherents of Ministers rest their claim to approbation, and advance it boldly in defiance of the outcry raised against the Government, on account of the burthens which the situation of Europe compelled it to lay upon the people.

In matters of taste, it is a process attended with little advantage, and often injurious, to compare one set of artists, or writers, with another. But, in estimating the merits of public men, especially of two Parties acting in direct opposition, it is not only expedient, but indispensible, that both should be kept constantly in sight. The truth or fallacy of French principles, and the tendency, good or bad, of the Revolution which sprang out of them; and the necessity, or non-necessity—the policy, or impolicy—of resisting by war the encroachments of republican and imperial France; these were the opposite grounds upon which each Party staked their credit: here we behold them in full contrast with each other—To whom shall the crown be given? On whom has the light fallen? and who are covered by shade and thick darkness?

The magnanimity which resolved, that for principle's sake no efforts should be spared to crush a bestial despotism, was acknowledged by every manly spirit whom Party degenerating into Faction had not vitiated. That such was the dictate of confiding *wisdom* had long been inwardly felt; and the *prudence* of the course was evinced by the triumphant issue; but to the very completeness of this triumph may be indirectly attributed no small portion of the obloquy now heaped upon those advisers through whom it was achieved. The power of Napoleon Buonaparte was overthrown—his person has disappeared from the theatre of Europe—his name has almost deserted the columns of her daily and weekly Journals—but as he has left no Successor, as there is no foreign Tyrant of sufficient importance to attract hatred by exciting fear, many honest English Patriots must either find, or set up, something at home for the employment of those affections. This is too natural to occasion surprise; thousands are so framed, that they are but languidly conscious of their love of an object, unless while they feel themselves in an active state of aversion to something which they can regard as its opposite.—Thus we see Men, who had been proud of their attachment to his Majesty's Ministers, during the awful struggle, as soon as it was over, allowing on the first temptation that proud attachment to be converted into immoderate suspicion, and a long experienced gratitude into sudden alienation.—Through this infirmity, many were betrayed into taking part with the Men whom they had heretofore despised or condemned; and assisted them in reviling their own Government for suffering, among the States of the Continent, institutions to remain which the respective nations (surely the best, if not the only judges in the case) were unwilling to part with; and for having permitted things to be done, either just and proper in themselves, or if indeed abuses, abuses of that kind which Great Britain had neither right to oppose, nor power to prevent. Not a Frenchman is in arms in Spain! But (alas for the credit of the English Cabinet!) Ferdinand, though a lawful, appears to be a sorry King; and the Inquisition, though venerated by the People of Spain as a holy tribunal, which has spread a protecting shade over their religion for hundreds of years, is, among Protestants, an abomination! Is that, however, a reason why we should not rejoice that Spain is restored to the rank of an Independent nation; and that her resources do not continue at the disposal of a foreign Tyrant, for the annoyance of Great Britain? Prussia no longer receives decrees from the Tuilleries; but nothing, we are told, is gained by this deliverance; because the Sovereign of that Country has not participated, as far as became him, a popular effervescence; and has withheld from his subjects certain privileges which they have proved themselves, to all but heated judgments, not yet qualified to receive. Now, if numbers can blame, without cause, the British Cabinet for events falling below their wishes, in cases remote from their immediate concerns, the reasonableness of their opinions may well be questioned in points where selfish passion is touched to the quick.—Yes, in spite of the outcry of such Men to the contrary, every enlightened Politician and discerning Patriot, however diffident as to what was the exact line of prudence in such arduous circumstances, will reprobate the conduct of those who were for reducing public expenditure with a precipitation that might have produced a convulsion in the State. The Habeas Corpus Act is also our own near concern; it was suspended, some think without sufficient cause; not so, however, the Persons who had the best means of ascertaining the state of the Country; for they could have been induced to have recourse to a measure, at all times so obnoxious, by nothing less than a persuasion of its expediency. 'But persuasion (an Objector will say) is produced in many ways; and even that degree of it which in these matters passes for conviction, depends less upon external testimony than on the habits and feelings of those by whom the testimony is to be weighed and decided upon. A council for the administration of affairs is far from being as favourably circumstanced as a tribunal of law; for the Party, which is to pronounce upon the case, has had to procure the evidence, the sum and quality of which must needs have been affected by previously existing prejudices, and by any bias received in the process of collecting it.—The privileges of the subject, one might think, would never be unjustifiably infringed, if it were only from considerations of self-interest; but power is apt to resort to unnecessary rigour in order to supply the deficiencies of *authority* forfeited by remissness; it is also not unfrequently exerted merely to shew that it is possessed; to show this to others while power is a novelty, and when it has long ceased to be so, to prove it to ourselves. Impatience of mind, moreover, puts men upon the use of strong and coarse tools, when those of lighter make and finer edge, with due care, might execute the work much better. Above all, timidity flies to extremes;—if the elements were at our command, how often would an inundation be called for, when a fire-engine would have proved equal to the service!—Much more might be urged in this strain, and similar suggestions are all that the question will admit of; for to suppose a gross appetite of tyranny in Government, would be an insult to the reader's understanding. Happily for the Inhabitants of Westmorland, as no dispositions existing among them could furnish a motive for this restrictive measure, so they will not be sorry that their remoteness from scenes of public confusion, has placed them where they will be slow to give an unqualified opinion upon its merits. Yet it will not escape their discernment, that, if doubts might have been entertained whether the ignorant and distressed multitude, in other parts of the Island, were actually brought to a state that justified the suspension of this law, such doubts must have been weakened, if not wholly removed, by the subsequent behaviour of those in the upper ranks of society, who, in order to arraign the Government, and denounce the laws, have seized every opportunity of palliating sedition, if not of exculpating treason. O far better to employ bad men in the detection of foul conspiracies, than to excuse and shelter—(would that I were allowed to confine myself to these words)—than to reward and honour—every one that can contrive to make himself conspicuous by courses which, wherever they are not branded with infamy, find the national character in a state of degradation, ominous (if it should spread) for the existence of all that ought to be dear to Englishmen.

But there are points of domestic policy in which his Majesty's Ministers, not appearing in counterview with their Opponents, are seen less to their honour. Speaking as an Individual, and knowing that here I differ from many Freeholders with whom it is an honour to co-operate in the present struggle, I must express my disapprobation of the patronage afforded by several persons in power, to a Society by which is virtually propagated the notion that Priesthood, and of course our own inestimable Church Establishment, is superfluous. I condemn their sanction (and this attaches to the whole body) of the malevolent and senseless abuse heaped upon the Clergy, in the matter of Tythes, through the medium of papers circulated by the Agricultural Board. I deprecate the course which some among them take in the Catholic Question, as unconstitutional; and deplore the want of discernment evinced by men who persuade themselves that the discontents prevalent in Ireland will be either removed or abated by such concession. With these errors and weaknesses the Members of the Administration (as appears to me) may be justly reproached; and a still heavier charge will lie against them, if the correction of the Poor Laws be longer deferred. May they exhibit, in treating this momentous subject, a tenderness of undeceived humanity on the one side, and a sternness of enlightened state-policy on the other! Thus, and thus only, can be checked immediately, and in due course of time perhaps removed, an evil by which one claim and title is set in array against another, in a manner, and to an extent, that threatens utter subversion to the ancient frame of society.

This is the heaviest burthen that now lies upon England! —Here is a necessity for reform which, as it cannot prosper unless it begin from the Government and the upper ranks in society, has no attraction for demagogues and mob-exciting patriots. They understand their game; and, as if the people could in no way be so effectually benefited as by rendering their Government suspected, they declaim against taxes; and, by their clamours for reduction of public expenditure, drown the counter-suggestions from the 'still small voice' of moderation appealing to circumstances. 'Cry aloud, and spare not!

—Retrench and lop off!' and so they proceeded with the huzza of the multitude at their heels, till they had produced an extreme embarrassment in the Government, and instant distress and misery among the People.

One of the most importunate of that class of Economists which Parliament contained, now Gentlemen, solicits the honour of representing you; and merit may perhaps be claimed for him for his exertions upon that occasion. If it be praise-worthy to have contributed to cast shoals of our deserving countrymen adrift, without regard to their past services, that praise cannot be denied him; if it be commendable to have availed himself of inordinate momentary passion to carry measures whereby the general weal was sacrificed, whether designedly for the attainment of popularity, or in the self-applauding sincerity of a heated mind, that praise is due to Mr. Brougham and his coadjutors. But, to the judicious Freeholders of Westmorland, whether Gentry or Yeomanry, rich or poor, he will in vain adduce this, or any other part of the recent conduct of Opposition, as a motive for strengthening their interests amongst us. No, Freeholders, we must wait; assuring them that they shall have a reasonable portion of our support as soon as they have proved that they deserve it!

Till that time comes, it will not grieve us that this County should supply two Representatives to uphold the Servants of the Crown, even if both should continue, through unavoidable circumstances, to issue from one Family amongst us. Till that change takes place, we will treat with scorn the senseless outcry for the recovery of an independence which has never been lost. We are, have been, and will remain, independent; and the host of men, respectable on every account, who have publicly avowed their desire to maintain our present Representatives in their seats, deem it insolence to assert the contrary. They are independent in every rational sense of the word; acknowledging, however, that they rest upon a principle, and are incorporated with an interest; and this they regard as a proof that their affections are sane, and their understandings superior to illusion. But in certain vocabularies liberty is synonymous with licence; and to be free, as explained by some, is to live and act without restraint. In like manner, independence, according to the meaning of their interpretation, is the explosive energy of conceit—making blind havoc with expediency. It is a presumptuous spirit at war with all the passive worth of mankind. The independence which they boast of despises habit, and time-honoured forms of subordination; it consists in breaking old ties upon new temptations; in casting off the modest garb of private obligation to strut about in the glittering armour of public virtue; in sacrificing, with jacobinical infatuation, the near to the remote, and preferring, to what has been known and tried, that which has no distinct existence, even in imagination; in renouncing, with voluble tongue and vain heart, every thing intricate in motive, and mixed in quality, in a downright passion of love for absolute, unapproachable patriotism! In short, the independence these Reformers bawl for is the worthy precursor of the liberty they adore;—making her first essay by starting out of the course for the pleasure of falling into the ditch; and asserting her heaven-born vigour by soaring *above* the level of humanity in profession, that it may more conspicuously appear how far she can fall *below* it in practice.

To this spurious independence the Friends of our present Representatives lay no claim. They assert in the face of the world that those Representatives hold their seats by free election.—*That* has placed them there; and why should we wish to change what we do not disapprove of—that which could not have been without our approbation? But this County has not for a long time been disturbed by electioneering contests.—Is there no species of choice, then, but that which is accompanied with commotion and clamour? Do silent acquiescence and deliberate consent pass for nothing? Being contented, what could we seek for more? Being satisfied, why should we stir for stirring's sake? Uproar and disorder, even these we could tolerate on a justifying occasion; but it is no sign of prudence to court them unnecessarily, nor of temper to invite them wantonly. He who resorts to substantial unruliness for the redress of imaginary grievances, provokes certain mischief; and often, in the end, produces calamity which would excite little compassion, could it be confined to its original author.

Let those who think that they are degraded proclaim their own dishonour. *They* choose to regard themselves as shackled Conscripts:—*we* know that we are self-equipped Volunteers. If they cannot be easy without branding themselves as slaves, we would endeavour to dissuade them from such abuse of their free-agency; but if they persist, we cannot interfere with their humour: only do not let them apply the iron to our foreheads! They cry out that they have been in a lethargy; why do they not add that they would have been asleep to this hour, if they had not been roused, in their vales and on their moors, by an officious and impertinent call from the dirty alleys and obscure courts of the Metropolis?

If there be any honour in England, the composition of the Lowther Party must be loyal and honourable. Its adversaries have admitted that a large majority, they might have added nearly the whole, of the leading Gentry; that the Magistracy—all but a single Individual; that the Clergy and the Members of the other liberal Professions—with very few exceptions; and a vast body of Tradesmen and Manufacturers, and of substantial Yeomen, the honest Grey-coats of Westmorland, have already declared themselves of one mind upon this appeal to their judgments. Looking to a distance, they see the worth and opulence, the weight of character, and the dignity and respectability of station, that distinguish the numerous list of Freeholders resident in London, who have jointly and publicly testified their satisfaction in the conduct of our present Representatives. The discontented see and know these things; and are well aware also that the Lowthers cannot justly be accused of inordinate and disrespectful family ambition, inasmuch as it was not their wish that the County should be represented by two Members of their House. It has long been no secret that if any other Gentleman of the County properly qualified, whose *political principles did not substantially differ from their own,* would have come forward, he would have been *sure of their support.* If they resist to the utmost persons of *opposite* principles, the points in dispute being scarcely less than vital, the more must they be respected by every zealous Patriot and conscientious Man.

From what has been said, it appears that the political influence of the family of Lowther in Westmorland is the natural and reasonable consequence of a long-continued possession of large property—furnishing, with the judicious Nobleman at its head, an obvious support, defence, and *instrument* for the intelligent patriotism of the County. I have said instrument, and laid an emphasis upon the word; because they who do not perceive that such is the truth are ignorant what shape, in these cases, social combinations must take, in order to be efficient and be preserved. Every great family which many have rallied round from congeniality of public sentiment, and for a political purpose, seems in course of time to direct, and in ordinary cases does direct, its voluntary adherents; but, if it should violate their wishes and shock their sense of right, it would speedily be reduced to such support only as it could *command;* and then would be seen who had been Principal, and who Secondary; to whom had belonged in reality the place of Agent, to whom that of the Employer. The sticklers for *emancipation* (a fashionable word in our times, when rational acquiescence is deemed baseness of spirit, and the most enlightened service passes for benighted servility!) have been free on numerous occasions to make the effort they are now making. Could any considerable person have been found to share their feeling, they might have proposed a Representative unacceptable to the Family whose ascendancy they complain of, with a certainty of securing his election, had the good-will of the Freeholders been on their side. What could possibly have prevented this trial? But they talk as if some mysterious power had been used to their injury. Some call it 'a thraldom from without'—some 'a drowsiness within.'—Mr. Brougham's Kendal Committee find fault with others—the Chairman of the Appleby Committee is inclined to fix the blame nearer home. An accredited organ of their Kendal Committee tells you dogmatically, from the Bill of Rights, that '*Elections shall be free;*' and, if asked how the citation bears upon the case, his answer would most likely prove him of opinion, that, as noise is sometimes an accompaniment of freedom, so there can be no freedom without noise. Or, does the erudite Constitutionalist take this method of informing us, that the Lord Lieutenant has been accustomed to awe and controul the Voters of this County, as Charles the Second and his Brother attempted to awe and controul those of the whole kingdom? If such be the meaning of the Writer and his Employers, what a pity Westmorland has not a Lunatic Asylum for the accommodation of the whole Body! In the same strain, and from the same quarter, we are triumphantly told 'that no Peer of Parliament shall interfere in Elections.' How injurious then to these Monitors and their Cause the report of the Hereditary

High Sheriff's massy subscription, and his zealous countenance! Let him be entreated formally to contradict it;—or would they have one law for a Peer who is a Friend to Administration, and another for such as are its enemies? Is the same act to pass for culpable or praiseworthy, just as it thwarts, or furthers, the wishes of those who pronounce a judgment upon it?

The approvers of that order of things in which we live and move, at this day, as free Englishmen, are under no temptation to fall into these contradictions. They acknowledge that the general question is one of great delicacy: they admit that laws cannot be openly slighted without a breach of decorum, even when the relations of things are so far altered that Law looks one way—and Reason another. Where such disagreement occurs in respect to those Statutes which have the dignity of constitutional regulations, the less that is said upon the subject the better for the Country. But writers, who in such a case would gladly keep a silent course, are often forced out of it by wily hypocrites, and by others, who seem unconscious that, as there are Pedants in Literature, and Bigots in Religion, so are there Precisians in Politics—men without experience, who contend for limits and restraints when the Power which those limits and restraints were intended to confine is long since vanished. In the Statute-books Enactments of great name stand unrepealed, which may be compared to a stately oak in the last stage of decay, or a magnificent building in ruins. Respect and admiration are due to both; and we should deem it profaneness to cut down the one, or demolish the other. But are we, therefore, to be sent to the sapless tree for may-garlands, or reproached for not making the mouldering ruin our place of abode? Government is essentially a matter of expediency; they who perceive this, and whose knowledge keeps pace with the changes of society, lament that, when Time is gently carrying what is useless or injurious into the back-ground, he must be interrupted in the process by Smatterers and Sciolists—intent upon misdirecting the indignation of the simple, and feeding the ill-humours of the ignorant. How often do such men, for no better purpose, remind their disciples of the standing order that declares it to be 'a high infringement of the liberties and privileges of the Commons, for any Lord of Parliament to concern himself in the election of members, to serve for the Commons in Parliament.'—This vote continues to be read publicly at the opening of every Session,—but practice rises up against it; and, without censuring the Custom, or doubting that it might be salutary when first established, (though it is not easily reconcileable with the eligibility of the eldest sons of Peers to the lower House, without any other qualification than their birth,) we may be permitted to be thankful that subsequent experience is not rendered useless to the living by the formal repetition of a voice from the tombs. Better is it that laws should remain till long trial has proved them an incumbrance, than that they should be too hastily changed; but this consideration need not prevent the avowal of an opinion, which every practical Statesman will confirm, that, if the property of the Peers were not, according to the will and by the care of the owners, substantially represented by Commoners, to a proportionate extent under their influence, their large Estates would be, for them, little better than sand liable to be blown about in the desart, and their privileges, however useful to the country, would become fugitive as foam upon the surface of the sea.—(*See Note.*)

I recollect a picture of Diogenes going about in search of an honest man. The philosopher bore a staff in one hand, and a lantern in the other. Did the latter accompaniment imply that he was a persevering Spirit who would continue his labour by night as well as by day? Or was it a stroke of satire on the part of the painter, indicating that, as Diogenes was a surly and conceited Cynic, he preferred darkness for his time of search, and a scanty and feeble light of his own carrying, to the bounteous assistance of the sun in heaven? How this might be with Diogenes, I know not; but assuredly thus it fares with our Reformers:—The Journal of some venal or factious scribbler is the black and smoky lantern they are guided by; and the sunshine spread over the face of a happy country is of no use in helping them to find any object they are in search of.—The plea of the degraded state of the Representation of Westmorland has been proved to be rotten;—if certain discontented persons desire to erect a building on a new plan, why not look about for a firm foundation? The dissatisfied ought honestly to avow, that their aim is to elect a Man, whose principles differ from those of the present Members to an extreme which takes away all hope, or even wish, that the interest he is to depend upon should harmonize with the interest hitherto prevalent in the County. Every thing short of this leaves them subject to a charge of acting upon false pretences, unless they prefer being accused of harbouring a pharisaical presumption, that would be odious were it not ridiculous. If the state of society in Westmorland be as corrupt as they describe, what, in the name of wonder, has preserved *their* purity? Away then with hypocrisy and hollow pretext; let us be no longer deafened with a rant about throwing off intolerable burthens, and repelling injuries, and avenging insults! Say at once that you disapprove of the present Members, and would have others more to your own liking; you have named your Man, or rather necessity has named him for you. Your ship was reduced to extremities; it would have been better to abandon her—you thought otherwise; will you listen then while I shew that the Pilot, who has taken charge of the vessel, is ignorant of the soundings, and that you will have cause to be thankful if he does not prove very desperate in the management of the helm?

The Lands of England, you will recollect, Gentlemen, are originally supposed to be holden by grants from the King, our liege Lord; and the Constitution of the Country is accordingly a mellowed feudality. The oldest and most respectable name for a County Representative is, KNIGHT OF THE SHIRE. In the reign of Queen Anne it was enacted, that every Knight of the Shire (the eldest sons of Peers and a few others excepted) shall have a clear estate of Freehold or Copyhold to the value of £600 per annum. The same qualification continues to be required at this day; and, if the depreciation of money and other causes have injuriously affected the *Letter* of the Statute, the *Spirit* of it has not only been preserved in practice, but carried still higher. Hence we scarcely scruple to take for granted that a County Representative is a man of substantial landed property; or stands in such known relation to a conspicuous Estate that he has in it a valuable interest; and that, whoever be the possessor, such Estate may be looked upon as a pledge for his conduct.

The basis of the elective Franchise being property, the legal condition of eligibility to a seat in Parliament is the same. Our ancestors were not blind to the *moral* considerations which, if they did not suggest these ordinances, established a confidence in their expediency. Knowing that there could be no *absolute* guarantee for integrity, and that there was no *certain* test of discretion and knowledge, for bodies of men, the prudence of former times turned to the best substitute human nature would admit of, and civil society furnished. This was property; which shewed that a man had something that might be impaired or lost by mismanagement; something which tended to place him above dependence from need; and promised, though it did not insure, some degree of education to produce requisite intelligence. To be a Voter required a fixed Property, or a defined privilege; to be voted for, required more; and the scale of demand rose with the responsibility incurred. A Knight of the Shire must have double the Estate required from a Representative of a Borough. This is the old Law; and the course of things since has caused, as was observed above, that high office to devolve almost exclusively on Persons of large Estate, or their near connections. And why is it desirable that we should not deviate from this track? If we wish for honesty, we shall select men who, not being subject to one of the strongest temptations to be otherwise than honest, will incur heavier disgrace, and meet with less indulgence, if they disappoint us. Do we wish for sage conduct, our choice will fall upon those who have the wisdom that lurks in circumstances, to supply what may be deficient in their personal accomplishments. But, if there *be* a deficiency, the fault must lie with the Electors themselves. When persons of large property are confided in, we cannot plead want of opportunities for being acquainted with them. Men of large estates cannot but be men of wide concerns; and thus it is that they become known in proportion. Extensive landed property entails upon the possessor many duties, and places him in divers relations, by which he undergoes a public trial. Is a man just in his dealings? Does he keep his promises? Does he pay his debts punctually? Has he a feeling for the poor? Is his Family well governed? Is he a considerate Landlord? Does he attend to his own affairs; and are those of others, which have fallen under his care, diligently and judiciously managed? Answers to these questions, where the Subject of them has but an inconsiderable landed Property, can only be expected from a very narrow circle of Neighbours;—but place him at the head of a large Estate, and knowledge of what he is in these particulars must spread to a distance; and it will be further known how he has acted as a Magistrate, and in what manner he has fulfilled the duties of every important office which he may have been called to, by virtue of his possessions.

Such are the general principles of reason which govern law, and justify practice in this weighty matter. The decision is not to take place upon imagination or conjecture. It is not to rest upon professions of the Candidate, or protestations of his Friends. As a County Representative is to be voted for by many—many must have opportunities of knowing him; or, failing that intimate knowledge, we require the pledge of condition, the bond and seal of circumstance. Otherwise we withhold our confidence, and cannot be prevailed upon to give, to the opinions of an Individual unbacked by these advantages, the countenance and authority which they might derive from being supposed to accord with those of numerous Constituents scattered over a wide Country, and therefore less liable to be affected by partial views, or sudden and transitory passion—to diminish their value.

The Freeholders of past times knew that their rights were most likely to repose in safety, under the shade of rank and property. Adventurers had no estimation among them; there was no room for them—no place for them to appear in.—Think of this, and ask if your Fathers, could they rise from their tombs, would not have stared, with no small degree of wonder, upon the Person who now solicits the Suffrages of the County of Westmorland. What are his Rents—Where are his comings in? He is engaged in an undertaking of great expence—how is that expence supplied? From his own purse? Impossible! Where are the golden sinews which this Champion of Independence depends upon? If they be furnished by those who have no natural connection with the County, are we simple enough to believe that they dip their hands into their pockets out of pure good-will to us? May they not rather justly be suspected of a wish to embroil us for some sinister purpose? At all events, it might be some satisfaction would they shew themselves, so that, if we are to have a Subscription-candidate, we may know what sort of Persons he is indebted to, and at least be able to *guess* what they will require of him.

The principles that have been laid down, and the facts which have been adverted to, might seem to render it superfluous to retrace the public conduct of Mr. Brougham, and to enquire whether, in Parliament or at the London Tavern, in Palace Yard or elsewhere, those acts and courses, to which he himself refers as his *only* recommendation, do not still more unfit him for the trust which he covets. But Persons fond of novelty make light of deficiencies which would have admitted of no compensation in the judgment of our Ancestors; and the Candidate, being in no respect remarkable for deference to public opinion, is willing to avail himself of new-fangled expectations. Hence it becomes necessary to consider what would be the *political value of the Freeholds of Westmorland*, if the system of Annual Parliaments and Universal Suffrage (countenanced by Mr. Brougham) should be acted upon. But, as there has been much saying and unsaying on this subject, let us review the case.

In the House of Commons, on the 17th of February, 1817, Lord Cochrane affirmed, that, on a certain day which he named, Mr. Brougham, at a dinner given at the London Tavern, to the Friends of Parliamentary Reform, used the following words, or words to the same effect:—'As often as we have required that Parliaments should be chosen yearly, and that the elective Franchise should be extended to all who pay taxes, we have been desired to wait, for the enemy was at the gate, and ready to avail himself of the discords attending our political contests, in order to undermine our national independence. This argument is gone, and our Adversaries must now look for another. He had mentioned the two radical doctrines of *yearly election*, and the *Franchise enjoyed by all paying taxes;* but it would be superfluous to reason in favour of them here, where all are agreed on the subject.'

When this, and other passages of like import, were produced by Lord C. in a paper declared to be in Mr. Brougham's handwriting, and to be a report made by himself of the speech then and there delivered, did Mr. Brougham deny that the handwriting was his, and that those words had fallen from his pen, as the best image that his own memory could furnish of what he had uttered? No—he gave vent only to a vague complaint of groundless aspersions; and accused certain persons of rashness and imprudence, and of not waiting only for a few days longer, when they would have had a full and fair opportunity of hearing his sentiments on this momentous subject. He then acknowledged that some observations had fallen from him *similar* to what had been read by the Noble Lord; and added, that he then said, or at least meant to be understood as saying, (he takes no notice of what he wrote or meant to be understood as writing,) *what he still maintained*—'that the power of election should be limited *to those who paid direct taxes*;' in other and more faithful words, should be *extended* to all persons in that condition. Mr. B. proceeded manfully to scout the notion, that the mere production of a speech delivered by him at a Tavern would make him swerve from the line of his duty, from the childish desire of keeping up an appearance of consistency!

What then is the amount? On the 23d of June, 1814, (it cannot be unfair to state as a fact, that a vacancy in the Representation of Westminster was at that time looked for,) Mr. B. either was, or wished to be, accounted an Advocate of Annual Parliaments and Suffrage to be enjoyed by all paying taxes; and on the 17th of February, 1817, when Mr. B. in another place is reminded of these, his avowed opinions, he is utterly mute upon the subject of Annual Parliaments, on the expediency of which he had before harangued at length, and confines himself to announce, as the sum of his then opinion, that suffrage should *be co-extensive with direct taxation!* The question had two faces, and Mr. B. chooses only to look at one. Hard pressed as he was, we cannot grant him this indulgence. He has, indeed, denounced, on other occasions, the *combined* doctrines of Annual Parliaments and Universal Suffrage as chimerical and absurd; though how near he came to the point of recommending both, at the London Tavern, he is any thing but explicit; (in fact both, as Lord C. shewed, *were* virtually recommended by him.) But what does he think of Annual Parliaments, in *conjunction* with his rectified opinion of Suffrage, co-extensive with direct taxation? Here he leaves us wholly in the dark; but if the turbulent workings of Mr. Brougham's mind, and his fondness for contentious exhibition, manifested on all possible occasions, may be admitted as positive evidence, to corroborate the negative which his silence on this point implies, we are justified in believing that his passions were on that side, whatever might be the bent of his cooler judgment. But this is of little import.

Introduce suffrage co-extensive with direct taxation, and Annual Parliaments must unavoidably follow. The clumsy simplicity of the one arrangement would, in the eyes of its Admirers, match strikingly with the palpable expediency of the other. Such a union is equally suitable to an age of gross barbarism and an age of false philosophy. It is amusing to hear this plan of suffrage for all who pay direct taxes recommended as consonant to the genius and spirit of the British Constitution, when, in fact, though sufficiently rash and hazardous, it is no better than a timid plagiarism from the doctrine of the Rights of Man. Upon the model of that system, it begins with flagrant injustice to *chartered* rights; for if it were adopted, the elective Franchises that now exist would be depreciated accordingly; an invidious process for those who would lose by the alteration; and still more invidious for those to whom the privilege would not be suffered to descend. Alas! I am trifling with the subject! If the spirit of a People, composed as that of England now is, were once put into a ferment, by organizing a democracy on this scheme, and to this extent, with a Press as free and licentious as our's has long been, what a flimsy barrier would remain to check the impetus of the excluded! When, in thousands, they bore down upon the newly constituted House of Assembly, demanding to be placed upon a level with their fellow-subjects, it would avail little to send a Peace-officer to enquire—where are your vouchers? Shew us that the Tax-gatherer has been among you! As soon as the petty Artizans, Shop-keepers, and Pot-house Keepers, of our over-grown Manufacturing Towns and our enormous Cities, had each and all been invested with the right of voting, the infection would spread like a plague.—Our neighbours on the Continent tried this plan of direct taxation; and, in the beginning of the third year of *their* Reform, Universal Suffrage, which had long ruled in spirit, lorded it in form also, from the Pyrenees to the Rhine, and from the Straits of Calais to the Shores of the Mediterranean. Down went the throne of France! and, if we should take the same guide, the Throne of England must submit a second time to a like destiny. Most of us would deem this a considerable evil—the greatest political evil that could befal the Land! Not so, however, our new Candidate! unless his opinion, if, indeed, he ever *held* what may be called an opinion upon any thing, has undergone important changes since the time when he expressed himself in the following words:—' When trade and the arts of civilized life have been carried to a certain length, war is the greatest calamity that can befal a community. Any state in modern Europe would be so completely ruined by the contests which Athens and Carthage easily supported, that it would be a matter of total indifference, whether the war was a series of victories or disasters. The return of Peace to France or England, after half so long a contest as either the Peloponnesian or the Punic wars, *would be cheaply purchased by any conquest or revolution, any change of dynasty or overthrow of Government.*'—See vol. i. p. 13, of *Colonial Policy*, by H. Brougham.

The above was given to the world when we were at war with Bonaparte; and that part of the English nation, who might read the book or hear of this author's doctrines, was plainly told, that, in *his* estimation, our Constitutional liberties were not worthy of being defended at the cost of a 14 years' war! But the unsuspecting, humane, and hope-cherishing adherents of the new Candidate will tell you, this does not prove that Mr. B. sets a small price on the Constitution and Laws of England; it only shews his tender-heartedness, and his extreme aversion to the horrors and devastation of war.—Hear then Mr. B. on these points also. Let his *serious* Friends take from his pen this pleasant description, which proves at least that he can be *jocular* upon a subject that makes most men grave; although they may not think twice seven years' war so great a calamity as *any* conquest or *Revolution*, any change of dynasty or *overthrow* of *Government.*—'A species of pecuniary commutation,' he tells us, 'has been contrived, by which the operations of war are rendered very harmless; they are performed by some hundreds of sailors fighting *harmlessly* on the barren plains of the ocean, and some thousands of soldiers carrying on a scientific, and regular, and *quiet* system of warfare, in countries *set apart for the purpose*, and resorted to as the arena where the disputes of nations may be determined. The prudent policy had been adopted of *purchasing defeat* at a distance rather than victory at home; in this manner we *paid our allies for being vanquished; a few useless millions, and a few more useless lives were sacrificed;* and the result was, that we were amply rewarded by safety, increased resources, and real addition of power.' (*Edinburgh Review*, No. II., and ascertained to be the writing of Mr. Brougham, by his having incorporated it in his *Colonial Policy*.)

The new Candidate challenges the strictest scrutiny into his public life, so that had we gone much farther than the above retrospect, we should only have been fulfilling his own wishes. Personal enmity towards the Subject, the Writer has none; being, in all that concerns the feelings of private life, friendly to Mr. Brougham, rather than otherwise. That his talents and habits of application entitle him to no common respect, must be universally acknowledged; but talents in *themselves merely* are, in the eyes of the judicious, no recommendation. If a sword be sharp, it is of the more importance to ask—What use it is likely to be put to? In government, if we can keep clear of mischief, good will come of itself. Fitness is the thing to be sought; and unfitness is much less frequently caused by general incapacity than by absence of that kind of capacity which the charge demands. Talent is apt to generate presumption and self-confidence; and no qualities are so necessary, in a Legislator, as the opposites of these—which, if they do not imply the existence of sagacity, are the best substitutes for it—whether they produce, in the general disposition of the mind, an humble reliance on the wisdom of our Forefathers, and a sedate yielding to the pressure of existing things; or carry the thoughts still higher, to religious trust in a superintending Providence, by whose permission laws are ordered and customs established, for other purposes than to be perpetually found fault with.

These suggestions are recommended to the consideration of our new Aspirant, and of all those public men whose judgments are perverted, and tempers soured, by long struggling in the ranks of opposition, and incessant bustling among the professors of Reform. I shall not recal to notice further particulars, because time, by softening asperities or removing them out of sight, is a friend to benevolence. Although a rigorous investigation has been invited, it is well that there is no need to run through the rash assertions, the groundless accusations, and the virulent invectives that disfigure the speeches of this never-silent Member. All these things, offensive to moderate men, are too much to the taste of many of Mr. Brougham's partizans in Westmorland. But I call upon those who relish these deviations from fair and honourable dealing—upon those also of his adherents who are inwardly ashamed of their Champion, on this account—and upon all the Freeholders concerned in the general question, to review what has been laid before them. Having done this, they cannot but admit that Mr. Brougham's *independence* is a dark *dependence*, which no one understands—and, that if a jewel *has* been lost in Westmorland, his are not the eyes by which it is to be found again. If the dignity of Knight of the Shire is to be conferred, *he* cannot be pronounced a fit person to receive it. For whether, my Brother Freeholders, you look at the humbleness of his situation amongst Country Gentlemen; or at his amphibious habits, in the two elements of Law and Authorship, and the odd vagaries he has played in both; or whether he be tried by the daring opinions which, by his own acknowledgment, he has maintained in Parliament, and at public meetings, on the subject of the elective Franchise; we meet with concurring proofs that HE IS ALTOGETHER UNFIT TO REPRESENT THIS, OR ANY OTHER COUNTY!

If, notwithstanding the truth of this inference, Mr. Brougham's talents, information, and activity make it desirable that he should have a place in the House of Commons, why cannot they who are of this opinion be content, since he is already there? What service he is capable of rendering may be as effectually performed, should he never aspire beyond re-election to one of those seats which he now fills. The good, if any is to be looked for, may then be obtained with much less risk of evil. While he continues a Member for a close Borough, his dangerous opinions are left mainly to the support of his own character, and the arguments which his ingenuity can adduce to recommend them; but should they derive that degree of sanction from the Freeholders of a County, which success in his present undertaking would imply, they might become truly formidable!—Let every one, then, who cannot accompany Mr. B. in his bold theories, and does not go the length of admiring the composition of his political life, be cautious how he betakes himself to such help, in order to reduce, within what he may deem due bounds, the influence of a Family prominent in the civil service of the County from the earliest times. It is apparent, if the Writer has not employed his pen in vain, that against this influence there is no just ground of complaint. They who think with him will continue to uphold it, as long as the Family proves that it understands its own interest and honour by a judicious attention to our's. And should it forfeit our respect by misconduct, in the unavoidable decline of its political importance which would ensue, we should not envy that House its splendid possessions or its manifold privileges; knowing that some Families must be permanently great and opulent, or there would be no security for the possessions of the middle ranks, or of the humble Proprietor. But, looking at the present constitution and measure of this influence, you cannot but perceive, Gentlemen, that, if there were *indeed* any thing in it that could justly be complained of, our duty might still be to bear with the local evil, as correcting an opposite extreme in some other quarter of the Island;—as a counterpoise of some weight elsewhere pressing injuriously upon the springs of social order. How deplorable would be the ignorance, how pitiful the pride, that could prevent us from submitting to a partial evil for the sake of a general good! In fine, if a comprehensive survey enjoined no such sacrifice, and even if all that the unthinking, the malevolent, and the desperate, all that the deceivers and the deceived, have conjointly urged at this time against the House of Lowther, were literally true, you would be cautious how you sought a remedy for aristocratic oppression, by throwing yourselves into the arms of a flaming democracy!

Government and civil Society are things of infinite complexity, and rash Politicians are the worst enemies of mankind; because it is mainly through them that rational liberty has made so little progress in the world. You have heard of a Profession to which the luxury of modern times has given birth, that of Landscape-Gardeners, or Improvers of Pleasure-grounds. A competent Practitioner in this elegant art begins by considering every object, that he finds in the place where he is called to exercise his skill, as having a right to remain, till the contrary be proved. If it be a deformity he asks whether a slight alteration may not convert it into a beauty; and he destroys nothing till he has convinced himself by reflection that no alteration, no diminution or addition, can make it ornamental. Modern Reformers reverse this judicious maxim. If a thing is before them, so far from deeming that it has on that account a claim to continue and be deliberately dealt with, its existence with them is a sufficient warrant for its destruction. Institutions are to be subverted, Practices radically altered, and Measures to be reversed. All men are to change their places, not because the men are objectionable, or the place is injurious, but because certain Pretenders are eager to be at work, being tired of both. Some are forward, through pruriency of youthful talents—and Greybeards hobble after them, in whom number of years is a cloak for poverty of experience. Some who have much leisure, because every affair of their own has withered under their mismanagement, are eager to redeem their credit, by stirring gratis for the public;—others, having risen a little in the world, take *swimmingly* to the trade of factious Politics, on their original stock of base manners and vulgar opinions. Some are theorists hot for practice, others hacknied Practitioners who never had a theory; many are vain, and must be busy; and almost as many are needy—and the spirit of justice, deciding upon their own merits, will not suffer them to remain at rest.

The movement made among us, my countrymen of Westmorland, was preceded, announced, and prepared, by *such* Agitators, disseminating falsehoods and misrepresentations, equally mischievous, whether they proceeded from wilful malice or presumptuous ignorance. Take warning in time. Be not persuaded to unite with them who, whether they intend you injury or not, cannot but prove your enemies. Let not your's be the first County in England, which, since the days of Wilkes, and after the dreadful example of France, has given countenance to principles congenial to the vice, profligacy, and half-knowledge of Westminster; but which formerly were unheard of among us, or known only to be detested. Places, Pensions, and formidable things, if you like! but far better these, with our King and Constitution, with our quiet fire-sides and flourishing fields, than proscription and confiscation, without them! Long wars, and their unavoidable accompaniment, heavy taxes—both these evils are liable to intemperate exaggeration; but, be they what they may, would there be less of war and lighter taxes, as so many grumblers loudly preach, and too many submissive spirits fondly believe, if the House of Commons were altered into one of more popular frame, with more frequent opportunities given of changing the persons sent thither? A reference to the twenty years which succeeded the Revolution, may suffice to shew the fallacy of such expectations. Parliaments were then triennial, and democratic principles fashionable even among the Servants of the Crown. Yet, during that space of time, wars were almost incessant; and never were burthens imposed so far above the apparent ability of the Nation to support them. Having adverted to the warlike measures of those reigns merely to support my argument, I cannot forbear to applaud the high-spirited Englishmen of that age. Our forefathers were tried, as we have been tried—and their virtue did not sink under the duties which the decrees of Providence imposed upon it. They triumphed, though less signally than we have done;—following their example, let us now cultivate fortitude, encourage hope and chearful industry; and give way to enterprise. So will prosperity return. The stream, which has been checked, will flow with recruited vigour—and, when another century shall have passed away, the ambition of France will be as little formidable to our then-existing Posterity as it is now to us. But the lessons of History must be studied;—they teach us that, under every form of civil polity, war will contrive to lift up its head, and most pertinaciously in those States where the People have most sway. When I recur to these admonitions, it is to entreat that the discontented would exercise their understandings, rather than consult their passions; first separating real from mistaken grievances, and then endeavouring to ascertain (which cannot be done with a glance of the mind) how much is fairly attributable to the Government; how much to ourselves; and how large a portion of what we have to endure has been forced upon us by a foreign Power, over whom we could exercise no controul but by arms. The course here recommended will keep us, as we are, free and happy—will preserve us from what, through want of these and like precautions, other Nations have been hurried into—domestic broils, sanguinary tribunals, civil slaughter in the field, anarchy, and (sad cure and close of all!) tranquillity under the iron grasp of military despotism. Years before this catastrophe, what would have become of your Elective Franchise, Freeholders of Westmorland? The Coadjutors of the obscure Individuals who, from a distance, first excited this movement under a pretence of recovering your Rights, would have played the whirlwind among your Property, and crushed you, less perhaps out of malice, than because, in their frenzy, they could not help it.

A conviction that the subject is ill understood by those who were unprepared for what has just been said, is the excuse to my own mind, Gentlemen, for having made so protracted a demand upon your attention. The ruinous tendencies of this self-flattering enterprize can only be checked by timely and general foresight. The contest in which we are engaged has been described by Persons noticing it from a distance, as the work of a Cabal of Electioneering Jobbers, who have contrived to set up the Thanet against the Lowther interests, that both Parties might spend their money for the benefit of those who cared for neither. The Thanet interest in the County of Westmorland! —one might almost as well talk of an interest in the moon! The Descendant of the Cliffords has not thought it worth while to recommend himself to the Electors, by the course either of his public or his private life; and therefore, though his purse may have weight, and his possessions are considerable, he himself, in reference to the supposed object, is nothing. If this had been really an attempt made by a numerous body of malcontent Freeholders to carry their wishes for a change into effect, by placing at their head some *approved* Chief of an ancient Family, possessed of real consequence in the County, the proceeding, considered in the abstract, could not have been objected to. This County is, and ever was, open to fair and honourable contest, originating in principles sanctioned by general practice; and carried on by means which, if universally adopted, would not be injurious to the State. But the present measure stands not upon any such grounds; it is an attempt, no matter with what ultimate view, TO EFFECT A TOTAL CHANGE IN THE CHARACTER OF COUNTY ELECTIONS; beginning here with the expectation, as is openly avowed, of being imitated elsewhere. It *reverses* the order hitherto pursued. Instead of aiming to influence the less wealthy and less instructed Freeholders through the medium of those whom they have been accustomed to confide in—instead of descending by legitimate gradations from high to lower, from the well-instructed and widely-experienced to those who have not had equal advantages—it commences at the bottom; far beneath the degree of the poorest Freeholders; and works upwards, with an inflammatory appeal to feelings that owe their birth to previous mistatement of facts. Opulence, rank, station, privilege, distinction, intellectual culture—the notions naturally following upon these in a Country like England are protection, succour, guidance, example, dissemination of knowledge, introduction of improvements, and all the benefits and blessings that among Freemen are diffused, where authority like the parental, from a sense of community of interest and the natural goodness of mankind, is softened into brotherly concern. This is no Utopian picture of the characteristics of elevated rank, wealth, competence, and learned and liberal education in England; for, with the liberty of speech and writing that prevails amongst us, if such rays of light and love did not generally emanate from superiority of station, possessions, and accomplishment, the frame of society, which we behold, could not subsist. Yes—in spite of pride, hardness of heart, grasping avarice, and other selfish passions, the not unfrequent concomitants of affluence and worldly prosperity, the mass of the people are justly dealt with, and tenderly cherished;—accordingly, gratitude without servility; dispositions to prompt return of service, undebased by officiousness; and respectful attachment, that, with small prejudice to the understanding, greatly enriches the heart: such are the sentiments with which Englishmen of the humblest condition have been accustomed to look up towards their Friends and Benefactors. Among the holders of fixed property (whether labourers in the field or artisans); among those who are fortunate enough to have an interest in the soil of their Country; these human sentiments of civil life are strengthened by additional dependencies.—I am aware how much universal habits of rapacious speculation, occasioned by fluctuations in the value of produce during the late war—how much the spread of manufactories and the baleful operation of the Poor Laws, have done to impair these indigenous and salutary affections. I am conscious of the sad deterioration, and no one can lament it more deeply; but sufficient vitality is left in the Stock of ancient virtue to furnish hope that, by careful manuring, and skilful application of the knife to the withered branches, fresh shoots might thrive in their place—were it not for the base artifices of Malignants, who, pretending to invigorate the tree, pour scalding water and corrosive compounds among its roots; so that the fibres are killed in the mould by which they have been nourished.

That for years such artifices have been employed in Westmorland, and in a neighbouring County, with unremitting activity, must be known to all. Whatever was disliked has been systematically attacked, by the vilifying of persons connected with it. The Magistrates and public Functionaries, up to the Lord Lieutenant himself, have been regularly traduced—as unfaithful to their trust; the Clergy habitually derided—as time-servers and slavish dependants; and the Gentry, if conspicuous for attachment to the Government, stigmatized—as Men without honour or patriotism, and leagued in conspiracy against the Poor. After this manner have the Provincial Newspapers (the chief agents in this local mischief,) concurred with the disaffected London Journals, who were playing the same part towards laws and institutions, and general measures of State, by calumniating the principal Authorities of the Kingdom. Hence, instead of gratitude and love, and confidence and hope, are resentment and envy, mistrust and jealousy, and hatred and rancour, inspired:—and the drift of all is, to impress the Body of the People with a belief that neither justice can be expected, nor benevolence hoped for, unless power be transferred to Persons least resembling those who now hold it; that is—to Demagogues and Incendiaries!

It will be thought that this attempt is too extravagant to be dangerous; inasmuch as every member of society, possessed of weight and authority, must revolt from such a transfer, and abhor the issues to which it points. Possessed of weight and authority—with whom? These Agitators *have* weight and authority there, where they seek for it, that is with no small portion of what they term the physical strength of the Country. The People have ever been the dupes of extremes. VAST GAINS WITH LITTLE PAINS, is a jingle of words that would be an appropriate inscription for the insurrectionary banner of unthinking humanity. To walk—to wind—towards a thing that is coveted—how unattractive an operation compared with leaping upon it at once!—Certainly no one possessed of *legitimate authority* can desire such a transfer as we have been forced to contemplate; but he may aid in bringing it about, without desiring it. Numerous are the courses of civil action in which men of pure dispositions and honourable aims, are tempted to take part with those who are utterly destitute of both. Be not startled, if, merely glancing at the causes of this deplorable union, as it is now exhibited in this part of England, I observe, that there is no necessary connection between public spirit and political sagacity. How often does it happen that right intention is averse to inquiry as casting a damp upon its own zeal, and a suspicion upon the intrinsic recommendation of its object! Good men turn instinctively from inferences unfavourable to human nature. But there are facts which are not to be resisted, where the understanding is sound. The self-styled Emancipators have tried their strength; if there were any thing promising to England in their efforts, we should have seen this Country arrayed in opposite Parties resembling each other in quality and composition. Little of that appears. The promoters of the struggle did not hope for such a result; and many of them would not have wished for it, could they have expected to be carried through by that ruinous division of the upper from the lower ranks of society, on which they mainly relied.

But, Freeholders, wicked devices have not done the service that was expected from them. You are upon your guard; the result of this canvass has already shewn that a vast majority of you are proof against assault, and remain of sound mind. Such example of Men abiding by the rules of their Forefathers cannot but encourage others, who yet hesitate, to determine in favour of the good cause. The more signal the victory the greater will be the honour paid to fixed and true principles, and the firmer our security against the recurrence of like innovations. At all events, enough, I trust, has been effected by the friends of our present Representatives to protect those who have been deceived, and may not in time awaken from their delusion. May their eyes be opened, and at no distant day; so that, perceiving the benefits which the laws, as now enacted and administered, ensure to their native Land, they may feel towards you who make the wiser choice the gratitude which you will have deserved.—The beginnings of great troubles are mostly of comparative insignificance;—a little spark can kindle a mighty conflagration, and a small leak will suffice to sink a stately vessel. To that loyal decision of the event now pending, which may be confidently expected, Britain may owe the continuance of her tranquillity and freedom; the maintenance of the justice and equity for which she is pre-eminent among nations; and the preservation of her social comforts, her charitable propensities, her morals and her religion. Of this, as belonging to the future, we cannot speak with certainty; but not a doubt can exist that the practices which led to the destruction of all that was venerable in a neighbouring Country, have upon this occasion been industriously, unscrupulously, eagerly resorted to.—But my last words shall be words of congratulation and thanksgiving—upon a bright prospect that the wishes will be crossed, and the endeavours frustrated, of those amongst us who, without their own knowledge, were ready to relinquish every good which they and we possess, by uniting with overweening Reformers—to compose the VANGUARD OF A FEROCIOUS REVOLUTION!

A FREEHOLDER.

Westmorland, February 24, 1818.

NOTE.

I HAVE not scrupled to express myself strongly on this subject, perceiving what use is made by the Opposite Party of those resolutions of the House of Commons. In support of my opinion I quote the following from the 'CARLISLE PATRIOT' of the 14th of February, premising, with the Author of the Letter from which it is extracted, that by far the greatest number of opulent Landholders are Members of the upper House, and that the richest subjects are some of its Peers:—

'The Peers of Great Britain, stripped as they now are of the overgrown importance which they derived from the Feudal System, have made no acquisition of political influence to compensate for the loss of it, by an increasing extension of patronage, either collectively or individually, like the crown; nor have the various circumstances operated upon their body in any considerable degree, which have effected such a radical and powerful accumulation of consequence and importance in the Lower House. Add to this, that the general sentiment or feeling that commonly exists between them and the body of the people bears no analogy to the vivid principles of affectionate loyalty that tend so strongly to secure and guard the person and rights of the King, or the reciprocal sympathy of congenial interests that acts and directs so powerfully betwixt the Commons and the Community in general. On the contrary, the spirit that exists betwixt the Peers as a collectively distinct body, and the people at large, is a spirit of *repulsion* rather than of attraction. In a corporate light, they are viewed with no sentiments of kindly affection, and therefore upon the supposition of a political contest betwixt them and either of the other two Estates, they would inevitably labour under the disadvantage of carrying it on against all the force of the prejudices, which to a great extent always directs popular opinion; hence, amidst all the contests and struggles which have agitated or convulsed the Kingdom since the Reign of Henry the Seventh, the political importance of the Peers, considered as an Estate of Parliament, has been rather diminished than increased; and were such a democratical House of Commons as our modern Patriots so loudly call for, to be efficiently formed, the constitutional equilibrium of our envied public system would be infallibly destroyed, and the spirit of our Legislative Body, which in a great measure awards influence in proportion to property, completely abrogated:—and it is in vain to suppose that if even such a change was desirable, it could possibly be effected without producing a train of incalculable miseries that would much more than overbalance any partial good which could reasonably be expected from the alteration.' . . . . . .

'As property then is incontestibly the foundation-stone of political right in Britain, it follows, as an inevitable consequence, that the ratio of these rights should be in some measure commensurate to the extent of the property, otherwise the immutable maxims of justice, as well as the spirit of the Constitution, is violated; for it would be palpably unjust to put a man who possessed a great stake in the welfare of the Country, and paid comparatively a greater proportion of its public revenue, on a level with the inferior freeholders, who, not possessing any thing like an equal extent of property, cannot possibly have the means of equally contributing to the exigencies of the State. . . . . . .

'Now if any considerate conscientious man will calmly reflect upon the power of the House of Commons in the imposition of taxes, and in how many ways the public burthen affects the landed interest, either directly or indirectly, he must acknowledge the expediency, as well as the necessity and justice of the system, which, *steadily though silently*, protects the great landholders in exercising an appropriate influence in the election of the Representatives of the People.—Phocion.'

Previous to the Reign of Henry the Seventh, the Peers defended their property and their privileges through the means of armed Retainers. That politic Prince, by laws directed against the number of these Retainers; by bringing in use the making of leases; and by statutes framed for the purpose of 'unfettering more easily the Estates of his powerful Nobility, and laying them more open to alienation,' prepared the way for reducing the power of an Order which had been too strong for the Crown. The operation of these laws, in course of time, would have brought the Peers, as an Estate of the Realm, to utter insignificance, had not the practice of supplying the Peerage with new Members, through creation by patent without intervention of Parliament, been substituted for the only mode previously tolerated by the great Barons for the exercise of this royal prerogative, namely, by authority of Parliament. Thus did the consequence of the Order, notwithstanding the diminution of its power, continue to be maintained;—rich Commoners and Royal Favourites being introduced to supply the places of extinguished Families, or those whose wealth had fallen into decay. This prerogative grew without immoderate exercise till the close of the Reign of Queen Elizabeth. The first of the Stuarts employed it lavishly, not considering the changes that had taken place. His predecessors of the House of Tudor, by breaking down the feudal strength of the Lords, and by transfer (through the Reformation) of the Spiritual supremacy to themselves as temporal Sovereigns, had come into possession of a superfluity of power which enabled the Crown to supply what was wanted in the Peers for their own support. But through remote operation of the same causes, the Commons were rising fast into consequence, with a puritanical spirit of republicanism spreading rapidly amongst them. Hence the augmentation of the number of Peers, made by James the First, notwithstanding the addition of property carried by it to the Upper House, did not add sufficient strength to that body to compensate for the distastefulness of the measure to the people; and, as far as the property of the New Peers was but the creature of prodigal grants from the Crown, the conjoint strength of the two Estates received no increase. In the meanwhile surrenders were made of the power of the Crown with infatuated facility; till the Commons became so strong that the right of creating Boroughs, being openly disputed, was almost abandoned; and the speedy consequence of the whole was that the two parliamentary Estates of King and Lords fell before the intemperance of the third. After the restoration, the disputes about the bounds of Liberty and Prerogative were revived; but Prerogative was gradually abandoned for the less obnoxious and less obvious operations of influence. The numerous creations of Peers were complained of; but, whatever motive might have governed those creations, they were justified by the necessity of things. Large as were the additions made to the number of Peers they were insufficient to give the House its due weight as a separate Estate in the Legislature. Through the reigns of Charles, William, and Anne, whether the Crown was disposed to tyranny, or the Commons were venal, factious, or arbitrary, we see too many proofs of the Lords wanting natural strength to maintain their rights, and carry their patriotic wishes into effect, even when they were supported by marked expressions of popular opinion in their favour. If the changes which had taken place in the structure of Society would have allowed them to act regularly as an independent body upon its intrinsic resources, a deathblow was given to such expectation towards the close of the reign of Queen Anne, when twelve Peers were created in one day. This act, deservedly made one of the articles of impeachment against Lord Oxford, shewed that their sentiments, as a Body, were at the mercy of any unprincipled Administration, and *compelled* them to look about for some other means of being attended to;—and the most obvious was the best for the Country and themselves—That of taking care of, and augmenting, the influence which they possessed in the House of Commons. Reformers plead against this practice, constitutional resolutions still existing. The slight review which has been given demonstrates its necessity if the Constitution is to be preserved. The only question which a practical politician can tolerate for a moment relates to the *degree* of this influence;—has it been carried too far? The considerations which put me upon writing the present note (for the length of which I ought to apologise) do not require the discussion of this point. The amicable reader will rejoice with me that, in spite of mutual shocks and encroachments, the three Orders of the State are preserved in salutary equipoise, although the mode of bringing this about has unavoidably changed with change of circumstances. The spirit of the Constitution remains unimpaired, nor have the essential parts of its frame undergone any alteration. May both endure as long as the Island itself!

V. OF THE CATHOLIC RELIEF BILL,

1829.

NOTE.

See Preface in the present volume for details on this 'Letter;' which was addressed to the Bishop of London (Blomfield). This is printed from the original Manuscript. G.

My Lord,

I have been hesitating for the space of a week, whether I should take the liberty of addressing you; but as the decision draws near my anxiety increases, and I cannot refrain from intruding upon you for a few minutes. I will try to be brief, throwing myself upon your indulgence, if what I have to say prove of little moment.

The question before us is, Can Protestantism and Popery —or, somewhat narrowing the ground, Can the Church of England (including that of Ireland) and the Church of Rome—be co-ordinate powers in the constitution of a free country, and at the same time Christian belief be in that country a vital principle of action? The States of the Continent afford no proof whatever that the existence of Protestantism and Romanism under the specified conditions is practicable; nor can they be rationally referred to as furnishing a guide for us. In France, the most conspicuous of these States and the freest, the number of Protestants in comparison with Catholics is insignificant, and unbelief and superstition almost divide the country between them. In Prussia, there is no legislative Assembly; the Government is essentially military; and excepting the countries upon the Rhine, recently added to that Power, the proportion of Catholics is inconsiderable. In Hanover, Jacob speaks of the Protestants as more than ten to one; here, indeed, is a legislative Assembly, but its powers are ill defined. Hanover had, and still may have, a censorship of the press—an indulgent one; it can afford to be so through the sedative virtue of the standing army of the country, and that of the Germanic League to back the executive in case of commotion. No sound-minded Englishman will build upon the short-lived experience of the kingdom of the Netherlands. In Flanders a benighted Papacy prevails, which defeated the attempts of the king to enlighten the people by education; and I am well assured that the Protestant portion of Holland have small reason to be thankful for the footing upon which they have been there placed. If that kingdom is to last, there is great cause for fear that its government will incline more and more to Romanism as the religion of a great majority of its subjects, and as one which by its slavish spirit makes the people more manageable. If so, it is to be apprehended that Protestantism will gradually disappear before it; and the ruling classes, in a still greater degree than they now are, will become infidels, as the easiest refuge in their own minds from the debasing doctrines of Papacy.

Three great conflicts* are before the progressive nations, between Christianity and Infidelity, between Papacy and Protestantism, and between the spirit of the old feudal and monarchical governments and the representative and republican system, as established in America. The Church of England, in addition to her infidel and Roman Catholic assailants, and the politicians of the anti-feudal class, has to contend with a formidable body of Protestant Dissenters. Amid these several and often combined attacks, how is she to maintain herself? From which of these enemies has she most to fear? Some are of opinion that Papacy is less formidable than Dissent, whose bias is republican, which is averse to monarchy, to a hierarchy, and to the tything system—to all which Romanism is strongly attached. The abstract principles embodied in the creed of the Dissenters' catechism are without doubt full as politically dangerous as those of the Romanists; but fortunately their creed is not their practice. They are divided among themselves, they acknowledge no foreign jurisdiction, their organisation and discipline are comparatively feeble; and in times long past, however powerful they proved themselves to overthrow, they are not likely to be able to build up. Whatever the Presbyterian form, as in the Church of Scotland, may have to recommend it, we find that the sons of the nobility and gentry of Scotland who choose the sacred profession almost invariably enter into the Church of England; and for the same reason, viz. the want of a hierarchy (you will excuse me for connecting views so humiliating with divine truth), the rich Dissenters, in the course of a generation or two, fall into the bosom of our

* In this classification I anticipate matter which Mr. Southey has in the press, the substance of a conversation between us.

Church. As holding out attractions to the upper orders, the Church of England has no advantages over that of Rome, but rather the contrary. Papacy will join with us in preserving the form, but for the purpose and in the hope of seizing the substance for itself. Its ambition is upon record; it is essentially at enmity with light and knowledge; its power to exclude these blessings is not so great as formerly, though its desire to do so is equally strong, and its determination to exert its power for its own exaltation by means of that exclusion is not in the least abated. The See of Rome justly regards England as the head of Protestantism; it admires, it is jealous, it is envious of her power and greatness. It despairs of being able to destroy them, but it is ever on the watch to regain its lost influence over that country; and it hopes to effect this through the means of Ireland. The words of this last sentence are not my own, but those of the head of one of the first Catholic families of the county from which I write, spoken without reserve several years ago. Surely the language of this individual must be greatly emboldened when he sees the prostrate condition in which our yet Protestant Government now lies before the Papacy of Ireland. 'The great Catholic interest,' 'the old Catholic interest,' I know to have been phrases of frequent occurrence in the mouth of a head of the first Roman Catholic family of England; and to descend far lower, 'What would satisfy you?' said, not long ago, a person to a very clever lady, a dependent upon another branch of that family. 'That church,' replied she, pointing to the parish church of the large town where the conversation took place. Monstrous expectation! yet not to be overlooked as an ingredient in the compound of Papacy. This 'great Catholic interest' we are about to embody in a legislative form. A Protestant Parliament is to turn itself into a canine monster with two heads, which, instead of keeping watch and ward, will be snarling at and bent on devouring each other.

Whatever enemies the Church of England may have to struggle with now and hereafter, it is clear that at this juncture she is specially called to take the measure of her strength as opposed to the Church of Rome—that is her most pressing enemy. The Church of England, as to the point of private judgment, standing between the two extremes of Papacy and

Dissent, is entitled to heartfelt reverence; and among thinking men, whose affections are not utterly vitiated, never fails to receive it. Papacy will tolerate no private judgment, and Dissent is impatient of anything else. The blessing of Providence has thus far preserved the Church of England between the shocks to which she has been exposed from those opposite errors; and notwithstanding objections may lie against some parts of her Liturgy, particularly the Athanasian Creed, and however some of her articles may be disputed about, her doctrines are exclusively scriptural, and her practice is accommodated to the exigencies of our weak nature. If this be so, what has she to fear? Look at Ireland, might be a sufficient answer. Look at the disproportion between her Catholic and Protestant population. Look at the distempered heads of the Roman Catholic Church insisting upon terms which in France, and even in Austria, dare not be proposed, and which the Pope himself would probably relinquish for a season. Look at the revenues of the Protestant Church; her cathedrals, her churches, that once belonged to the Romanists, and where, *in imagination*, their worship has never ceased to be celebrated. Can it be doubted that when the yet existing restrictions are removed, that the disproportion in the population and the wealth of the Protestant Church will become more conspicuous objects for discontent to point at; and that plans, however covert, will be instantly set on foot, with the aid of new powers, for effecting an overthrow, and, if possible, a transfer? But all this is too obvious; I would rather argue with those who think that by excluding the Romanists from political power we make them more attached to their religion, and cause them to unite more strongly in support of it. Were this true to the extent maintained, we should still have to balance between the unorganised power which they derive from a sense of injustice, real or supposed, and the legitimate organised power which concession would confer upon surviving discontent; for no one, I imagine, is weak enough to suppose that discontent would disappear. But it is a deception, and a most dangerous one, to conclude that if a free passage were given to the torrent, it would lose, by diffusion, its ability to do injury. The checks, as your Lordship well knows, which are after a time necessary to provoke other sects to activity, are not wanted here. The Roman Church stands independent of them through its constitution, so exquisitely contrived, and through its doctrine and discipline, which give a peculiar and monstrous power to its priesthood. In proof of this, take the injunction of celibacy, alone separating the priesthood from the body of the community, and the practice of confession, making them masters of the conscience, while the doctrines give them an absolute power over the will. To submit to such thraldom men must be bigoted in its favour; and that we see is the case of Spain, in Portugal, in Austria, in Italy, in Flanders, in Ireland, and in all countries where you have Papacy in full blow. And does not history prove, that however other sects may have languished under the relaxing influence of good fortune, Papacy has ever been most fiery and rampant when most prosperous?

But many, who do not expect that conciliation will be the result of concession, have a farther expedient on which they rely much. They propose to take the Romish Church in Ireland into pay, and expect that afterwards its clergy will be as compliant to the Government as the Presbyterians in that country have proved. This measure is, in the first place, too disingenuous not to be condemned by honest men; for the Government acting on this policy would degrade itself by offering bribes to men of a sacred calling to act contrary to their sense of duty. If they be sincere, as priests and truly spiritual-minded, they will find it impossible to accept of a stipend, known to be granted with such expectation. If they be worldlings and false of heart, they will practise double-dealing, and seem to support the Government while they are actually undermining it; for they know that if they be suspected of sacrificing the interests of the Church they will lose all authority over their flocks. Power and consideration are more valued than money. The priests will not be induced to risk their sway over the people for any sums that our Government would venture to afford them out of the exhausted revenues of the empire. Surely they would prefer to such a scanty hire the hope of carving for themselves from the property of the Protestant Church of their country, or even the gratification of stripping usurpation—for such they deem it—of its gains, though there may be no hope to win what others are deprived of. Many English favourers of this scheme are reconciled to what they call a modification of the Irish Protestant Establishment in an application of a portion of the revenues to the support of the Romish Church. This they deem reasonable; shortly it will be openly aimed at, and they will rejoice should they accomplish their purpose. But your Lordship will agree with me that, if that happen, it would be one of the most calamitous events that ignorance has in our time given birth to. After all, could the secular clergy be paid out of this spoliation, or in any other way? The Regulars would rise in consequence of their degradation; and where would be the influence that could keep them from mischief? They would swarm over the country to prey upon the people still more than they now do. In all the reasonings of the friends to this bribing scheme, the distinctive character of the Papal Church is overlooked.

But they who expect that tranquillity will be a permanent consequence of the Relief Bill dwell much upon the mighty difference in opinion and feeling between the upper and lower ranks of the Romish communion. They affirm that many keep within the pale of the Church as a point of honour; that others have notions greatly relaxed, and though not at present prepared to separate, they will gradually fall off. But what avail the inward sentiments of men if they are convinced that by acting upon them they will forfeit their outward dignity and power? As long as the political influence which the priests now exercise shall endure, or anything like it, the great proprietors will be obliged to dissemble, and to conform in their action to the demands of that power. Such will be the conduct of the great Roman Catholic proprietors; nay, farther, I agree with those who deem it probable that, through a natural and reasonable desire to have their property duly represented, many landholders who are now Protestant will be tempted to go over to Papacy. This may be thought a poor compliment to Protestantism, since religious scruples, it is said, are all that keep the Papists out; but is not the desire to be in, pushing them on almost to rebellion at this moment? We are taking, I own, a melancholy view of both sides; but human nature, be it what it may, must by legislators be looked at as it is.

In the treatment of this question we hear perpetually of wrong; but the wrong is all on one side. If the political power of Ireland is to be a transfer from those who are of the State religion of the country to those who are not, there is nothing gained on the score of justice. We hear also much of STIGMA; but this is not to be done away unless all offices, the Privy Council and the Chancellorship, be open to them; that is, unless we allow a man to be eligible to keep the King's conscience who has not his own in his keeping; unless we open the throne itself to men of this soul-degrading faith.

The condition of Ireland is indeed, and long has been, wretched. Lamentable is it to acknowledge, that the mass of the people are so grossly uninformed, and from that cause subject to such delusions and passions, that they would destroy each other were it not for restraints put upon them by a power out of themselves. This power it is that protracts their existence in a state for which otherwise the course of nature would provide a remedy by reducing their numbers through mutual destruction; so that English civilisation may fairly be said to have been the shield of Irish barbarism. And now these swarms of degraded people, which could not have existed but through the neglect and misdirected power of the sister island, are by a withdrawing of that power to have their own way, and to be allowed to dictate to us. A population, vicious in character as unnatural in immediate origin (for it has been called into birth by short-sighted landlords, set upon adding to the number of votes at their command, and by priests who for lucre's sake favour the increase of marriages), is held forth as constituting a claim to political power strong in proportion to its numbers, though in a sane view that claim is in an inverse ratio to them. Brute force indeed wherever lodged, as we are too feelingly taught at present, must be measured and met—measured with care, in order to be met with fortitude.

The chief proximate causes of Irish misery and ignorance are Papacy—of which I have said so much—and the tenure and management of landed property, and both these have a common origin, viz. the imperfect conquest of the country. The countries subjected by the ancient Romans, and those that in the middle ages were subdued by the Northern tribes, afford striking instances of the several ways in which nations may be improved by foreign conquest. The Romans by their superiority in arts and arms, and, in the earlier period of their history, in virtues also, may seem to have established a moral right to force their institutions upon other nations, whether under a process of decline or emerging from barbarism; and this they effected, we all know, not by overrunning countries as Eastern conquerors have done, and Bonaparte in our own days, but by completing a regular subjugation, with military roads and garrisons, which became centres of civilisation for the surrounding district. Nor am I afraid to add, though the fact might be caught at as bearing against the general scope of my argument, that both conquerors and conquered owed much to the participation of civil rights which the Romans liberally communicated. The other mode of conquest, that pursued by the Northern nations, brought about its beneficial effects by the settlement of a hardy and vigorous people among the distracted and effeminate nations against whom their incursions were made. The conquerors transplanted with them their independent and ferocious spirit to reanimate exhausted communities, and in their turn received a salutary mitigation, till in process of time the conqueror and conquered, having a common interest, were lost in each other. To neither of these modes was unfortunate Ireland subject, and her insular territory, by physical obstacles, and still more by moral influences arising out of them, has aggravated the evil consequent upon independence lost as hers was. The writers of the time of Queen Elizabeth have pointed out how unwise it was to transplant among a barbarous people, not half subjugated, the institutions that time had matured among those who too readily considered themselves masters of that people. It would be presumptuous in me to advert in detail to the exacerbations and long-lived hatred that have perverted the moral sense in Ireland, obstructed religious knowledge, and denied to her a due share of English refinement and civility. It is enough to observe, that the Reformation was ill supported in that country, and that her soil became, through frequent forfeitures, mainly possessed by men whose hearts were not in the land where their wealth lay.

But it is too late, we are told, for retrospection. We have no choice between giving way and a sanguinary war. Surely it is rather too much that the country should be required to take the measure of the threatened evil from a Cabinet which by its being divided against itself, which by its remissness and fear of long and harassing debates in the two Houses, has for many years past fostered the evil, and in no small part created the danger, the extent of which is now urged as imposing the necessity of granting their demands.

Danger is a relative thing, and the first requisite for being in a condition to judge of what we have to dread from the physical force of the Romanists is to be in sympathy with the Protestants. Had our Ministers been truly so, could they have suffered themselves to be bearded by the Catholic Association for so many years as they have been?

I speak openly to you, my Lord, though a member of his Majesty's Privy Council; and begging your pardon for detaining you so long, I hasten to a conclusion.

The civil disabilities, for the removal of which Mr. O'Connell and his followers are braving the Government, cannot but be indifferent to the great body of the Irish nation, except as means for gaining an end. Take away the intermediate power of the priests, and an insurrection in Brobdignag at the call of the King of Lilliput might be as hopefully expected as that the Irish people would stir as they are now prepared to do at the call of a political demagogue. Now these civil disabilities do not directly affect the priests; they therefore must have ulterior views, and though it must be flattering to their vanity to shew that they have the Irish representation in their own hands, and though their worldly interest and that of their connections will, they know, immediately profit by that dominion, what they look for principally is the advancement of their religion at the cost of Protestantism; that would bring everything else in its train. While it is obvious that the political agitators could not rouse the people without the intervention of the priests, it is true that the priests could not excite the people without a hope that from the exaltation of their Church their social condition would be improved. What in Irish interpretation these words would mean we may tremble to think of.

In whatever way we look, religion is so much mixed up in this matter, that the guardians of the Episcopal Church of the Empire are imperiously called upon to show themselves worthy of the high trust reposed in them. You, my Lord, are convinced that, in spite of the best securities that can be given, the admission of Roman Catholics into the Legislature is a dangerous experiment. Oaths cannot be framed that will avail here; the only securities to be relied upon are what we have little hope to see—the Roman Church reforming itself, and a Ministry and a Parliament sufficiently sensible of the superiority of the one form of religion over the other to be resolved, not only to preserve the present rights and immunities of the Protestant Church inviolate, but prepared by all fair means for the extension of its influence, with a hope that it may gradually prevail over Papacy.

It is, we trust, the intention of Providence that the Church of Rome should in due time disappear; and come what may on the Church of England, we have the satisfaction of knowing that in defending a Government resting upon a Protestant basis —say what they will, the other party have abandoned—we are working for the welfare of humankind, and supporting whatever there is of dignity in our frail nature.

Here I might stop; but I am above measure anxious for the course which the bench of bishops may take at this crisis. They are appealed to, and even by the Heir Presumptive to the throne from his seat in Parliament. There will be attempts to brow-beat them on the score of humanity; but humanity is, if it deserves the name, a calculating and prospective quality; it will on this occasion balance an evil at hand with a far greater one that is sure, or all but sure, to come. Humanity is not shewn the less by firmness than by tenderness of heart. It is neither deterred by clamour, nor enfeebled by its own sadness; but it estimates evil and good to the best of its power, acts by the dictates of conscience, and trusts the issue to the Ruler of all things.

If, my Lord, I have seemed to write with over-confidence on any opinions I have above given, impute it to a wish of avoiding cumbrous qualifying expressions.

Sincerely do I pray that God may give your Lordship and the rest of your brethren light to guide you and strength to walk in that light.

I am, my Lord, &c.

II. ETHICAL.

I. OF LEGISLATION FOR THE POOR, THE WORKING CLASSES, AND THE CLERGY: APPENDIX TO POEMS.

1835.

NOTE.

On the several portions of this division of the Prose see Preface in the present volume. G.

OF LEGISLATION FOR THE POOR, THE WORKING CLASSES, AND THE CLERGY.

APPENDIX TO POEMS.

In the present Volume, as in those that have preceded it, the reader will have found occasionally opinions expressed upon the course of public affairs, and feelings given vent to as national interests excited them. Since nothing, I trust, has been uttered but in the spirit of reflective patriotism, those notices are left to produce their own effect; but, among the many objects of general concern, and the changes going forward, which I have glanced at in verse, are some especially affecting the lower orders of society: in reference to these, I wish here to add a few words in plain prose.

Were I conscious of being able to do justice to those important topics, I might avail myself of the periodical press for offering anonymously my thoughts, such as they are, to the world; but I feel that, in procuring attention, they may derive some advantage, however small, from my name, in addition to that of being presented in a less fugitive shape. It is also not impossible that the state of mind which some of the foregoing poems may have produced in the reader, will dispose him to receive more readily the impression which I desire to make, and to admit the conclusions I would establish.

I. The first thing that presses upon my attention is the Poor Law Amendment Act. I am aware of the magnitude and complexity of the subject, and the unwearied attention which it has received from men of far wider experience than my own; yet I cannot forbear touching upon one point of it, and to this I will confine myself, though not insensible to the objection which may reasonably be brought against treating a portion of this, or any other, great scheme of civil polity separately from the whole. The point to which I wish to draw the reader's attention is, that *all* persons who cannot find employment, or procure wages sufficient to support the body in health and strength, are entitled to a maintenance by law.

This dictate of humanity is acknowledged in the Report of the Commissioners: but is there not room for apprehension that some of the regulations of the new Act have a tendency to render the principle nugatory by difficulties thrown in the way of applying it? If this be so, persons will not be wanting to show it, by examining the provisions of the Act in detail,—an attempt which would be quite out of place here; but it will not, therefore, be deemed unbecoming in one who fears that the prudence of the head may, in framing some of those provisions, have supplanted the wisdom of the heart, to enforce a principle which cannot be violated without infringing upon one of the most precious rights of the English people, and opposing one of the most sacred claims of civilised humanity.

There can be no greater error, in this department of legislation, than the belief that this principle does by necessity operate for the degradation of those who claim, or are so circumstanced as to make it likely they may claim, through laws founded upon it, relief or assistance. The direct contrary is the truth: it may be unanswerably maintained that its tendency is to raise, not to depress; by stamping a value upon life, which can belong to it only where the laws have placed men who are willing to work, and yet cannot find employment, above the necessity of looking for protection against hunger and other natural evils, either to individual and casual charity, to despair and death, or to the breach of law by theft or violence.

And here, as in the Report of the Commissioners, the fundamental principle has been recognised, I am not at issue with them any farther than I am compelled to believe that their 'remedial measures' obstruct the application of it more than the interests of society require.

And calling to mind the doctrines of political economy which are now prevalent, I cannot forbear to enforce the justice of the principle, and to insist upon its salutary operation.

And first for its justice: If self-preservation be the first law of our nature, would not every one in a state of nature be morally justified in taking to himself that which is indispensable to such preservation, where, by so doing, he would not rob another of that which might be equally indispensable to *his* preservation? And if the value of life be regarded in a right point of view, may it not be questioned whether this right of preserving life, at any expense short of endangering the life of another, does not survive man's entering into the social state; whether this right can be surrendered or forfeited, except when it opposes the divine law, upon any supposition of a social compact, or of any convention for the protection of mere rights of property?

But, if it be not safe to touch the abstract question of man's right in a social state to help himself even in the last extremity, may we not still contend for the duty of a christian government, standing *in loco parentis* towards all its subjects, to make such effectual provision, that no one shall be in danger of perishing either through the neglect or harshness of its legislation? Or, waiving this, is it not indisputable that the claim of the State to the allegiance, involves the protection of the subject? And, as all rights in one party impose a correlative duty upon another, it follows that the right of the State to require the services of its members, even to the jeoparding of their lives in the common defence, establishes a right in the people (not to be gainsaid by utilitarians and economists) to public support when, from any cause, they may be unable to support themselves.

Let us now consider the salutary and benign operation of this principle. Here we must have recourse to elementary feelings of human nature, and to truths which from their very obviousness are apt to be slighted, till they are forced upon our notice by our own sufferings or those of others. In the Paradise Lost, Milton represents Adam, after the Fall, as exclaiming, in the anguish of his soul—

> Did I request Thee, Maker, from my clay
> To mould me man; did I solicit Thee
> From darkness to promote me?
> . . . . . . My will
> Concurred not to my being.

Under how many various pressures of misery have men been driven thus, in a strain touching upon impiety, to expostulate with the Creator! and under few so afflictive as when the source and origin of earthly existence have been brought back to the mind by its impending close in the pangs of destitution. But as long as, in our legislation, due weight shall be given to this principle, no man will be forced to bewail the gift of life in hopeless want of the necessaries of life.

Englishmen have, therefore, by the progress of civilisation among them, been placed in circumstances more favourable to piety and resignation to the divine will, than the inhabitants of other countries, where a like provision has not been established. And as Providence, in this care of our countrymen, acts through a human medium, the objects of that care must, in like manner, be more inclined towards a grateful love of their fellow-men. Thus, also, do stronger ties attach the people to their country, whether while they tread its soil, or, at a distance, think of their native Land as an indulgent parent, to whose arms even they who have been imprudent and undeserving may, like the prodigal son, betake themselves, without fear of being rejected.

Such is the view of the case that would first present itself to a reflective mind; and it is in vain to show, by appeals to experience, in contrast with this view, that provisions founded upon the principle have promoted profaneness of life, and dispositions the reverse of philanthropic, by spreading idleness, selfishness, and rapacity: for these evils have arisen, not as an inevitable consequence of the principle, but for want of judgment in framing laws based upon it; and, above all, from faults in the mode of administering the law. The mischief that has grown to such a height from granting relief in cases where proper vigilance would have shewn that it was not required, or in bestowing it in undue measure, will be urged by no truly enlightened statesman, as a sufficient reason for banishing the principle itself from legislation.

Let us recur to the miserable states of consciousness that it precludes.

There is a story told, by a traveller in Spain, of a female who, by a sudden shock of domestic calamity, was driven out of her senses, and ever after looked up incessantly to the sky, feeling that her fellow-creatures could do nothing for her relief. Can there be Englishmen who, with a good end in view, would, upon system, expose their brother Englishmen to a like necessity of looking upwards only; or downwards to the earth, after it shall contain no spot where the destitute can demand, by civil right, what by right of nature they are entitled to?

Suppose the objects of our sympathy not sunk into this blank despair, but wandering about as strangers in streets and ways, with the hope of succour from casual charity; what have we gained by such a change of scene? Woful is the condition of the famished Northern Indian, dependent, among winter snows, upon the chance passage of a herd of deer, from which one, if brought down by his rifle-gun, may be made the means of keeping him and his companions alive. As miserable is that of some savage Islander, who, when the land has ceased to afford him sustenance, watches for food which the waves may cast up, or in vain endeavours to extract it from the inexplorable deep. But neither of these is in a state of wretchedness comparable to that which is so often endured in civilised society: multitudes, in all ages, have known it, of whom may be said:—

> Homeless, near a thousand homes they stood,
> And near a thousand tables pined, and wanted food.

Justly might I be accused of wasting time in an uncalled-for attempt to excite the feelings of the reader, if systems of political economy, widely spread, did not impugn the principle, and if the safeguards against such extremities were left unimpaired. It is broadly asserted by many, that every man who endeavours to find work, *may* find it. Were this assertion capable of being verified, there still would remain a question, what kind of work, and how far may the labourer be fit for it? For if sedentary work is to be exchanged for standing; and some light and nice exercise of the fingers, to which an artisan has been accustomed all his life, for severe labour of the arms; the best efforts would turn to little account, and occasion would be given for the unthinking and the unfeeling unwarrantably to reproach those who are put upon such employment, as idle, froward, and unworthy of relief, either by law or in any other way! Were this statement correct, there would indeed be an end of the argument, the principle here maintained would be superseded. But, alas! it is far otherwise. That principle, applicable to the benefit of all countries, is indispensable for England, upon whose coast families are perpetually deprived of their support by shipwreck, and where large masses of men are so liable to be thrown out of their ordinary means of gaining bread, by changes in commercial intercourse, subject mainly or solely to the will of foreign powers; by new discoveries in arts and manufactures; and by reckless laws, in conformity with theories of political economy, which, whether right or wrong in the abstract, have proved a scourge to tens of thousands, by the abruptness with which they have been carried into practice.

But it is urged,—refuse altogether compulsory relief to the able-bodied, and the number of those who stand in need of relief will steadily diminish through a conviction of an absolute necessity for greater forethought, and more prudent care of a man's earnings. Undoubtedly it would, but so also would it, and in a much greater degree, if the legislative provisions were retained, and parochial relief administered under the care of the upper classes, as it ought to be. For it has been invariably found, that wherever the funds have been raised and applied under the superintendence of gentlemen and substantial proprietors, acting in vestries and as overseers, pauperism has diminished accordingly. Proper care in that quarter would effectually check what is felt in some districts to be one of the worst evils in the Poor Law system, viz. the readiness of small and needy proprietors to join in imposing rates that seemingly subject them to great hardships, while, in fact, this is done with a mutual understanding, that the relief each is ready to bestow upon his still poorer neighbours will be granted to himself or his relatives, should it hereafter be applied for.

But let us look to inner sentiments of a nobler quality, in order to know what we have to build upon. Affecting proofs occur in every one's experience, who is acquainted with the unfortunate and the indigent, of their unwillingness to derive their subsistence from aught but their own funds or labour, or to be indebted to parochial assistance for the attainment of any object, however dear to them. A case was reported, the other day, from a coroner's inquest, of a pair who, through the space of four years, had carried about their dead infant from house to house, and from lodging to lodging, as their necessities drove them, rather than ask the parish to bear the expense of its interment;—the poor creatures lived in the hope of one day being able to bury their child at their own cost. It must have been heart-rending to see and hear the mother, who had been called upon to account for the state in which the body was found, make this deposition. By some, judging coldly, if not harshly, this conduct might be imputed to an unwarrantable pride, as she and her husband had, it is true, been once in prosperity. But examples, where the spirit of independence works with equal strength, though not with like miserable accompaniments, are frequently to be found even yet among the humblest peasantry and mechanics. There is not, then, sufficient cause for doubting that a like sense of honour may be revived among the people, and their ancient habits of independence restored, without resorting to those severities which the new Poor Law Act has introduced.

But even if the surfaces of things only are to be examined, we have a right to expect that lawgivers should take into account the various tempers and dispositions of mankind: while some are led, by the existence of a legislative provision, into idleness and extravagance, the economical virtues might be cherished in others by the knowledge that, if all their efforts fail, they have in the Poor Laws a 'refuge from the storm and a shadow from the heat.' Despondency and distraction are no friends to prudence: the springs of industry will relax, if cheerfulness be destroyed by anxiety; without hope men become reckless, and have a sullen pride in adding to the heap of their own wretchedness. He who feels that he is abandoned by his fellow-men will be almost irresistibly driven to care little for himself; will lose his self-respect accordingly, and with that loss what remains to him of virtue?

With all due deference to the particular experience and general intelligence of the individuals who framed the Act, and of those who in and out of Parliament have approved of and supported it; it may be said, that it proceeds too much upon the presumption that it is a labouring man's own fault if he be not, as the phrase is, beforehand with the world. But the most prudent are liable to be thrown back by sickness, cutting them off from labour, and causing to them expense: and who but has observed how distress creeps upon multitudes without misconduct of their own; and merely from a gradual fall in the price of labour, without a correspondent one in the price of provisions; so that men who may have ventured upon the marriage state with a fair prospect of maintaining their families in comfort and happiness, see them reduced to a pittance which no effort of theirs can increase? Let it be remembered, also, that there are thousands with whom vicious habits of expense are not the cause why they do not store up their gains; but they are generous and kind-hearted, and ready to help their kindred and friends; moreover, they have a faith in Providence that those who have been prompt to assist others will not be left destitute, should they themselves come to need. By acting from these blended feelings, numbers have rendered themselves incapable of standing up against a sudden reverse. Nevertheless, these men, in common with all who have the misfortune to be in want, if many theorists had their wish, would be thrown upon one or other of those three sharp points of condition before adverted to, from which the intervention of law has hitherto saved them.

All that has been said tends to show how the principle contended for makes the gift of life more valuable, and has, it may be hoped, led to the conclusion that its legitimate operation is to make men worthier of that gift: in other words, not to degrade but to exalt human nature. But the subject must not be dismissed without adverting to the indirect influence of the same principle upon the moral sentiments of a people among whom it is embodied in law. In our criminal jurisprudence there is a maxim, deservedly eulogised, that it is better that ten guilty persons should escape, than that one innocent man should suffer; so, also, might it be maintained, with regard to the Poor Laws, that it is better for the interests of humanity among the people at large, that ten undeserving should partake of the funds provided, than that one morally good man, through want of relief, should either have his principles corrupted, or his energies destroyed; than that such a one should either be driven to do wrong, or be cast to the earth in utter hopelessness. In France, the English maxim of criminal jurisprudence is reversed; there, it is deemed better that ten innocent men should suffer, than one guilty escape: in France, there is no universal provision for the poor; and we may judge of the small value set upon human life in the metropolis of that country, by merely noticing the disrespect with which, after death, the body is treated, not by the thoughtless vulgar, but in schools of anatomy, presided over by men allowed to be, in their own art and in physical science, among the most enlightened in the world. In the East, where countries are overrun with population as with a weed, infinitely more respect is shown to the remains of the deceased: and what a bitter mockery is it, that this insensibility should be found where civil polity is so busy in minor regulations, and ostentatiously careful to gratify the luxurious propensities, whether social or intellectual, of the multitude! Irreligion is, no doubt, much concerned with this offensive disrespect shown to the bodies of the dead in France; but it is mainly attributable to the state in which so many of the living are left by the absence of compulsory provision for the indigent so humanely established by the law of England.

Sights of abject misery, perpetually recurring, harden the heart of the community. In the perusal of history and of works of fiction, we are not, indeed, unwilling to have our commiseration excited by such objects of distress as they present to us; but, in the concerns of real life, men know that such emotions are not given to be indulged for their own sakes: there, the conscience declares to them that sympathy must be followed by action; and if there exist a previous conviction that the power to relieve is utterly inadequate to the demand, the eye shrinks from communication with wretchedness, and pity and compassion languish, like any other qualities that are deprived of their natural aliment. Let these considerations be duly weighed by those who trust to the hope that an increase of private charity, with all its advantages of superior discrimination, would more than compensate for the abandonment of those principles, the wisdom of which has been here insisted upon. How discouraging, also, would be the sense of injustice, which could not fail to arise in the minds of the well-disposed, if the burden of supporting the poor, a burden of which the selfish have hitherto by compulsion borne a share, should now, or hereafter, be thrown exclusively upon the benevolent.

By having put an end to the Slave Trade and Slavery, the British people are exalted in the scale of humanity; and they cannot but feel so, if they look into themselves, and duly consider their relation to God and their fellow-creatures. That was a noble advance; but a retrograde movement will assuredly be made, if ever the principle, which has been here defended, should be either avowedly abandoned or but ostensibly retained.

But after all, there may be a little reason to apprehend permanent injury from any experiment that may be tried. On the one side will be human nature rising up in her own defence, and on the other prudential selfishness acting to the same purpose, from a conviction that, without a compulsory provision for the exigencies of the labouring multitude, that degree of ability to regulate the price of labour, which is indispensable for the reasonable interest of arts and manufactures, cannot, in Great Britain, be upheld.

II. In a poem of the foregoing collection, allusion is made to the state of the workmen congregated in manufactories. In order to relieve many of the evils to which that class of society are subject, and to establish a better harmony between them and their employers, it would be well to repeal such laws as prevent the formation of joint-stock companies. There are, no doubt, many and great obstacles to the formation and salutary working of these societies, inherent in the mind of those whom they would obviously benefit. But the combinations of masters to keep down, unjustly, the price of labour would be fairly checked by them, as far as they were practicable; they would encourage economy, inasmuch as they would enable a man to draw profit from his savings, by investing them in buildings or machinery for processes of manufacture with which he was habitually connected. His little capital would then be working for him while he was at rest or asleep; he would more clearly perceive the necessity of capital for carrying on great works: he would better learn to respect the larger portions of it in the hands of others; he would be less tempted to join in unjust combinations: and, for the sake of his own property, if not for higher reasons, he would be slow to promote local disturbance, or endanger public tranquillity; he would, at least, be loth to act in that way *knowingly:* for it is not to be denied that such societies might be nurseries of opinions unfavourable to a mixed constitution of government, like that of Great Britain. The democratic and republican spirit which they might be apt to foster would not, however, be dangerous in itself, but only as it might act without being sufficiently counterbalanced, either by landed proprietorship, or by a Church extending itself so as to embrace an ever-growing and ever-shifting population of mechanics and artisans. But if the tendencies of such societies would be to make the men prosper who might belong to them, rulers and legislators should rejoice in the result, and do their duty to the State by upholding and extending the influence of that Church to which it owes, in so great a measure, its safety, its prosperity, and its glory.

This, in the temper of the present times, may be difficult, but it is become indispensable, since large towns in great numbers have sprung up, and others have increased tenfold, with little or no dependence upon the gentry and the landed proprietors; and apart from those mitigated feudal institutions, which, till of late, have acted so powerfully upon the composition of the House of Commons. Now it may be affirmed that, in quarters where there is not an attachment to the Church, or the landed aristocracy, and a pride in supporting them, *there* the people will dislike both, and be ready, upon such incitements as are perpetually recurring, to join in attempts to overthrow them. There is no neutral ground here: from want of due attention to the state of society in large towns and manufacturing districts, and ignorance or disregard of these obvious truths, innumerable well-meaning persons became zealous supporters of a Reform Bill, the qualities and powers of which, whether destructive or constructive, they would otherwise have been afraid of: and even the framers of that bill, swayed as they might be by party resentments and personal ambition, could not have gone so far, had not they too been lamentably ignorant or neglectful of the same truths both of fact and philosophy.

But let that pass; and let no opponent of the Bill be tempted to compliment his own foresight, by exaggerating the mischiefs and dangers that have sprung from it: let not time be wasted in profitless regrets; and let those party distinctions vanish to their very names that have separated men who, whatever course they may have pursued, have ever had a bond of union in the wish to save the limited monarchy, and those other institutions that have, under Providence, rendered for so long a period of time this country the happiest and worthiest of which there is any record since the foundation of civil society.

III. A philosophic mind is best pleased when looking at religion in its spiritual bearing; as a guide of conduct, a solace under affliction, and a support amid the instabilities of mortal life; but the Church having been forcibly brought by political considerations to my notice, while treating of the labouring classes, I cannot forbear saying a few words upon that momentous topic.

There is a loud clamour for extensive change in that department. The clamour would be entitled to more respect if they who are the most eager to swell it with their voices were not generally the most ignorant of the real state of the Church, and the service it renders to the community. *Reform* is the word employed. Let us pause and consider what sense it is apt to carry, and how things are confounded by a lax use of it. The great religious Reformation, in the sixteenth century, did not profess to be a new construction, but a restoration of something fallen into decay, or put out of sight. That familiar and justifiable use of the word seems to have paved the way for fallacies with respect to the term reform, which it is difficult to escape from. Were we to speak of improvement and the correction of abuses, we should run less risk of being deceived ourselves, or of misleading others. We should be less likely to fall blindly into the belief, that the change demanded is a renewal of something that has existed before, and that, therefore, we have experience on our side; nor should we be equally tempted to beg the question, that the change for which we are eager must be advantageous. From generation to generation, men are the dupes of words; and it is painful to observe, that so many of our species are most tenacious of those opinions which they have formed with the least consideration. They who are the readiest to meddle with public affairs, whether in Church or State, fly to generalities, that they may be eased from the trouble of thinking about particulars; and thus is deputed to mechanical instrumentality the work which vital knowledge only can do well.

'Abolish pluralities, have a resident incumbent in every parish,' is a favourite cry; but, without adverting to other obstacles in the way of this specious scheme, it may be asked what benefit would accrue from its *indiscriminate* adoption to counterbalance the harm it would introduce, by nearly extinguishing the order of curates, unless the revenues of the Church should grow with the population, and be greatly increased in many thinly peopled districts, especially among the parishes of the North.

The order of curates is so beneficial, that some particular notice of it seems to be required in this place. For a Church poor as, relatively to the numbers of people, that of England is, and probably will continue to be, it is no small advantage to have youthful servants, who will work upon the wages of hope and expectation. Still more advantageous is it to have, by means of this order, young men scattered over the country, who being more detached from the temporal concerns of the benefice, have more leisure for improvement and study, and are less subject to be brought into secular collision with those who are under their spiritual guardianship. The curate, if he reside at a distance from the incumbent, undertakes the requisite responsibilities of a temporal kind, in that modified way which prevents him, as a new-comer, from being charged with selfishness: while it prepares him for entering upon a benefice of his own, with something of a suitable experience. If he should act under and in co-operation with a resident incumbent, the gain is mutual. His studies will probably be assisted; and his training, managed by a superior, will not be liable to relapse in matters of prudence, seemliness, or in any of the highest cares of his functions; and by way of return for these benefits to the pupil, it will often happen that the zeal of a middle-aged or declining incumbent will be revived, by being in near communion with the ardour of youth, when his own efforts may have languished through a melancholy consciousness that they have not produced as much good among his flock as, when he first entered upon the charge, he fondly hoped.

Let one remark, and that not the least important, be added. A curate, entering for the first time upon his office, comes from college after a course of expense, and with such inexperience in the use of money, that, in his new situation, he is apt to fall unawares into pecuniary difficulties. If this happens to him, much more likely is it to happen to the youthful incumbent; whose relations, to his parishioners and to society, are more complicated; and, his income being larger and independent of another, a costlier style of living is required of him by public opinion. If embarrassment should ensue, and with that unavoidably some loss of respectability, his future usefulness will be proportionably impaired: not so with the curate, for he can easily remove and start afresh with a stock of experience and an unblemished reputation; whereas the early indiscretions of an incumbent being rarely forgotten, may be impediments to the efficacy of his ministry for the remainder of his life. The same observations would apply with equal force to doctrine. A young minister is liable to errors, from his notions being either too lax or overstrained. In both cases it would prove injurious that the error should be remembered, after study and reflection, with advancing years, shall have brought him to a clearer discernment of the truth, and better judgment in the application of it.

It must be acknowledged that, among the regulations of ecclesiastical polity, none at first view are more attractive than that which prescribes for every parish a resident incumbent. How agreeable to picture to one's self, as has been done by poets and romance writers, from Chaucer down to Goldsmith, a man devoted to his ministerial office, with not a wish or a thought ranging beyond the circuit of its cares! Nor is it in poetry and fiction only that such characters are found; they are scattered, it is hoped not sparingly, over real life, especially in sequestered and rural districts, where there is but small influx of new inhabitants, and little change of occupation. The spirit of the Gospel, unaided by acquisitions of profane learning and experience in the world,—that spirit and the obligations of the sacred office may, in such situations, suffice to effect most of what is needful. But for the complex state of society that prevails in England, much more is required, both in large towns, and in many extensive districts of the country. A minister should not only be irreproachable in manners and morals, but accomplished in learning, as far as is possible without sacrifice of the least of his pastoral duties. As necessary, perhaps more so, is it that he should be a citizen as well as a scholar; thoroughly acquainted with the structure of society and the constitution of civil government, and able to reason upon both with the most expert; all ultimately in order to support the truths of Christianity, and to diffuse its blessings.

A young man coming fresh from the place of his education, cannot have brought with him these accomplishments; and if the scheme of equalising Church incomes, which many advisers are much bent upon, be realised, so that there should be little or no secular inducement for a clergyman to desire a removal from the spot where he may chance to have been first set down:

surely not only opportunities for obtaining the requisite qualifications would be diminished, but the motives for desiring to obtain them would be proportionably weakened. And yet these qualifications are indispensable for the diffusion of that knowledge, by which alone the political philosophy of the New Testament can be rightly expounded, and its precepts adequately enforced. In these time, when the press is daily exercising so great a power over the minds of the people, for wrong or for right as may happen, *that* preacher ranks among the first of benefactors who, without stooping to the direct treatment of current politics and passing events, can furnish infallible guidance through the delusions that surround them; and who, appealing to the sanctions of Scripture, may place the grounds of its injunctions in so clear a light, that disaffection shall cease to be cultivated as a laudable propensity, and loyalty cleansed from the dishonour of a blind and prostrate obedience.

It is not, however, in regard to civic duties alone, that this knowledge in a minister of the Gospel is important; it is still more so for softening and subduing private and personal discontents. In all places, and at all times, men have gratuitously troubled themselves, because their survey of the dispensations of Providence has been partial and narrow; but now that readers are so greatly multiplied, men judge as they are *taught*, and repinings are engendered everywhere, by imputations being cast upon the government; and are prolonged or aggravated by being ascribed to misconduct or injustice in rulers, when the individual himself only is in fault. If a Christian pastor be competent to deal with these humours, as they may be dealt with, and by no members of society so successfully, both from more frequent and more favourable opportunities of intercourse, and by aid of the authority with which he speaks; he will be a teacher of moderation, a dispenser of the wisdom that blunts approaching distress by submission to God's will, and lightens, by patience, grievances which cannot be removed.

We live in times when nothing, of public good at least, is generally acceptable, but what we believe can be traced to preconceived intention, and specific acts and formal contrivances of human understanding. A Christian instructor thoroughly accomplished would be a standing restraint upon such presumptuousness of judgment, by impressing the truth that—

In the unreasoning progress of the world
A wiser spirit is at work for us,
A better eye than ours.—MS.

Revelation points to the purity and peace of a future world; but our sphere of duty is upon earth; and the relations of impure and conflicting things to each other must be understood, or we shall be perpetually going wrong, in all but goodness of intention; and goodness of intention will itself relax through frequent disappointment. How desirable, then, is it, that a minister of the Gospel should be versed in the knowledge of existing facts, and be accustomed to a wide range of social experience! Nor is it less desirable for the purpose of counterbalancing and tempering in his own mind that ambition with which spiritual power is as apt to be tainted as any other species of power which men covet or possess.

It must be obvious that the scope of the argument is to discourage an attempt which would introduce into the Church of England an equality of income and station, upon the model of that of Scotland. The sounder part of the Scottish nation know what good their ancestors derived from their Church, and feel how deeply the living generation is indebted to it. They respect and love it, as accommodated in so great a measure to a comparatively poor country, through the far greater portion of which prevails a uniformity of employment; but the acknowledged deficiency of theological learning among the clergy of that Church is easily accounted for by this very equality. What else may be wanting there, it would be unpleasant to inquire, and might prove invidious to determine: one thing, however, is clear; that in all countries the temporalities of the Church Establishment should bear an analogy to the state of society, otherwise it cannot diffuse its influence through the whole community. In a country so rich and luxurious as England, the character of its clergy must unavoidably sink, and their influence be everywhere impaired, if individuals from the upper ranks, and men of leading talents, are to have no inducements to enter into that body but such as are purely spiritual. And this 'tinge of secularity' is no reproach to the clergy, nor does it imply a deficiency of spiritual endowments. Parents and guardians, looking forward to sources of honourable maintenance for their children and wards, often direct their thoughts early towards the Church, being determined partly by outward circumstances, and partly by indications of seriousness, or intellectual fitness. It is natural that a boy or youth, with such a prospect before him, should turn his attention to those studies, and be led into those habits of reflection, which will in some degree tend to prepare him for the duties he is hereafter to undertake. As he draws nearer to the time when he will be called to these duties, he is both led and compelled to examine the Scriptures. He becomes more and more sensible of their truth. Devotion grows in him; and what might begin in temporal considerations will end (as in a majority of instances we trust it does) in a spiritual-mindedness not unworthy of that Gospel, the lessons of which he is to teach, and the faith of which he is to inculcate. Not inappositely may be here repeated an observation which, from its obviousness and importance, must have been frequently made—viz. that the impoverishing of the clergy, and bringing their incomes much nearer to a level, would not cause them to become less worldly-minded: the emoluments, howsoever reduced, would be as eagerly sought for, but by men from lower classes in society; men who, by their manners, habits, abilities, and the scanty measure of their attainments, would unavoidably be less fitted for their station, and less competent to discharge its duties.

Visionary notions have in all ages been afloat upon the subject of best providing for the clergy; notions which have been sincerely entertained by good men, with a view to the improvement of that order, and eagerly caught at and dwelt upon, by the designing, for its degradation and disparagement. Some are beguiled by what they call the *voluntary system*, not seeing (what stares one in the face at the very threshold) that they who stand in most need of religious instruction are unconscious of the want, and therefore cannot reasonably be expected to make any sacrifices in order to supply it. Will the licentious, the sensual, and the depraved, take from the means of their gratifications and pursuits, to support a discipline that cannot advance without uprooting the trees that bear the fruit which they devour so greedily? Will *they* pay the price of that seed whose harvest is to be reaped in an invisible world? A voluntary system for the religious exigencies of a people numerous and circumstanced as we are! Not more absurd would it be to expect that a knot of boys should draw upon the pittance of their pocket-money to build schools, or out of the abundance of their discretion be able to select fit masters to teach and keep them in order! Some, who clearly perceive the incompetence and folly of such a scheme for the agricultural part of the people, nevertheless think it feasible in large towns, where the rich might subscribe for the religious instruction of the poor. Alas! they know little of the thick darkness that spreads over the streets and alleys of our large towns. The parish of Lambeth, a few years since, contained not more than one church and three or four small proprietary chapels, while dissenting chapels of every denomination were still more scantily found there; yet the inhabitants of the parish amounted at that time to upwards of 50,000. Were the parish church, and the chapels of the Establishment existing there, an *impediment* to the spread of the Gospel among that mass of people? Who shall dare to say so? But if any one, in the face of the fact which has just been stated, and in opposition to authentic reports to the same effect from various other quarters, should still contend, that a voluntary system is sufficient for the spread and maintenance of religion, we would ask, what kind of religion? wherein would it differ, among the many, from deplorable fanaticism?

For the preservation of the Church Establishment, all men, whether they belong to it or not, could they perceive their true interest, would be strenuous: but how inadequate are its provisions for the needs of the country! and how much is it to be regretted that, while its zealous friends yield to alarms on account of the hostility of Dissent, they should so much overrate the danger to be apprehended from that quarter, and almost overlook the fact that hundreds of thousands of our fellow-countrymen, though formally and nominally of the Church of England, never enter her places of worship, neither have they communication with her ministers! This deplorable state of things was partly produced by a decay of zeal among the rich and influential, and partly by a want of due expansive power in the constitution of the Establishment as regulated by law. Private benefactors, in their efforts to build and endow churches, have been frustrated, or too much impeded by legal obstacles: these, where they are unreasonable or unfitted for the times, ought to be removed; and, keeping clear of intolerance and injustice, means should be used to render the presence and powers of the Church commensurate with the wants of a shifting and still-increasing population.

This cannot be effected, unless the English Government vindicate the truth, that, as her Church exists for the benefit of all (though not in equal degree), whether of her communion or not, all should be made to contribute to its support. If this ground be abandoned, cause will be given to fear that a moral wound may be inflicted upon the heart of the English people, for which a remedy cannot be speedily provided by the utmost efforts which the members of the Church will themselves be able to make.

But let the friends of the Church be of good courage. Powers are at work by which, under Divine Providence, she may be strengthened and the sphere of her usefulness extended; not by alterations in her Liturgy, accommodated to this or that demand of finical taste, nor by cutting off this or that from her articles or Canons, to which the scrupulous or the overweening may object. Covert schism, and open nonconformity, would survive after alterations, however promising in the eyes of those whose subtilty had been exercised in making them. Latitudinarianism is the parhelion of liberty of conscience, and will ever successfully lay claim to a divided worship. Among Presbyterians, Socinians, Baptists, and Independents, there will always be found numbers who will tire of their several creeds, and some will come over to the Church. Conventicles may disappear, congregations in each denomination may fall into decay or be broken up, but the conquests which the National Church ought chiefly to aim at, lie among the thousands and tens of thousands of the unhappy outcasts who grow up with no religion at all. The wants of these cannot but be feelingly remembered. Whatever may be the disposition of the new constituencies under the Reformed Parliament, and the course which the men of their choice may be inclined or compelled to follow, it may be confidently hoped that individuals, acting in their private capacities, will endeavour to make up for the deficiencies of the Legislature. Is it too much to expect that proprietors of large estates, where the inhabitants are without religious instruction, or where it is sparingly supplied, will deem it their duty to take part in this good work; and that thriving manufacturers and merchants will, in their several neighbourhoods, be sensible of the like obligation, and act upon it with generous rivalry?

Moreover, the force of public opinion is rapidly increasing: and some may bend to it, who are not so happy as to be swayed by a higher motive: especially they who derive large incomes from lay-impropriations, in tracts of country where ministers are few and meagerly provided for. A claim still stronger may be acknowledged by those who, round their superb habitations, or elsewhere, walk over vast estates which were lavished upon their ancestors by royal favouritism or purchased at insignificant prices after church-spoliation; such proprietors, though not conscience-stricken (there is no call for that), may be prompted to make a return for which their tenantry and dependents will learn to bless their names. An impulse has been given; an accession of means from these several sources, co-operating with a *well*-considered change in the distribution of some parts of the property at present possessed by the Church, a change scrupulously founded upon due respect to law and justice, will, we trust, bring about so much of what her friends desire, that the rest may be calmly waited for, with thankfulness for what shall have been obtained.

Let it not be thought unbecoming in a layman to have treated at length a subject with which the clergy are more intimately conversant. All may, without impropriety, speak of what deeply concerns all: nor need an apology be offered for going over ground which has been trod before so ably and so often: without pretending, however, to any thing of novelty, either in matter or manner, something may have been offered to view, which will save the writer from the imputation of having little to recommend his labour, but goodness of intention.

It was with reference to thoughts and feelings expressed in verse, that I entered upon the above notices, and with verse I will conclude. The passage is extracted from my MSS. written above thirty years ago: it turns upon the individual dignity which humbleness of social condition does not preclude, but frequently promotes. It has no direct bearing upon clubs for the discussion of public affairs, nor upon political or trade-unions; but if a single workman—who, being a member of one of those clubs, runs the risk of becoming an agitator, or who, being enrolled in a union, must be left without a will of his own, and therefore a slave—should read these lines, and be touched by them, I should indeed rejoice, and little would I care for losing credit as a poet with intemperate critics, who think differently from me upon political philosophy or public measures, if the sober-minded admit that, in general views, my affections have been moved, and my imagination exercised, under and *for* the guidance of reason.

Here might I pause, and bend in reverence
To Nature, and the power of human minds;
To men as they are men within themselves.
How oft high service is performed within,
When all the external man is rude in show;
Not like a temple rich with pomp and gold,
But a mere mountain chapel that protects
Its simple worshippers from sun and shower!
Of these, said I, shall be my song; of these.
If future years mature me for the task,
Will I record the praises, making verse
Deal boldly with substantial things—in truth
And sanctity of passion speak of these,
That justice may be done, obeisance paid
Where it is due. Thus haply shall I teach
Inspire, through unadulterated ears
Pour rapture, tenderness, and hope; my theme
No other than the very heart of man,
As found among the best of those who live,
Not unexalted by religious faith,
Nor uninformed by books, good books, though few
In Nature's presence: thence may I select
Sorrow that is not sorrow, but delight,
And miserable love that is not pain
To hear of, for the glory that redounds
Therefrom to human kind, and what we are.
Be mine to follow with no timid step
Where knowledge leads me; it shall be my pride
That I have dared to tread this holy ground,
Speaking no dream, but things oracular,
Matter not lightly to be heard by those
Who to the letter of the outward promise
Do read the invisible soul; by men adroit
In speech, and for communion with the world
Accomplished, minds whose faculties are then
Most active when they are most eloquent,
And elevated most when most admired.
Men may be found of other mould than these;
Who are their own upholders, to themselves
Encouragement and energy and will;
Expressing liveliest thoughts in lively words
As native passion dictates. Others, too,
There are, among the walks of homely life,

Still higher, men for contemplation framed;
Shy, and unpractised in the strife of phrase;
Meek men, whose very souls perhaps would sink
Beneath them, summoned to such intercourse.
Theirs is the language of the heavens, the power,
The thought, the image, and the silent joy:
Words are but under-agents in their souls;
When they are grasping with their greatest strength
They do not breathe among them; this I speak
In gratitude to God, who feeds our hearts
For His own service, knoweth, loveth us,
When we are unregarded by the world.

II. ADVICE TO THE YOUNG.

(*a*) Letter to the Editor of 'The Friend,' signed 'Mathetes.'

(*b*) Answer to the Letter of 'Mathetes.'

1809.

ADVICE TO THE YOUNG.

INTRODUCTION TO 'THE FRIEND,' VOL. III. (1850).

(*a*) LETTER TO THE EDITOR BY 'MATHETES.'

Παρὰ Σέξτου——τὴν ἔννοιαν τοῦ κατὰ φύσιν ζῆν, καὶ τὸ σεμνὸν ἀπλάστως,——ὥϛε κολακείας μὲν πάσης προσηνεϛέραν εἶναι τὴν ὁμιλίαν αὐτοῦ, αἰδεσιμώτατον δὲ παρ' αὐτὸν ἐκεῖνον τὸν καιρὸν εἶναι· καὶ ἅμα μὲν ἀπαθέϛατον εἶναι, ἅμα δὲ φιλοϛοργότατον· καὶ τὸ ἰδεῖν ἄνθρωπον σαφῶς ἐλάχιϛον τῶν ἑαυτοῦ καλῶν ἡγούμενον τὴν αὐτοῦ πολυμαθίην.

M. ANTONINUS.*

From Sextus, and from the contemplation of his character, I learned what it was to live a life in harmony with nature; and that seemliness and dignity of deportment, which insured the profoundest reverence at the very same time that his company was more winning than all the flattery in the world. To him I owe likewise that I have known a man at once the most dispassionate and the most affectionate, and who of all his attractions set the least value on the multiplicity of his literary acquisitions.

To the Editor of 'The Friend.'

SIR,

I hope you will not ascribe to presumption the liberty I take in addressing you on the subject of your work. I feel deeply interested in the cause you have undertaken to support; and my object in writing this letter is to describe to you, in part from my own feelings, what I conceive to be the state of many minds, which may derive important advantage from your instructions.

I speak, Sir, of those who, though bred up under our unfavourable system of education, have yet held at times some intercourse with nature, and with those great minds whose works have been moulded by the spirit of nature; who, therefore, when they pass from the seclusion and constraint of early study, bring with them into the new scene of the world much of the pure sensibility which is the spring of all that is greatly good in thought and action. To such the season of that entrance into the world is a season of fearful importance; not for

* L. i. 9. But the passage is made up from, rather than found in, Antoninus. Ed. of *Friend*.

the seduction of its passions, but of its opinions. Whatever be their intellectual powers, unless extraordinary circumstances in their lives have been so favourable to the growth of meditative genius, that their speculative opinions must spring out of their early feelings, their minds are still at the mercy of fortune: they have no inward impulse steadily to propel them: and must trust to the chances of the world for a guide. And such is our present moral and intellectual state, that these chances are little else than variety of danger. There will be a thousand causes conspiring to complete the work of a false education, and by inclosing the mind on every side from the influences of natural feeling, to degrade its inborn dignity, and finally bring the heart itself under subjection to a corrupted understanding. I am anxious to describe to you what I have experienced or seen of the dispositions and feelings that will aid every other cause of danger, and tend to lay the mind open to the infection of all those falsehoods in opinion and sentiment, which constitute the degeneracy of the age.

Though it would not be difficult to prove, that the mind of the country is much enervated since the days of her strength, and brought down from its moral dignity, it is not yet so forlorn of all good,—there is nothing in the face of the times so dark and saddening and repulsive—as to shock the first feelings of a generous spirit, and drive it at once to seek refuge in the elder ages of our greatness. There yet survives so much of the character bred up through long years of liberty, danger, and glory, that even what this age produces bears traces of those that are past, and it still yields enough of beautiful, and splendid, and bold, to captivate an ardent but untutored imagination. And in this real excellence is the beginning of danger: for it is the first spring of that excessive admiration of the age which at last brings down to its own level a mind born above it. If there existed only the general disposition of all who are formed with a high capacity for good, to be rather credulous of excellence than suspiciously and severely just, the error would not be carried far: but there are, to a young mind, in this country and at this time, numerous powerful causes concurring to inflame this disposition, till the excess of the affection above the worth of its object is beyond all computation. To trace these causes it will be necessary to follow the history of a pure and noble mind from the first moment of that critical passage from seclusion to the world, which changes all the circumstances of its intellectual existence, shows it for the first time the real scene of living men, and calls up the new feeling of numerous relations by which it is to be connected with them.

To the young adventurer in life, who enters upon his course with such a mind, every thing seems made for delusion. He comes with a spirit the dearest feelings and highest thoughts of which have sprung up under the influences of nature. He transfers to the realities of life the high wild fancies of visionary boyhood: he brings with him into the world the passions of solitary and untamed imagination, and hopes which he has learned from dreams. Those dreams have been of the great and wonderful and lovely, of all which in these has yet been disclosed to him: his thoughts have dwelt among the wonders of nature, and among the loftiest spirits of men, heroes, and sages, and saints;—those whose deeds, and thoughts, and hopes, were high above ordinary mortality, have been the familiar companions of his soul. To love and to admire has been the joy of his existence. Love and admiration are the pleasures he will demand of the world. For these he has searched eagerly into the ages that are gone; but with more ardent and peremptory expectation he requires them of that in which his own lot is cast: for to look on life with hopes of happiness is a necessity of his nature, and to him there is no happiness but such as is surrounded with excellence.

See first how this spirit will affect his judgment of moral character, in those with whom chance may connect him in the common relations of life. It is of those with whom he is to live, that his soul first demands this food of her desires. From their conversation, their looks, their actions, their lives, she asks for excellence. To ask from all and to ask in vain, would be too dismal to bear: it would disturb him too deeply with doubt and perplexity and fear. In this hope, and in the revolting of his thoughts from the possibility of disappointment, there is a preparation for self-delusion: there is an unconscious determination that his soul shall be satisfied; an obstinate will to find good every where. And thus his first study of mankind is a continued effort to read in them the expression of his own feelings. He catches at every uncertain shew and shadowy resemblance of what he seeks; and unsuspicious in innocence, he is first won with those appearances of good which are in fact only false pretensions. But this error is not carried far: for there is a sort of instinct of rectitude, which, like the pressure of a talisman given to baffle the illusions of enchantment, warns a pure mind against hypocrisy. There is another delusion more difficult to resist and more slowly dissipated. It is when he finds, as he often will, some of the real features of excellence in the purity of their native form. For then his rapid imagination will gather round them all the kindred features that are wanting to perfect beauty; and make for him, where he could not find, the moral creature of his expectation; peopling, even from this human world, his little circle of affection with forms as fair as his heart desired for its love.

But when, from the eminence of life which he has reached, he lifts up his eyes, and sends out his spirit to range over the great scene that is opening before him and around him, the whole prospect of civilised life so wide and so magnificent;—when he begins to contemplate, in their various stations of power or splendour, the leaders of mankind, those men on whose wisdom are hung the fortunes of nations, those whose genius and valour wield the heroism of a people;—or those, in no inferior pride of place, whose sway is over the mind of society, chiefs in the realm of imagination, interpreters of the secrets of nature, rulers of human opinion;—what wonder, when he looks on all this living scene, that his heart should burn with strong affection, that he should feel that his own happiness will be for ever interwoven with the interests of mankind? Here then the sanguine hope with which he looks on life, will again be blended with his passionate desire of excellence; and he will still be impelled to single out some, on whom his imagination and his hopes may repose. To whatever department of human thought or action his mind is turned with interest, either by the sway of public passion or by its own impulse, among statesmen, and warriors, and philosophers, and poets, he will distinguish some favoured names on which he may satisfy his admiration. And there, just as in the little circle of his own acquaintance, seizing eagerly on every merit they possess, he will supply more from his own credulous hope, completing real with imagined excellence, till living men, with all their imperfections, become to him the representatives of his perfect ideal creation;—till, multiplying his objects of reverence, as he enlarges his prospect of life, he will have surrounded himself with idols of his own hands, and his imagination will seem to discern a glory in the countenance of the age, which is but the reflection of its own effulgence.

He will possess, therefore, in the creative power of generous hope, a preparation for illusory and exaggerated admiration of the age in which he lives: and this predisposition will meet with many favouring circumstances, when he has grown up under a system of education like ours, which (as perhaps all education must that is placed in the hands of a distinct and embodied class, who therefore bring to it the peculiar and hereditary prejudices of their order) has controlled his imagination to a reverence of former times, with an unjust contempt of his own. For no sooner does he break loose from this control, and begin to feel, as he contemplates the world for himself, how much there is surrounding him on all sides that gratifies his noblest desires, than there springs up in him an indignant sense of injustice, both to the age and to his own mind; and he is impelled warmly and eagerly to give loose to the feelings that have been held in bondage, to seek out and to delight in finding excellence that will vindicate the insulted world, while it justifies, too, his resentment of his own undue subjection, and exalts the value of his new found liberty.

Add to this, that secluded as he has been from knowledge, and, in the imprisoning circle of one system of ideas, cut off from his share in the thoughts and feelings that are stirring among men, he finds himself, at the first steps of his liberty, in a new intellectual world. Passions and powers which he knew not of start up in his soul. The human mind, which he had seen but under one aspect, now presents to him a thousand unknown and beautiful forms. He sees it, in its varying powers, glancing over nature with restless curiosity, and with impetuous energy striving for ever against the barriers which she has placed around it; sees it with divine power creating from dark materials living beauty, and fixing all its high and transported fancies in imperishable forms. In the world of knowledge, and science, and art, and genius, he treads as a stranger: in the confusion of new sensations, bewildered in delights, all seems beautiful;

all seems admirable. And therefore he engages eagerly in the pursuit of false or insufficient philosophy; he is won by the allurements of licentious art; he follows with wonder the irregular transports of undisciplined imagination. Nor, where the objects of his admiration are worthy, is he yet skilful to distinguish between the acquisitions which the age has made for itself, and that large proportion of its wealth which it has only inherited: but in his delight of discovery and growing knowledge, all that is new to his own mind seems to him newborn to the world. To himself every fresh idea appears instruction; every new exertion, acquisition of power: he seems just called to the consciousness of himself, and to his true place in the intellectual world; and gratitude and reverence towards those to whom he owes this recovery of his dignity, tend much to subject him to the dominion of minds that were not formed by nature to be the leaders of opinion.

All the tumult and glow of thought and imagination, which seize on a mind of power in such a scene, tend irresistibly to bind it by stronger attachment of love and admiration to its own age. And there is one among the new emotions which belong to its entrance on the world, one almost the noblest of all, in which this exaltation of the age is essentially mingled. The faith in the perpetual progression of human nature towards perfection gives birth to such lofty dreams, as secure to it the devout assent of the imagination; and it will be yet more grateful to a heart just opening to hope, flushed with the consciousness of new strength, and exulting in the prospect of destined achievements. There is, therefore, almost a compulsion on generous and enthusiastic spirits, as they trust that the future shall transcend the present, to believe that the present transcends the past. It is only on an undue love and admiration of their own age that they can build their confidence in the melioration of the human race. Nor is this faith, which, in some shape, will always be the creed of virtue, without apparent reason, even in the erroneous form in which the young adopt it. For there is a perpetual acquisition of knowledge and art, an unceasing progress in many of the modes of exertion of the human mind, a perpetual unfolding of virtues with the changing manners of society: and it is not for a young mind to compare what is gained with what has passed away; to discern that amidst the incessant intellectual activity of the race, the intellectual power of individual minds may be falling off; and that amidst accumulating knowledge lofty science may disappear; and still less, to judge, in the more complicated moral character of a people, what is progression, and what is decline.

Into a mind possessed with this persuasion of the perpetual progress of man, there may even imperceptibly steal both from the belief itself, and from many of the views on which it rests, something like a distrust of the wisdom of great men of former ages, and with the reverence, which no delusion will ever overpower in a pure mind, for their greatness, a fancied discernment of imperfection and of incomplete excellence, which wanted for its accomplishment the advantages of later improvements: there will be a surprise that so much should have been possible in times so ill prepared; and even the study of their works may be sometimes rather the curious research of a speculative inquirer, than the devout contemplation of an enthusiast,—the watchful and obedient heart of a disciple listening to the inspiration of his master.

Here then is the power of delusion that will gather round the first steps of a youthful spirit, and throw enchantment over the world in which it is to dwell; hope realising its own dreams; ignorance dazzled and ravished with sudden sunshine; power awakened and rejoicing in its own consciousness; enthusiasm kindling among multiplying images of greatness and beauty, and enamoured, above all, of one splendid error; and, springing from all these, such a rapture of life and hope and joy, that the soul, in the power of its happiness, transmutes things essentially repugnant to it into the excellence of its own nature: these are the spells that cheat the eye of the mind with illusion. It is under these influences that a young man of ardent spirit gives all his love, and reverence, and zeal, to productions of art, to theories of science, to opinions, to systems of feeling, and to characters distinguished in the world, that are far beneath his own original dignity.

Now as this delusion springs not from his worse but his better nature, it seems as if there could be no warning to him from within of his danger: for even the impassioned joy which he draws at times from the works of nature, and from those of her mightier sons, and which would startle him from a dream of unworthy passion, serves only to fix the infatuation :—for those deep emotions, proving to him that his heart is uncorrupted, justify to him all its workings, and his mind, confiding and delighting in itself, yields to the guidance of its own blind impulses of pleasure. His chance, therefore, of security is the chance that the greater number of objects occurring to attract his honourable passions may be worthy of them. But we have seen that the whole power of circumstances is collected to gather round him such objects and influences as will bend his high passions to unworthy enjoyment. He engages in it with a heart and understanding unspoiled: but they cannot long be misapplied with impunity. They are drawn gradually into closer sympathy with the falsehoods they have adopted, till, his very nature seeming to change under the corruption, there disappears from it the capacity of those higher perceptions and pleasures to which he was born: and he is cast off from the communion of exalted minds, to live and to perish with the age to which he has surrendered himself.

If minds under these circumstances of danger are preserved from decay and overthrow, it can seldom, I think, be to themselves that they owe their deliverance. It must be to a fortunate chance which places them under the influence of some more enlightened mind, from which they may first gain suspicion and afterwards wisdom. There is a philosophy, which, leading them by the light of their best emotions to the principles which should give life to thought and law to genius, will discover to them, in clear and perfect evidence, the falsehood of the errors that have misled them, and restore them to themselves. And this philosophy they will be willing to hear and wise to understand; but they must be led into its mysteries by some guiding hand; for they want the impulse or the power to penetrate of themselves the recesses.

If a superior mind should assume the protection of others just beginning to move among the dangers I have described, it would probably be found, that delusions springing from their own virtuous activity were not the only difficulties to be encountered. Even after suspicion is awakened, the subjection to falsehood may be prolonged and deepened by many weaknesses both of the intellectual and moral nature; weaknesses that will sometimes shake the authority of acknowledged truth. There may be intellectual indolence; an indisposition in the mind to the effort of combining the ideas it actually possesses, and bringing into distinct form the knowledge, which in its elements is already its own: there may be, where the heart resists the sway of opinion, misgivings and modest self-mistrust in him who sees that, if he trusts his heart, he must slight the judgment of all around him:—there may be too habitual yielding to authority, consisting, more than in indolence or diffidence, in a conscious helplessness and incapacity of the mind to maintain itself in its own place against the weight of general opinion; and there may be too indiscriminate, too undisciplined, a sympathy with others, which by the mere infection of feeling will subdue the reason. There must be a weakness in dejection to him who thinks with sadness, if his faith be pure, how gross is the error of the multitude, and that multitude how vast;—a reluctance to embrace a creed that excludes so many whom he loves, so many whom his youth has revered;—a difficulty to his understanding to believe that those whom he knows to be, in much that is good and honourable, his superiors, can be beneath him in this which is the most important of all;—a sympathy pleading importunately at his heart to descend to the fellowship of his brothers, and to take their faith and wisdom for his own. How often, when under the impulses of those solemn hours, in which he has felt with clearer insight and deeper faith his sacred truths, he labours to win to his own belief those whom he loves, will he be checked by their indifference or their laughter! And will he not bear back to his meditations a painful and disheartening sorrow, a gloomy discontent in that faith which takes in but a portion of those whom he wishes to include in all his blessings? Will he not be enfeebled by a distraction of inconsistent desires, when he feels so strongly that the faith which fills his heart, the circle within which he would embrace all he loves—would repose all his wishes and hopes, and enjoyments—is yet incommensurate with his affections?

Even when the mind, strong in reason and just feeling united, and relying on its strength, has attached itself to truth, how much is there in the course and accidents of life that is for ever silently at work for its degradation. There are pleasures deemed harmless, that lay asleep the recollections of innocence: there are pursuits held honourable, or imposed by duty, that oppress the moral spirit: above all there is that perpetual connection with ordinary minds in the common intercourse of society; that restless activity of frivolous conversation, where men of all characters and all pursuits mixing together, nothing may be talked of that is not of common interest to all;—nothing, therefore, but those obvious thoughts and feelings that float over the surface of things: and all which is drawn from the depth of nature, all which impassioned feeling has made original in thought, would be misplaced and obtrusive. The talent that is allowed to shew itself is that which can repay admiration by furnishing entertainment: and the display to which it is invited is that which flatters the vulgar pride of society, by abasing what is too high in excellence for its sympathy. A dangerous seduction to talents, which would make language, given to exalt the soul by the fervid expression of its pure emotions, the instrument of its degradation. And even when there is, as in the instance I have supposed, too much uprightness to choose so dishonourable a triumph, there is a necessity of manners, by which every one must be controlled who mixes much in society, not to offend those with whom he converses by his superiority; and whatever be the native spirit of a mind, it is evident that this perpetual adaptation of itself to others, this watchfulness against its own rising feelings, this studied sympathy with mediocrity, must pollute and impoverish the sources of its strength.

From much of its own weakness, and from all the errors of its misleading activities, may generous youth be rescued by the interposition of an enlightened mind: and in some degree it may be guarded by instruction against the injuries to which it is exposed in the world. His lot is happy who owes this protection to friendship; who has found in a friend the watchful guardian of his mind. He will not be deluded, having that light to guide; he will not slumber, with that voice to inspire; he will not be desponding or dejected, with that bosom to lean on. But how many must there be whom Heaven has left unprovided, except in their own strength; who must maintain themselves, unassisted and solitary, against their own infirmities and the opposition of the world! For such there may yet be a protector. If a teacher should stand up in their generation, conspicuous above the multitude in superior power, and still more in the assertion and proclamation of disregarded truth;—to him, to his cheering or summoning voice, all those would turn, whose deep sensibility has been oppressed by the indifference, or misled by the seduction, of the times. Of one such teacher who has been given to our own age you have described the power when you said, that in his annunciation of truths he seemed to speak in thunders. I believe that mighty voice has not been poured out in vain; that there are hearts that have received into their inmost depths all its varying tones; and that even now, there are many to whom the name of Wordsworth calls up the recollection of their weakness and the consciousness of their strength.

To give to the reason and eloquence of one man this complete control over the minds of others, it is necessary, I think, that he should be born in their own times. For thus whatever false opinion of preeminence is attached to the age becomes at once a title of reverence to him: and when with distinguished powers he sets himself apart from the age, and above it, as the teacher of high but ill-understood truths, he will appear at once to a generous imagination in the dignity of one whose superior mind outsteps the rapid progress of society, and will derive from illusion itself the power to disperse illusions. It is probable too, that he who labours under the errors I have described, might feel the power of truth in a writer of another age, yet fail in applying the full force of his principles to his own times: but when he receives them from a living teacher, there is no room for doubt or misapplication. It is the errors of his own generation that are denounced; and whatever authority he may acknowledge in the instructions of his master, strikes, with inevitable force, at his veneration for the opinions and characters of his own times. And finally there will be gathered round a living teacher, who speaks to the deeper soul, many feelings of human love that will place the infirmities of the heart peculiarly under his control; at the same time that they blend with and animate the attachment to his cause. So that there will flow from him something of the peculiar influence of a friend: while his doctrines will be embraced and asserted and vindicated with the ardent zeal of a disciple, such as can scarcely be carried back to distant times, or connected with voices that speak only from the grave.

I have done what I proposed. I have related to you as much as I have had opportunities of knowing of the difficulties from within and from without, which may oppose the natural development of true feeling and right opinion in a mind formed with some capacity for good; and the resources which such a mind may derive from an enlightened contemporary writer. If what I have said be just, it is certain that this influence will be felt more particularly in a work, adapted by its mode of publication to address the feelings of the time, and to bring to its readers repeated admonition and repeated consolation.

I have perhaps presumed too far in trespassing on your attention, and in giving way to my own thoughts; but I was unwilling to leave any thing unsaid which might induce you to consider with favour the request I was anxious to make, in the name of all whose state of mind I have described, that you would at times regard us more particularly in your instructions. I cannot judge to what degree it may be in your power to give the truth you teach a control over understandings that have matured their strength in error; but in our class I am sure you will have docile learners.

MATHETES.

(b) ANSWER TO THE LETTER OF MATHETES.

The Friend might rest satisfied that his exertions thus far have not been wholly unprofitable, if no other proof had been given of their influence, than that of having called forth the foregoing letter, with which he has been so much interested, that he could not deny himself the pleasure of communicating it to his readers. In answer to his correspondent, it need scarcely here be repeated, that one of the main purposes of his work is to weigh, honestly and thoughtfully, the moral worth and intellectual power of the age in which we live; to ascertain our gain and our loss; to determine what we are in ourselves positively, and what we are compared with our ancestors; and thus, and by every other means within his power, to discover what may be hoped for future times, what and how lamentable are the evils to be feared, and how far there is cause for fear. If this attempt should not be made wholly in vain, my ingenious correspondent, and all who are in a state of mind resembling that of which he gives so lively a picture, will be enabled more readily and surely to distinguish false from legitimate objects of admiration: and thus may the personal errors which he would guard against be more effectually prevented or removed by the development of general truth for a general purpose, than by instructions specifically adapted to himself or to the class of which he is the able representative. There is a life and spirit in knowledge which we extract from truths scattered for the benefit of all, and which the mind, by its own activity, has appropriated to itself,—a life and spirit, which is seldom found in knowledge communicated by formal and direct precepts, even when they are exalted and endeared by reverence and love for the teacher.

Nevertheless, though I trust that the assistance which my correspondent has done me the honour to request, will in course of time flow naturally from my labours, in a manner that will best serve him, I cannot resist the inclination to connect, at present, with his letter a few remarks of direct application to the subject of it; remarks, I say,—for to such I shall confine myself, —independent of the main point out of which his complaint and request both proceed; I mean the assumed inferiority of the present age in moral dignity and intellectual power to those which have preceded it. For if the fact were true, that we had even surpassed our ancestors in the best of what is good, the main part of the dangers and impediments which my correspondent has feelingly portrayed, could not cease to exist for minds like his, nor indeed would they be much diminished; as they arise out of the constitution of things, from the nature of youth, from the laws that govern the growth of the faculties, and from the necessary condition of the great body of mankind. Let us throw ourselves back to the age of Elizabeth, and call up to mind the heroes, the warriors, the statesmen, the poets, the divines, and the moral philosophers, with which the reign of the virgin queen was illustrated. Or if we be more strongly attracted by the moral purity and greatness, and that sanctity of civil and religious duty, with which the tyranny of Charles I. was struggled against, let us cast our eyes, in the hurry of admiration, round that circle of glorious patriots: but do not let us be persuaded, that each of these, in his course of discipline, was uniformly helped forward by those with whom he associated, or by those whose care it was to direct him. Then, as now, existed objects to which the wisest attached undue importance; then, as now, judgment was misled by factions and parties, time wasted in controversies fruitless, except as far as they quickened the faculties; then, as now, minds were venerated or idolized, which owed their influence to the weakness of their contemporaries rather than to their own power. Then, though great actions were wrought, and great works in literature and science produced, yet the general taste was capricious, fantastical, or grovelling; and in this point, as in all others, was youth subject to delusion, frequent in proportion to the liveliness of the sensibility, and strong as the strength of the imagination. Every age hath abounded in instances of parents, kindred, and friends, who, by indirect influence of example, or by positive injunction and exhortation, have diverted or discouraged the youth, who, in the simplicity and purity of nature, had determined to follow his intellectual genius through good and through evil, and had devoted himself to knowledge, to the practice of virtue and the preservation of integrity, in slight of temporal rewards. Above all, have not the common duties and cares of common life at all times exposed men to injury from causes the action of which is the more fatal from being silent and unremitting, and which, wherever it was not jealously watched and steadily opposed, must have pressed upon and consumed the diviner spirit?

There are two errors into which we easily slip when thinking of past times. One lies in forgetting in the excellence of what remains the large overbalance of worthlessness that has been swept away. Ranging over the wide tracts of antiquity, the situation of the mind may be likened to that of a traveller* in some unpeopled part of America, who is attracted to the burial place of one of the primitive inhabitants. It is conspicuous upon an eminence, 'a mount upon a mount!' He digs into it, and finds that it contains the bones of a man of mighty stature; and he is tempted to give way to a belief, that as there were giants in those days, so all men were giants. But a second and wiser thought may suggest to him that this tomb would never have forced itself upon his notice, if it had not contained a body that was distinguished from others,—that of a man who had been selected as a chieftain or ruler for the very reason that he surpassed the rest of his tribe in stature, and who now lies thus conspicuously inhumed upon the mountain-top, while the bones of his followers are laid unobtrusively together in their burrows upon the plain below. The second habitual error is, that in this comparison of ages we divide time merely into past and present, and place these in the balance to be weighed against each other; not considering that the present is in our estimation not more than a period of thirty years, or half a century at most, and that the past is a mighty accumulation of many such periods, perhaps the whole of recorded time, or at least the whole of that portion of it in which our own country has been distinguished. We may illustrate this by the familiar use of the words ancient and modern, when applied to poetry. What can be more inconsiderate or unjust than to compare a few existing writers with the whole succession of their progenitors? The delusion, from the moment that our thoughts are directed to it, seems too gross to deserve mention; yet men will talk for hours upon poetry, balancing against each other the words ancient and modern, and be unconscious that they have fallen into it.

These observations are not made as implying a dissent from

* See Ashe's *Travels in America*.

the belief of my correspondent, that the moral spirit and intellectual powers of this country are declining; but to guard against unqualified admiration, even in cases where admiration has been rightly fixed, and to prevent that depression which must necessarily follow, where the notion of the peculiar unfavourableness of the present times to dignity of mind has been carried too far. For in proportion as we imagine obstacles to exist out of ourselves to retard our progress, will, in fact, our progress be retarded. Deeming, then, that in all ages an ardent mind will be baffled and led astray in the manner under contemplation, though in various degrees, I shall at present content myself with a few practical and desultory comments upon some of those general causes, to which my correspondent justly attributes the errors in opinion, and the lowering or deadening of sentiment, to which ingenuous and aspiring youth is exposed. And first, for the heart-cheering belief in the perpetual progress of the species towards a point of unattainable perfection. If the present age do indeed transcend the past in what is most beneficial and honourable, he that perceives this, being in no error, has no cause for complaint; but if it be not so, a youth of genius might, it should seem, be preserved from any wrong influence of this faith by an insight into a simple truth, namely, that it is not necessary, in order to satisfy the desires of our nature, or to reconcile us to the economy of providence, that there should be at all times a continuous advance in what is of highest worth. In fact it is not, as a writer of the present day has admirably observed, in the power of fiction to portray in words, or of the imagination to conceive in spirit, actions or characters of more exalted virtue, than those which thousands of years ago have existed upon earth, as we know from the records of authentic history. Such is the inherent dignity of human nature, that there belong to it sublimities of virtues which all men may uttain, and which no man can transcend: and though this be not true in an equal degree of intellectual power, yet in the persons of Plato, Demosthenes, and Homer, and in those of Shakespeare, Milton, and Lord Bacon, were enshrined as much of the divinity of intellect as the inhabitants of this planet can hope will ever take up its abode among them. But the question is not of the power or worth of individual minds, but of the general moral or intellectual merits of an age, or a people, or of the human race. Be it so. Let us allow and believe that there is a progress in the species towards unattainable perfection, or whether this be so or not, that it is a necessity of a good and greatly-gifted nature to believe it; surely it does not follow that this progress should be constant in those virtues and intellectual qualities, and in those departments of knowledge, which in themselves absolutely considered are of most value, things independent and in their degree indispensable. The progress of the species neither is nor can be like that of a Roman road in a right line. It may be more justly compared to that of a river, which, both in its smaller reaches and larger turnings, is frequently forced back towards its fountains by objects which cannot otherwise be eluded or overcome; yet with an accompanying impulse that will insure its advancement hereafter, it is either gaining strength every hour, or conquering in secret some difficulty, by a labour that contributes as effectually to further it in its course, as when it moves forward uninterrupted in a line, direct as that of the Roman road with which I began the comparison.

It suffices to content the mind, though there may be an apparent stagnation, or a retrograde movement in the species, that something is doing which is necessary to be done, and the effects of which will in due time appear; that something is unremittingly gaining, either in secret preparation or in open and triumphant progress. But in fact here, as every where, we are deceived by creations which the mind is compelled to make for itself; we speak of the species not as an aggregate, but as endued with the form and separate life of an individual. But human kind,—what is it else than myriads of rational beings in various degrees obedient to their reason; some torpid, some aspiring; some in eager chase to the right hand, some to the left; these wasting down their moral nature, and those feeding it for immortality? A whole generation may appear even to sleep, or may be exasperated with rage,—they that compose it, tearing each other to pieces with more than brutal fury. It is enough for complacency and hope, that scattered and solitary minds are always labouring somewhere in the service of truth and virtue; and that by the sleep of the multitude the energy of the multitude may be prepared; and that by the fury of the people the chains of the people may be broken. Happy moment was it for

England when her Chaucer, who has rightly been called the morning star of her literature, appeared above the horizon; when her Wicliffe, like the sun, shot orient beams through the night of Romish superstition! Yet may the darkness and the desolating hurricane which immediately followed in the wars of York and Lancaster, be deemed in their turn a blessing, with which the Land has been visited.

May I return to the thought of progress, of accumulation, of increasing light, or of any other image by which it may please us to represent the improvement of the species? The hundred years that followed the usurpation of Henry IV., were a hurling-back of the mind of the country, a dilapidation, an extinction; yet institutions, laws, customs, and habits, were then broken down, which would not have been so readily, nor perhaps so thoroughly destroyed by the gradual influence of increasing knowledge; and under the oppression of which, if they had continued to exist, the virtue and intellectual prowess of the succeeding century could not have appeared at all, much less could they have displayed themselves with that eager haste, and with those beneficent triumphs, which will to the end of time be looked back upon with admiration and gratitude.

If the foregoing obvious distinctions be once clearly perceived, and steadily kept in view, I do not see why a belief in the progress of human nature towards perfection should dispose a youthful mind, however enthusiastic, to an undue admiration of his own age, and thus tend to degrade that mind.

But let me strike at once at the root of the evil complained of in my correspondent's letter. Protection from any fatal effect of seductions and hindrances which opinion may throw in the way of pure and high-minded youth, can only be obtained with certainty at the same price by which every thing great and good is obtained, namely, steady dependence upon voluntary and self-originating effort, and upon the practice of self-examination, sincerely aimed at and rigorously enforced. But how is this to be expected from youth? Is it not to demand the fruit when the blossom is barely put forth, and is hourly at the mercy of frosts and winds? To expect from youth these virtues and habits, in that degree of excellence to which in mature years they may be carried, would indeed be preposterous. Yet has youth many helps and aptitudes for the discharge of these difficult duties, which are withdrawn for the most part from the more advanced stages of life. For youth has its own wealth and independence; it is rich in health of body and animal spirits, in its sensibility to the impressions of the natural universe, in the conscious growth of knowledge, in lively sympathy and familiar communion with the generous actions recorded in history, and with the high passions of poetry; and, above all, youth is rich in the possession of time, and the accompanying consciousness of freedom and power. The young man feels that he stands at a distance from the season when his harvest is to be reaped; that he has leisure and may look around, and may defer both the choice and the execution of his purposes. If he makes an attempt and shall fail, new hopes immediately rush in and new promises. Hence, in the happy confidence of his feelings, and in the elasticity of his spirit, neither worldly ambition, nor the love of praise, nor dread of censure, nor the necessity of worldly maintenance, nor any of those causes which tempt or compel the mind habitually to look out of itself for support; neither these, nor the passions of envy, fear, hatred, despondency, and the rankling of disappointed hopes, (all which in after life give birth to, and regulate, the efforts of men and determine their opinions) have power to preside over the choice of the young, if the disposition be not naturally bad, or the circumstances have not been in an uncommon degree unfavourable.

In contemplation, then, of this disinterested and free condition of the youthful mind, I deem it in many points peculiarly capable of searching into itself, and of profiting by a few simple questions, such as these that follow. Am I chiefly gratified by the exertion of my power from the pure pleasure of intellectual activity, and from the knowledge thereby acquired? In other words, to what degree do I value my faculties and my attainments for their own sakes? or are they chiefly prized by me on account of the distinction which they confer, or the superiority which they give me over others? Am I aware that immediate influence and a general acknowledgment of merit are no necessary adjuncts of a successful adherence to study and meditation in those departments of knowledge which are of most value to mankind;—that a recompense of honours and emoluments is far less to be expected; in fact, that there is little natural connection between them? Have I perceived this truth; and, perceiving it, does the countenance of philosophy continue to appear as bright and beautiful in my eyes?—Has no haze bedimmed it? Has no cloud passed over and hidden from me that look which was before so encouraging? Knowing that it is my duty, and feeling that it is my inclination, to mingle as a social being with my fellow men; prepared also to submit cheerfully to the necessity that will probably exist of relinquishing, for the purpose of gaining a livelihood, the greatest portion of my time to employments where I shall have little or no choice how or when I am to act; have I, at this moment, when I stand as it were upon the threshold of the busy world, a clear intuition of that preeminence in which virtue and truth (involving in this latter word the sanctities of religion) sit enthroned above all denominations and dignities which, in various degrees of exaltation, rule over the desires of men? Do I feel that, if their solemn mandates shall be forgotten, or disregarded, or denied the obedience due to them when opposed to others, I shall not only have lived for no good purpose, but that I shall have sacrificed my birth-right as a rational being; and that every other acquisition will be a bane and a disgrace to me? This is not spoken with reference to such sacrifices as present themselves to the youthful imagination in the shape of crimes, acts by which the conscience is violated; such a thought, I know, would be recoiled from at once, not without indignation; but I write in the spirit of the ancient fable of Prodicus, representing the choice of Hercules. Here is the World, a female figure approaching at the head of a train of willing or giddy followers: her air and deportment are at once careless, remiss, self-satisfied, and haughty: and there is Intellectual Prowess, with a pale cheek and serene brow, leading in chains Truth, her beautiful and modest captive. The one makes her salutation with a discourse of ease, pleasure, freedom, and domestic tranquillity; or, if she invite to labour, it is labour in the busy and beaten track, with assurance of the complacent regards of parents, friends, and of those with whom we associate. The promise also may be upon her lip of the huzzas of the multitude, of the smile of kings, and the munificent rewards of senates. The other does not venture to hold forth any of these allurements; she does not conceal from him whom she addresses the impediments, the disappointments, the ignorance and prejudice which her follower will have to encounter, if devoted, when duty calls, to active life; and if to contemplative, she lays nakedly before him a scheme of solitary and unremitting labour, a life of entire neglect perhaps, or assuredly a life exposed to scorn, insult, persecution, and hatred; but cheered by encouragement from a grateful few, by applauding conscience, and by a prophetic anticipation, perhaps, of fame—a late, though lasting, consequence. Of these two, each in this manner soliciting you to become her adherent, you doubt not which to prefer; but oh! the thought of moment is not preference, but the degree of preference; the passionate and pure choice, the inward sense of absolute and unchangeable devotion.

I spoke of a few simple questions. The question involved in this deliberation is simple, but at the same time it is high and awful; and I would gladly know whether an answer can be returned satisfactory to the mind. We will for a moment suppose that it can not; that there is a startling and a hesitation. Are we then to despond,—to retire from all contest,—and to reconcile ourselves at once to cares without a generous hope, and to efforts in which there is no more moral life than that which is found in the business and labours of the unfavoured and unaspiring many? No. But if the inquiry have not been on just grounds satisfactorily answered, we may refer confidently our youth to that nature of which he deems himself an enthusiastic follower, and one who wishes to continue no less faithful and enthusiastic. We would tell him that there are paths which he has not trodden; recesses which he has not penetrated; that there is a beauty which he has not seen, a pathos which he has not felt, a sublimity to which he hath not been raised. If he have trembled because there has occasionally taken place in him a lapse of which he is conscious; if he foresee open or secret attacks, which he has had intimations that he will neither be strong enough to resist, nor watchful enough to elude, let him not hastily ascribe this weakness, this deficiency, and the painful apprehensions accompanying them, in any degree to the virtues or noble qualities with which youth by nature is furnished; but let him first be assured, before he looks about for the means of attaining the insight, the discriminating powers, and the confirmed wisdom of manhood, that his soul has more to demand of the appropriate excellencies of youth, than youth has yet supplied to it; that the evil under which he labours is not a superabundance of the instincts and the animating spirit of that age, but a falling short, or a failure. But what can he gain from this admonition? He cannot recall past time; he cannot begin his journey afresh; he cannot untwist the links by which, in no undelightful harmony, images and sentiments are wedded in his mind. Granted that the sacred light of childhood is and must be for him no more than a remembrance. He may, notwithstanding, be remanded to nature, and with trustworthy hopes, founded less upon his sentient than upon his intellectual being; to nature, as leading on insensibly to the society of reason, but to reason and will, as leading back to the wisdom of nature. A re-union, in this order accomplished, will bring reformation and timely support; and the two powers of reason and nature, thus reciprocally teacher and taught, may advance together in a track to which there is no limit.

We have been discoursing (by implication at least) of infancy, childhood, boyhood, and youth, of pleasures lying upon the unfolding intellect plenteously as morning dew-drops,—of knowledge inhaled insensibly like the fragrance,—of dispositions stealing into the spirit like music from unknown quarters,—of images uncalled for and rising up like exhalations,—of hopes plucked like beautiful wild flowers from the ruined tombs that border the highways of antiquity, to make a garland for a living forehead;—in a word, we have been treating of nature as a teacher of truth through joy and through gladness, and as a creatress of the faculties by a process of smoothness and delight. We have made no mention of fear, shame, sorrow, nor of ungovernable and vexing thoughts; because, although these have been and have done mighty service, they are overlooked in that stage of life when youth is passing into manhood—overlooked, or forgotten. We now apply for the succour which we need to a faculty that works after a different course; that faculty is reason; she gives more spontaneously, but she seeks for more; she works by thought through feeling; yet in thoughts she begins and ends.

A familiar incident may elucidate this contrast in the operations of nature, may render plain the manner in which a process of intellectual improvements, the reverse of that which nature pursues, is by reason introduced. There never perhaps existed a school-boy, who, having, when he retired to rest, carelessly blown out his candle, and having chanced to notice, as he lay upon his bed in the ensuing darkness, the sullen light which had survived the extinguished flame, did not, at some time or other, watch that light as if his mind were bound to it by a spell. It fades and revives, gathers to a point, seems as if it would go out in a moment, again recovers its strength, nay becomes brighter than before: it continues to shine with an endurance, which in its apparent weakness is a mystery; it protracts its existence so long, clinging to the power which supports it, that the observer, who had lain down in his bed so easy-minded, becomes sad and melancholy; his sympathies are touched; it is to him an intimation and an image of departing human life; the thought comes nearer to him; it is the life of a venerated parent, of a beloved brother or sister, or of an aged domestic, who are gone to the grave, or whose destiny it soon may be thus to linger, thus to hang upon the last point of mortal existence, thus finally to depart and be seen no more. This is nature teaching seriously and sweetly through the affections, melting the heart, and, through that instinct of tenderness, developing the understanding. In this instance the object of solicitude is the bodily life of another. Let us accompany this same boy to that period between youth and manhood, when a solicitude may be awakened for the moral life of himself. Are there any powers by which, beginning with a sense of inward decay that affects not however the natural life, he could call to mind the same image and hang over it with an equal interest as a visible type of his own perishing spirit? Oh! surely, if the being of the individual be under his own care, if it be his first care, if duty begin from the point of accountableness to our conscience, and, through that, to God and human nature; if without such primary sense of duty, all secondary care of teacher, of friend, or parent, must be baseless and fruitless; if, lastly, the motions of the soul transcend in worth those of the animal functions, nay, give to them their sole value; then truly are there such powers; and the image of the dying taper may be recalled and contemplated, though with no sadness in the nerves, no disposition to tears, no unconquerable sighs, yet with a melancholy in the soul, a sinking inward into ourselves from thought to thought, a steady remonstrance, and a high resolve. Let then the youth go back, as occasion will permit, to nature and to solitude, thus admonished by reason, and relying upon this newly acquired support. A world of fresh sensations will gradually open upon him as his mind puts off its infirmities, and as instead of being propelled restlessly towards others in admiration, or too hasty love, he makes it his prime business to understand himself. New sensations, I affirm, will be opened out, pure, and sanctioned by that reason which is their original author; and precious feelings of disinterested, that is self-disregarding, joy and love may be regenerated and restored; and, in this sense, he may be said to measure back the track of life he has trodden.

In such disposition of mind let the youth return to the visible universe, and to conversation with ancient books, and to those, if such there be, which in the present day breathe the ancient spirit; and let him feed upon that beauty which unfolds itself, not to his eye as it sees carelessly the things which cannot possibly go unseen, and are remembered or not as accident shall decide, but to the thinking mind; which searches, discovers, and treasures up, infusing by meditation into the objects with which it converses an intellectual life, whereby they remain planted in the memory, now and for ever. Hitherto the youth, I suppose, has been content for the most part to look at his own mind, after the manner in which he ranges along the stars in the firmament with naked unaided sight: let him now apply the telescope of art, to call the invisible stars out of their hiding places; and let him endeavour to look through the system of his being, with the organ of reason, summoned to penetrate, as far as it has power, in discovery of the impelling forces and the governing laws.

These expectations are not immoderate; they demand nothing more than the perception of a few plain truths; namely, that knowledge, efficacious for the production of virtue, is the ultimate end of all effort, the sole dispenser of complacency and repose. A perception also is implied of the inherent superiority of contemplation to action. The Friend does not in this contradict his own words, where he has said heretofore, that 'doubtless to act is nobler than to think.'* In those words, it was

* 'The Friend,' vol. i. p. 158 (ed. 1850). G.

his purpose to censure that barren contemplation, which rests satisfied with itself in cases where the thoughts are of such quality that they may, and ought to, be embodied in action. But he speaks now of the general superiority of thought to action; as proceeding and governing all action that moves to salutary purposes; and, secondly, as leading to elevation, the absolute possession of the individual mind, and to a consistency or harmony of the being within itself, which no outward agency can reach to disturb or to impair; and lastly, as producing works of pure science; or of the combined faculties of imagination, feeling, and reason; works which, both from their independence in their origin upon accident, their nature, their duration, and the wide spread of their influence, are entitled rightly to take place of the noblest and most beneficent deeds of heroes, statesmen, legislators, or warriors.

Yet, beginning from the perception of this established superiority, we do not suppose that the youth, whom we wish to guide and encourage, is to be insensible to those influences of wealth, or rank, or station, by which the bulk of mankind are swayed. Our eyes have not been fixed upon virtue which lies apart from human nature, or transcends it. In fact there is no such virtue. We neither suppose nor wish him to undervalue or slight these distinctions as modes of power, things that may enable him to be more useful to his contemporaries; nor as gratifications that may confer dignity upon his living person, and, through him, upon those who love him; nor as they may connect his name, through a family to be founded by his success, in a closer chain of gratitude with some portion of posterity, who shall speak of him as among their ancestry, with a more tender interest than the mere general bond of patriotism or humanity would supply. We suppose no indifference to, much less a contempt of, these rewards; but let them have their due place; let it be ascertained, when the soul is searched into, that they are only an auxiliary motive to exertion, never the principal or originating force. If this be too much to expect from a youth who, I take for granted, possesses no ordinary endowments, and whom circumstances with respect to the more dangerous passions have favoured, then, indeed, must the noble spirit of the country be wasted away; then would our institutions be deplorable, and the education prevalent among us utterly vile and debasing?

But my correspondent, who drew forth these thoughts, has said rightly, that the character of the age may not without injustice be thus branded. He will not deny that, without speaking of other countries, there is in these islands, in the departments of natural philosophy, of mechanic ingenuity, in the general activities of the country, and in the particular excellence of individual minds, in high stations civil or military, enough to excite admiration and love in the sober-minded, and more than enough to intoxicate the youthful and inexperienced. I will compare, then, an aspiring youth, leaving the schools in which he has been disciplined, and preparing to bear a part in the concerns of the world, I will compare him in this season of eager admiration, to a newly-invested knight appearing with his blank unsignalized shield, upon some day of solemn tournament, at the court of the Faery-queen, as that sovereignty was conceived to exist by the moral and imaginative genius of our divine Spenser. He does not himself immediately enter the lists as a combatant, but he looks round him with a beating heart, dazzled by the gorgeous pageantry, the banners, the impresses, the ladies of overcoming beauty, the persons of the knights, now first seen by him, the fame of whose actions is carried by the traveller, like merchandize, through the world, and resounded upon the harp of the minstrel. But I am not at liberty to make this comparison. If a youth were to begin his career in such an assemblage, with such examples to guide and to animate, it will be pleaded, there would be no cause for apprehension; he could not falter, he could not be misled. But ours is, notwithstanding its manifold excellences, a degenerate age; and recreant knights are among us far outnumbering the true. A false Gloriana in these days imposes worthless services, which they who perform them, in their blindness, know not to be such; and which are recompensed by rewards as worthless, yet eagerly grasped at, as if they were the immortal guerdon of virtue.

I have in this declaration insensibly overstepped the limits which I had determined not to pass: let me be forgiven; for it is hope which hath carried me forward. In such a mixed assemblage as our age presents, with its genuine merit and its large overbalance of alloy, I may boldly ask into what errors, either with respect to person or thing, could a young man fall, who had sincerely entered upon the course of moral discipline which has been recommended, and to which the condition of youth, it has been proved, is favourable? His opinions could no where deceive him beyond the point up to which, after a season, he would find that it was salutary for him to have been deceived. For as that man cannot set a right value upon health who has never known sickness, nor feel the blessing of ease who has been through his life a stranger to pain, so can there be no confirmed and passionate love of truth for him who has not experienced the hollowness of error. Range against each other as advocates, oppose as combatants, two several intellects, each strenuously asserting doctrines which he sincerely believes; but the one contending for the worth and beauty of that garment which the other has outgrown and cast away. Mark the superiority, the ease, the dignity, on the side of the more advanced mind, how he overlooks his subject, commands it from centre to circumference, and hath the same thorough knowledge of the tenets which his adversary, with impetuous zeal, but in confusion also, and thrown off his guard at every turn of the argument, is labouring to maintain. If it be a question of the fine arts (poetry for instance) the riper mind not only sees that his opponent is deceived; but, what is of far more importance, sees how he is deceived. The imagination stands before him with all its imperfections laid open; as duped by shows, enslaved by words, corrupted by mistaken delicacy and false refinement, as not having even attended with care to the reports of the senses, and therefore deficient grossly in the rudiments of its own power. He has noted how, as a supposed necessary condition, the understanding sleeps in order that the fancy may dream. Studied in the history of society, and versed in the secret laws of thought, he can pass regularly through all the gradations, can pierce infallibly all the windings, which false taste through ages has pursued, from the very time when first, through inexperience, heedlessness, or affectation, the imagination took its departure from the side of truth, its original parent. Can a disputant thus accoutred be withstood?—one to whom, further, every movement in the thoughts of his antagonist is revealed by the light of his own experience; who, therefore, sympathizes with weakness gently, and wins his way by forbearance; and hath, when needful, an irresistible power of onset, arising from gratitude to the truth which he vindicates, not merely as a positive good for mankind, but as his own especial rescue and redemption.

I might here conclude: but my correspondent towards the close of his letter, has written so feelingly upon the advantages to be derived, in his estimation, from a living instructor, that I must not leave this part of the subject without a word of direct notice. The Friend cited, some time ago,* a passage from the prose works of Milton, eloquently describing the manner in which good and evil grow up together in the field of the world almost inseparably; and insisting, consequently, upon the knowledge and survey of vice as necessary to the constituting of human virtue, and the scanning of error to the confirmation of truth.

If this be so, and I have been reasoning to the same effect in the preceding paragraph, the fact, and the thoughts which it may suggest, will, if rightly applied, tend to moderate an anxiety for the guidance of a more experienced or superior mind. The advantage, where it is possessed, is far from being an absolute good: nay, such a preceptor, ever at hand, might prove an oppression not to be thrown off, and a fatal hindrance. Grant that in the general tenor of his intercourse with his pupil he is forbearing and circumspect, inasmuch as he is rich in that knowledge (above all other necessary for a teacher) which cannot exist without a liveliness of memory, preserving for him an unbroken image of the winding, excursive, and often retrograde course, along which his own intellect has passed. Grant that, furnished with these distinct remembrances, he wishes that the mind of his pupil should be free to luxuriate in the enjoyments, loves, and admirations appropriated to its age; that he is not in haste to kill what he knows will in due time die of itself; or be transmuted, and put on a nobler form and higher faculties otherwise unattainable. In a word, that the teacher is governed habitually by the wisdom of patience waiting with pleasure. Yet perceiving how much the outward help of art can facilitate the progress of nature, he may be betrayed into many unnecessary or pernicious mistakes where he deems his interference war-

* 'The Friend,' vol. i. p. 96 (ed. 1850). G.

ranted by substantial experience. And in spite of all his caution, remarks may drop insensibly from him which shall wither in the mind of his pupil a generous sympathy, destroy a sentiment of approbation or dislike, not merely innocent but salutary; and for the inexperienced disciple how many pleasures may be thus off, what joy, what admiration, and what love! While in their stead are introduced into the ingenuous mind misgivings, a mistrust of its own evidence, dispositions to affect to feel where there can be no real feeling, indecisive judgments, a superstructure of opinions that has no base to support it, and words uttered by rote with the impertinence of a parrot or a mocking-bird, yet which may not be listened to with the same indifference, as they cannot be heard without some feeling of moral disapprobation.

These results, I contend, whatever may be the benefit to be derived from such an enlightened teacher, are in their degree inevitable. And by this process, humility and docile dispositions may exist towards the master, endued as he is with the power which personal presence confers; but at the same time they will be liable to overstep their due bounds, and to degenerate into passiveness and prostration of mind. This towards him; while, with respect to other living men, nay even to the mighty spirits of past times, there may be associated with such weakness a want of modesty and humility. Insensibly may steal in presumption and a habit of sitting in judgment in cases where no sentiment ought to have existed but diffidence or veneration. Such virtues are the sacred attributes of youth; its appropriate calling is not to distinguish in the fear of being deceived or degraded, not to analyze with scrupulous minuteness, but to accumulate in genial confidence; its instinct, its safety, its benefit, its glory, is to love, to admire, to feel, and to labour. Nature has irrevocably decreed, that our prime dependence in all stages of life after infancy and childhood have been passed through (nor do I know that this latter ought to be excepted) must be upon our own minds; and that the way to knowledge shall be long, difficult, winding, and oftentimes returning upon itself.

What has been said is a mere sketch, and that only of a part of the interesting country into which we have been led; but my correspondent will be able to enter the paths that have been pointed out. Should he do this and advance steadily for a while, he needs not fear any deviations from the truth which will be finally injurious to him. He will not long have his admiration fixed upon unworthy objects; he will neither be clogged nor drawn aside by the love of friends or kindred, betraying his understanding through his affections; he will neither be bowed down by conventional arrangements of manners producing too often a lifeless decency; nor will the rock of his spirit wear away in the endless beating of the waves of the world; neither will that portion of his own time, which he must surrender to labours by which his livelihood is to be earned or his social duties performed, be unprofitable to himself indirectly, while it is directly useful to others; for that time has been primarily surrendered through an act of obedience to a moral law established by himself, and therefore he moves them also along the orbit of perfect liberty.

Let it be remembered, that the advice requested does not relate to the government of the more dangerous passions, or to the fundamental principles of right and wrong as acknowledged by the universal conscience of mankind. I may therefore assure my youthful correspondent, if he will endeavour to look into himself in the manner which I have exhorted him to do, that in him the wish will be realized, to him in due time the prayer granted, which was uttered by that living teacher of whom he speaks with gratitude as of a benefactor, when in his character of philosophical poet, having thought of morality as implying in its essence voluntary obedience, and producing the effect of order, he transfers in the transport of imagination, the law of moral to physical natures, and having contemplated, through the medium of that order, all modes of existence as subservient to one spirit, concludes his address to the power of duty in the following words:

> To humbler functions, awful power!
> I call thee: I myself commend
> Unto thy guidance from this hour;
> Oh, let my weakness have an end!
> Give unto me, made lowly wise,
> The spirit of self-sacrifice;
> The confidence of reason give,
> And in the light of truth thy bondman let me live!

III. OF EDUCATION.

(a) On the Education of the Young: Letter to a Friend, 1806.
(b) Of the People, their Ways and Needs: Letter to Archdeacon Wrangham, 1808.
(c) Education: two Letters to the Rev. H. J. Rose, 1828.
(d) Education of Duty: Letter to Rev. Dr. Wordsworth, 1830.
(e) Speech on laying the Foundation-Stone of the new School in the Village of Bowness, Windermere, 1836.

(a) ON THE EDUCATION OF THE YOUNG.

Letter to a Friend [1806].

My dear Sir,

I am happy to hear of the instructions which you are preparing for parents, and feel honoured by your having offered to me such an opportunity of conveying to the public any information I may possess upon the subject; but, in truth, I am so little competent in the present unarranged state of my ideas to write any thing of value, that it would be the highest presumption in me to attempt it. This is not mock modesty, but rigorous and sober truth. As to the case of your own child, I will set down a few thoughts, which I do not hope will throw much light on your mind, but they will show my willingness to do the little that is in my power.

The child being the child of a man like you, what I have to say will lie in small compass.

I consider the facts which you mention as indicative of what is commonly called sensibility, and of quickness and talent, and shall take for granted that they are so; you add that the child is too much noticed by grown people, and apprehend selfishness.

Such a child will almost always be too much noticed; and it is scarcely possible entirely to guard against the evil: hence vanity, and under bad management selfishness of the worst kind. And true it is, that under better and even the best management, such constitutions are liable to selfishness; not showing itself in the shape of tyranny, caprice, avarice, meanness, envy, skulking, and base self-reference; but selfishness of a worthier kind, yet still rightly called by that name. What I mean I shall explain afterwards.

Vanity is not the necessary or even natural growth of such a temperament; quite the contrary. Such a child, if neglected and suffered to run wild, would probably be entirely free from vanity, owing to the liveliness of its feelings, and the number of its resources. It would be by nature independent and sufficient for itself. But as such children, in these times in particular, are rarely if ever neglected, or rather rarely if ever not far too much noticed, it is a hundred to one your child will have more vanity than you could wish. This is one evil to be guarded against. Formerly, indeed till within these few years, children were very carelessly brought up; at present they too early and too habitually feel their own importance, from the solicitude and unremitting attendance which is bestowed upon them. A child like yours, I believe, unless under the wisest guidance, would prosper most where she was the least noticed and the least made of; I mean more than this where she received the least cultivation. She does not stand in need of the stimulus of praise (as much as can benefit her, *i.e.* as much as her nature requires, it will be impossible to withhold from her); nor of being provoked to exertion, or, even if she be not injudiciously thwarted, to industry. Nor can there be any need to be *sedulous* in calling out her affections; her own lively enjoyments will do all this for her, and also point out what is to be done to her. But take all the pains you can, she will be too much noticed. Other evils will also beset her, arising more from herself; and how are these to be obviated? But, first, let us attempt to find what these evils will be.

Observe, I put all gross mismangement out of the question, and I believe they will then probably be as follows: first, as mentioned before, a considerable portion of vanity. But if the child be not constrained too much, and be left sufficiently to her own pursuits, and be not too anxiously tended, and have not her mind planted over by art with likings that do not spring naturally up in it, this will by the liveliness of her independent enjoyment almost entirely disappear, and she will become modest and diffident; and being not apt from the same ruling cause,—I mean the freshness of her own sensations—to compare herself with others, she will hold herself in too humble estimation. But she will probably still be selfish; and this brings me to the explanation of what I hinted at before, viz., in what manner she will be selfish.

It appears, then, to me that all the permanent evils which you have to apprehend for your daughter, supposing you should live to educate her yourself, may be referred to this principle,—an undue predominance of present objects over absent ones, which, as she will surely be distinguished by an extreme love of those about her, will produce a certain restlessness of mind, calling perpetually for proofs of ever-living regard and affection: she must be loved as much and in the same way as she loves, or she will not be satisfied. Hence, quickness in taking offence, petty jealousies and apprehensions lest she is neglected or loses ground in people's love, a want of a calm and steady sense of her own merits to secure her from these fits of imagined slights; for, in the first place, she will, as is hinted at before, be in general deficient in this just estimation of her own worth, and will further be apt to forget everything of that kind in the present sense of supposed injury. She will (all which is referable to the same cause) in the company of others have too constant a craving for sympathy up to a height beyond what her companions are capable of bestowing; this will often be mortifying to herself, and burthensome to others; and should circumstances be untoward, and her mind be not sufficiently furnished with ideas and knowledge, this craving would be most pernicious to herself, preying upon mind and body. She will be too easily pleased, apt to overrate the merits of new acquaintances, subject to fits of over-love and over-joy, in absence from those she loves full of fears and apprehensions, &c., injurious to her health; her passions for the most part will be happy and good, but she will be too little mistress of them. The distinctions which her intellect will make will be apt, able, and just, but in conversation she will be prone to overshoot herself, and commit eloquent blunders through eagerness. In fine, her manners will be frank and ardent, but they will want dignity; and a want of dignity will be the general defect of her character.

Something of this sort of character, which I have thus loosely sketched, and something of the sort of selfishness to which I have adverted, it seems to me that under the best management you have reason to apprehend for your daughter. If she should happen to be an only child, or the only sister of brothers who would probably idolize her, one might prophesy almost with absolute confidence that most of these qualities would be found in her in a great degree. How then is the evil to be softened down or prevented? Assuredly, not by mortifying her, which is the course commonly pursued with such tempers; nor by preaching to her about her own defects; nor by overrunning her infancy with books about good boys and girls, and bad boys and girls, and all that trumpery; but (and this is the only important thing I have to say upon the subject) by putting her in the way of acquiring without measure or limit such knowledge as will lead her out of herself, such knowledge as is interesting for its own sake; things known because they are interesting, not interesting because they are known; in a word, by leaving her at liberty to luxuriate in such feelings and images as will feed her mind in silent pleasure. This nourishment is contained in fairy tales, romances, the best biographies and histories, and such parts of natural history relating to the powers and appearances of the earth and elements, and the habits and structure of animals, as belong to it, not as an art or science, but as a magazine of form and feeling. This kind of knowledge is purely good, a direct antidote to every evil to be apprehended, and food absolutely necessary to preserve the mind of a child like yours from morbid appetites. Next to these objects comes such knowledge as, while it is chiefly interesting for its own sake, admits the fellowship of another sort of pleasure, that of complacence from the conscious exertion of the faculties and love of praise. The accomplishments of dancing, music, and drawing, rank under this head; grammar, learning of languages, botany probably, and out of the way knowledge of arts and manufactures, &c. The second class of objects, as far as they tend to feed vanity and self-conceit, are evil; but let them have their just proportion in the plan of education, and they will afterwards contribute to destroy these, by furnishing the mind with power and independent gratification: the vanity will disappear, and the good will remain.

Lastly comes that class of objects which are interesting almost solely because they are known, and the knowledge may be displayed; and this unfortunately comprehends three fourths of what, according to the plan of modern education, children's heads are stuffed with; that is, minute, remote, or trifling facts in geography, topography, natural history, chronology, &c., or acquisitions in art, or accomplishments which the child makes by rote, and which are quite beyond its age; things of no value in themselves, but as they show cleverness; things hurtful to any temper, but to a child like yours absolute poison. Having said thus much, it seems almost impertinent to add that your child, above all, should, I might say, be chained down to the severest attention to truth,—I mean to the minutest accuracy in every thing which she relates; this will strike at the root of evil by teaching her to form correct notions of present things, and will steadily strengthen her mind. Much caution should be taken not to damp her natural vivacity, for this may have a very bad effect; and by the indirect influence of the example of manly and dignified manners any excessive wildnesses of her own will be best kept under. Most unrelaxing firmness should from the present hour be maintained in withstanding such of her desires as are grossly unreasonable. But indeed I am forgetting to whom I am speaking, and am ashamed of these precepts; they will show my good will, and in that hope alone can I suffer them to stand. Farewell, there is great reason to congratulate yourself in having a child so promising; and you have my best and most ardent wishes that she may be a blessing to her parents and every one about her.*

* *Memoirs*, vol. ii. pp. 164-70. G.

(b) OF THE PEOPLE, THEIR WAYS AND NEEDS.

Letter to Archdeacon Wrangham.

Grasmere, June 5, 1808.

MY DEAR WRANGHAM,

I have this moment received your letter.

—— is a most provoking fellow; very kind, very humane, very generous, very ready to serve, with a thousand other good qualities, but in the practical business of life the arrantest mar-plan that ever lived. When I first wrote to you, I wrote also to him, sending the statement which I sent to you, and begging his exertions *among his friends*. By and by comes back my statement, having undergone a *rifacimento* from his hands, and *printed*, with an accompanying letter, saying that if some of the principal people in this neighbourhood who had already subscribed would put their names to this paper, testifying that this was a proper case for charitable interferences, or that the *persons mentioned were proper objects of charity*, that he would have the printed paper inserted in the public newspapers, &c. Upon which, my sister wrote to him, that in consequence of what had been already subscribed, and what we had reason to expect from those friends who were privately stirring in the business, among whom we chiefly alluded to you, in our own minds, as one on whom we had most dependence, that there would be no necessity *for public advertisements*, but that if among his private friends he could raise any money for us, we should be very glad to receive it. And upon this does he write to you in this (what shall I call it? for I am really vexed!) blundering manner! I will not call upon you to undertake the awkward task of rebuilding that part of the edifice which —— has destroyed, but let what remains be preserved; and if a little could be added, there would be no harm. I must request you to transmit the money to me, with the names of the persons to whom we are obliged.

. . . .

With regard to the more important part of your letter, I am under many difficulties. I am writing from a window which gives me a view of a little boat, gliding quietly about upon the surface of our basin of a lake. I should like to be in it, but what could I do with such a vessel in the heart of the Atlantic Ocean? As this boat would be to that navigation, so is my letter to the subject upon which you would set me afloat. Let me, however, say, that I have read your sermon (which I lately received from Longman) with much pleasure; I only gave it a cursory perusal, for since it arrived our family has been in great confusion, we having removed to another house, in which we are not yet half settled. The Appendix I had received before in a frank, and of that I feel myself more entitled to speak, because I had read it more at leisure. I am entirely of accord with you in chiefly recommending religious books for the poor; but of many of those which you recommend I can neither speak in praise nor blame, as I have never read them. Yet, as far as my own observation goes, which has been mostly employed upon agricultural persons in thinly-peopled districts, I cannot find that there is much disposition to read among the labouring classes, or much occasion for it. Among manufacturers and persons engaged in sedentary employments, it is, I know, very different. The labouring man in agriculture generally carries on his work either in solitude or with his own family—with persons whose minds he is thoroughly acquainted with, and with whom he is under no temptation to enter into discussions, or to compare opinions. He goes home from the field, or the barn, and within and about his own house he finds a hundred little jobs which furnish him with a change of employment which is grateful and profitable; then comes supper, and bed. This for week-days. For sabbaths, he goes to church with us often or mostly twice a day; on coming home, some one turns to the Bible, finds the text, and probably reads the chapter whence it is taken, or perhaps some other; and in the afternoon the master or mistress frequently reads the Bible, if alone; and on this day the mistress of the house *almost always* teaches the children to read, or as they express it, hears them a lesson; or if not thus employed, they visit their neighbours, or receive them in their own houses as they drop in, and keep up by the hour a slow and familiar chat. This kind of life, of which I have seen much, and which I know would be looked upon with little complacency by many religious persons, is peaceable, and as innocent as (the frame of society and the practices of government being what they are) we have a right to expect; besides, it is much more intellectual than a careless observer would suppose. One of our neighbours, who lives as I have described, was yesterday walking with me; and as we were pacing on, talking about indifferent matters, by the side of a brook, he suddenly said to me, with great spirit and a lively smile, 'I *like* to walk where I can hear the sound of a beck!' (the word, as you know, in our dialect for a brook). I cannot but think that this man, without being conscious of it, has had many devout feelings connected with the appearances which have presented themselves to him in his employment as a shepherd, and that the pleasure of his heart at that moment was an acceptable offering to the Divine Being. But to return to the subject of books. I find among the people I am speaking of, halfpenny ballads and penny and two-penny histories in great abundance; these are often bought as charitable tributes to the poor persons who hawk them about (and it is the best way of procuring them). They are frequently stitched together in tolerably thick volumes, and such I have read; some of the contents, though not often religious, very good; others objectionable, either for the superstition in them, such as prophecies, fortune-telling, &c., or more frequently for indelicacy. I have so much felt the influence of these straggling papers, that I have many a time wished that I had talents to produce songs, poems, and little histories that might circulate among other good things in this way, supplanting partly the bad flowers and useless herbs, and to take place of weeds. Indeed, some of the poems which I have published were composed, not without a hope that at some time or other they might answer this purpose. The kind of library which you recommend would not, I think, for the reasons given above, be of much direct use in any of the agricultural districts of Cumberland and Westmoreland with which I am acquainted, though almost every person here can read; I mean of general use as to morals or behaviour. It might, however, with individuals, do much in awakening enterprise, calling forth ingenuity, and fostering genius. I have known several persons who would eagerly have sought, not after these books merely, but *any* books, and would have been most happy in having such a collection to repair to. The knowledge thus acquired would also have spread, by being dealt about in conversation among their neighbours, at the door, and by the fireside; so that it is not easy to foresee how far the good might extend; and harm I can see none which would not be greatly overbalanced by the advantage. The situation of manufacturers is deplorably different. The monotony of their employments renders some sort of stimulus, intellectual or bodily, absolutely necessary for them. Their work is carried on in clusters,—men from different parts of the world, and perpetually changing; so that every individual is constantly in the way of being brought into contact with new notions and feelings, and being unsettled in his own accordingly; a select library, therefore, in such situations may be of the same use as a public dial, keeping everybody's clock in some kind of order.

Besides contrasting the manufacturer with the agriculturalist, it may be observed, that he has much more leisure; and in his over hours, not having other pleasant employment to turn to, he is more likely to find reading a relief. What, then, are the books which should be put in his way? Without being myself a clergyman, I have no hesitation in saying, chiefly religious ones; though I should not go so far as you seemed inclined to do, excluding others because they are not according to the letter or in the spirit of your profession. I, with you, feel little disposed to admire several of those mentioned by Gilbert Burns, much less others which you name as having been recommended. In Gilbert B.'s collection there may be too little religion, and I should fear that you, like all other clergymen, may confine yourself too exclusively to that concern which you justly deem the most important, but which by being exclusively considered can never be thoroughly understood. I will allow, with you, that a religious faculty is the eye of the soul; but, if we would have successful soul-oculists, not merely that organ, but the general anatomy and constitution of the intellectual frame must be studied; for the powers of that eye are affected by the general state of the system. My meaning is, that piety and religion will be the best understood by him who takes the most comprehensive view of the human mind, and that, for the most part, they will strengthen with the general strength of the mind, and that this is best promoted by a due mixture of direct and indirect nourishment and discipline. For example, *Paradise Lost,* and *Robinson Crusoe,* might be as serviceable as Law's *Serious Call,* or Melmoth's *Great Importance of a Reli-*

gious Life; at least, if the books be all good, they would mutually assist each other. In what I have said, though following my own thoughts merely as called forth by your Appendix, is *implied* an answer to your request that I would give you 'half an idea upon education as a national object.' I have only kept upon the surface of the question, but you must have deduced, that I deem any plan of national education in a country like ours most difficult to apply to practice. In Switzerland, or Sweden, or Norway, or France, or Spain, or anywhere but Great Britain, it would be comparatively easy. Heaven and hell are scarcely more different from each other than Sheffield and Manchester, &c., differ from the plains and valleys of Surrey, Essex, Cumberland, or Westmoreland. We have mighty cities, and towns of all sizes, with villages and cottages scattered everywhere. We are mariners, miners, manufacturers in tens of thousands, traders, husbandmen, everything. What form of discipline, what books or doctrines—I will not say would equally suit all these—but which, if happily fitted for one, would not perhaps be an absolute nuisance in another? You will, also, have deduced that nothing romantic can be said with truth of the influence of education upon the district in which I live. We have, thank heaven, free schools, or schools with some endowment, almost everywhere; and almost every one can read. But not because we have free or endowed schools, but because our land is, far more than elsewhere, tilled by men who are the owners of it; and as the population is not over crowded, and the vices which are quickened and cherished in a crowded population do not therefore prevail, parents have more ability and inclination to send their children to school; much more than in manufacturing districts, and also, though in a less degree, more than in agricultural ones where the tillers are not proprietors. If in Scotland the children are sent to school, where the parents have not the advantage I have been speaking of, it is chiefly because their labour can be turned to no account at home. Send among them manufacturers, or farmers on a large scale, and you may indeed substitute Sunday-schools or other modes of instructing them; but the ordinary parish schools will be neglected. The influence of our schools in this neighbourhood can never be understood, if this, their connection with the state of landed property, be overlooked. In fact, that influence is not striking. The people are not habitually religious, in the common sense of the word, much less godly. The effect of their schooling is chiefly seen by the activity with which the young persons emigrate, and the success attending it; and at home, by a general orderliness and gravity, with habits of independence and self-respect: nothing obsequious or fawning is ever to be seen amongst them.

It may be added, that this ability (from the two causes, land and schools) of giving their children instruction contributes to spread a respect for scholarship through the country. If in any family one of the children should be quicker at his book, or fonder of it than others, he is often marked out in consequence for the profession of a clergyman. This (before the mercantile or manufacturing employments held out such flattering hopes) very generally happened; so that the schools of the North were the great nurseries of curates, several of whom got forward in their profession, some with and others without the help of a university education; and, in all instances, such connection of families (all the members of which lived in the humblest and plainest manner, working with their own hands as labourers) with a learned and dignified profession, assisted (and still does, though in a less degree) not a little to elevate their feelings, and conferred importance on them in their own eyes. But I must stop, my dear Wrangham. Begin your education at the top of society; let the head go in the right course, and the tail will follow. But what can you expect of national education conducted by a government which for twenty years resisted the abolition of the slave trade, and annually debauches the morals of the people by every possible device? holding out temptation with one hand, and scourging with the other. The distilleries and lotteries are a standing record that the government cares nothing for the morals of the people, and that all which they want is their money. But wisdom and justice are the only true sources of the revenue of a people; preach this, and may you not preach in vain!

Wishing you success in every good work, I remain your affectionate friend, W. WORDSWORTH.

Thanks for your inquiries about our little boy, who is well, though not yet quite strong.*

* *Memoirs*, vol. ii. pp. 171-9. G.

(c) EDUCATION.

Two Letters to the Rev. Hugh James Rose, Horsham, Sussex.

Rydal Mount, Dec. 11. 1828.

My dear Sir,

I have read your excellent sermons delivered before the University* several times. In nothing were my notions different from yours as there expressed. It happened that I had been reading just before Bishop Bull's sermon,† of which you speak so highly: it had struck me just in the same way as an inestimable production. I was highly gratified by your discourses, and cannot but think that they must have been beneficial to the hearers, there abounds in them so pure a fervour. I have as yet bestowed less attention upon your German controversy‡ than so important a subject deserves.

Since our conversation upon the subject of Education, I have found no reason to alter the opinions I then expressed. Of those who seem to me to be in error, two parties are especially prominent; they, the most conspicuous head of whom is Mr. Brougham, who think that sharpening of intellect and attainment of knowledge are things good in themselves, without reference to the circumstances under which the intellect *is* sharpened, or to the quality of the knowledge acquired. 'Knowledge,' says Lord Bacon, 'is power,' but surely not less for evil than for good. Lord Bacon spoke like a philosopher; but they who have that maxim in their mouths the oftenest have the least understanding of it.

The other class consists of persons who are aware of the importance of religion and morality above everything; but, from

* *On the Commission and consequent Duties of the Clergy*, preached before the University of Cambridge, in April 1826, and published in 1828. G.

† The title of which is *The Priest's Office difficult and dangerous.* It will be found in vol. i. p. 137. of Dr. Burton's edition of the bishop's works. G.

‡ *The State of the Protestant Religion in Germany*, a series of discourses preached before the University of Cambridge, by the Rev. Hugh James Rose; Lond. 1825: and his *Letter to the Bishop of London, in reply to Mr. Pusey's work on that subject*; Lond. 1829. G.

not understanding the constitution of our nature and the composition of society, they are misled and hurried on by zeal in a course which cannot but lead to disappointment. One instance of this fell under my own eyes the other day in the little town of Ambleside, where a party, the leaders of which are young ladies, are determined to set up a school for girls on the Madras system, confidently expecting that these girls will in consequence be less likely to go astray when they grow up to women. Alas, alas! they may be taught, I own, more quickly to read and write under the Madras system, and to answer more readily, and perhaps with more intelligence, questions put to them, than they could have done under dame-teaching. But poetry may, with deference to the philosopher and the religionist, be consulted in these matters; and I will back Shenstone's schoolmistress, by her winter fire and in her summer garden-seat, against all Dr. Bell's sour-looking teachers in petticoats that I have ever seen.

What is the use of pushing on the education of girls so fast, and mainly by the stimulus of Emulation, who, to say nothing worse of her, is cousin-german to Envy? What are you to do with these girls? what demand is there for the ability that they may have prematurely acquired? Will they not be indisposed to bend to any kind of hard labour or drudgery? and yet many of them must submit to it, or do wrong. The mechanism of the Bell system is not required in small places; praying after the *fugleman* is not like praying at a mother's knee. The Bellites overlook the difference: they talk about moral discipline; but wherein does it encourage the imaginative feelings, without which the practical understanding is of little avail, and too apt to become the cunning slave of the bad passions. I dislike *display* in everything; above all in education. . . . The old dame did not affect to make theologians or logicians; but she taught to read; and she practised the memory, often, no doubt, by rote; but still the faculty was improved: something, perhaps, she explained, and trusted the rest to parents, to masters, and to the pastor of the parish. I am sure as good daughters, as good servants, as good mothers and wives, were brought up at that time as now, when the world is so much less humble-minded. A hand full of employment, and a head not above it, with such principles and habits as may be acquired without the

Madras machinery, are the best security for the chastity of wives of the lower rank.

Farewell. I have exhausted my paper.

Your affectionate
W. WORDSWORTH.*

Of the Same to the Same.

MY DEAR SIR,

I have taken a folio sheet to make certain minutes upon the subject of EDUCATION.

. . . .

As a Christian preacher your business is with man as an immortal being. Let us imagine you to be addressing those, and those only, who would gladly co-operate with you in any course of education which is most likely to ensure to men a happy immortality. Are you satisfied with that course which the most active of this class are bent upon? Clearly not, as I remember from your conversation, which is confirmed by your last letter. Great principles, you hold, are sacrificed to shifts and expedients. I agree with you. What more sacred law of nature, for instance, than that the mother should educate her child? yet we felicitate ourselves upon the establishment of infant-schools, which is in direct opposition to it. Nay, we interfere with the maternal instinct before the child is born, by furnishing, in cases where there is no necessity, the mother with baby-linen for her unborn child. Now, that in too many instances a lamentable necessity may exist for this, I allow; but why should such charity be obtruded? Why should so many excellent ladies form themselves into committees, and rush into an almost indiscriminate benevolence, which precludes the poor mother from the strongest motive human nature can be actuated by for industry, for forethought, and self-denial? When the stream has thus been poisoned at its fountain-head, we proceed, by separating, through infant-schools, the mother from the child, and from the rest of the family, disburthening them of all care of the little-one for perhaps eight hours of the day. To those who think this an evil, but a necessary one,

* *Memoirs*, vol. ii. pp. 180-3. G.

much might be said, in order to qualify unreasonable expectations. But there are thousands of stirring people now in England, who are so far misled as to deem these schools *good in themselves*, and to wish that, even in the smallest villages, the children of the poor should have what *they* call 'a good education' in this way. Now, these people (and no error is at present more common) confound *education* with *tuition*.

Education, I need not remark to you, is everything that *draws out* the human being, of which *tuition*, the teaching of schools especially, however important, is comparatively an insignificant part. Yet the present bent of the public mind is to sacrifice the greater power to the less—all that life and nature teach, to the little that can be learned from books and a master. In the eyes of an enlightened statesman this is absurd; in the eyes of a pure lowly-minded Christian it is monstrous.

The Spartan and other ancient communities might disregard domestic ties, because they had the substitution of country, which we cannot have. With us, country is a mere name compared with what it was to the Greeks; first, as contrasted with barbarians; and next, and above all, as that *passion* only was strong enough to preserve the individual, his family, and the whole State, from ever-impending destruction. Our course is to supplant domestic attachments without the possibility of substituting others more capacious. What can grow out of it but selfishness?

Let it then be universally admitted that infant-schools are an evil, only tolerated to qualify a greater, viz., the inability of mothers to attend to their children, and the like inability of the elder to take care of the younger, from their labour being wanted in factories, or elsewhere, for their common support. But surely this is a sad state of society; and if these expedients of tuition or education (if that word is not to be parted with) divert our attention from the fact that the remedy for so mighty an evil must be sought elsewhere, they are most pernicious things, and the sooner they are done away with the better.

But even as a course of tuition, I have strong objections to infant-schools; and in no small degree to the Madras system also. We must not be deceived by premature adroitness. The *intellect* must not be trained with a view to what the infant or child may perform, without constant reference to what that performance promises for the man. It is with the mind as with the body. I recollect seeing a German babe stuffed with beer and beef, who had the appearance of an infant Hercules. *He* might have enough in him of the old Teutonic blood to grow up to a strong man; but tens of thousands would dwindle and perish after such unreasonable cramming. Now I cannot but think, that the like would happen with our modern pupils, if the views of the patrons of these schools were realised. The diet they offer is not the natural diet for infant and juvenile minds. The faculties are over-strained, and not exercised with that simultaneous operation which ought to be aimed at as far as is practicable. Natural history is taught in infant-schools by pictures stuck up against walls, and such mummery. A moment's notice of a red-breast pecking by a winter's hearth is worth it all.

These hints are for the negative side of the question: and for the positive,—what conceit, and presumption, and vanity, and envy, and mortification, and hypocrisy, &c. &c., are the unavoidable result of schemes where there is so much display and contention! All this is at enmity with Christianity; and if the practice of sincere churchmen in this matter be so, what have we not to fear when we cast our eyes upon other quarters where religious instruction is deliberately excluded? The wisest of us expect far too much from school teaching. One of the most innocent, contented, happy, and, in his sphere, most useful men whom I know, can neither read nor write. Though learning and sharpness of wit must exist somewhere, to protect, and in some points to interpret the Scriptures, yet we are told that the Founder of this religion rejoiced in spirit, that things were hidden from the wise and prudent, and revealed unto babes: and again, 'Out of the mouths of babes and sucklings Thou hast perfected praise.' Apparently, the infants here contemplated were under a very different course of discipline from that which many in our day are condemned to. In a town of Lancashire, about nine in the morning, the streets resound with the crying of infants, wheeled off in carts and other vehicles (some ladies, I believe, lending their carriages for this purpose) to their school-prisons.

But to go back a little. Human learning, as far as it tends to breed pride and self-estimation (and that it requires constant vigilance to counteract this tendency we must all feel), is against the spirit of the Gospel. Much cause then is there to lament that inconsiderate zeal, wherever it is found, which whets the intellect by blunting the affections. Can it, in a *general* view, be good, that an infant should learn much which its *parents do not know?* Will not the child arrogate a superiority unfavourable to love and obedience?

But suppose this to be an evil only for the present generation, and that a succeeding race of infants will have no such advantage over their parents; still it may be asked, should we not be making these infants too much the creatures of society when we cannot make them more so? Here would they be for eight hours in the day like plants in a conservatory. What is to become of them for the other sixteen hours, when they are returned to all the influences, the dread of which first suggested this contrivance? Will they be better able to resist the mischief they may be exposed to from the bad example of their parents, or brothers and sisters? It is to be feared not, because, though they must have heard many good precepts, their condition in school is artificial; they have been removed from the discipline and exercise of humanity, and they have, besides, been subject to many evil temptations within school and peculiar to it.

In the present generation I cannot see anything of an harmonious co-operation between these schools and home influences. If the family be thoroughly bad, and the child cannot be removed altogether, how feeble the barrier, how futile the expedient! If the family be of middle character, the children will lose more by separation from domestic cares and reciprocal duties, than they can possibly gain from captivity with such formal instruction as may be administered.

We are then brought round to the point, that it is to a physical and not a moral necessity that we must look, if we would justify this disregard, I had almost said violation, of a primary law of human nature. The link of eleemosynary tuition connects the infant school with the national schools upon the Madras system. Now I cannot but think that there is too much indiscriminate gratuitous instruction in this country; arising out of the misconception above adverted to, of the real power of school teaching, relatively to the discipline of life; and out of an over-value of talent, however exerted, and of knowledge prized for its own sake, and acquired in the shape of knowledge. The latter clauses of the last sentence glance rather at the London University and the Mechanics' Institutes than at the Madras schools, yet they have some bearing upon these also. Emulation, as I observed in my last letter, is the master-spring of that system. It mingles too much with all teaching, and with all learning; but in the Madras mode it is the great wheel which puts every part of the machine into motion.

But I have been led a little too far from gratuitous instruction. If possible, instruction ought never to be altogether so. A child will soon learn to feel a stronger love and attachment to its parents, when it perceives that they are making sacrifices for its instruction. All that precept can teach is nothing compared with convictions of this kind. In short, unless book-attainments are carried on by the side of moral influences they are of no avail. Gratitude is one of the most benign of moral influences; can a child be grateful to a corporate body for its instruction? or grateful even to the Lady Bountiful of the neighbourhood, with all the splendour which he sees about her, as he would be grateful to his poor father and mother, who spare from their scanty provision a mite for the culture of his mind at school? If we look back upon the progress of things in this country since the Reformation, we shall find, that instruction has never been severed from moral influences and purposes, and the natural action of circumstances, in the way that is now attempted. Our forefathers established, in abundance, free grammar schools; but for a distinctly understood religious purpose. They were designed to provide against a relapse of the nation into Popery, by diffusing a knowledge of the languages in which the Scriptures are written, so that a sufficient number might be aware how small a portion of the popish belief had a foundation in Holy Writ.

It is undoubtedly to be desired that every one should be able to read, and perhaps (for that is far from being equally apparent) to write. But you will agree with me, I think, that these attainments are likely to turn to better account where they are not gratuitously lavished, and where either the parents and connections are possessed of certain property which enables them to procure the instruction for their children, or where, by their frugality and other serious and self-denying habits, they contribute, as far as they can, to benefit their offspring in this way. Surely, whether we look at the usefulness and happiness of the individual, or the prosperity and security of the State, this, which was the course of our ancestors, is the better course. Contrast it with that recommended by men in whose view knowledge and intellectual adroitness are to do everything of themselves.

We have no guarantee on the social condition of these *well* informed pupils for the use they may make of their power and their knowledge: the scheme points not to man as a religious being; its end is an unworthy one; and its means do not pay respect to the order of things. Try the Mechanics' Institutes and the London University, &c. &c. by this test. The powers are not co-ordinate with those to which this nation owes its virtue and its prosperity. Here is, in one case, a sudden formal abstraction of a vital principle, and in both an unnatural and violent pushing on. Mechanics' Institutes make discontented spirits and insubordinate and presumptuous workmen. Such at least was the opinion of Watt, one of the most experienced and intelligent of men. And instruction, where religion is expressly excluded, is little less to be dreaded than that by which it is trodden under foot. And, for my own part, I cannot look without shuddering on the array of surgical midwifery lectures, to which the youth of London were invited at the commencement of this season by the advertisements of the London University. Hogarth understood human nature better than these professors: his picture I have not seen for many long years, but I think his last stage of cruelty is in the dissecting room.

But I must break off, or you will have double postage to pay for this letter. Pray excuse it; and pardon the style, which is, purposely, as meagre as I could make it, for the sake of brevity. I hope that you can gather the meaning, and that is enough. I find that I have a few moments to spare, and will, therefore, address a word to those who may be inclined to ask, what is the use of all these objections? The schoolmaster is, and will remain, abroad. The thirst of knowledge is spreading and will spread, whether virtue and duty go along with it or no. Grant it; but surely these observations may be of use if they tend to check unreasonable expectations. One of the most difficult tasks is to keep benevolence in alliance with beneficence. Of the former there is no want, but we do not see our way to the latter. Tenderness of heart is indispensable for a good man, but a certain sternness of heart is as needful for a wise one. We are as impatient under the evils of society as under our own, and more so; for in the latter case, necessity enforces submission. It is hard to look upon the condition in which so many of our fellow creatures are born, but they are not to be raised from it by partial and temporary expedients: it is not enough to rush headlong into any new scheme that may be proposed, be it Benefit Societies, Savings' Banks, Infant Schools, Mechanic Institutes, or any other. Circumstances have forced this nation to do, by its manufacturers, an undue portion of the dirty and unwholesome work of the globe. The revolutions among which we have lived have unsettled the value of all kinds of property, and of labour, the most precious of all, to that degree, that misery and privation are frightfully prevalent. We must bear the sight of this, and endure its pressure, till we have by reflection discovered the cause, and not till then can we hope even to palliate the evil. It is a thousand to one but that the means resorted to will aggravate it.

Farewell, ever affectionately yours,

W. Wordsworth.

Quere.—Is the education in the parish schools of Scotland gratuitous, or if not, in what degree is it so?*

* *Memoirs*, vol. ii. pp. 183-92. G.

(d) EDUCATION OF DUTY.

Letter to the Rev. Dr. Wordsworth.

Rydal Mount, April 27. 1830.

MY DEAR BROTHER,

Was Mr. Rose's course of sermons upon education? The more I reflect upon the subject, the more I am convinced that positive instruction, even of a religious character, is much over-rated. The education of man, and above all of a Christian, is the education of *duty*, which is most forcibly taught by the business and concerns of life, of which, even for children, especially the children of the poor, book-learning is but a small part. There is an officious disposition on the part of the upper and middle classes to precipitate the tendency of the people towards intellectual culture in a manner subversive of their own happiness, and dangerous to the peace of society. It is mournful to observe of how little avail are lessons of piety taught at school, if household attentions and obligations be neglected in consequence of the time taken up in school tuition, and if the head be stuffed with vanity from the gentlemanliness of the employment of reading. Farewell.

W. W.*

* *Memoirs*, vol. ii. p. 193. G.

(e) SPEECH ON LAYING THE FOUNDATION-STONE OF THE NEW SCHOOL IN THE VILLAGE OF BOWNESS, WINDERMERE, 1836.

STANDING here as Mr. Bolton's substitute, at his own request, an honour of which I am truly sensible, it gives me peculiar pleasure to see in spite of this stormy weather, so numerous a company of his friends and neighbours upon this occasion. How happy would it have made him to have been eye-witness of an assemblage which may fairly be regarded as a proof of the interest felt in his benevolent undertaking, and an earnest that the good work will not be done in vain. Sure I am, also, that there is no one present who does not deeply regret the cause why that excellent man cannot appear among us. The public spirit of Mr. Bolton has ever been remarkable both for its comprehensiveness and the judicious way in which it has been exerted. Many years ago when we were threatened with foreign invasion, he equipped and headed a body of volunteers, for the defence of our country. Not long since the inhabitants of Ulverston (his native place I believe) were indebted to him for a large contribution towards erecting a church in that town. His recent munificent donations to the public charities of Liverpool are well known; and I only echo the sentiments of this meeting, when I say that every one would have rejoiced to see a gentleman (who has completed his 80th year) taking the lead in this day's proceedings, for which there would have been no call, but for his desire permanently to benefit a district in which he has so long been a resident proprietor. It may be gathered from old documents, that, upwards of 200 years ago, this place was provided with a school, which early in the reign of Charles II. was *endowed* by the liberality of certain persons of the neighbourhood. The building, originally small and low, has long been in a state which rendered the erection of a new one very desirable; this Mr. Bolton has undertaken to do at his sole expense. The structure, which is to supersede the old school-house, will have two apartments, airy, spacious, and lofty, one for boys the other for girls, in which they will be instructed by respective teachers, and not crowded together as in the old school-room, under one and the same person; each room will be capable of containing at least 100 children; within the enclosure there will be spacious and separate play-grounds for the boys and girls, with distinct covered sheds to play in in wet weather. There will also be a library-room for the school, and to contain books for the benefit of the neighbourhood; and, in short, every arrangement that could be desired. It may be added, that the building, from the elegance of its architecture, and its elevated, conspicuous situation, will prove a striking ornament to the beautiful country in the midst of which it will stand. Such being the advantages proposed, allow me to express a hope that they will be turned to the best possible account. The privilege of the school being free, will not, I trust, tempt parents to withdraw their children from punctual attendance upon slight and trivial occasions; and they will take care, as far as depends upon themselves, that the wishes of the present benefactor may be met, and his intentions fulfilled. Those wishes and intentions I will take upon me to say, are consonant to what has been expressed in the original trust-deed of the pious and sensible men already spoken of, who in that instrument declare that they have provided a fund 'towards the finding and maintenance of an able schoolmaster, and repairing the school-house from time to time, for ever; for teaching and instructing of youth within the said hamlets, in grammar, writing, reading, and other good learning and discipline meet and convenient for them; for the honour of God, for the better advancement and preferment of the said youth, and to the perpetual and thankful remembrance of the founders and authors of so good a work.' The effect of this beautiful summary upon your minds will not, I hope, be weakened if I make a brief comment upon the several clauses of it, which will comprise nearly the whole of what I feel prompted to say upon this occasion. I will take the liberty, however, of inverting the order in which the purposes of these good men are mentioned, beginning at what they end with. '*The perpetual and thankful remembrance of the founders and authors of so good a work.*' Do not let it be supposed that your forefathers, when they looked onwards to this issue, did so from vanity and love of applause, uniting with local attachment; they wished their good works to be remembered principally because they were conscious that such remembrance would be beneficial to the hearts of those whom they desired to serve, and would effectually promote the particular good they had in view. Let me add *for* them, what their modesty and humility would have prevented their insisting upon, that such tribute of grateful recollection was, and is still, their *due;* for if gratitude be not the most perfect shape of justice, it is assuredly her most beautiful crown,—a halo and glory with which she delights to have her brows encircled. So much of this gratitude as those good men hoped for, I may bespeak for your neighbour, who is now animated by the same spirit, and treading in their steps.

The second point to which I shall advert is that where it is said that such and such things shall be taught '*for the better advancement and preferment of the said youth.*' This purpose is as honourable as it is natural, and recalls to remembrance the time when the northern counties had, in this particular, great advantages over the rest of England. By the zealous care of many pious and good men, among whom I cannot but name (from his connection with this neighbourhood, and the benefits he conferred upon it) Archbishop Sandys, free schools were founded in these parts of the kingdom in much greater numbers than elsewhere. The learned professions derived many ornaments from this source; but a more remarkable consequence was that till within the last 40 years or so, merchants' counting-houses, and offices, in the lower departments of which a certain degree of scholastic attainment was requisite, were supplied in a great measure from Cumberland and Westmorland. Numerous and large fortunes were the result of the skill, industry, and integrity, which the young men thus instructed, carried with them to the Metropolis. That superiority no longer exists; not so much, I trust, from a slackening on the part of the teachers, or an indisposition of the inhabitants to profit by their free schools, but because the kingdom at large has become sensible of the advantages of school instruction; and we of the north consequently have competitors from every quarter. Let not this discourage, but rather stimulate us to more strenuous endeavours, so that if we do not keep a-head of the rest of our countrymen, we may at least take care not to be left behind in the race of honourable ambition. But after all, worldly advancement and preferment neither are, nor ought to be the *main* end of instruction, either in schools or elsewhere, and particularly in those which are in rural places, and scantily endowed. It is in the order of Providence, as we are all aware, that *most* men must end their temporal course pretty much as they began it; nor will the thoughtful repine at this dispensation. In lands where nature in the many is not trampled upon by injustice, feelingly may the peasant say to the courtier—

> The sun that bids your diamond blaze
> To deck our lily deigns.

Contentment, according to the common adage, is better than riches; and why is it better? Not merely because there can be no happiness without it, but for the sake, also, of its moral dignity. Mankind, we know, are placed on earth to have their hearts and understandings exercised and improved, some in one sphere and some in another, to undergo various trials, and to perform divers duties; *that* duty which, in the world's estimation may seem the least, often being the most important in the eyes of our heavenly Father. Well and wisely has it been said, in words which I need not scruple to quote here, where extreme poverty and abject misery are unknown—

> God doth not need
> Either man's work or his own gifts; who best
> Bear his mild yoke, they serve him best; his state
> Is kingly—thousands at his bidding speed
> And post o'er land and ocean without rest;
> They also serve who only stand and wait.

Thus am I naturally led to the third and last point in the declaration of the ancient trust-deed, which I mean to touch upon: —'*Youth shall be instructed in grammar, writing, reading, and other good discipline, meet and convenient for them, for the honour of God.*' Now, my friends and neighbours, much as we must admire the zeal and activity which have of late years been shewn in the teaching of youth, I will candidly ask those among you, who have had sufficient opportunities to observe, whether the instruction given in many schools *is*, in fact, *meet and convenient?* In the building about to be erected here, I have not the smallest reason for dreading that it will be otherwise. But I speak in the hearing of persons who may be active in the management of schools elsewhere; and they will excuse me for saying, that many are conducted at present so as to afford melancholy proof that instruction is neither *meet nor convenient* for the pupils there taught, nor, indeed, for the human mind in any rank or condition of society. I am not going to say that religious instruction, the most important of all, is neglected; far from it; but I affirm, that it is too often given with reference, less to the affections, to the imagination, and to the practical duties, than to subtile distinctions in points of doctrine, and to facts in scripture history, of which a knowledge may be brought out by a catechetical process. This error, great though it be, ought to be looked at with indulgence, because it is a tempting thing for teachers unduly to exercise the understanding and memory, inasmuch as progress in the departments in which these faculties are employed, is most obviously proved to the teacher himself, and most flatteringly exhibited to the inspectors of schools and casual lookers on. A still more lamentable error which proceeds much from the same cause, is an overstrained application to mental processes of arithmetic and mathematics; and a too minute attention to departments of natural and civil history. How much of trick may mix with this we will not ask, but the display of precocious intellectual power in these branches, is often astonishing; and, in proportion as it is so, may, for the most part, be pronounced not only useless, but injurious. The training that fits a boxer for victory in the ring, gives him strength that cannot, and is not required, to be kept up for ordinary labour, and often lays the foundation of subsequent weakness and fatal disease. In like manner there being in after life no call for these extraordinary powers of mind, and little use for the knowledge, the powers decay, and the knowledge withers and drops off. Here is then not only a positive injury, but a loss of opportunities for culture of intellect and acquiring information, which, as being in a course of regular demand, would be hereafter, the one strengthened and the other naturally increased. All this mischief, my friends, originates in a decay of that feeling which our fathers had uppermost in their hearts, viz., that the business of education should be conducted for *the honour of God*. And here I must direct your attention to a fundamental mistake, by which this age, so distinguished for its marvellous progress in arts and sciences, is unhappily characterized—a mistake, manifested in the use of the word *education*, which is habitually confounded with *tuition* or school instruction; this is indeed a very important part of education, but when it is taken for the whole, we are deceived and betrayed. Education, according to the derivation of the word, and in the only use of which it is strictly justifiable, comprehends all those processes and influences, come from whence they may, that conduce to the best development of the bodily powers, and of the moral, intellectual, and spiritual faculties which the position of the individual admits of. In this just and high sense of the word, the education of a sincere Christian, and a good member of society upon Christian principles, does not terminate with his youth, but goes on to the last moment of his conscious earthly existence—an education not for time but for eternity. To education like this, is indispensably necessary, as co-operating with schoolmasters and ministers of the gospel, the never-ceasing vigilance of parents; not so much exercised in superadding their pains to that of the schoolmaster or minister in teaching lessons or catechisms, or by enforcing maxims or precepts (though this part of their duty ought to be habitually kept in mind), but by care over their *own* conduct. It is through the silent operation of example in their own well-regulated behaviour, and by accustoming their children early to the discipline of daily and hourly life, in such offices and employment as the situation of the family requires, and as are suitable to tender years, that parents become infinitely the most important tutors of their children, without appearing, or positively meaning to be so. This education of circumstances has happily, in this district, not yet been much infringed upon by experimental novelties; parents here are anxious to send their offspring to those schools where knowledge substantially useful is inculcated, and those arts most carefully taught for which in after life there will be most need; this is especially true of the judgments of parents respecting the instruction of their daughters, which *I know* they would wish to be confined to reading, writing, and arithmetic, and plain needlework, or any other art favourable to economy and home-comforts. Their shrewd sense perceives that hands full of employment, and a head not above it, afford the best protection against restlessness and discontent, and all the perilous temptations to which, through them, youthful females are exposed. It is related of Burns, the celebrated Scottish poet, that once while in the company of a friend, he was looking from an eminence over a wide tract of country, he said, that the sight of so many smoking cottages gave a pleasure to his mind that none could understand who had not witnessed, like himself, the happiness and worth which they contained. How were those *happy* and *worthy* people educated? By the influence of hereditary good example at home, and by their parochial schoolmasters opening the way for the admonitions and exhortations of their clergy; that was at a time when knowledge was perhaps better than now distinguished from smatterings of information, and when knowledge itself was more thought of in due subordination to wisdom. How was the evening before the sabbath then spent by the families among which the poet was brought up? He has himself told us in imperishable verse. The Bible was brought forth, and after the father of the family had reverently laid aside his bonnet, passages of scripture were read, and the poet thus describes what followed:—

> Then kneeling down to Heaven's Eternal King,
> The saint, the father, and the husband prays;
> Hope springs exulting on triumphant wing,
> That thus they all shall meet in future days:
> There ever bask in uncreated rays,
> No more to sigh or shed the bitter tear
> Together hymning their Creator's praise,
> In such society, yet still more dear;
> While circling time moves round in an eternal sphere.

May He who enlightened the understanding of those cottagers with a knowledge of Himself for the entertainment of such hope, 'who sanctified their affections that they might love Him, and put His fear into their hearts that they might dread to offend Him'—may He who, in preparing for these blessed effects, disdained not the humble instrumentality of parochial schools, enable this of ours, by the discipline and teaching pursued in it, to sow seeds for a like harvest! In this wish, I am sure, my friends, you will all fervently join; and now, after renewing our expression of regret that the benevolent founder is not here to perform the ceremony himself, we will proceed to lay the first stone of the intended edifice.

NOTES AND ILLUSTRATIONS.

I. Political.

i. *Apology for the French Revolution.*

P. 3, l. 5. 'A sublime allegory.' 'The Vision of Mirza' of Addison, originally published in 'The Spectator' (No. 159, Sept. 1, 1711).

P. 4, ll. 38-9. 'A bishop, a man of philosophy and humanity, as distinguished as your lordship.' This was the Abbé Grégoire, whom Schlosser describes as the 'good-natured, pious, and visionary bishop;' and again, 'particular attention must be paid to the speeches of the pious Grégoire and his dreams of Utopian virtue.' ('History of the 18th Century,' vol. vi. pp. 263-434). Cf. Alison's 'History of the French Revolution,' vol. ii. c. vii. pp. 81-2 (ed. 1853); vol. xii. p. 3, *et alibi.*

P. 7, l. 26. 'The hero of the necklace.' Prince de Rohan. More exactly the Cardinal de Rohan, but who was of the princely house of De Rohan. Carlyle has characteristically told the story of 'the diamond necklace' in one of his Essays. Cf. Alison, as before, i. p. 177; and Schlosser, *s.n.*

P. 8, l. 22. 'Mr. Burke, in a philosophic lamentation over the extinction of chivalry,' &c. The famous apostrophe in relation to Marie Antoinette in his 'Reflections on the Revolution in France' (1790).

P. 9, ll. 8-12. The author gives no reference whatever to the source of this French quotation.

P. 14, l. 34. 'The Rights of Man.' The famous (or notorious) book of Thos. Paine, published in 1791-2 as 'The Rights of Man; being an Answer to Mr. Burke's Attack on the French Revolution.' See p. 21 for Wordsworth's vehement denunciation of Burke in the work which Paine answers, viz. 'The Reflections,' &c. But Wordsworth's ultimate estimate of Burke is the splendid praise of 'The Prelude,' book vii. ll. 513-544.

ii. *The Convention of Cintra.*

Title-page. 'Qui didicit,' &c. From Horace, 'De Arte Poetica,' ll. 312, 314, 315.

Verso of title-page. Quotation from Bacon. From 'Advertisement touching the Controversies of the Church of England (4th paragraph), Spedding's Letters and Life,' vol. i. p. 76.

P. 55, l. 40. 'General Loison.' A French general of cavalry. He was known by the nickname of Maneta, the bloody one-handed. He was the Alaric of Evora. 'His misdeeds,' says Southey, 'were never equalled or paralleled in the dark ages.' It was from Orense that Soult invaded Portugal, having Loison and Foy for his lieutenants.

P. 56, l. 26. 'M. le duc d'Abrantés.' Andoche Junot, duc d'Abrantés, born 23d Oct. 1771, and died by his own hand 29th July 1813. He was created duke by Napoleon when he was sent by him to command the French army in Portugal (1808); defeated by Sir Arthur Wellesley (Wellington) at Vimiera, 21st August 1808.

P. 65, l, 27. 'Massaredo.' Rather Mazaredo, a Spanish general. He had lived much in England. He cleansed and repaired Sir John Moore's tomb at Corunna, and planted the ground for a public Alameda (walk).

P. 59, ll. 25-6. 'General Morla.' At wind-blown Fuencanal (one league from

Madrid) is an old mansion of the Mendoza family, in which Buonaparte lodged from Dec. 2, 1808, until Dec. 22; and here, Dec. 3, he received the Madrid deputation headed by the traitor Morla. 'On the 4th Dec. 1808, General Morla and General Don Fernando de Vera, governor of the town (Madrid), presented themselves, and at ten o'clock General Belliard took the command of Madrid. All the posts were put into the hands of the French, and a general pardon was proclaimed' (Southey, *s.n.*).

P. 60, l. 15. 'The names of Pelayo and The Cid,' &c. (1) *Pelayo*. The Moorish descent was made in great force near Gibraltar in 711. The battle of the Gaudalete (fought near Jerez de la Frontera) followed immediately; and in the course of three years they (the Moors) had conquered the whole of Spain except the north-west region (Biscay and Asturias), behind whose mountains a large body of Chŕtians under Pelayo retreated. Seven years later he (Pelayo) defeated the Moors, seized Léon, and became the first king of the Asturias. (2) *The Cid*. Rodrigo Ruy Diaz of Vibar, born in 1026, is the prince the champion of Spain, El Cid Campeador, and the Achilles and Aeneas of Gotho-Spanish epos. Thus, as Schlegel says, 'he is worth a whole library for the understanding the spirit of his age and the character of the old Castilian.' 'Cast in the stern mould of a disputed and hostile invasion, when men fought for their God and their fatherland, for all they had or hoped for in this world and the next, the Cid possessed the vices and virtues of the mediæval Spaniard, and combined the daring personal valour, the cool determination and perseverance of the Northman, engrafted on the subtle perfidy and brilliant chivalry of the Oriental.'

P. 63, l. 15. 'Ferdinand VII.' King of Spain; born 1784; died 1833. Father of Isabella II., the present ex-queen of Spain. In opposition to his father and his best advisers, he solicited the protection of Napoleon, for which he was imprisoned (1807); compelled to renounce his rights (1808); resided at Bayonne, where he servilely subjected himself to Napoleon, 1808 to 1813; restored 1814, when he abolished the Cortes and revived the Inquisition. By the help of a French army he put down an insurrection, and reëstablished absolute despotism (1823). He married Christiana of Naples (now Duchess Rianzanes), 1829. Abolished Salic law in favour of his daughter, 1830.

P. 84, l. 35. 'Radice in Tartara tendit.' From Virgil, Georg. ii. 292.

P. 92, l. 28. 'General Dupont.' In June 1808, Dupont, commanding the French army, had marched from Madrid to Andalusia, in the south of Spain, given Cordova up to pillage, and committed atrocities which roused the Spanish people to fury. The Spanish general Leastaños (afterwards created Duque de Baylen), with an army sent by the Junta of Seville, won the sanguinary battle of Baylen, and compelled the French to surrender at discretion on the 21st July 1808.

P. 96, l. 37. 'General Friere.' More accurately, Froyere, viz. Manuel Freyere, a Spanish general; born 1795; died 1834. He distinguished himself in the War of Independence, 1809-1813. He helped much in gaining the victory at Toulouse, 10th April 1814. Faithful to constitutional principles, he retired from public life in 1820.

P. 109, ll. 12-16. Quotation from Milton. Adapted from 'Paradise Lost,' book x. ll. 294-7.

P. 117, l. 33. 'The Boy of Saragossa.' Probably a *lapsus* for the *Maid* of Saragossa, Angustina. This Amazon (in a good, soft sense), although a mere itinerant seller of cool drinks, vied in heroism with the noble Condeya de Burita, who amid the crash of war tended the sick and wounded, resembling in looks and deeds a ministering angel. She (Angustina) snatched the match from a dying artillery-man's hand, and fired the cannon at the French; hence she was called La Artillera.

P. 122, ll. 8-10. Latin quotation. Virgil, Eclogae, iv. 6.

P. 149, ll. 16-19. Quotation from Milton, viz. 'Paradise Lost,' book iii. ll. 455-7.

P. 149, l. 40. 'The Sicilian Vespers.' The historical name given to the massacre of the French in Sicily, commenced at Palermo 30th March 1282. The late Earl of Ellesmere wrote a monograph on the subject.

P. 160, ll. 11-13. Quotation in Italian. From Dante, 'Inferno,' c. iii. ll. 1-3.

P. 165, ll. 30-1. Saying of Pyrrhus. More exactly, 'Another such victory, and I must return to Epeirus alone' (said of the renowned battle on the bank of the Siris). See 'Plutarch and Dionysius,' and Droysen, 'Geschichte des Hellenismus,' *s.n.*

P. 166, l. 31. 'Onward.' Sir Philip Warwick. His 'Memoirs' were reprinted and edited by Sir Walter Scott (1702). His 'portraiture' of Cromwell is among the commonplaces of history.

P. 167, l. 30. 'Padre St. Iago Sass.' He is introduced into Wilkie's famous picture of the 'Maid of Saragossa.'

P. 167, l. 31. 'Palafox.' José Palafox y Chelzi, Duke of Saragossa, was born in 1780; heroically defended Saragossa against the attack of the French, 27th July 1808; sent prisoner to France 21st Feb. 1809; released 11th Dec. 1813; died 16th Feb. 1847.

P. 173-4. 'Petrarch.' From his Epistolae, *s.v.*—'Milton.' Apparently a somewhat loose recollection from memory of a passage in 'The Ready and Easy Way to establish a Free Commonwealth,' &c. (1659-60), commencing 'It may be well thought strange,' &c.

III. *Vindication of Opinions in the Treatise on the Convention of Cintra.*

P. 205, foot-note. Latin quotation. Read, 'Totis imperii viribus [contra mirmillonem] consurgitur.' Florus, iii. 20.

II. Ethical.

I. *Of Legislation for the Poor.*

P. 275, ll. 28 onward. Quotation from Milton. From 'Paradise Lost,' book x. ll. 743-747, but changed somewhat in meaning.

P. 277, ll. 16-17. Quotation. Adapted from 'Guilt and Sorrow,' st. xli. ll. 8-9.

II. (*e*) *Speech on Laying the Foundation-stone of the New School, &c.*

On this occasion a prayer was offered by the Rev. R. P. Graves, M.A., (then) the curate, which—as admirably suitable, and as having made a profound impression at the time, the bowed head and reverent look of the venerable Poet as he joined in it remaining 'pleasures of memory' still—it is deemed expedient to preserve permanently. I derive it from the same source as the full Speech itself, and give the context: 'Mr. Wordsworth then descended a step-ladder to the foundation-stone, and deposited the bottle in the cavity, which was covered with a brass plate, having inscribed on it the name of the founder, date, &c. Being furnished with a trowel and mortar by the master mason, Mr. John Holme, he spread it; another massy stone was then let down upon the first, and adjusted to its position, Mr. Wordsworth handling the rule, plumb-line, and mallet, and patting the stone he retired. The Rev. R. P. Graves next offered up the following prayer for the welfare and success of the undertaking: "The foundation-stone of the new parochial school-house of Bowness being now laid, it remains that, as your minister, I should invoke upon the work that blessing of God, without which no human undertaking can prosper,—O Lord God, Who dwellest on high, Whose throne is the Heaven of heavens, and Who yet deignest to look down with goodness and mercy on Thy children of earth, look down, we beseech Thee, with favour upon us who now implore Thy gracious benediction on the work which is before Thee. The building which Thou hast put into the heart of Thy servant to erect grant that, as it is happily begun, it may be successfully completed, and that it may become a fountain-head of blessing to this place and neighbourhood. Thou hast directed us, O Lord, to bring up our children in Thy nurture and admonition; bless, we pray Thee, this effort to secure the constant fulfilment of so important a duty, one so entirely bound up with our own and our children's welfare. Grant that here, from age to age, the youth of these hamlets may receive such faithful instruction as may fit them for usefulness in this life, and for happiness in the next. Grant that the one school may send out numbers endued with such principles and knowledge as may make them, in their several callings, industrious, upright, useful men; in society, peaceful neighbours, contented citizens, loyal subjects; in their families, affectionate sons, and husbands, and fathers; in the Church, dutiful members of that pure and Scriptural Establishment with which Thou hast blessed our Land; and, as crowning and including all, resolved and pious followers of our Redeemer Christ. Grant too, O Lord, that the females which shall be educated in the other school shall receive there such valuable principles and such convenient knowledge as may fit them to make happy the homes of such men; that, with Thy blessing on their instruction, they may become obedient and dutiful children, modest and virtuous women, faithful and affectionate wives and mothers, pious and unassuming Christians; so that with regard to both it may be widely and gratefully owned that here was sown the good seed which shall have borne fruit abundantly in all the relations of life, and which at the great day of harvest hereafter shall, according to Thy word, be gathered into Thy garner. Such, O Lord God, Thou knowest to be the good objects contemplated by the original founders of the school, and the promotion of which is at the heart of him whose benefaction we have this day seen auspiciously begun. Trusting, therefore, O Lord, with full assurance that Thou dost favourably allow and regard these pious designs, I now undertake, as God's minister, and in His name, to bless and dedicate for ever this spot of ground, and the building which, with the Divine permission, will be here erected, and of which this is the foundation-stone, to the sound and religious training up of youth from generation to generation, to the continued grateful remembrance of the pious benefactor, and to the everlasting glory of God Most High, the Father, the Son, and the Holy Spirit. And let all the people say, Amen."'

P. 288, ll. 1-3. These lines might have gone into the closing book of 'The Prelude,' but I have failed to trace or recall them.

P. 223. Long verse-quotation. From 'The Prelude,' book xiii. ll. 220-277.

P. 311, footnote °, viz. Captain T. Ashe's 'Travels in America in the year 1806, for the purpose of exploring the rivers of Alleghanny, Monongahela, Ohio, and the Mississippi, and ascertaining the Produce and Condition of their Banks and Vicinity.' 3 vols. 12mo, 1808. Alexander Wilson, the 'Ornithologist,' vainly sought to accompany Ashe. Had he done so the incredibilities of these Travels had probably been omitted. (See his Works by me, 2 vols. 8vo, 1875.)

P. 326. Verse-quotation at close. From close of 'Ode to Duty' (xix. 'Poems of Sentiment and Reflection').

P. 353, ll. 7-8. Verse-quotation. Whence? It sounds familiarly.

P. 353, ll. 20-25. From Milton, 'Sonnet xiv.'

P. 356, ll. 16-24. Verse-quotation. From Burns' 'Cottar's Saturday Night.' It may be noted here that the 'saint, the father, and the husband' of this imperishable celebration of lowly Scottish godliness was William Burns (or Burness), father of the Poet; and whilst this note is being written a copy of a most interesting MS. (about to be published) by William Burness, prepared by him for his children, reaches me. It is entitled, 'Manual of Religious Belief, by William Burness, in the form of a Dialogue between a Father and his Son.' G.

END OF VOL. I.

LONDON: ROBSON AND SONS, PRINTERS, PANCRAS ROAD, N.W.

www.ingramcontent.com/pod-product-compliance
Lightning Source LLC
Chambersburg PA
CBHW022258280326
41932CB00010B/903

* 9 7 8 3 7 4 4 6 8 7 9 6 6 *